RECORD COPY
Do not remove from office

Governors
AND THE
Progressive
Movement

Governors
AND THE
Progressive Movement

David R. Berman

UNIVERSITY PRESS OF COLORADO
Louisville

© 2019 by University Press of Colorado

Published by University Press of Colorado
245 Century Circle, Suite 202
Louisville, Colorado 80027

All rights reserved
Printed in the United States of America

 The University Press of Colorado is a proud member of the Association of University Presses.

The University Press of Colorado is a cooperative publishing enterprise supported, in part, by Adams State University, Colorado State University, Fort Lewis College, Metropolitan State University of Denver, University of Colorado, University of Northern Colorado, Utah State University, and Western State Colorado University.

∞ This paper meets the requirements of the ANSI/NISO Z39.48-1992 (Permanence of Paper).

ISBN: 978-1-60732-915-2 (cloth)
ISBN: 978-1-60732-916-9 (ebook)
DOI: https://doi.org/10.5876/9781607329169

Library of Congress Cataloging-in-Publication Data

Names: Berman, David R., author.
Title: Governors and the Progressive movement / by David R. Berman.
Description: Louisville, Colorado : University Press Of Colorado, [2018] | Includes bibliographical references and index.
Identifiers: LCCN 2019005808| ISBN 9781607329152 (cloth) | ISBN 9781607329169 (ebook)
Subjects: LCSH: Governors—United States—States—History. | Progressivism (United States politics)—History. | Populism—United States—States—History. | Progressive Party (U.S. : 1912) | Populist Party (U.S. : 1892-1908)
Classification: LCC JK2447 .B45 2018 | DDC 973.91092/2—dc23
LC record available at https://lccn.loc.gov/2019005808

Cover photographs, clockwise from top left: Oswald West, Stephen Hogg, Robert La Follette, Joseph Folk, Hiram Johnson, Theodore Roosevelt, Woodrow Wilson, Charles Evan Hughes. All images courtesy of the Library of Congress.

To the Progressive governors who led the way

CONTENTS

Preface   ix

1 Progressive Reform and the Governors   3
2 The Flow of Party Politics and Reform, 1890–1920   18
3 Midwesterners Paving the Way: Altgeld, Pingree, La Follette, with Follow-ups by Deneen, Dunne, Osborn, and McGovern   36
4 More from the Midwest: Cummins, Johnson, Folk, Harmon, Cox, and Marshall   56
5 Raising Hell on the Plains: Lewelling, Hoch, Stubbs, Sheldon, Burke, and Norbeck   75
6 Mixing Race and Reform in the South: The Deep South, with Tillman, Blease, Vardaman, Bilbo, Hoke Smith, and Comer   94
7 The Southern Periphery: Broward, Davis, Hogg, and Haskell   114
8 The Upper South: Not So Southern, a Succession of Progressive Governors   133

9	Going East: Roosevelt, Hughes, Al Smith, Governing and Dealing with the Bosses	152
10	Wilson of New Jersey, Scholar and Tactician, Confronting the Bosses	167
11	The Rest of the East: Republican and Conservative, Doing What Could Be Done with Boss and Corporate Control and Only Limited Power	181
12	Western "Radicalism": Hiram Johnson, Curtailing the Railroads, Getting beyond Politics as Usual	201
13	Agitation and Activity in the Northwest: Chamberlain, West, Rogers, and Carey	215
14	The Southwest: Shafroth, Bamberger, and Hunt	234
15	Governors and Reform: The Record and the Legacy	253
	Bibliography	273
	Index	293

PREFACE

America's "Age of Reform," roughly from 1890 to 1920, was one in which reform-minded politicians, spurred on by scores of crusading organizations and individuals, set out to accomplish a wide variety of goals. This book focuses on one set of actors who played a crucial role in the development of the movement for reform and the enactment or failure of many policy proposals: the governors of the various states.

The idea for this book grew out of some of my own research, especially a study I did on Governor Hunt of Arizona, published in 2015, which raised several questions in my mind about the behavior, role, and accomplishments of governors in regard to the unfolding of reform during the Populist-Progressive reform era (I think of the Populist and Progressive movements in many ways as constituting one continuous movement). I decided to find out more about what other governors were doing in the same period. This was one of those projects that took on a life of its own. It kept growing as I continued to find more governors I wanted to know more about.

I sought information on their personal histories, political careers, personalities, leadership qualities, governing styles, orientation toward reform, reform packages they put together, role in regard to the drive for Progressive reform in their states, and accomplishments as reformers along with a general account of the conditions under which they served. I paid attention to their stands on a broad range of issues, including those involving corporate regulation and taxation, labor protection, participation in the political process, governmental organization, moral uplift, the criminal justice system, education, transportation, and public health. I looked into their performance not simply in terms of legislation but as chief administrators in charge of the prison system and other state institutions, as commanders in chief of the state militia or National Guard in their handling of labor disputes, riots, and lynching and as chief magistrates issuing pardons and commutations. I paid particular attention to how racism played into the Progressive movement and the decisions governors had to make. I found many governors worthy of praise, but did not ignore their limitations and imperfections. Some were very disagreeable people.

Preparation of this manuscript involved analyzing letters, speeches, and documents gathered from archives around the country and examining and integrating many secondary studies. I drew upon several well-known newspapers and a host of relatively rare and unexplored ones owned and operated by people in small towns and rural areas and ones written by and for minority group members, labor activists, and those on both the far right and far left. Many of these papers were found online through the Library of Congress. In exploring the secondary literature I looked for informed biographies of individual governors and, in shaping the context for understanding and attempting to explain their activities, I drew upon the insights of scholars from various academic disciplines. In particular this work draws upon scholarship in the fields of history, political science, and public policy and aims to contribute to the literature in each of these areas.

After an initial review of gubernatorial activity in each of the forty-eight states in existence at the time, I proceeded to put together an overview of which governors were doing what in regard to reform in each state, using a regional framework. More attention is paid to some governors than others in the following pages. I've highlighted those who, based on the information I was able to gather, struck me as particularly significant in terms of ideas, experiences, or accomplishments. I have given special attention to governors who stood out because of their reputations as Progressives in the eyes of respected historians and contemporary observers, supplemented by what I was able to discover through my own examination of primary materials. Much of the focus is on the highly proactive types who assumed leadership and challenged entrenched political party and economic leaders in an effort to bring about a package of fundamental political, economic, and social changes.

There were assertive reform-minded governors in the 1890s and before, but the early 1900s brought the emergence of a larger set of strong governors who exerted considerable influence over their political parties and the legislatures in their states. Though it has been common to think of only a few exceptional figures such as Robert La Follette of Wisconsin, Hiram Johnson of California, and Woodrow Wilson of New Jersey as falling into this category, examination of the evidence during this period suggests that many governors around the nation assumed leadership positions and pushed through significant reforms. Much of what happened in Wisconsin, California, and New Jersey also happened elsewhere around the country.

These "new governors" with a Progressive bent played a special role in bringing change. Citizen reformers, academics, and journalistic muckrakers were outsiders looking in, but the governors, while cognizant of outside forces, were exceptionally pivotal insiders. Outsiders could stand as unflinching and unbending proponents of their causes and were expected to do so, but governors operated in a more restrictive environment, being hemmed in by concerns with electoral pressures on them or their political party and with practical problems of political and economic feasibility when it came to pursuing various courses of action. Sitting at the hub of reform activity, they sorted out the demands of various groups, compiled their own reform packages, submitted them to their legislatures, and worked for their adoption.

Governors during the period 1890–1920 sought to revamp the political system in regard to voting rights, election machinery, the operation of the legislature, and the powers and duties of the governor's office. On issues involving social and economic reform, governors saw the need for more spending, especially on education and transportation, more regulation and taxation of large business enterprises, more labor protection, more attention to a variety of morality issues involving such matters as drinking and gambling and extending to prizefighting and even human sterilization, and more concern for a host of criminal justice issues, particularly prison reform and the abolition of the death penalty.

This work represents the first effort to put together an overview of the unfolding of the Progressive movement at the state level, covering every state in existence at the time, as evidenced in the eyes and actions of state governors. Previous research provided me with useful information concerning the backgrounds and careers of governors who served in this period and gave me some inclination of how variations in occupational status prior to taking office as governor may have contributed to the outlook and style of governors as Progressive leaders. In this volume I expand upon this research and further explore the various roles governors played in the unfolding of Progressive reform in their states, their reform packages, and their personal qualities that had a bearing on their style and success and their overall contribution to the movement. While there were a multitude of active governors, they were a very diverse group and made different contributions in bringing reform.

My general goals are to further understanding of the growth in the office of governor, the leading role many governors played in bringing reform during the Progressive years, and more about the nature of the Progressive movement in general. The work offers a state-level view of the national impact of the movement, the problems to which it was addressed, the activity of state governments, much of which was highly innovative in nature, and salient regional or subregional variations. It also reviews and examines debates over the role of government and issues involving corporate power, racism, voting rights, and gender equality, which have continued to characterize American politics. We enter a world of greedy corporations, political bosses, corrupt legislators, and conflict along racial, class, labor-management, urban-rural, and state-local lines. This was a time when insurgent Republicans set out to save their party from the railroads and reform-minded Democrats set out to save their party from the Populists. It was also a time when states, often led by Progressive governors, functioned as laboratories of experimentation, devising programs later adopted on the national level.

The following two chapters present an overview of the book, relevant literature, and the broader historical, political, and policymaking context in which governors functioned from 1890 to 1920 (though events connected with the First World War are only slightly touched upon). Following these, I examine gubernatorial activity in all the states, starting with those in the Midwest and moving on to the South, the East, and West in that order. The final chapter offers concluding observations on the personal qualities and accomplishments of governors active during this period and the legacy they left behind.

As always, I am appreciative of the help given by several archivists over the years and my wife Susan for her proofreading skills. I would also like to acknowledge the support of the Emeritus College, Arizona State University, Professors Dan Herman and Phil Vandermeer, and the anonymous reviewers.

Governors
AND THE
Progressive Movement

1

PROGRESSIVE REFORM AND THE GOVERNORS

The Populist and Progressive movements in the United States, starting in the last decade of the nineteenth century and running through the first two of the twentieth century, though differing in their base of support, had some common themes. Among the most central of these were the need to purify and democratize the governmental system through political and structural reforms, the need to rein in the political and economic power of giant corporations, and, more broadly, the need to bring to power an energetic and positive government that would serve the interests of the many rather than a privileged few.[1]

Though reform activity first took root on the local level in many states, much of the critical action from 1890 to 1920 took place at the state level.[2] The states had the authority—they could act in a variety of areas, and their willingness to do so was of extreme importance to a flood of reformers, organizations, and interest groups. The initial problem was getting the states to respond. Throughout the country reformers on the state level strove to democratize and purify state political systems. Once the choke hold of the corrupting special interests on government was broken and power was turned over to the people, reformers felt they could move on to address matters of basic economic and social justice.

In a time of rapid industrialization and urbanization, reform meant more spending on such matters as public education, roads, health protection, and to help out those who needed help, even though this meant departing from the norm of individualism, increasing the functions of government, and raising taxes. Reform also meant not only harnessing the power of large corporations but distributing economic benefits more widely and shifting more of the tax burden to the wealthy through personal income, inheritance, and corporate taxes. On the labor front it involved hour and wage regulations, factory and mine inspection, worker's compensation, and ending injunctions against organizing unions. Reformers too thought in terms of improving morality by curbing or banning drinking and gambling, and many went off in the direction of perfecting the population through eugenics legislation. Many focused on prison reform and the abolition of the death penalty, protecting the rights of workers on industrial battlegrounds, and coping with violent vigilante actions and riots in minority areas.

INTERESTS, MACHINES, LEGISLATORS, DIVISIONS AMONG REFORMERS

Much of the initial and continuing focus of reformers was on destroying the network of special interest politics and corruption formed by leading business interests, political machines associated with the major parties, and officeholders, especially state legislators. They saw corrupt governing systems throughout the country.

Reformers targeted a variety of large businesses, including those engaged in railroading, telephone and telegraph services, the provision of gas and electricity, transit, insurance, banking, mining, and timber. Railroads were an early and special target just about everywhere. Charges against them included not paying their fair share of the taxes, setting excessive and discriminatory passenger and freight rates, being partial to particular shippers, hording land allocated to them by the federal or state governments needed for development, mistreatment of their employees, and through means ranging from giving free railroad passes to direct cash bribes to politicians and lavishly entertaining them, corrupting the political system. Meanwhile, on the local level public utilities, especially local street railway (aka traction) companies got unlimited franchises and everything else they wanted through the bribery of city officials.

During the 1890s and early 1900s reformers put a great deal of emphasis on the corrupting effects of the railroad pass. A leading Populist, for example, argued that "the power for evil of the Free Pass Bribery System is far greater than bribery with money. Few men can be bribed with money, but many men can be bribed with a free railroad pass."[3] All this led to a situation in which "Instead of public officials compelling railroads to obey the law, the railroads compel the public officials to serve them and betray the people."[4]

Railroad officials and other spokespeople for large corporations saw the problem differently. To many a business person, paying off legislators was simply a routine cost of doing business and businesspeople were not the only ones to be blamed. As mining entrepreneur William A. Clark, who routinely bribed state legislators, said in his own defense: "I never bought a man who wasn't for sale."[5] Often legislators took the initiative and "sandbagged" businesspeople by threatening to push for laws detrimental to them if no bribe was forthcoming. In 1904 an observer in Missouri compared the sandbagger to the "corrupt and unscrupulous" highwayman who "places not a revolver" but a "legislative bill to the head of his victim and demands money."[6]

In the period 1890–1920, as now, people used the term "political machine" as a pejorative to put a bad label on a political organization they did not like. Still, in many parts of the country those who used the term had a clear vision of a particular type of political organization associated with either the Republican or Democratic Party headed by a boss who was able to deliver enough votes to heavily influence, if not control, the actions of elected state and local officials. As boss Tom Pendergast of Kansas City, Missouri, put it: "The delivery of the votes is what counts... Politics is a business, just like anything else."[7]

Bosses were in the business of controlling party nominations and winning elections. They thrived by rewarding those who worked for them with governmental jobs and by selling their ability to control legislation and administrative decisions to those willing to pay for their services.

Party bosses did not always oppose Progressive reform—some were "easy bosses" willing to go along, especially when championing change looked like it would facilitate getting their candidates elected, but they could be expected to draw the line when it came to proposals directly affecting the welfare of their organization, such as ending patronage, or those deemed harmful to clients they represented.

While power in some states rested in highly organized political organizations controlled by a party boss or a few bosses, in others one found less formal networks of party officeholders and workers aligned with prominent officeholders. Often considerable control was in the hands of a clique headed by a US senator who led the dominant faction within one of the major parties. Conflict in these cases took the form of a struggle between two factions of the same party, one side trying to bring change, while the other, being tied to the status quo and being close to the dominant economic interests, opposed change. The story in much of the western part of the country, a region where party organizations were relatively weak, was not so much one of reformers attacking party bosses or highly structured and disciplined political party machines as it was one of reformers directly attacking the corporate interests, often the railroads and the mines, and their allies or stooges in office.

Throughout the country reformers of the late 1890s and early 1900s strove to clean up corruption and combat special interest influence through direct primaries, which gave ordinary party members or registered voters at large an opportunity to choose the nominees of political parties for various offices, including state legislative seats, taking that power away from party bosses meeting with corporate representatives in the proverbial "smoke-filled rooms" at party conventions. They also sought an end to patronage appointments through civil service laws and corrupt-practices acts that put limitations on campaign contributions and required disclosure of where the money came from and how it was spent.

Many saw malfunctioning state legislators to be at the heart of the problem of governance. In addition to the safeguards regarding campaigns and elections, reformers called for laws putting limits on lobbying and requiring disclosure of who was lobbying for what. Some reformers also proposed to improve the legislative process by increasing research and bill drafting services, reducing the number of legislators, or creating smaller, more efficient, and transparent one-house legislative bodies. Another and broader thrust of the reform effort was to shift more of the responsibility for governing from state legislatures to the people directly, the governor, or neutral, nonpolitical, competent experts in administrative agencies, though there was little agreement on which of the three directions was most preferable. As a consequence, the movement was filled with contradictory ideas. For example, while promoting the idea of popular control of government, some Progressives also wanted to do away with several elective offices and also called for a greater shift of responsibility to nonelected expert administrators under civil service protection.

As far as the legislators were concerned, high among the most objectionable proposed reforms were those allowing citizens to completely bypass the legislature and make their own laws through the initiative process, challenge what the legislature had done through a referendum procedure that subjected these decisions to a vote of the people, and, if necessary, to recall legislators, as well as other elected officials, from office prior to the expirations of their terms if they were not meeting citizen expectations as to performance and conduct.

Progressives drew upon widespread feelings that government responded to the interests of a privileged few rather than to those of ordinary people and that there was a need for an activist government at the state level that would protect the many from the few and the weak from the strong. They saw a need for a crusade against injustice, corruption, the special influence of big business, and the invisible government of special interests that ran things.

They faced the opposition of reactionary stand-pat politicians, defenders of the party machines and the corporate interests, and others who benefited from the status quo or believed in only limited reform. Within the Republican Party the conflict was commonly defined as between the Progressive "insurgents" who were out to wrest control of the party from the leading corporate interests in their states and the conservative "Standpatters" who liked things the way they were. Opponents of reform on the Republican side were also commonly called "Stalwart Republicans."

One group of limited reformers—known by a variety of titles, including Cleveland or Bourbon Democrats, Mugwump Republicans, Independents, good government people (goo-goos), and structural reformers—believed in honesty and efficiency in government but did not seek far-ranging political, economic, or social change and, indeed, often opposed those who did.[8] Populists and Progressives also favored honesty and efficiency but had a far broader focus. They believed in fundamental reform and considered the honesty and efficiency types to be narrow-minded conservatives and as much of an enemy to meaningful reform as the reactionaries in both parties. For their part, the honesty and efficiency types, as defenders of individualism and laissez-faire, were frightened by what they saw as the extreme radicalism of the Populists and the Progressive reformers who followed in their footsteps. Many of these underlying issues were found in the division between Bryan and Cleveland Democrats (see chapter 2).

RISE OF THE GOVERNORS

This office of governor had been a strong one in the colonial period. Usually appointed by the Crown, the governor had virtually complete control over legislative matters, enjoyed full appointive powers when filling governmental positions, and in some places even headed the highest court in the colony. Over time, however, governors became the central target of the colonists' hostility toward the Crown. This history contributed to the willingness of the framers of most of the first state constitutions to limit the power of the office. As a result, governors were usually appointed by the legislature, served only one-year terms, and lacked the power to veto legislation. New York and Massachusetts were exceptions when it came to the strength of the office. In these states governors were elected by the voters and had the veto power.

During the first half of the nineteenth century poor performance on the part of state legislatures prompted state constitutional changes improving the legal status of the governor: the office became popularly elective everywhere, and governors were given longer terms, veto authority, and more power to appoint. With the liberalization of suffrage restrictions for white males, governors also gained the opportunity to strengthen their status as political leaders by developing a large statewide constituency.[9]

At the same time, however, the movement toward greater democracy stimulated by Andrew Jackson also reduced the ability of the governor to act as chief administrator. Jacksonian democracy brought the election not only of the governor but a large number of other state administrators. Proponents argued that democracy depended not only on how many could vote but on how many officials they could vote for, even though the people who were elected, such as the state treasurer, had little discretionary authority. The result was to seriously fragment executive authority, making it virtually impossible for the governor or any other single executive to control the executive branch as a whole. The problem of control worsened as the states responded to each problem they had to address with the creation of a new administrative agency headed by a board whose members had terms that put them beyond the control of any single governor serving one or two short terms.

While more independent of the legislature, the office of governor continued throughout the nineteenth century to be a weak and relatively unattractive one. Writing in the late 1880s, the best thing British observer James Bryce felt could be said was that the state governor was "not yet a nonentity" but close to it because of the dominance of the state legislature.[10] Many of those who served as governor during the nineteenth century did so in the Whig tradition of a dignified but generally passive, low-key chief executive who was willing to let the legislature do most of the governing. To some, the governor was, at best, "a great office manager."[11]

In 1891, John Altgeld, a future governor of Illinois, expressed his skepticism over the value of the office of governor as a position to lead the cause of reform. He claimed no governor in the last decade had done anything "of an enduring character for their country or for the progress of civilization ... anything that can be regarded as raising the standard of public morals, creating a healthy public sentiment, or solving in a proper manner any of the great questions, both economic and social, that are calling for solution."[12] Altgeld suggested that the problem was largely due to a lack of leadership—the simple failure of the people who held the office to stand up and do the right thing—rather than the weakness of the office itself. They could and should do more. Other critics around this time supplied a different reason for the failure of governors to do much of anything worthwhile: they were simply the stooges of political bosses and the special interests that were ripping off the public.

To some, matters had not improved by the turn of the century. Writing in 1904, muckraker Lincoln Steffens concluded that Robert La Follette of Wisconsin was one of the few governors who actually qualified as "head of the State." To Steffens "most governors are simply 'safe men' set up as figureheads by the System, which is the actual government that is growing up in the United States in place of the 'government of the people, by the people, and for the people.'" Steffens viewed the "System" as one in which "the leading politicians of both parties conduct the government in the interest of those leading businesses which seek special privileges and pay for them with bribes and the 'moral' support of graft."[13]

Scholars were to add their own negative assessments of the office during the Progressive period. While noting that some governors like Robert La Follette, Hiram Johnson, and Woodrow Wilson had succeeded as legislative leaders, political scientist Austin Macdonald saw these few leaders as exceptions who "were endowed with unusual powers of leadership that captivated the public."[14] "Most governors," Macdonald concluded in 1927, "have not possessed to such a high degree the rare quality of leadership, and so have been rewarded with nothing but popular disapproval. The governorship may sometimes be a stepping-stone to fame; usually it is a toboggan to political oblivion."[15] He saw the office as essentially a weak one that offered little in terms of compensation or an opportunity for accomplishment. It fell far short of offering anything "to make the job sufficiently attractive to draw the type of men we need."[16]

Joining in, political scientist W. Brooke Graves concluded in regard to those who served in the Progressive period: "While there were instances in which conspicuously able men came to the governorship, they were the exception rather than the rule. There was little about the office, save the honor attached to it, to challenge the interest and creative ability of able men."[17] In one of the pioneering studies on the American governor, written in 1939, Leslie Lipson came to a similar conclusion: "The La Follettes and Johnsons, the Hughes' [sic] or the Wilsons, were not of the ordinary stamp of governors. They were exceptional men. One needs, therefore, to qualify the statement that there was a renaissance of the governor in the first decade of the twentieth century. In the forty-six states that then composed the Union only a few were of this mold." Lipson saw only the possibility of executive leadership at the state level during the Progressive period.[18]

Contrary to the generally negative assessment of the office and the people who served as governor from 1900 to 1920, this work provides numerous examples of reform-minded and effective governors during this time span—demonstrating that when it comes to executive leadership we are not talking about simply a few individuals with exceptional talents or something that happened only in Wisconsin, California, New Jersey, and a few other states.[19] Governors throughout the nation encouraged and rode the wave of public demand for reform. Governors played a special role in bringing about reform in most states. They deserve far more attention than they have received. And more of them deserve attention. We can still say, as Nicholas Burckel wrote more than forty years ago, that scholars have given insufficient attention to Progressive governors outside those few who established national reputations, such as Robert La Follette of Wisconsin, Hiram Johnson of California, and Woodrow Wilson of New Jersey.[20]

Reform-minded and assertive governors did not just suddenly emerge in the early 1900s. One can, for example, look back to the 1870s during the Granger revolt and find governors stirred into action by banking failures, the inability of farmers to get credit, and the abuses of large corporations, especially railroads. One example was Horace Austin, Republican governor of Minnesota, 1870–74, who robustly declared: "It is time to take those robber corporations by the scuff of their neck and shake them over hell!"[21] In the late 1890s and first decade of the twentieth century, several observers pick up on the movement toward more independent and assertive governors. An evaluation of twenty-five governors elected in 1896, by a prominent national political magazine, drawing upon the observations of private correspondents in the various states, concluded that only three of the victors were tied to political machines while the rest, including a half-dozen Populists, were graded good if not outstanding in terms of character and their likely performance.[22] In 1905, contrary to the assessment of Steffens a year earlier, William Allen White, Progressive journalist and author, noted the emergence of several governors, especially in the Middle West in addition to Ls Follette, who were already making a difference and that "the type is multiplying rapidly."[23]

Five years later, an overview of the national scene concluded that matters had developed to the point where "the old-fashioned and perfunctory governor is no longer attractive to the intelligent citizen voters. The voters are wanting business results and moral influence from the state government. They understand that the governor, as the head of the state administration, gives the trend to public affairs." They were looking for "a positive, courageous and progressive governor" who "sets the pace and stirs the public conscience into action" and "turns the searchlight into dark corners that would otherwise be overlooked."[24] More and more governors appeared to be playing that role.

During the 1890s Populist governors enjoyed some success at the state level, but as much of the literature on the subject suggests, they had considerable difficulty in getting anything through the legislature. They were often inexperienced in governing and frequently in a weak position because their opponents controlled one or both legislative houses. They also had a difficult time holding together the coalition that had been formed to get them elected because of disagreements over patronage and policy matters. Yet, while they made few legislative gains, they set the stage for meaningful reform.[25]

The new governors coming to power in the late 1890s and early 1900s throughout the country as Democrats or Republicans picked up on the basic Populist-Progressive themes and programs and enjoyed considerable success, culminating in the years 1910–15. They helped usher in an era in politics in the states where political party organizations played a reduced role, a larger number of groups made demands for governmental action, the states assumed a greater number of functions, and much of the work of the states shifted from the legislative branch to the executive branch and administrative agencies. They helped the states play a major role as innovators, acting in advance of federal action in regard to labor protection, bank deposit guaranties, securities regulation, woman suffrage, prohibition, and other areas. In 1911 one observer, who was particularly impressed by Wilson's accomplishments, saw the movement led by strong governors ushering in a new era in state government in which it would be evident that the states could do much of the job of governing and, because of this, there was less need to shift functions and powers to the federal government.[26]

Although there were aggressive, reform-minded governors during the Granger and Populist eras, there were more numerous and more successful ones in terms of accomplishment starting in the early 1900s and not just in a handful of states. Separating themselves as best they could from the existing power structure in their own political party, they pushed ahead, drawing on their own popularity and personal political machines and the powers of their office. Rather than playing a largely passive role of approving or rejecting what the legislature did, they recommended legislation and lobbied for its adoption, sometimes taking their case to the people directly. In justifying such actions, governors could and did claim that compared to legislators they spoke for the people of the state rather than some area within the state. They also used their executive powers to get involved in other areas where they could act relatively free from the legislature. Especially attractive to many was the field of prison reform.

Governors always had the potential to lead in terms of legislation, and from 1900 to 1920 many did so, one might argue, because of public support for executive action. To many, the political system had failed. State legislatures were part of a corrupt system and were not responding to pressing public problems. Politics as usual had to go. Governors were less touched than legislators by charges of corruption. A swelling of public sentiment for reform put governors in the driver's seat should they choose to try to push their states in a Progressive direction.

The "new governor" was a product of this reform sentiment. To some extent, the emergence of executive leadership at the state level was also stimulated by the demonstration of the importance of executive leadership to the cause of reform at the local level. Governors, in turn, provided examples of executive leadership for future presidents. Two Populist-Progressive-era governors, Theodore Roosevelt and Woodrow Wilson, carried their experiences directly into the White House.[27]

During the 1890–1920 period governors were deeply involved in the dissemination of reform ideas. They were in contact with other governors, muckrakers, legislators, academics, citizen reformers, national and state reform organizations, and a growing list of interest groups, all seeking reform of one type or another. Contact among governors came through the mails, campaign events, and various meetings. Going through the papers of governors in various state archives, one often finds a host of letters from one governor to another, involving such matters as an upcoming conference, past or pending legislation, or gubernatorial speeches on various topics or for various events. Some governors looked for all the help they could get. For example, in 1912, L. B. Hanna wrote the governor of Idaho: "I have recently been elected Governor of North Dakota and would appreciate it if you would kindly [send] me copies of the messages that have been sent by you or former Governors to your legislature for the past two or three sessions."[28] Not all requests had to do with monumental matters. For example, a secretary to Washington governor Ernest Lister wrote to W. E. Lindsey, governor of New

Mexico, in 1917: "Governor Lister has received the copy of your Arbor and Bird Day Proclamation which you were kind enough to send to him, and desires to thank you very much for the same."[29]

Governors during the Progressive era seem genuinely excited about the opportunity to gather with their colleagues from around the country and to promote greater interstate cooperation.[30]

They had a variety of organizations to facilitate their interaction. Some were general discussion conclaves for governors while others were dedicated to specific reform causes or regional or national political objectives. One formal means of interaction was the Conference of Governors, known early on as the "House of Governors." This organization grew out of a meeting of governors from around the country in 1908, called by President Theodore Roosevelt in an effort to line up the support for his stand on conservation matters. From 1910 onward, governors initiated the conference themselves.

At the organization's first meeting Governor Joseph W. Folk of Missouri noted: "It would not have been possible for so many Governors to have come together in any other period of history. Prior to the Civil War the transportation facilities were not sufficient. After the Civil War the feeling between the sections was not such as would make such a meeting very harmonious or very happy. But we have met here now as one large family."[31] At the same meeting Kentucky governor Augustus E. Willson expressed his appreciation of having the opportunity to get together with other governors: "There are many matters in which a new Governor at least, like myself, feels he needs counsel and help about from other Governors—matters like extradition, matters of general public policy, matters to decide what one should do in certain emergencies that come to all of us. I have four years ahead of me, and I feel that I needed this Conference; and I feel glad that I am here, and am glad that I have had the opportunity of meeting the Governors."[32] The main function of the organization was to facilitate interstate cooperation and the dissemination of information on such matters as the reorganization of state government, prison administration, and political reform measures such as the direct primary.[33] Along with exchanging views on policy issues and talking shop, governors got together in little groups and talked politics, not simply their own personal situations or in their state, but what was happening elsewhere and on the presidential level.[34]

In addition to the governors' conference there were several regional bodies that facilitated communication and cooperation among governors on a regular basis and many more in which governors got together to consider common problems. Here too one could find good advice. At a meeting of western governors Governor Joseph Carey of Wyoming humorously cautioned: "Now, if you open your doors to everybody, you will have speeches from worse cranks that any of us (laughter), and it will take you days to arrive at a conclusion."[35] The "House of Southern Governors" brought chief executives in the region together to consider such problems as those affecting commerce, public health, and, usually in executive session, racial relations.[36] A regional approach was often imperative in New England, given the small size of the states and the geographical scope of the problems they faced. As one paper noted in regard to a meeting of New England governors in 1913 to study railroad problems: "The fundamental reason for this conference is that there are five states too many in New England for the satisfactory handling of the transportation problem created by the railroad monopoly."[37]

BACKGROUNDS, LABELS, AND MOTIVES

Studies, though done some time ago, give us a general picture of the backgrounds and careers of those who served as governor during the first two decades of the twentieth century. One by political scientist Austin Macdonald of the 187 governors, all of whom were male, who served from 1900 to 1910 found that about half of them were college graduates and lawyers and that more than 80 percent of them had held some political office prior to becoming governor—of the 187, 132 had served in the state legislature, 27 had been judges of state courts, 25 had been in the US House, and one had been in the US Senate. The study found that 70 percent of the governors who served in this period never went on to serve in another office after serving as governor. Among the 57 who continued to serve, 30 went to Congress (23 to the Senate and 7 to the House), 6 entered the diplomatic service, 2 became vice-presidents, and one became president.[38]

Another study indicates that during the period 1900–1920, two trends regarding the political careers of governors that began in the 1870s continued to be felt. One, likely reflecting the loss of confidence in state legislatures, was a continuing decline in the percentage of governors who had served as legislators or who had jumped directly from a position in the legislature to the office of governor. In the same period there was a rise in the percentage of governors who had some law enforcement experience (a public attorney or a judge at the state or local level) and who had such positions immediately prior to becoming governor and used that service as a springboard.[39] Sensational cases relating to governmental corruption and illegal business activities appear to have given public prosecutors and judges exceptional opportunities for political advancement. Using their obligation to enforce the law gave them "a political shield" of nonpartisan neutrality free from self-aggrandizement and created an image, often associated with Governor Joseph Folk of Missouri, of a "lone warrior for righteousness."[40]

Deciding what ideological labels to put on governors and other political figures active during this period is no easy task. Scholars are not certain, for example, whether Governors Teddy Roosevelt and Charles Evans Hughes of New York should be considered dynamic conservatives or positive liberals.[41] Roosevelt himself seemed to have been confused about whether he was a conservative radical or a radical conservative.[42] Looking back at the results of the 1912 Republican presidential primaries, Roosevelt noted: "The amusing thing is that in the Dakotas I am being opposed on the ground that I am a conservative and in the East on the ground that I am a radical."[43] Seeking to move in a more Progressive direction during his 1910 campaign for governor of New Jersey, Woodrow Wilson probably confused everyone by announcing he was "a conservative with a move on."[44] While running for president in 1912, he declared that being a Progressive meant "not getting caught standing still when everything else is moving."[45]

Scholars, as a whole, have been little help in sorting out Progressives from non-Progressives. As political scientist Howard Reiter once noted, "it is almost impossible to find a significant party leader [during the 1900–1920 period] who has *not* been considered Progressive by at least one historian."[46] Given the popularity of reform, most every governor who served from 1890 to 1920 took some positions that most people would consider Progressive. Sometimes the reputation apparently rests on the governor's association with one or two pieces of legislation or simply their general opposition to "machine rule." In this work, as a working definition, a truly Progressive governor is viewed, rather loosely, as a person who, as indicated by a conscientious examination of relevant materials, called for a broad package of fundamental political, economic, and social reforms going beyond honesty and efficiency.

A somewhat related matter involves disputes over the underlying motivations of those who sought to be identified as Progressives. Was a particular governor a true believer or simply posing as a Progressive because there was political gain in doing so? The question was frequently asked during the period under review. This was a time when it was useful to be known as a Progressive, and many of those politicians who emerged sounding like true believers suffered in terms of credibility because their conversion to the creed came suddenly and was in stark contrast to what they had been saying or how they had been voting or by what might be inferred by their association with party bosses and machines.

There is no sure-fire test to determine the sincerity of those who advocated various reforms in this period or any other period. Passing the test of sincerity is easier if a researcher has reason to know that a politician realizes that what he or she is proposing is not likely to be popular. On the other hand, one cannot simply write off a politician who proposes reforms that he or she thinks is popular as an opportunist—politicians can sincerely believe that something that is likely to be well received by the public is worth doing.

This is not to deny that Progressivism had its bandwagon effect; many hopped on, hoping to use the "Progressive stands" they took to help them win office. With reform sentiment in full swing, more than one ambitious politician saw becoming at least a "rhetorical Progressive" as key to winning election. Like businesspeople, they offered popular programs in exchange for votes. But politics, then as now, had as much to do with religion and conviction as it did with economics and self-interest. Progressive governors often seemed highly motivated crusaders out on a holy mission.

While one cannot come to any firm conclusions about the underlying motivations of those governors who championed (or, for that matter, opposed) reform, it seems reasonable to assume that when it comes to finding determined and uncompromising true believers during this period, one is more likely to find them among academics and citizen groups than among governors. Compared with the others, governors were in a highly practical business in which it paid to be concerned about strategic considerations regarding elections and the political and economic feasibility of pursing various objectives, a business in which a positive outcome often required compromise and the balancing of competing interests.

All in all, it also seemed reasonable to proceed on the assumption that the policy stands of governors in this period reflected their own values as well as their ties to various groups, perceptions of public opinion, and what was best for their political parties or their individual political fortunes. Picking and choosing out of the broad and far-ranging set of ideas that were floating around, governors are viewed as putting together their own particular package of reforms that satisfied their values and practical concerns. I also anticipated that their general outlook and assessment of the value of specific reforms affiliated would often differ considerably from that of the Progressive outsiders, the intellectuals, ideologues, muckrakers, and other true believers.

The discussion of individual governors in the following pages is necessarily abbreviated because of their large number and because of limitations on information and space. Far more attention is given to some governors than others. Some are of interest primarily in tracing the course of reform in their states. Special attention is given, though, to the backgrounds, personalities, and governing styles of several governors, especially the most productive. Research indicates that personality and experience have a great deal to do with the success of presidents and governors.[47] We look into these qualities and the importance of the economic, social, and political conditions in which the governors functioned. As the following chapters indicate, this environment differed, often on a regional or subregional basis, in regard to such matters as labor and racial tensions, gubernatorial powers, party competition, and the strength of political party organizations. We first look at the general historical context in which reform took place.

NOTES

1. Valuable reviews of the vast amount of literature on the Progressive movement are found in Link and McCormick, *Progressivism*; and Rodgers, "In Search of Progressivism." More recent

works that also provide literature reviews are McGerr, *A Fierce Discontent*; and Stromquist, *Reinventing "The People."*

2. While Progressivism was often first manifested on the local level, there were exceptions, such as in Kansas and New Hampshire, where the state level was initially more important when it came to meaningful action. See Wright, *Progressive Yankees*, xix, and La Forte, *Leaders of Reform*, 5.

3. Berge, *Free Pass Bribery System*, xi.

4. Ibid., vii.

5. Malone, *Battle for Butte*, 113.

6. "Hon. Harry B. Hawes," *Iron County Register*, January 21, 1904, 10.

7. Gunther, *Inside U.S.A.*, 590.

8. On Mugwumps see generally Tucker, *Mugwumps*. On structural versus social reformers, especially in regard to local politics, see Holli, *Reform in Detroit*; Morton, *Justice and Humanity*; and Warner, *Progressivism in Ohio*. A discussion of the rise of honesty and efficiency "independents" and more broad-scale reformers in New York City is found in McCormick, *Realignment to Reform*, 106–8. For a history and analysis of the struggles between the Cleveland and Bryan wings of the Democratic Party see Hollingsworth, *Whirligig of Politics*.

9. Lambert, "The Executive Article," 186–87. In 1906 James Bryce reported that the term of office for governors was four years in twenty-one states, three years in one state, two years in twenty-one states, and one year in two states (Massachusetts and Rhode Island). Some states limited the number of terms a governor could serve, "but in those which do not there seems to exist no tradition forbidding a third term of office similar to that which has prevailed in the Federal government since the days of Washington." Bryce, *American Commonwealth*, 199.

10. Bryce, *American Commonwealth*, 532.

11. "What Is a Governor?" *The Outlook*, December 24, 1910, 893–94.

12. Barnard, *Eagle Forgotten*, 173, citing *Chicago Evening Post*, July 31, 1891.

13. Steffens, *Struggle for Self-Government*, 79.

14. Macdonald, "American Governors," 718.

15. Ibid.

16. Ibid.

17. Graves, *American State Government*, 317.

18. Lipson, *American Governor*, 61.

19. This theme was advanced in the pioneering study by Nicholas Burckel, "Progressive Governors in the Border States." Though only partially concerned with the Progressive era, some useful essays, relating to the leading role played by governors generally in this period and referred to in later notes, are found in Sribnick, *A Legacy of Innovation*.

20. Burckel, "Progressive Governors in the Border States."

21. Quoted by Barnard, *Eagle Forgotten*, 33.

22. See "The New Governors."

23. White, "Political Signs of Promise," 668–69.

24. "The Difference in Governors," *Evening Times-Republican*, August 4, 1910, 4, taken from *Sioux City Tribune*.

25. See generally Argersinger, *Limits of Agrarian Radicalism*; Hicks, *Populist Revolt*; and Griffiths, *Populism in the Western United States*.

26. Mathews "The New Stateism."

27. See Ambar, *How Governors Built the Modern American Presidency*.

28. L. B. Hanna to James H. Hawley, November 29, 1912, James Hawley Papers, Idaho State Historical Society.

29. [Illegible name] to W. E. Lindsey, March 27, 1917, Governor Washington E. Lindsey Collection, New Mexico State Records Center and Archives.

30. Brooks, *A Legacy of Leadership*, 9.

31. McGee, *Proceedings of a Conference of Governors*, 157.
32. Ibid., 218.
33. Brooks, *When Governors Convene*, 21–22.
34. See, for example, "Poll of Governors on 1912," *New York Times*, September 14, 1911, 1.
35. *Proceedings of the Conference of Western Governors, Held at Denver*, 102.
36. "House of Southern Governors," *Public Ledger*, October 7, 1915, 4; "Governors Invited," *Richmond Times-Dispatch*, July 13, 1915, 1; and "Race Questions Up by Governors," *Pensacola Journal*, December 10, 1919, 2.
37. "Interstate Control of Interstate Commerce," *Burlington Weekly Free Press*, January 30, 1913, 8.
38. Macdonald, "American Governors."
39. Schlesinger, *How They Became Governor*.
40. Ibid., 51, 81; Nolette, "Litigating the 'Public Interest' in the Gilded Age"; and Geiger, *Joseph W. Folk of Missouri*, 64.
41. Roper, "The Governorship in History."
42. White, *Roosevelt the Reformer*, 1. White cites a letter from Roosevelt to John Strachey, March 9, 1901.
43. Roosevelt to Hadley, quoted in Martin, *Ballots and Bandwagons*, 46.
44. "Woodrow Wilson Talks on Big Public Questions," *New York Times*, December 24, 1911, SM1.
45. Baker, *Woodrow Wilson*, 274.
46. Reiter, "The Bases of Progressivism," 84.
47. See, example, Barber, *Presidential Character*; Crew, "Gubernatorial Leadership"; and Gross, "Governors and Policymaking."

2

THE FLOW OF PARTY POLITICS AND REFORM, 1890–1920

National political trends deeply influenced developments on the state level during the Populist-Progressive years. Governors and other state politicians were caught up in strong national shifts in public opinion, changing political alliances, and shifts in public policy. Demands for reform produced splits in both major parties on the national level and contributed to the creation or growth of third parties. Democrats started with a falling out between the followers of Grover Cleveland and William Jennings Bryan. Insurgency spread in the Republican Party from the efforts of relatively isolated reform-minded individuals to capture a nomination over the objections of a conservative establishment, to the growth of a faction within a political party that favored Robert La Follette or Theodore Roosevelt over President William Howard Taft, to the birth of a new political party.[1] Reform came in many places when major parties, attempting to build, retain, or gain support, adopted popular programs being offered by third parties, such as the Populists, Bull Moose Progressives, and the more radical Nonpartisan League. This period of party disruption, which represented a turn to the left, was accompanied by a tidal wave of reform legislation and reform activity in the states.

CLEVELAND, POPULISTS, BRYAN, AND WILSON

Grover Cleveland, whom New York voters made governor in 1882, ran a frugal businesslike administration and earned the respect of the "honesty and efficiency" group by curbing spending and refusing to bow to the leaders of the Tammany Hall Democratic Party machine when deciding who should receive various appointments and how to handle matters of public policy. He made a complete break with the machine by leading a successful effort to defeat the reelection of the organization's leader in the state senate. As part of the battle, he also successfully pushed for a civil service law, putting a crimp in the patronage system depended upon by the political machines. At the same time, he showed his limited-government, pro-business side by vetoing a bill to reduce the fares charged to ride the elevated trains owned by the unpopular railroad baron Jay Gould in New York City. Eastern Republican Mugwumps saw a kindred spirit in Cleveland. In 1884 they asserted their independence by rejecting the scandal-damaged Republican presidential nominee, James G. Blaine, and rallying behind Cleveland in his bid for the presidency. Their support, especially strong in New York, helped swing the election to Cleveland.[2]

Voters turned down Cleveland in his bid for reelection as president in 1888, but he came back to win the office in 1892. Trouble began for him shortly after his reelection with the advent of a deep recession bringing business failures and unemployment caused by the Panic of 1893. During the severe depression, various groups of unemployed workers set out for Washington, DC, to protest the failure of the federal government to do anything about the unemployment problem. Some hijacked trains in trying to make their way to Washington. The most publicized protest group was led by Ohio businessman and Populist agitator Jacob S. Coxey. Coxey left Massillon, Ohio, on March 25, 1894, with about 100 followers and reached the nation's capital on May 1 with about 500 men, having picked up followers along the way. Coxey demanded that Congress alleviate the unemployment problem by initiating a vast program of public works, such as road building, to provide jobs. President Cleveland and Congress ignored the demands made by "Coxey's Army." The protest drive came to a humiliating end soon after police arrested Coxey for walking on the grass at the US Capitol. Coxey spent a month in jail for this offense.

The economic downturn prompted Cleveland to call a special session of Congress to repeal the Sherman Silver Purchase Act, which had been adopted in 1890. He felt that the act had dangerously depleted the government's gold resources and, with this, contributed to the "financial distrust and fear" that had suddenly sprung up and would cause more damage if not repealed.[3] After a long and bitter debate Congress repealed the act. Cleveland's action and, more broadly, his belief in a single gold standard brought him into conflict with many in his own party who sought a bimetallic monetary standard of gold and silver. Cleveland's suppression of the Pullman Strike in 1894 further angered a large segment of his party. With only a bit of exaggeration it can be said that Richard Olney, Cleveland's attorney general, who also was serving on several railroad boards, "used every instrument of federal power except the navy" to break the strike.[4]

While several issues, including corporate regulation, the rights of labor, and democratizing the political process, emerged in the 1890s and early 1900s, "free silver" dominated political discourse. Supporters of free silver demanded that the federal government return to the bimetallic gold and silver standard it had abandoned in 1873 and purchase silver bullion for conversion into silver dollars without limit (freely), with sixteen grains of silver equaling the value of one grain of gold.

The movement for the free coinage of silver was popular as a general inflationary policy that would allow debtors to pay off their creditors with less valuable dollars. This made the cause popular to many debt-ridden farmers. In much of the West free coinage of silver was valued as a way of reviving the silver mining industry. Free silver was something both mine owners and mine workers could agree upon. More broadly, a long line of reformers in the anti-monopoly tradition saw free silver as a way of ensuring economic opportunity, striking back at the railroads, bankers, and other creditors, and pursuing the theme that "government is to be used, not for the few, but for the many."[5] Ohio Progressive reformer Tom Johnson declared shortly before his death in 1911 that he had joined the cause in the belief that "the free silver fight was the first great protest of the American people against monopoly—the first great struggle of the masses in our country against the privileged classes." He went on to note: "It was not free silver that frightened the plutocratic leaders. What they feared then, what they fear now, is free men."[6]

The adoption of a bimetallic monetary system of silver and gold was one of the most popular "talking points" of the Populist or People's Party, which came to life in a meeting in 1892 when grassroots farmer organizations, called Farmers' Alliances, and the nation's leading labor organization, the Knights of Labor, got together in St. Louis and decided to merge their efforts. The party held its first convention that same year in Omaha, Nebraska. The Populist Party largely disappeared after merging with the Democratic Party in 1896 behind William Jennings Bryan, who lost the presidential election to Republican William McKinley that year.

Some of those attracted to the Populist Party were primarily interested in the silver issue, while others, known as middle-of-the roaders or mid-roaders, were committed, and often uncompromisingly so, to the broad set of more fundamental reforms found in the Populist platform, including public control of railroads and other corporations, the protection of the rights of labor, and a variety of political reforms, including the popular election of US senators, the initiative, and the referendum. Populism was more labor oriented in the West, especially the mountain regions, than in the South and Midwest. In the latter two regions, Populism was far more farmer based.

Populists tended to be skeptical of representative government. In their view, corporate lobbyists dominated city councils and had, if anything, an even more corrupting influence on state legislatures.[7] Populists, unlike many Progressives to come, were also distrustful of a strong executive. Rather than concentrate power in the office of governor, they placed their hope on the force of direct public control through such means as the initiative and referendum as a remedy for legislative corruption and failure.

Many Democrats who wound up opposing Cleveland had much in common with the Populists on the silver and other economic and political issues. This was especially true of Bryan, who emerged as a leader of the anti-Cleveland faction in the Democratic Party. In addition to differences over silver and other policy issues, the Bryan and Cleveland factions had basic underlying philosophical differences. The Cleveland Democrats, in contrast to the Bryan types, were strongly attached to free enterprise, individualism, limited government, and the notion that "the better elements" should rule society. They were less sympathetic than the Bryanites to those in poverty, seeing this condition as something brought on by a lack of effort or immorality. To Cleveland Democrats, government had no obligation to interfere with the natural course of economic or social affairs and to do so would be contrary to the general welfare.[8] As Cleveland put it succinctly in 1887, "the lesson should be constantly enforced that though the people support the Government the Government should not support the people."[9]

Those in the Bryan wing, like the Populists and, later, the Progressives, moved away from laissez-faire, individualism, and limited government and generally took the position that poverty was the product of conditions over which the poor had no control or, borrowing from the Populists, that the poor were that way because the rich were stealing from them. Bryan sought to bring the good life to all people, not simply the privileged. He pledged to break up the monopolies, regulate or nationalize the railroads, democratize the political system so that the common people could rule, and shift more of the costs of government to those who could afford to pay. Many people, including Theodore Roosevelt and Woodrow Wilson, who eventually picked up many of his ideas, initially saw him as a dangerous revolutionary.[10] As the following pages suggest, Bryan was everywhere, unstoppable, irrepressible, a dominant personality in the period under review, interacting with a host of governors, mostly Democrats, but also some Republicans, campaigning for them, and pushing for reform measures in states throughout the country.

Bryan had worked his way up in the Nebraska Democratic Party as a friend of J. Sterling Morton, an anti-Populist, Cleveland Democrat who failed several times in his bid for the governorship. Morton supported Bryan's successful bid for Congress in 1890, but Bryan had moved away from Morton and the free-enterprise position by the time he came up for reelection in 1892. He managed to win that election, though, by only a small margin.[11]

Bryan and his followers made plans to capture the Democratic Party in the summer of 1893 after Congress, with Cleveland's help, repealed the Sherman

Silver Purchase Act of 1890. By 1896, Bryan, borrowing much from the Populists, had assumed leadership of the Democratic Party and was steering it on to the broad cause of basic political, social, and economic reform.[12] He lost in 1896 and again in 1900 in a bid for the presidency. In 1904 the party turned away from him and went conservative, hoping to win corporate backing with the nomination of a Cleveland Democrat, Judge Alton Parker, for president. Parker went down to a disastrous defeat, and the Bryanites rebounded back into power four years later.

In the states, meanwhile, a long string of Populist and Democratic governors pushed for change. During the 1890s voters chose several Populist governors who ran either on Populist tickets or, more commonly, on tickets representing the combined efforts of the Populist Party, the Democratic Party, and, in some instances, the Silver Republican Party (Republicans who supported the silver cause). In Oregon a governor who was elected as a Democrat changed his affiliation to the Populist Party after his election. In 1892 the major Populist victories took place in Kansas, North Dakota, and Colorado. These were followed in 1894, 1896, and 1898 by less spectacular breakthroughs in Nebraska, Idaho, Montana, South Dakota, Washington, and Minnesota and in Kansas, where the fusion ticket was reelected. Populists also ran strongly in the South, sometimes in biracial alliances with the Republican Party, but were able to elect a governor only in North Carolina. Populist influence and gains in the several southern states, however, prompted Democratic and Republican leaders to try to offset their appeal by taking up the case against railroads and other reforms that Populists had made popular. Along with this, though, came a called for white unity behind the Democratic Party.

Governors leading the drive for reform from the Democratic side during the 1890s included Ben Tillman in South Carolina, James Hogg in Texas, and John Peter Altgeld in Illinois—each of which, like other Democratic reformers, blunted the strength of the Populists in their states by adopting much of the Populist program. By the early 1900s, Progressive Democrats could boast of several governors who were dynamic leaders, such as Joseph Folk of Missouri, John A. Johnson of Minnesota, John Burke of North Dakota, Judson Harmon in Ohio, Hoke Smith of Georgia, Napoleon Broward of Florida, Braxton Comer of Alabama, and Luis Garvin of Rhode Island.

Bryan, looking for another bid in 1908, was not reluctant to attack Democratic governors who thought about seeking the Democratic nomination, though he seemed a bit softer when it came to candidates like Folk, whom he had long supported. Bryan went on to lose to Republican William Howard Taft. Democrats, though, saw some hope in the returns with the gubernatorial victories of Harmon in Ohio, Thomas Marshall in Indiana, John Shafroth in Colorado, and John Johnson, once more in Minnesota. Progressive Democrats were further stimulated by the prospect that a corporate-friendly Taft administration would give them an opportunity to march to victory as the party of reform (Roosevelt had been difficult to oppose on this basis). They also saw the split in Republican ranks between insurgents and conservatives as helping them make inroads, and, indeed, they were to benefit considerably at the polls because of this division.

In 1910 came Democratic Progressive gubernatorial victories for Woodrow Wilson in New Jersey, John Dix in New York, Simeon Baldwin in Connecticut, and Frederick Plaisted in Maine and Harmon's reelection in Ohio. The following year Progressive-minded Democrats came to power with the admission of two new states to the union: Arizona, where George Hunt became governor, and New Mexico, where W. C. McDonald won the gubernatorial contest. In 1912 Wilson's successful run for the presidency and the Republican split between Roosevelt and Taft helped elect or reelect Democratic gubernatorial candidates William Sulzer in New York, Simeon Baldwin in Connecticut, Edward Dunne in Illinois, Woodbridge Ferris in Michigan, Samuel Stewart in Montana, Samuel Felker in New Hampshire, James Cox in Ohio, and Ernest Lister in Washington.

Wilson, with the benefit of a Congress controlled by members of his party who were perhaps even more committed to change than he was, fulfilled his "New Freedom" pledges, made during his run for the presidency, with the passage of a strong line of Progressive reforms. These included the cutting of tariff rates that had long benefited monopolies, the creation of a Federal Reserve System to better manage the economy and protect against bank panics, legislation establishing a progressive income tax, the Federal Trade Commission to combat unfair business practices, the Clayton Act, which both benefited unions and further regulated business practices, and various labor laws.

REPUBLICAN INSURGENTS, LA FOLLETTE AND ROOSEVELT

Republicans had their own reform-minded revolution, starting in the late 1890s with insurgent governors such as Hazen Pingree in Michigan and Theodore Roosevelt in New York and extending into the early 1900s with Charles Evans Hughes in New York, Coe Crawford in South Dakota, Albert Cummins in Iowa, Robert La Follette in Wisconsin, and Hiram Johnson in California. Several of these governors went on to join other Republicans as insurgents in Congress, working to make the party one of reform.

Moving up from the vice-presidency to the presidency following the assassination of President McKinley, Roosevelt did not challenge the conservative Republicans who controlled Congress but, acting on his own, initiated an antitrust action through his attorney general to break up the Northern Securities trust. Progressives also applauded his handling of the Pennsylvania anthracite coal strike in 1902 when he threatened to use federal troops to take control of the mines if mine owners continued to refuse to negotiate with striking miners, forcing an arbitration decision very favorable to the miners. Elected to a full term over conservative Democrat Alton Parker in 1904, Roosevelt proceeded with more antitrust activity and sided with Progressive Republicans in Congress to strengthen railroad regulation through the Hepburn Act and to adopt the Pure Food and Drug Act.

Roosevelt backed Taft for president in 1908, seeing him as his heir, and the Republican Progressives went along with this recommendation, taking some comfort in finding that conservatives were unhappy with the selection. Taft defeated Bryan, who was making his third bid for the presidency, but he did not deliver to the satisfaction of Roosevelt and the insurgent Republicans. Several Republican governors joined the movement of insurgents to take over the GOP prior to the presidential election of 1912.

The Progressive rebellion within the party led into the creation of the National Progressive Republican League (NPRL) to strengthen the insurgent faction in the Republican Party, encourage the adoption of Progressive reforms, and, many suspected, help boost former governor Robert M. La Follette's effort to challenge President Taft for the 1912 Republican presidential nomination. The organization was born in a meeting in the Washington, DC, home of Senator La Follette on January 21, 1911.[13] Nine US senators, thirteen members of the US House of Representatives, and six governors signed on as charter members of La Follette's league. The governors were Chester Aldrich of Nebraska, Joseph Carey of Wyoming, Hiram Johnson of California, Francis E. McGovern of Wisconsin, Chase Osborn of Michigan, and W. R. Stubbs of Kansas. Governor Osborn was also an officer in the organization, as was a noted citizen reformer, George L. Record of New Jersey. Theodore Roosevelt, no doubt suspecting something was being plotted by his rival La Follette, refused to sign on, as did Roosevelt supporter and Progressive governor Robert P. Bass of New Hampshire.[14]

Roosevelt, after much hesitation, decided to make a bid for the Republican nomination. As for his likely opponent, Roosevelt felt that "Taft means well, but he means well feebly."[15] Several governors had encouraged Roosevelt to make a firm commitment to run, so he asked the governors to frame a letter urging his candidacy that they could all sign and to which he would publicly respond in the affirmative. He got the state party chair in Michigan to draft the letter and secure the signatures of the governors.[16] On February 10, 1912, four governors who were charter members of the NPRL—Aldrich, Carey, Osborn, and Stubbs—joined Republican governors Bass of New Hampshire, Herbert Hadley of Missouri, and William Glasscock of West Virginia in signing the letter and publicly urging Roosevelt to make a run at securing the Republican presidential nomination in 1912.[17] Roosevelt's affirmative response to the letter, which had been prepared well in advance of receiving it, came as a declaration of candidacy on February 25.

Roosevelt in 1912 did well in several presidential primaries but lost contested delegations at the Republican national convention, held in Chicago in June;

Figure 2.1. Theodore Roosevelt. Courtesy of the Library of Congress, Prints & Photographs Division, LC-DIG-ppmsca-36121.

realizing he was not going to secure the nomination, he bolted the meeting and went on to form the National Progressive Party (aka the Bull Moose Party) behind his candidacy for president. Roosevelt was set to challenge Taft and whomever the Democrats nominated. Several governors, such as Bass of New Hampshire and Carey of Wyoming, Robert Vessey of South Dakota, and Hiram Johnson of California, joined the Bull Moosers, with Johnson accepting the new party's nomination for the vice-presidency.

Roosevelt's campaign, however, received a blow when Democrats nominated Woodrow Wilson for president. The Bull Moosers had hoped the Democrats would go for a more conservative candidate than Wilson and, thus, push Democratic Party reformers to Roosevelt. With Wilson's nomination, several Progressives backed away from their support of a Progressive third party headed by Roosevelt. They took the position that Wilson's draw on the Progressive vote would make it impossible for Roosevelt to win the election and that the third party was not really needed and could do considerable damage to the Republican ticket.[18]

Roosevelt lost several of the governors who had supported him, including Stubs, Aldrich, Hadley, and Glasscock. Osborn wound up campaigning for Roosevelt, but not in Michigan, and would not join the Bull Moose Party. Several were fearful that Roosevelt's candidacy and a Bull Moose Party ticket would have devastating effects on Republican Party candidates in their state. In several cases, the Republican split did, indeed, facilitate the election of Progressive Democrats.[19]

Starting in 1916 and going into the 1920s, another reform-minded third party, the Nonpartisan League (NPL), enjoyed considerable influence in several states. Inspired in part by the La Follette–led movement in Wisconsin, it came to life in North Dakota in 1915 under the leadership of Arthur Townley, a former organizer for the Socialist Party who organized small farmers into a political movement directed at establishing several state-owned enterprises. In North Dakota much of the wrath of the farmers was directed against out-of-state companies, especially banking, milling, and railway interests located in Minnesota.

Townley saw little hope in trying to bring about change through third-party activity but saw the direct primary as offering a means through which reformers could put up and campaign for a candidate or slate of candidates in the primary of the dominant major party. In 1916 his league with a program not unlike that of the Socialist Party backed a slate of candidates who entered the Republican Party primary. One of these, a virtually unknown farmer, won the party's nomination for governor and went on to win the general election. Success in North Dakota stimulated a similar movement of farmers in South Dakota, Colorado, Idaho, Montana, Minnesota, and other states and had an indirect effect on public policy in some of these, especially South Dakota, but did not produce governors in any other state.[20]

REFORM IN THE STATES, POLICIES AND CONCERNS

While the major parties and factions within the major parties were battling it out from 1890 to 1920, state governments were considering a host of reform issues, being spurred on by various groups and in many places by the exposure of wrongdoing by journalistic "muckrakers." Changing directions took place through state constitutional conventions and the initiative process as well as by legislation and administrative action. In regard to constitutional changes, from 1898 to 1914 eight states, including three just joining the union, adopted new constitutions, and close to a thousand amendments were made to the constitutions of other states.[21]

One result of all the activity was increased spending. Even when accounting for population growth and inflation, the spending of state and local governments doubled from 1902 to 1922, with especially large increases for education and highways but also significant amounts for health, corrections, and social welfare.[22] As the functions of the states grew, so did taxes, though Progressives sought to shift as much of the burden as possible to large business enterprises and wealthy individuals. Increased corporate taxation came in large part by shifting the evaluation of railroad and other corporate property from local assessors, where the property was commonly underassessed, to state tax commissions that increased these assessments. Effective state-level personal income taxes were adopted in nine states between 1911 and 1919. Wisconsin led the way.[23]

One trailblazing breakthrough in the area of welfare came in the form of mothers' pension laws (aka widows' pensions, mothers' aid, and mothers' allowances laws), which authorized local governments to provide financial aid on a regular basis to mothers to take care of their children in their own homes when there was no adult male to provide income. Keeping children with their mothers was seen as providing a better environment for the children and being less costly for the government than sending children to orphanages or providing foster care for them. Laws of this nature first passed on a statewide basis in Illinois in 1911 and spread rapidly around the country, being adopted in various forms in thirty-nine states by 1919. The movement was driven by women's clubs, child welfare reformers, and juvenile court judges and had only token opposition, largely from private charities. This cause did not play much of a role in the calculations or concerns of politicians. It was seldom addressed in party platforms or given much attention by party leaders when they listed their accomplishments. It was a widely popular cause, essentially bipartisan in nature, and advocates sought with considerable success to keep it out of partisan politics.[24]

Many of the reform proposals during the Progressive period called for changing the way states elected public officials, structured their governing institutions, and went about doing their business. This drive, as one observer noted, represented a multifaceted effort to "better organize democracy" at the state level so that democracy would no longer be the easy "prey of organized privilege." In this Progressives were following the burst of a similar reform activity that had taken place on the municipal level.[25] Other reforms had to do with efforts to rein in corporation practices, provide labor protection, and address issues of morality, penal reform, and law and order.

Prominent among the political system reforms proposed during this period and discussed in the following pages—and perhaps the most important in terms of both its short- and long-term impacts—was the direct primary to eliminate the control of political bosses over the nomination of candidates. The direct primary moved the nomination process out of party conventions and opened it up to the voters, though, most often, only those aligned with a particular political party. Noted political scientist Austin Ranney, writing in 1975, considered the direct primary "the most radical of all the party reforms adopted in the whole course of American history."[26] The direct primary was a major Progressive-era reform. From 1901 to 1917, starting with Wisconsin in 1904 and shortly followed by Oregon the same year, forty-six of the forty-eight states adopted various versions of the system.[27]

Most of the states that were to eventually adopt the widely heralded reform of direct legislation—the initiative and referendum—did so during the period under review. Statewide adoption began in South Dakota in 1898, followed by Utah in 1900, Oregon in 1902, and Montana in 1906. By 1918 nineteen states had the initiative and referendum, and two other states had the referendum only.[28] Many viewed the initiative and referendum as leading indicators of the radical direction in which the country was going. The recall of elected officials, including judges, was considered even more radical. Oregon was the first to adopt the innovation statewide in 1908, and ten other states followed its lead over the next six years.[29]

The Progressive period also brought two election-related movements on the state level that ultimately led to amendments to the US Constitution. One took the choice of US senators away from state legislators and gave it directly to the voters—a movement that ultimately resulted in the adoption of the Seventeenth Amendment to the US Constitution in 1913. Oregon in 1908 was the first to make the election of US senators dependent on popular vote. Over thirty state legislatures adopted resolutions calling on Congress to submit a constitutional amendment calling for direct election. Woman suffrage advocates enjoyed victories in Wyoming, Utah, Colorado, Washington, California, Kansas, Oregon, Arizona, and Illinois, roughly in that order, prior to the adoption of the suffrage amendment to the US Constitution in 1920. Regionally, the battle appeared to some contemporaries as a "psychic contest between the spirit of radicalism in the West," where support was strong, "conservatism in the South," where support was weak, and "cynicism in the North and Middle States," where support was mixed. Only in the South is another great issue involved—the latent fear of reviving "the negro question."[30]

In the area of campaign finance, reform activity prompted several states in the 1880s to adopt "publicity acts" that were predicated on the belief that effective regulation could be imposed through public disclosure of the source of funding, how much was spent, and how it was spent on a campaign. A few states went further and limited the amount of money that could be spent and how the money could be used. By the mid-1910s, nearly every state had enacted a corrupt-practices law regulating the purposes for which campaign funds could be spent, requiring the reporting and accounting of those funds and maintaining treasurers for political committees, prohibiting attempts to influence voters, and limiting the solicitation of funds from public employees or by corporations.[31]

Several other measures affecting the election system, governmental structures, and procedures were popular in reform circles during the 1890–1920 period but never really got off the ground. These included calls for nonpartisan state elections, one-house state legislatures, civil service, a "short ballot" that would eliminate statewide elective offices (in favor of having them appointed by the governor), and general state government reorganization. Nonpartisanship gains were confined to local and judicial elections. Between 1912 and 1919, legislators or voters in Oregon,

Kansas, Oklahoma, Minnesota, Arizona, Washington, and South Dakota gave the establishment of a one-house legislature serious consideration, but no state adopted the unicameral system during this period.[32]

Replacing patronage systems with civil service merit systems—which gave independent commissions the task of hiring governmental employees on the basis of their ability to do the job rather than on their political connections and protected employees from political pressures and removal—was a widely heralded reform but had only limited success in the states. New York acted in 1883, but it was more than twenty years before another state followed suit. In spite of local pressures and the activities of the National Civil Service Reform League, only four states adopted a civil service or merit system in the period from 1900 to 1920 and only one more did before 1936.[33]

In 1910 longtime citizen reformer Richard Childs managed the National Short Ballot Organization, which was dedicated to the cause of reducing the number of elected state administrative officials such as the state treasurer or state auditor and making them the appointees of the governor. This, proponents felt, would improve overall coordination, eliminate waste, take a burden off the voters, and shift the responsibility to someone who was better prepared to make the choice of who should serve in these offices.

Childs operated out of a small office in New York City. One day in December 1910, California governor Hiram Johnson decided to drop in. Childs later wrote: "Governor Johnson . . . visited our office unannounced. All of us were out to lunch! But an alert office boy did what he could, gave him everything we had, and he devoted one-sixth of his message to the legislature to the subject [of the short ballot] a few weeks later with verbatim quotations from our pamphlets."[34] Johnson, though, was only partially successful in getting this reform adopted (see chapter 12).

Getting results was also an uphill battle elsewhere. Childs, using 1912 as an example, noted that even though short-ballot planks appeared in the platforms of several state political parties (Democratic, Republican, and Progressive) and in the messages of eleven governors, nothing happened: "It seemed like a quick and favoring gale of astonishingly prompt response. Alas, it was all lip service; even in states where all three parties endorsed the idea the bills were pocketed in legislative committees."[35]

The short-ballot movement gradually blended into the broader task of not just getting rid of separately elected administrators and making them the appointees of the governor, but to one of generally reorganizing state government to improve the control of the governor in the interest of economy, efficiency, and overall management. State governments were not initially structured with the idea that they had a great deal to do. When they began to do things, they tended to create one agency at a time, without much regard to how what it did affected the tasks given to other agencies. Often too agencies and boards were created whose members had terms greater than those of the governors and could not be removed by them. Virtually nothing was done, however, to reorganize state governments and improve gubernatorial control over state agencies until 1917.[36] Along with increased attention to streamlining state government, reformers made an effort to give governors a greater role in the preparation of state budgets, but, again, by 1918 very little had been accomplished.[37]

Another central theme of Progressive reformers was that lawmakers need to base their decisions on actual societal facts, derived from objective investigations into the nature of various problems and what could be done about them, rather than abstract concepts about human behavior. Legislators and governors could identify problems but were largely amateurs when it came to researching and drafting sound legislation proposals. To help fill this void, several states followed the lead of Wisconsin in the adoption of legislative reference service bureaus to provide needed expertise.[38]

Much of the most noted reform activity on the state level during the Progressive period involved putting controls on large business enterprises. Railroads were a central target of early reformers virtually everywhere in the country. During the late 1860s and 1870s, farmers, organized as Grangers, along with businesspeople in urban areas successfully pushed for the regulation of the rates and various practices of the railroads. They were particularly effective in the midwestern states. Early gains against the railroads were often wiped out by court rulings, but agitation continued on through the Populist period of the 1890s and into the early 1900s when Progressive reformers began taking up the cause.

Fueled by disclosures of corruption, the years 1905–7 brought the establishment of fifteen new railroad commissions and the expansion of the authority of at least that many existing commissions. The commissions had the power to set rates and supervise services, safety, and financial matters, and their authority extended beyond railroads to other public utilities, including gas and electric companies, street railways, and telegraph and telephone companies.[39]

By 1907 the landslide of antirailroad legislation had prompted industry leaders to largely abandon the notion that the states could be depended upon to provide any kind of shelter against a pursuing federal government.[40]

The regulations kept coming. By one estimate, from 1902 to 1910, states passed more than 1,300 laws regulating railroads, and an additional 442 were passed in the next five years.[41] In 1913 alone legislatures in forty-two states passed 230 railroad laws affecting matters from hours of labor to grade crossings. Along with rail and public utility regulations came laws regulating insurance companies, guaranteeing banking depositions, "blue sky" laws against stock fraud, and improved antitrust measures to break up monopolies or monopolistic practices.

Though much of the traditional literature on Progressivism paints the cause as being, at best, lukewarm to labor, a great deal of labor legislation was enacted in the 1890–1920 period, particularly after 1900.[42] From 1911 to 1919, forty states adopted worker's compensation laws.[43] The period also brought laws limiting hours of work, protecting women and children, and factory and mine inspection protections against injuries on the job. While organized labor supported this type of legislation, it is fair to say that its adoption had more to do with the efforts of social welfare reform groups than labor groups and more to do with humanitarian concerns and an "awakened sense of social responsibility" than with concerns for the rights of labor.[44]

Hoping to elevate community morals, many states during the period under review prohibited the manufacture and sale of alcoholic beverages. At the turn of the twentieth century only five of the existing forty-five states had adopted prohibition. These were Maine, Kansas, North Dakota, New Hampshire, and Vermont. Four states, Pennsylvania, Tennessee, Idaho, and Nevada, relied heavily upon high license fees to regulate the liquor traffic. Elsewhere some states allowed local option on the prohibition question, but this system brought the closure of only a relatively few saloons.[45] Calls for prohibition commonly pitted older native stock, people in rural areas, Protestants, and middle-class reformers against newly arrived immigrants, urban dwellers, Catholics, and lower-class citizens.[46]

A surge for prohibition took place after 1900, especially in the South, where there was a high percentage of old, native stock.[47] Prohibition was also linked here to racial considerations. Many whites assumed alcohol "demoralized and debauched black men, reduced their efficiency as workers, and fueled their secret lust for white women."[48] Prohibition was advocated as a way of controlling the behavior of "undependable" and "criminally inclined" black people. Supporters also argued that prohibition would further cut down on the number of blacks voting, because the liquor interests had often been able to control the black vote.[49] In the South nearly all the leading Progressive reformers favored prohibition.[50] By the end of the first decade of the twentieth century, the issue was being debated throughout the country.[51]

Other types of morality legislation developed over the period in regard to gambling, prostitution, and prizefighting. During the Progressive era, eugenics, the sterilization of people who were considered deficient or undesirable, was also a popular cause. It caught on in several states beginning with Indiana in 1907. Sixteen states had adopted sterilization laws by 1917.[52] Eugenics was one of the many reforms floated around in this period that were promoted as being based on science. Adoption of such laws had less to do with public demand than with the testimony of experts in the fields of psychiatry and criminology and those who supervised state institutions for "the feebleminded" and prisoners. "It was primarily a movement of specialists rather than a popular crusade."[53]

During the Progressive period, several efforts were made to adopt reforms protecting people accused or convicted of crimes. One prominent movement was for the abolition of the death penalty. This enjoyed some success: from 1907 to 1917 ten states abolished capital punishment. These were Arizona, Colorado, Kansas, Minnesota, Missouri, North Dakota, Oregon, South Dakota, Tennessee, and Washington.[54] Related reforms included making greater use of parole, probation, and indeterminate sentencing (giving prisoners an opportunity to reduce their sentence because of good behavior) and the improvement of prison conditions. As reformers saw it, the central goal of prison was not punishment but rehabilitation. They hoped to modernize the correctional system by making it both more humane and more scientific.[55]

In the South reformers focused on eliminating the convict labor leasing system, which provided low-cost labor to private contractors engaged in large-scale farming and railroad building and other enterprises. This provided cheap labor to the contractors and a considerable amount of revenue for state governments. It also saved the states money by not having to build and maintain prison facilities. On the other hand, it was condemned largely on humanitarian grounds: "prisoners put to work in isolated locations" and "operators [who] were determined to get as much out of them as possible" produced "incredible conditions of cruelty, brutality, and degradation."[56]

Disputes over the criminal justice system also frequently involved the manner in which governors used their clemency powers. Given the possibility that the system of justice would not always work properly and that innocent people could get convicted or punished with undue severity, governors had been given the power to pardon those convicted of a crime or to commute (reduce) the severity of their sentence. Governors in the Progressive period often used their clemency powers for humane purposes, given the deplorable nature of prison conditions, but also for practical political purposes.[57]

The 1890–1920 period was one of disorder and violence, marked by lynching, race riots, and intense labor-management conflicts. Lynching was not confined to the South but was especially prevalent there, especially in Mississippi, Georgia, and Texas, and most of the people lynched in that region were African American men.[58] Lynching presented difficult situations for state officials because such events often had considerable support in the communities where they occurred, not only by the people at large but local police and city and county officials. If vigilantes were brought to court, jurors and judges were reluctant to punish them.

Difficult questions confronted state officials in handling race riots and using state troops in labor-management disputes. Much of the responsibility in these cases fell to the governor, who, as commander in chief, had control over the National Guard. Governors usually did not take personal command of the guard, leaving this to an adjutant general they appointed. The performance of the guard depended in large part on the ability and leadership of the adjutants general. Still, governors were deeply involved in the most serious events.[59]

Progressivism took place at a time when racism was a growing problem in the nation. The Progressive movement had little to offer minorities. Blacks, Hispanics, Asians, Native Americans, and other minorities suffered social, economic, and political discrimination. It is difficult for those who generally see Progressivism as a good thing to accept someone as a Progressive who was also a committed and virulent racist. Yet many otherwise worthy Progressives were that way. Somehow they saw no conflict between the racist views they held and their public quest for humanitarian causes, equality, and social justice.

Racism could be found in the North as well as the South. The South, however, stood out when it came to keeping blacks out of the voting booth and the amount of violence directed against blacks through vigilante activities.[60] The South also produced state and local Jim Crow laws mandating the separation of the blacks and whites in virtually all public facilities, including schools, trains and buses, theaters, parks, hospitals, restaurants, prisons, cemeteries, restrooms, and even telephone booths. Facilities for the races were to be "separate but equal," but, in fact, they were anything but equal as far as blacks were concerned. Southern leaders considered black disfranchisement and segregation necessary preconditions to Progressivism if not Progressive reforms in themselves. With the race issue "settled" by denying blacks the right to vote and separating them from whites in public facilities, the states, it was argued, could move on to reforms that would help the South catch up with the North.

The drive for reform in the states from 1890 to 1920 was deeply influenced by national movements and events. There was a great deal of borrowing of ideas and proposals from national reform organizations and groups representing public officials and much one-on-one exchange of information among candidates and officeholders around the country. Throughout the nation many of the same arguments were used both in support of and opposition to various programs, and there was much similarity in the measures adopted. Still, as the literature suggests and the following pages further illustrate, there were differences often occurring on a regional basis in the general context in which decisions were made, the overall approach to reform, and reform outputs.[61]

NOTES

1. Johansen and Gates, *Empire of the Columbia*, 471.
2. See generally Tucker, *Mugwumps*.
3. Grover Cleveland, "Special Session Message," August 8, 1893, in Richardson, *A Compilation of the Messages and Papers of the Presidents*, 9:401–5.
4. Beatty, *Age of Betrayal*, 193.
5. De Witt, *Progressive Movement*, 26–27.
6. Johnson, *My Story*, 109.
7. Postel, *Populist Vision*, 161.

8. On these differences see generally Hollingsworth, *Whirligig of Politics*, 5–6.

9. Veto message to the US House of Representatives, February 16, 1887, in Richardson, *A Compilation of the Messages and Papers of the Presidents*, 8:557.

10. Koenig, *Bryan*.

11. Folsom, *No More Free Markets or Free Beer*, 28–29.

12. On Bryan's debt to the Populists see Koenig, *Bryan*, 10.

13. On the creation of the league see La Follette, *La Follette's Autobiography*, 211–13. For a copy of the "personal and confidential" letter La Follette sent to those he felt might be interested in joining the league, see La Follette to Governor Carey, January 7, 1911, Carey Administrative Papers, Joseph M. Carey Papers, Wyoming State Archives.

14. "Republicans Launch Progressive League," *Hartford Courant*, January 24, 1911, 12.

15. Martin, *Ballots and Bandwagons*, 18.

16. Ibid., 33.

17. The governors signed the letter at a meeting of the National Roosevelt Committee, held in Chicago on February 10, 1912. In addition to Carey, Stubbs, Osborn, Hadley, Aldridge, Bass, and Glasscock, Governor Vessey of South Dakota was at the meeting but was called away before he had a chance to sign the letter. He did say, however, he was in complete agreement with it. See "Eight Governors in a Roosevelt League," *New York Times*, February 11, 1912, 1.

18. "Many Deserting Roosevelt Ranks," *New York Times*, July 4, 1912, 1.

19. See generally Gable, *Bull Moose Years*.

20. See generally Morlan, *Political Prairie Fire*; National Nonpartisan League Papers, State Historical Society of North Dakota.

21. Faulkner, *Quest For Social Justice*, 84–85.

22. Richards, "Half of Our Century," 83, 86; Howe and Reeb, "The Historical Evolution of State and Local Tax Systems," 113.

23. Mehrotra and Shreve, "To Lay and Collect."

24. See generally Leff, "Consensus for Reform." See also Skocpol et al., "Women's Associations and the Enactment of Mothers' Pensions."

25. Holcombe, "Organizing Democracy."

26. Ranney. *Cursing the Mischiefs of Faction*, 121.

27. Information concerning the dates when states adopted the direct primary and several other reforms covered in this study was taken from materials used in Walker, "The Diffusion of Innovations among the American States." The materials are found on line at http://www.icpsr.umich.edu/icpsrweb/ICPSR/ssvd/studies/66.

28. MacDonald, *State and Local Government*, 329. According to another source, between 1898 and 1918 twenty-two states adopted the initiative and referendum, and twelve states adopted the recall. See Noble, *New Jersey before Wilson*, 130.

29. Faulkner, *Quest for Social Justice*, 85–86.

30. "What America Thinks of Votes for Women," *Literary Digest*, October 9, 1915, 753.

31. Hohenstein, *Curbing Corruption*, 67.

32. Childs, *Civic Victories*, 119–22.

33. Walker, "The Diffusion of Innovations."

34. Childs, *Civic Victories*, 86.

35. Ibid., 88.

36. See generally Buck, *Reorganization of State Governments*.

37. See Willoughby, *Movement for Budgetary Reform*.

38. See the discussion in Burns, "The Legislative Reference Movement in Ohio."

39. Link and McCormick, *Progressivism*, 33; McCormick, *Realignment to Reform*, 225.

40. "States' Rights and Railroad Wrongs," *Literary Digest*, August 17, 1907, 219–20.

41. Kolko, *Railroads and Regulation*, 218.

42. On labor laws passed in this period see Fishback, Holmes, and Allen, "Lifting the Curse of Dimensionality."
43. Walker, "The Diffusion of Innovations."
44. Dulles and Dubofsky, *Labor in America*, 191–93.
45. Timberlake, *Prohibition and the Progressive Movement*, 149.
46. Ibid., 150–53.
47. Ibid.; Grantham *Southern Progressivism*, 160–77.
48. Grantham, *Southern Progressivism*, 176.
49. Timberlake, *Prohibition and the Progressive Movement*, 155.
50. Ibid., 175.
51. Ibid., 158. See also "Prohibition Fight Is Now National," *New York Times*, September 6, 1908, 4; "Prohibition the Issue of 1911 in Many States," *New York Times*, July 16, 1911, MS13.
52. Haller, *Eugenics*, 133–34.
53. Ibid., 124.
54. See Galliher, Ray, and Cook, "Abolition and Reinstatement of Capital Punishment"; and Filler, "Movements to Abolish the Death Penalty."
55. For a useful overview of this effort see Pillsbury, "Understanding Penal Reform." On the variety of penal reforms pursued in the Progressive era see Rothman, *Conscience and Convenience*.
56. Grantham, *Southern Progressivism*, 128.
57. See generally Jensen, *Pardoning Power*.
58. Cooper, *Rise of the National Guard*, 47.
59. Ibid., 81–82.
60. Keyssar, *Right to Vote*, 170.
61. One of the few studies that touch upon regional differences throughout the country is Link and McCormick, *Progressivism*.

3

MIDWESTERNERS PAVING THE WAY

Altgeld, Pingree, La Follette, with Follow-ups by Deneen, Dunne, Osborn, and McGovern

Russel Nye, author of a pioneering study of the Progressive movement in the Midwest, characterized the effort of reformers in this region as "moderate rather than revolutionary, aimed at planned experimentation rather than disintegration and upheaval." Reformers, he felt, came up with practical solutions to specific problems. Nye too noted: "It was always difficult for demagogues to gain a Midwestern following of any significance."[1]

While most of the reform-minded governors of the region were certainly less demagogic than one finds in the South and many might be justly considered moderate in their views, it is also true that many were more than willing to take on the dominant economic interests in their states and to experiment with innovative ideas concerning economic, social, and political reform in the interest of the many rather than a few.

Farmer unrest, evidenced in the Granger movement of the 1860s and 1870s, had a strong left-leaning impact on the development of a reform orientation in midwestern states such as Illinois, Iowa, Minnesota, Wisconsin, Kansas, and Nebraska. Farmers complained about low prices for their produce, high freight rates, high interest rates, exploitative middle men driving up their costs and eating into their profits, and corrupt legislators catering to the railroads and other corporations at their expense.

The Populist Party, building upon these grievances and offering solutions to the problems, was strong in much of the Midwest, especially Kansas, Nebraska, North

Dakota, South Dakota, and Minnesota, where Populist governors were elected. In much of the Midwest, however, the appeal of the Populist Party was diminished by the loyalty given to the two major parties, especially the Republican Party. Some states in the Midwest were as much one-party Republican as states in the South were one-party Democratic. Many resembled eastern states in regard to the importance of ethnic politics, and several were similar in regard to the importance of big-city political machines.

In this chapter we begin with a focus on the careers, character, and accomplishments of three Progressive trailblazers: Democrat John Peter Altgeld of Illinois and Republicans Hazen Pingree of Michigan and Robert La Follette of Wisconsin, each of whom shared the Mugwump approach in moving toward more fundamental reform. A biographer of Altgeld complained several years ago that this governor's many contributions in helping to keep his state "from becoming a laggard in the march of social progress" had been buried under the firestorm that his opponents had created out of his decision to pardon prisoners convicted for their part in the Haymarket bombing.[2] Here we discuss the pardons, but also focus more broadly on Altgeld the humanitarian, who was, indeed, in many respects a major agenda builder for governors to come in Illinois, especially Edward Dunne, and around the nation. Pingree, also a humanitarian, moved up from the office of mayor to the office of governor, bringing an urban agenda and a strong anticorporate outlook to the job. Though developing a national following, he found the job frustrating in terms of accomplishment. Still the machine that opposed him withered away, and subsequent governors, especially Republican Chase Osborn, were able to implement much of his agenda. La Follette, a Republican but a friend of William Jennings Bryan and someone who had considerable Democratic support, focused on political and economic reform and produced a wide range of measures that made him among the best-known Progressives in the country if not the best known. La Follette built a reform-orientated political machine that continued on well after he left for Washington for the US Senate in the administrations of Francis McGovern and others.

JOHN PETER ALTGELD: WAY BEYOND MUGWUMPISM

Born in Germany, John Peter Altgeld immigrated with his family as a three-month-old child to the United States. He grew up in poverty in Missouri, where he became a teacher, a lawyer, a county attorney, and a champion of the Granger cause. He won the county attorney office as a candidate of the Granger-backed "People's Party," which had fused with the Democratic Party. He came to Chicago in 1875 and opened a law practice. Largely because of his real estate investments, he became relatively wealthy. He was not considered a physically attractive man.

Slight, plagued by a twitch, he once joked about himself: "Hell, if I had to depend on my looks I'd have been hung long ago!"[3]

His initial entry into a political life in Illinois came in 1884 with the printing of a small book, *Our Penal Machinery and Its Victims*, in which he urged reform of the penal system in a more humane direction, focusing less on punishment and more on the rehabilitation of prisoners. He wrote: "The truth is, that the great multitudes annually arrested for the first time are of the poor, unfortunate, the young and neglected; of those that are weak and, to a greater extent, are the victims of unfavorable environments. In short, our penal machinery seems to recruit its victims from among those that are fighting an unequal fight in the struggle for existence."[4]

In the mid-1880s he also became attracted to the cause of working people and steadily built up his reputation as a leader in the battle for labor reform. The battle, he declared in 1890, was a dire one because the mass of workers are "in a condition where they are absolutely in the power of stronger class, where they are the slaves of adverse circumstances, and where individual action can accomplish absolutely nothing."[5]

In 1886 Altgeld won a position on the Cook County (Chicago) Superior Court as the nominee of the Democratic Party and the Union Labor Party. By 1891 he had built up considerable support in his drive to capture the Democratic Party nomination for governor. He had made some important political allies. One was George A. Shilling, a labor leader and reformer, also born in Germany, who had a background with the Knights of Labor and as a Socialist organizer. Another was lawyer Clarence Darrow, with whom Altgeld developed a strong personal friendship. He also had the backing of writer-muckraker Henry Demarest Lloyd. Overall, a Chicago-based set of social reformers and organized labor leaders stood solidly behind him both before and after he became governor.[6]

However, most important in terms of securing the nomination at the party convention in 1892 was saloon keeper "King Mike" McDonald, the most powerful Democratic boss in Chicago. McDonald took Altgeld under his wing and gave him the political boost he needed.

In many respects Altgeld was an ideal candidate. In 1891 Illinois adopted a secret ballot system, making it far more important for party leaders to find candidates who could attract actual votes and win an election honestly. Altgeld filled the bill because of his background and appeal to reformers and key groups, especially workers and farmers, caught up in the Populist current of the time. Party leaders also saw him as someone who would remember his friends should he win office when it came to jobs and other spoils. Another factor that attracted the bosses was that Altgeld was wealthy and could finance his own campaign, relieving the machine of much of the burden.

After the bosses got him the gubernatorial nomination in 1892, Altgeld went on to become the first Democratic governor of Illinois since 1852. He won in a relatively close race by drawing 425,498 votes compared with 402,666 for his Republican opponent, or around 49 percent of the vote to 46 percent.[7] During the campaign he conducted a hand-shaking tour of the state and did especially well with the German Lutheran vote because of his background, being born in Germany to Lutheran parents, his ties to labor, and his championing of parochial schools, a cause dear to Lutherans.[8] Illinois Democrats had discovered that the parochial school issue had worked well for the party in Wisconsin. In using it Altgeld was able to hide the fact until after the election that he had supported the parochial school act that he had condemned his opponent for supporting.[9]

Governor Altgeld did little to curtail the power of the political bosses. He recognized his obligation to the Democratic Party leaders who had helped elect him. He had no qualms about replacing Republican officeholders with Democratic officeholders, especially since the Democrats had been out of office for such a long time. When it came to specific appointments, he usually deferred to the judgment of party bosses as to who should have what office. He did, however, insist on the appointment of some Progressively-minded prison wardens, the highly qualified Shilling as head of the state labor board, and the equally well qualified Florence Kelley, who was recommended by Lloyd and Jane Addams of Hull House, as state factory inspector. Kelley used her position to campaign for laws to improve factory safety conditions and legislation regulating child labor.

Altgeld clearly was no Mugwump when it came to separating himself from the party bosses. He also differed from the Mugwumps by articulating the need for fundamental reform. He was not much interested in things being pushed by upper-class reformers—the elimination of patronage, more efficiency, and lower taxes. He felt more committed to the goal of improving the lives of ordinary people.[10] He presented a long list of reforms to the legislature, which was controlled by Democrats, but did not expect much to be adopted because of the strength of the corporations and his inability to even get the support of his own party. Difficult as things were in his first two years, they became even more difficult for Altgeld after 1894 when Republicans took over the legislature. The governor continued to push for a broad range of Progressive measures with hope that while immediate prospects were not good, he was at least building the agenda for action sometime in the future.

In the end, though, he accomplished a considerable amount in his years as governor, including an eight-hour day for women (though subsequently invalidated by the state supreme court), child labor protections, regulations on sweatshops, a labor arbitration board, a measure prohibiting discrimination against workers who joined a labor union, improvements in prison conditions, parole reform, indeterminate sentencing, an inheritance tax, a graduated income tax on corporations, antitrust legislation, and increased university funding He tried but was not able to get increased assessments on the property of wealthy corporations as a way of equalizing taxes.[11]

Altgeld supported education and, in particular, came to the rescue of the University of Illinois, hoping to make it a leading educational institution. He was motivated in part by the desire to give the children of not-so-wealthy families an opportunity to get a quality college education. He was also motivated by the fear, then commonly shared by Progressive reformers, that many of the country's endowed universities were being unduly influenced by contributions from large corporations. This view was fostered in Illinois by the generous contributions of John D. Rockefeller to the University of Chicago.[12] Altgeld feared that what he called the "Rockefeller University" in Chicago would be used to promote the policy views of Standard Oil and saw a strong state university as necessary to counter the influence of the private university. Democrats in the legislature saw considerable political value in being credited with putting the state university on its feet and taking on the University of Chicago and Rockefeller.[13]

Altgeld held the line a bit on corporations by using his veto power. Among his twenty-three vetoes was one in 1895 striking down legislation that would have given traction "baron" financier Charles T. Yerkes a fifty-year mass transit monopoly franchise in Chicago. Yerkes had attempted to bribe Altgeld and, when that failed, to override Altgeld's veto by bribing legislators. As the story goes, Yerkes was willing to bribe as many legislators as needed, a policy he had followed in getting the bill to Altgeld in the first place, but because of the growing costs involved, he wanted to economize as much as possible. To do this he gave some legislators as much as $10,000 but purchased the vote of several more for as little as $200. Altgeld's people found out about this disparity and spread the word among the legislators. Those who sold out for $200 were outraged. In protest of what they considered being swindled, enough of them changed their votes to defeat the override attempt.[14] After the session talk about the role money had played in the proceedings was revived when the speaker of the house died and several new thousand-dollar bills were found in his safe deposit box.[15]

Outside the area of legislation Altgeld demonstrated his instinct for justice in June of 1893 when he expressed his outrage at the mob lynching of a black man in Decatur, Illinois, who was being held under suspicion of committing a crime. The governor denounced "this cowardly and diabolical act as not only murder under our laws, but as a disgrace to our civilization and a blot upon the fair name of our State."[16] He offered a reward for the arrest and conviction for each one of those who took part in the lynching.

Shortly after his election, Darrow, Shilling, and others urged Altgeld to pardon three men sitting in prison who had been convicted of conspiracy in an 1886 bombing that took place at Haymarket Square in Chicago during a labor demonstration. The governor hesitated but after studying the record concluded that the prisoners had been wrongly convicted, and issued the pardons on June 26, 1893. Earlier he had written to Darrow: "I have not yet examined the record. I have no opinion about it. It is a big job. When I do examine it, I will do what I believe to be right, no matter what that is. But don't deceive yourself: If I conclude to pardon these men it will not meet with the approval that you expect; let me tell you, that from that day I will be a dead man politically."[17] As he predicted, newspapers and conservative politicians around the country condemned him for pardoning the "Haymarket Anarchists."[18] He never won another election.

As the result of the pardons Altgeld acquired the reputation of someone who would not hesitate to let dangerous people out of prison. In one case at least the notion that he would issue a pardon encouraged or served as an excuse for a double lynching. This occurred in Danville, Illinois, in 1895. Altgeld's fear of such future events may well have prompted him to do what he could to demonstrate that he was less lenient in regard to pardons than popularly perceived, even to the point of refusing to grant pardons he would have granted under other conditions. As it turned out, he granted fewer pardons than governors both before and after him.[19]

In 1894 his enemies found another reason to go after the governor. The triggering event was President Cleveland's sending federal troops into Chicago to put down a strike by railroad workers against the Pullman Company. Cleveland's action incensed Altgeld. He claimed that under the US Constitution the president had to get the consent of the governor or legislature before sending troops into a state. There was no request for federal troops. Cleveland had ignored state and local officials. Altgeld also noted that there had been no need for federal troops because the state militia under his direction and the Chicago police were able to handle the situation. In an exchange of telegrams and letters, Cleveland defended his action. The US Supreme Court eventually sided with the president.[20]

Altgeld received the strong support of noted reform governors of the period—Hogg of Texas, Lewelling of Kansas, Pennoyer of Oregon, and Waite of Colorado—for his stand against the sending of troops into Chicago, but the conservative press dismissed these governors as "Anarchists like Altgeld."[21] A Princeton professor, one Woodrow Wilson, was also highly critical of Altgeld for sympathizing with the strikers and doing nothing to avoid disorder.[22] New York assemblyman Theodore Roosevelt joined in declaring Altgeld "a foe of decent government" and also condemning the governors who supported Altgeld's position on the sending of troops.[23]

Altgeld by the mid-1890s had a strong following among Populists and had won several victories for Populist principles if not for the Populist Party.[24] He had become a champion of free silver, something he favored on its merits but also because he felt it was a useful tool to use against Cleveland personally and the control that Cleveland Democrats had over the Democratic Party. During the 1896 presidential campaign, Republicans commonly attacked Bryan because of his association with the much better known Altgeld. The governor was a perfect boogeyman for frightening men of wealth and winning them over to the Republican side. Out on the campaign trail for the Republicans, Theodore Roosevelt declared: "Mr. Altgeld is much more dangerous than Bryan. He is much slyer, much more intelligent, much less silly, much more free from all the restraints of public morality."[25]

In a more subtle fashion, a reporter for the *New York Times* painted the following unflattering, somewhat sinister portrait of Altgeld while in New York for a political event in October: "The pardoner of Anarchists is a little below the medium height. His head is round and his hair of faintly silver-black falls uncombed over a low forehead. His eyes are of a pale blue, with heavy lids, so heavy that they conceal, when he talks, what is considered one of the best indications of character . . . The governor wore a suit of blue. He was probably not present when it was cut . . . He is evidently of a fidgety, nervous temperament, for, while he talked, he shifted about and kept one or both hands pocketed most of the time."[26]

In June 1896, 1,069 delegates to the Illinois Democratic State Convention renominated Altgeld for governor. He, however, lost in the general election to a Republican Party machine candidate who ran well behind other candidates on his ticket and was likely carried into office by McKinley's popularity.[27] Altgeld had spent much of his time and energy trying to help Bryan.

In his retiring address, prepared for delivery at Springfield on January 11, 1897, Altgeld offered this thought: "In my judgment no epitaph can be written upon the tomb of a public man that will so surely win the contempt of the ages than to say of him that he held office all his life and never did anything for humanity."[28] In a 1902 commemorative ceremony, Darrow noted Altgeld's contribution in this regard and concluded: "John P. Altgeld, like many of the earth's greatest souls, was a solitary man. Life to him was serious and earnest—an endless tragedy. The earth was a great hospital of sick, wounded and suffering, and he a devoted surgeon, who had no right to waste one moment's time and whose duty was to cure them all."[29]

A succession of Republican governors followed Altgeld in office. One of these, Charles S. Deneen, served two terms, from 1905 to 1913, and, while not commonly considered a Progressive, helped usher in several reforms. These included a direct primary system, a presidential preference primary, a civil service program, and pure food and drug legislation. He also favored state approval of the federal income tax amendment. Deneen has been viewed as a man who lacked personal warmth but who was a capable politician when it came to building a personal political machine and making safe political moves: "His two outstanding traits as governor were an exceptional talent for organization and extreme caution." He talked with both reform and antireform Republicans and listened to their ideas but did not take action until he was certain the public would support him or, at least, not get in the way. He was always eager to do what he could to further his position as governor and party leader.[30]

In 1912 Democrat Edward Dunne, who had slowly emerged as leader of the Progressive cause in the Democratic Party while Altgeld was out of office, defeated

Deneen in his bid for a third term. Dunne, a former mayor of Chicago, came out of a circle of social reformers in that city similar to that which supported Altgeld.³¹ He championed several reforms during a term that lasted from 1913 to 1917, including strengthening the public utilities commission, upgrading the worker's compensation program, and providing for a Legislative Reference Bureau.³² He failed to get approval of a corrupt-practices act or to advance one of his major goals—the adoption of the initiative and referendum—when the House refused by one vote to submit the question to the voters.

Dunne joined a penal reform movement rapidly gaining support around the country by ending such prison practices as the rule of silence and the wearing of striped clothing. He called for improved sanitary conditions and giving inmates more letter-writing privileges and recreation. Dunne too made it clear that he opposed capital punishment—being among those, for example, who urged Governor Slaton of Georgia to commute the death sentence of Leo Frank (see chapter 6). While somewhat conservative when it came to the political role of women, he went along with a statutory measure giving women the right to vote.³³ This was a major breakthrough for the suffrage movement, the first victory in a major state east of the Mississippi and one coming after defeats in several midwestern states.

Dunne has been seen by his biographer as mild in temperament, open and honest, and someone the professional politicians never suspected of having ulterior motives or of being a major threat to their power. Some felt he was not tough enough. Still, his mild temperament could also help account for the successes he did enjoy, and there is room for doubt about whether a more messianic arm-twisting approach would have been more successful.³⁴

PINGREE: FROM CITY TO STATE, PUSHING FOR REFORM

Michigan during the early stages of the Progressive period produced Republican Hazen S. Pingree, who, as mayor of Detroit and governor in the 1890s, took on US senator James McMillan, leader of the conservative forces, in a struggle for control of the Republican Party.

Pingree, born in Maine, one of eight children in a poor family that could provide him with only limited education, came to Detroit after service for the North in the Civil War, during which he was held for five months as prisoner of war, and became a successful shoe manufacturer. Conservative business leaders in Detroit, seeing Pingree as one of their own, talked him into running for mayor. He was elected four times to the office, each time with increased majorities.³⁵

Pingree began his service following his election in 1889 as an honesty and efficiency type but after a few years on the job became a leading proponent of a broad-ranging political, social, and economic progressive program. This brought much opposition from the businesspeople and Republican political leaders who had put him office. As a contemporary politician noted: "They ran him for mayor. No one knew him as a great humanist; he did not even know it himself. . . . When Pingree began to find out how things were in a social and political way, he began to raise the dickens. This marked him as a troublemaker and undesirable by the machine."[36]

Much of his attention was on the streetcar companies that had bribed city officials to secure very lucrative franchises. He called for stricter control of transit and other franchises and refused to renew agreements without significant concessions from the companies. His pressure produced more transit competition and lower fares. Not satisfied with this, he went on to drive down the cost of gas, lighting, and water utilities and began a long campaign for city ownership and operation of its own transit system. He also shifted more of the tax burden to the wealthy. Other reforms as mayor included a city-owned electricity plant, better schools, more parks, and, during the economically depressed conditions of the early 1890s, the implementation of a "potato patch plan" under which hard-hit residents could farm vegetables on unused city property. With the depression brought on by the Panic of 1893 he began to sympathize with and champion the cause of the city's working-class and foreign-born residents, many of whom were in dire straits.

Michigan from the Civil War to the Great Depression of the 1930s was virtually a one-party Republican state. Getting the Republican Party nomination for an office was all one had to do to get elected. In Pingree's time, James H. McMillan of Detroit was the most powerful figure in the Republican Party, though to view him as a boss who headed a powerful statewide machine is somewhat of an exaggeration. More accurately, he was a central figure in an alliance of several groups, both economic and social.[37] McMillan amassed a fortune in the shipping business, turned to politics in the 1880s, and during the 1890s served as US senator and Republican state party chair. His influence came from his control of federal patronage when Republicans held the presidency and his own wealth, which he freely distributed to candidates whom he expected to be favorable to the railroad and shipping interests with which he was allied.[38] Pingree's attacks on the streetcar franchise owners, some of the wealthiest and most prominent Republicans in Detroit, had provoked McMillan's hostility to the mayor.[39]

Pingree sought the office of governor to both defend what he had done as mayor from negative state action and to extend Progressive programs to the state as a whole.[40] He put together an urban agenda, secured the backing of labor (he had, among other things, supported Altgeld's stand in the Pullman Strike), and put together a popular reform program calling for increased railroad regulation and taxation, antitrust action, and the adoption of an income tax.[41]

He failed in 1892 and 1894 to get the nomination for governor at the Republican state convention, losing out to McMillan's candidates. He finally won in 1896 thanks to a strong statewide organization he had built based on his personal popularity and contacts made on speaking tours throughout the state and the support of many local officials, including sheriffs, who shared his views.[42] Most helpful was the word from Republican political leader Mark Hanna to McMillan that Pingree's candidacy and his likely broad appeal were necessary to McKinley's carrying Michigan in 1896 in his bid for the presidency.[43] McMillan withdrew his opposition to Pingree, though this by no means meant he would go along with whatever Pingree wanted to do as governor. Pingree won the 1896 election with 56 percent of the vote, helping to carry the state for McKinley.

Pingree came into office with several reform ideas, highlighted by the direct primary and proposals unwelcomed by railroads and other corporations.[44] Conservatives in the legislature aligned with McMillan, however, blocked many of his proposals. At the end of his first session there was some newspaper speculation that Pingree, in disgust, might resign from the governor's office and run for mayor again. As a *New York Times* story put it: "The fact is that his Gubernatorial job has not come quite up to its occupant's expectations. The Legislature has failed to pass his pet bills, and he is said to be much dissatisfied with the situation."[45]

Disappointing his opponents, Pingree decided to run again and, following his victory, came back more insistent on reform than ever before, but he had only limited success. He was able to get a measure through that created a municipal-owned and -operated transit system in Detroit, but the legislation was invalidated in court. He urged passage of legislation that would require primary nominations for virtually all state offices, but this was shot down, the most frequent arguments against it being that it would destroy the Republican organization and give Detroit and other cities a monopoly over nominations at the expense of small towns and rural areas.[46] His major accomplishment was securing the adoption of a bill calling for an evaluation of railroad and corporate property in the state, which later dramatically increased the level of taxation on their properties.[47] Several other states followed his example by undertaking a statewide evaluation of corporate property.

When he delivered his farewell message to the legislature on January 4, 1901, Pingree made several extemporaneous remarks attacking the lawmakers and the wealthy corporate interests that ran the state. He said: "My experience during my political life, extending over a period of twelve years, has convinced me that in order to secure the full commendation of those who consider themselves the 'better classes' the Governor and other high officials must do nothing to antagonize the great corporations and the wealthy people." He felt he could have had that support and the support of the press generally "if I had upheld those who have for years attempted to control legislation in their own interests to the end that they might be relieved from sharing equally with the poor and lowly the burden of taxation. I would have been pronounced a good fellow and a great statesman."[48]

As he saw it, the large economic interests he antagonized in his fight for equal taxation and the newspapers they controlled diverted attention from the real issues by making malicious personal attacks on him "in order that the present system of unjust, inequitable, and iniquitous laws might still remain in force, to the detriment of the great masses of the laboring classes and farmers and those of small properties who are unable to speak and act for themselves." He predicted that without a change in the "present system of inequality in less than a quarter of a century there will be a bloody revolution in this great country of ours."[49] On another occasion Pingree declared: "I do not condemn corporations and rich men, but I would keep them within their proper spheres. It is not safe to entrust the government of the country to the influence of Wall Street."[50]

Along with his drive for corporate taxation and regulation, Pingree stood for woman suffrage and was not reluctant to appoint a woman to a high office.[51] Like Altgeld, he was accused of being too liberal with pardons. In defense, he pointed out that he gave fewer pardons than the previous governor but, more important, that he was well justified in granting the ones he did: "In studying the history of these convicts and the proceedings of our criminal courts I came to the conclusion that a very large percentage of the inmates of our three state prisons were wrongfully there; that the prisoners themselves were not receiving any benefit on account of long terms for excusable first offenses, nor was society being benefited by supporting them while their families were starving. . . . The consequences of overzealous inhumanity on the part of prosecuting attorneys and judges in criminal cases shocked me as I reviewed officially their conduct and procedure."[52]

Following McMillan's death in 1902, the alliance he led slowly began to fall apart and, with this, the opposition to reform began to fade. Movement toward Progressivism came with the 1904 election of Republican Fred Warner, a successful businessman and state senator who was reelected in 1906 and 1908. Warner broke with what was left of the alliance group and proceeded to push for more utility control, higher taxes on the railroads, direct primary expansion, improved labor protection, and other reforms. His conversion seems to have been a mixture of conviction and opportunism.[53]

The next highpoint in terms of Progressivism in Michigan came with the election of author-lecturer-politician Chase Osborn in 1910. Osborn won with the backing of some long-standing associates of McMillan but ran on a Progressive platform and upon taking office called for just about everything in the Progressive playbook. He initially had difficulty with the legislature, but the opposition "gradually wore down."[54] In his single two-year term he eliminated the state deficit and brought a flood of reforms, including a presidential primary law, worker's compensation legislation, more railroad and business regulation, and a move toward higher corporate property tax appraisals. A supporter of woman suffrage, he was outraged when it appeared that the liquor interests and "election crooks" had been able to defeat a suffrage proposal submitted to the voters in 1912.[55] Between 1910 and 1912 Osborn jumped around supporting various candidates for president. He started with La Follette, switched to Roosevelt, decided to endorse Wilson, and switched back to Roosevelt. In all the confusion he lost the GOP nomination for governor in 1912. He regained the nomination two years later but lost in the general election.

In 1912 Michigan voters put a Democrat in the office of governor for the first time in twenty years. Democrat Woodbridge Ferris won with little more than 35 percent of the vote over candidates from the Republican and Progressive Parties. Osborn came back to win the Republican Party nomination for governor in 1914 running as a Progressive, with lots of help from Democrats who took advantage of the state's open primary law that had been adopted in 1913. Osborn, however, lost the general election as conservatives from both parties supported Ferris's bid for reelection. While Ferris campaigned to attract the conservative vote in 1914, after the election he returned to a pattern of mild Progressivism he had established in his first term.[56]

His tenure brought improvements in the public health area and the adoption of a limited initiative and referendum measure. In dealing with the bitter Copper County strike of 1913–14 involving the Western Federation of Miners, Ferris has been given credit for ordering the National Guard to remain neutral and not serve as strikebreakers.[57] The perception from the left, however, quite different—one radical paper labeled Ferris "the servile tool of the mine owners."[58]

FIGHTING BOB LA FOLLETTE

In the 1880s and 1890s railroad and lumber interests were the dominant political power in Wisconsin. They "dictated to the governor and both houses of the legislature. At one time a railroad lobbyist boasted that no legislation ever had been or could be enacted without the permission of the railroads."[59] In 1874 a Granger-inspired legislature produced some railroad regulations, but these were undone in the next legislative session.

Proponents of the Australian or secret ballot law adopted in 1889 hoped that this reform would reduce the power of the special interests and the party bosses and politicians allied with them. What it did was to prompt them to shift their sights from the voters to the nomination system. The remedy was simple: if they could choose the candidates for office, what the voters did or did not do wasn't really all that important. The railroads and lumber interests proceeded to establish a monopoly on the selection of candidates—they were the only groups in the state with the wealth and organization needed to control the highly complicated convention system used to make party nominations for public offices. They were especially successful on the Republican side, the party with the largest number of followers.⁶⁰

Robert La Follette, a Wisconsin farm boy when the Granger movement was at its height, was deeply influenced by its anticorporate message and set off to challenge the political establishment. His rise reflected years of discontent among Republicans with their party leaders. In the late 1880s and early 1890s one found Republican urban reformers in the state demanding change and insurgent Republicans on the statewide level rallying behind Congressman Nils Haugen in challenging the party leaders and, in particular, demanding more railroad regulation and taxation.⁶¹

La Follette began his political career by running for the office of Dane County district attorney in 1880. He did this despite a warning from the local Republican boss, Colonel E. W. Keyes, that his machine had already chosen a candidate for that position and that La Follette's bid was not welcomed. Keyes demanded that La Follette respect the authority of the political machine. La Follette ignored him, campaigned around the county promising to clean house and reinvigorate the county attorney's office, and was able to build up enough support to win the nomination on the fifth ballot at the party county convention. He had learned a valuable lesson: the bosses could be beaten.⁶²

La Follette completed two terms as county attorney and ran for Congress in 1884, again doing so without the permission of party leaders. He was reelected in 1886 and 1888 but went down to defeat in the general election of 1890 as part of a Democratic landslide that year. He went back to Madison, started a law practice, and began stumping the state in an attempt to build an organization—in effect, a political machine of his own—to wrest control of the Republican Party from conservatives tied to the railroad and lumber interests. He failed in 1896 and 1898 in his bid for the gubernatorial nomination, but made some progress in breaking down the strength of the machine. In 1898 he got several anticorporate reforms and a direct primary into the state party platform. As Lincoln Steffens noted, however, the Stalwarts (regular or conservative Republicans) did not care about what was in the platform as long as they were the ones who would actually be making the decisions when legislature convened, and they fully expected to be in that position.⁶³

True to form, Republican legislators, returning to power after the 1898 election, repudiated most of what the party had said it stood for in its platform, though some reform legislation got through.

The governor at the time was Republican Edward Scofield, who had twice defeated La Follette for the Republican nomination for the office. Scofield, whose considerable wealth came from the lumber industry, was generally in the camp of the leading economic interests. Still, along with conducting a business-minded administration, he was not altogether unprogressive—he signed antirailroad legislation and a corrupt-practices act requiring the disclosure of campaign expenditures.⁶⁴

Figure 3.1. Robert La Follette. Courtesy of the Library of Congress, Prints & Photographs Division, LC-USZ62-106669.

La Follette, meanwhile, continued to build a political following, becoming something of a "reform boss" in putting together a coalition that included the big-city political machine in Milwaukee and various local organizations and cliques of politicians, many of whom were not particularly Progressive in their outlooks.[65] He went around the state appealing to Republican voters on the need for railroad and corporation regulation and for legislation to combat the evils of the political machine, especially a measure providing for the direct primary. He made many speeches and distributed reams of campaign literature.

In declaring his bid for the gubernatorial nomination in 1900, La Follette took a much more conciliatory approach than he had in the past. He assured corporate leaders that he was not all that radical and praised the accomplishments of the legislature and Governor Scofield. His tone of conciliation, friendliness, cooperation, and moderation plus a well-organized and well-funded campaign won over most elements in the party. Helping things along, one of his most determined and influential enemies, Phileutus Sawyer, died. The remaining bosses and influential conservatives gave up hope of beating La Follette and offered him their support. Scofield, though, was not won over. He remained bitter over past encounters and openly called La Follette a radical. La Follette, intent on maximizing harmony among Republicans, did not respond.

Seeking to minimize opposition, he had relatively little to say about the divisive direct primary issue until his nomination was virtually assured. He then made it clear that he would not stand on any platform that did not call for this reform. He had publicly advocated the direct primary since 1897, in part, because of his frustration with the boss-controlled convention system of making nominations. He believed he would have been nominated for governor in 1896 and 1898 if Republican voters had been able to make the nomination and, with this nomination, have been easily elected to that office.[66]

In 1900 delegates to the Republican state convention adopted a direct primary plank as part of a highly Progressive state platform on the same day that they nominated La Follette for governor by acclamation. The general election campaign was based mostly on national issues, especially the imperialistic policies of the McKinley administration. La Follette defended McKinley as part of the united Republican campaign.[67] He won the governorship by more than 100,000 votes, close to 60 percent of the total.

La Follette came into office ready to lead—to be, in his words, "a strong factor in securing legislation that should build into the life of the people a new order of things."[68] He initially failed, however, to get much of anything through the legislature. Conservatives blocked his proposals for a railroad commission, increased taxes on railroads, and a direct primary system. As they had in 1898, they turned against the Progressive party platform. As Steffens noted, railroad lobbyists were very active in offering legislators food and entertainment and lucrative positions with the railroads. Bribes were not off limits, though they came in somewhat subtle form: "It was said if a member would get into a poker game with a lobbyist, the member was sure to win."[69]

Shortly after the end of the legislative session several conservative legislators organized the Wisconsin Republican League to campaign against La Follette and prevent him from being renominated in 1902. La Follette fought back with a lively campaign in winning renomination. He was aided by an army of state workers. As he acknowledged years later, after he first became governor he "appointed supporters of the Progressive movement to offices whenever there were appointments to make. These men did all in their power for the success of our campaigns."[70] He made extensive political use of those who held all kinds of state jobs, be they clerks, factory inspectors, State Fair ticket sellers, guards, or game wardens.[71] La Follette won reelection in 1902 with 53 percent of the vote. The legislature elected along with him was more disposed to support his agenda. It gave him the direct primary (approved by the voters in 1904 as the first statewide direct primary law in the country) and an inheritance tax and took steps toward increasing railroad taxes.

From the Progressive point of view more was needed, and La Follette was willing to keep trying. He was able to overcome the no-holds-barred efforts of the Stalwarts to deny him the nomination in 1904. Determined to leave nothing to nature when it came to who was going to serve in the legislature, he campaigned around the state, hoping to prevent the renomination of Republican legislators who had opposed his proposals.[72] He coasted to victory with an eleven-point lead over this Democratic opponent. After his reelection, with ample support in the legislature, he got a strong Railroad Commission Act, drawing on laws passed in Texas and Iowa, an antilobbying measure, and a variety of other reforms.[73] Also, in 1905 before he left the state to take up his seat in the US Senate and notably during his last term in office, he was successful in securing a civil service law to wipe out the spoils system.[74] When it came to campaigning in both 1902 and 1904, La Follette made effective use of his power to make a wide variety of appointments and, as noted, create an army of campaign workers. He later downplayed the overall importance of patronage, however, claiming it gave opponents an effective campaign issue and, overall, did about as much harm as good.[75]

La Follette generally received the support of farmers and workers and did particularly well with Scandinavians in the northern part of the state, German Socialists in Milwaukee, and old-time Populists at election time.[76] He also had the backing of many Democrats. La Follette felt the votes he received from "fair minded" Democrats in general elections far exceeded the losses caused by bolting Republican conservatives. La Follette and William Jennings Bryan were friends, and the latter sometimes came to the state to line up Democratic voters and legislators behind La Follette's efforts.[77]

The "Wisconsin Idea," with which La Follette is associated, was one of a positive, proactive state government, freed up from corporate control, promoting the interests of the general public rather than just a special few and bringing more efficient and informed public policies. Central to his view of Progressivism was the need to base legislation directed at social and economic problems on solid research. To do so, he developed close ties between state agencies and experts at the University of Wisconsin. He had been an active alumnus of the university and had a following among the faculty, many of whom participated in the development of his reform program. His "brain trust" at the university included T. Ely, Edward A. Ross, and John R. Commons.

La Follette also signed off on the development of the Wisconsin Legislative Reference Library as a central research agency to assist both him and the legislature in probing problems and developing appropriate legislation. A great deal of the legislation passed while he was governor was developed in this agency.[78]

First and foremost La Follette focused on the problem of corporate power. As he saw it, great industrial organizations had taken "control of politics . . . They manage conventions, make platforms, dictate legislation. They rule through the very men elected to represent the people."[79] Though strong on the direct primary as a way for the people and the Progressive forces in the state to gain control, La Follette was late coming to direct legislation. Having become a legislative leader, he was in a strong position to implement his program and may have seen little need for innovations that threatened to circumvent his control.[80] At any rate, La Follette did not become interested in the initiative and referendum until he became a presidential candidate and sought to win over the support of western Republicans, many of whom favored these devices. Wisconsin voters finally got a chance to adopt direct legislation but turned it down in 1913.

La Follette is best looked on as an idealistic, tough-minded, reluctant-to-compromise reformer who stood behind policy positions grounded in research and offered practical solutions to identifiable problems that rose to the surface in the state. He opposed political bosses and monopolies but lacked a broader view of society and its problems; compared with Altgeld and Pingree, he was less of a humanitarian when it came to being concerned about those who were having a rough time.[81]

Overall La Follette had the reputation of being highly ambitious, a vigorous political organizer but somewhat cold in personal relationships and rigid in his views, someone who lacked the emotional and inspirational appeal of Bryan as a speaker and, unlike Theodore Roosevelt, did not find fun in politics.[82] According to one biographer: "In discussing issues his characteristic method was to reduce every question to its simplest terms and to picture the alternatives as black and white: the choice was between right and wrong."[83] One study, focusing on his personality, found La Follette a flawed crusader—a vain, self-righteous, uncompromising man who always questioned the motives of those who disagreed with him. He did, however, apparently listen to his wife, Belle Case La Follette, an active Progressive reformer in her own right. Belle, the first woman to graduate from law school at the University of Wisconsin, was a key advisor to her husband. Politically savvy, she was especially active in the woman suffrage movement and influenced her husband's view on the cause.[84]

The two Republican governors who followed La Follette continued to implement a Progressive agenda, though both had a falling out with La Follette. James Davidson, who moved up from lieutenant governor to governor when La Follette left for Washington, won the office on his own in 1906 and 1908. Considered a man with a "genial and easygoing" temperament, he got along well with the more conservative members of the party even though he was a strong believer in Progressive principles. He was a longtime friend of La Follette and had helped the Progressive cause because of his influence with his fellow Norwegians.[85]

In 1906, however, La Follette, now a US senator, preferred another candidate for governor in the Republican primary over Davidson. He liked Irving Lenroot, a young, aggressive speaker of the State Assembly. Davidson, who had expected to be easily nominated, was surprised and shocked but fought back and, finding considerable support, including that of the conservative Republicans who had no love for La Follette, easily won the nomination. La Follette had apparently overrated his ability to influence events. The two were able to patch up their differences, but Davidson later became a member of the Stalwart wing of the party.[86] He did, however, perform well from a Progressive perspective as governor. With Davidson came legislation involving the regulation of corporate stock issues, rail services and rates, and public utilities in addition to railroads.

La Follette backed Francis McGovern's successful bids for the governorship in 1910 and 1912, but the two had a falling out in 1913 after McGovern switched to La Follette's rival, Teddy Roosevelt, in the race for the presidential nomination. La Follette's supporters in the state legislature retaliated by opposing McGovern's proposals, and La Follette refused to support McGovern's bid for a US senate seat in 1914, helping to cost him the election. As governor, though, McGovern had an impressive Progressive record. Among the measures adopted in his years in office were several labor reforms, including a model worker's compensation law and laws regulating factory safety and limiting the hours of women and children. Along with these came a state income tax, water and forest conservation laws, and measures encouraging farm cooperatives and loans for farm improvements. McGovern also signed off on a sterilization law in 1913. In 1914 bitter strife among Republican Progressives led to the nomination of a longtime conservative opponent of La Follette, Emanuel L. Philipp, who went on to become governor. Voters returned him to office in 1916 and 1918. In the 1920s, though, the state once again moved in a Progressive direction.

NOTES

1. Nye, *Midwestern Progressive Politics*, 13.
2. Browne, *Altgeld of Illinois*, 175.
3. Barnard, *Eagle Forgotten*, 19.
4. Quoted by Browne, *Altgeld of Illinois*, 179.
5. Address given on Eight-Hour Movement, February 22, 1890, cited by Browne, *Altgeld of Illinois*, 189.
6. Wish, "Altgeld and the Progressive Tradition," 814.
7. Ginger, *Altgeld's America*, 72; Christman, *Mind and Spirit of John Peter Altgeld*, 8. Unless otherwise indicated, the source use here and for voting results in all gubernatorial elections was *Gubernatorial Elections*. Unless otherwise indicated, returns for national and other state elections came from *CQ Guide to U.S. Elections*.
8. Jensen, *Winning of the Midwest*, 160, 219–21; Merrill, *Bourbon Democracy*, 223, 235–38. On Altgeld's support among Germans, see, for example, "The Altgeld Movement," *Illinois Staats-Zeitung*, September 10, 1892, http://flps.newberry.org/article/5418474_11_1767. This is one of several similar translated articles on the Newberry Library's website.
9. Merrill, *Bourbon Democracy*, 236.
10. Ginger, *Altgeld's America*, 172.
11. Ibid., 75, 168–72; Barnard, *Eagle Forgotten*, 178.
12. Wish, "Altgeld and the Progressive Tradition," 829.
13. Barnard, *Eagle Forgotten*, 410; Browne, *Altgeld of Illinois*, 214–16.

14. Barnard, *Eagle Forgotten*, 403.
15. Steffens, *Struggle for Self-Government*, 56.
16. Ginger, *Altgeld's America*, 76; Barnard, *Eagle Forgotten*, 178.
17. Ginger, *Altgeld's America*, 77.
18. "They Call Altgeld an Alien," *New York Times*, June 29, 1893, 1.
19. Browne, *Altgeld of Illinois*, 245–54; Barnard, *Eagle Forgotten*, 261–62, Ginger, *Altgeld's America*, 170.
20. See correspondence between Altgeld and Cleveland in Nevins, *Letters of Grover Cleveland*, 357–62. The power of the president to send in federal troops without the permission of a governor—indeed, in spite of a governor's opposition—was upheld by the US Supreme Court in the opinion *In re Debs* (158 US 154, 1894).
21. Barnard, *Eagle Forgotten*, 301.
22. Ibid., 317.
23. Roosevelt, "True American Ideals," 746–47.
24. Nye, *Midwestern Progressive Politics*, 82, 86.
25. Cited in Hollingsworth, *Whirligig of Politics*, 89.
26. "Gov. Altgeld's Personality," *New York Times*, October 18, 1896, 8.
27. "The New Governors," 35.
28. "Retiring Address as Governor of Illinois," in Christman, *Mind and Spirit*, 177.
29. "Memorial Address by Clarence Darrow," delivered at Chicago, April 20, 1902, in ibid., 182.
30. Pegram, *Partisans and Progressives*, 169.
31. Morton, *Justice and Humanity*, 8–9, 15.
32. Ibid., 76, 77.
33. Morton, *Justice and Humanity*, 78, 79. See account in Harper, *History of Woman Suffrage*, 6:157.
34. Morton, *Justice and Humanity*, viii.
35. "The New Governors," 39.
36. Osborn, *Iron Hunter*, 127.
37. Sarasohn and Sarasohn, *Political Party Patterns*, 8–15.
38. Ibid., 10.
39. Baker, *Curbing Campaign Cash*, 67.
40. Holli, *Reform in Detroit*, 195.
41. Ibid., 191.
42. Sarasohn and Sarasohn, *Political Party Patterns*, 13–14.
43. Ibid.
44. "The New Governors," 39.
45. "Pingree Is Ousted as Mayor," *New York Times*, March 20, 1897, 1.
46. Millspaugh, "Direct Primary Legislation in Michigan," 21.
47. Lough, "Hazen S. Pingree," 81–82.
48. "Pingree Says Farewell" *New York Times*, January 4, 1901, 5.
49. Ibid.
50. Nye, *Midwestern Progressive Politics*, 205.
51. Harper, *History of Woman Suffrage*, 5:765, 766.
52. "Governor Pingree on Penal Reform," *Literary Digest*, February 2, 1901, 126.
53. See generally the account in Sarasohn and Sarasohn, *Political Party Patterns*, 16–17, and in greater detail in Fox, *"I Went to the People."*
54. Sarasohn and Sarasohn, *Political Party Patterns*, 17; Osborn, *Iron Hunter*, 251.
55. Harper, *History of Woman Suffrage*, 6:306–7, 315.
56. Sarasohn and Sarasohn, *Political Party Patterns*, 18–19.
57. Cooper, *Rise of the National Guard*, 150.

58. "Socialism vs. Anarchy, or the Perfidity of the Putrid Press," *Socialist and Labor Star*, September 26, 1913, 1. See also "The Strike in Michigan," *Miner's Magazine*, January 22, 1914, 8, and untitled item in the same, February, 12, 1914, 4.

59. Lovejoy, *La Follette*, 18.

60. Ibid., 18, 19.

61. La Follette, *La Follette's Autobiography*, 9; Thelen, *New Citizenship*.

62. La Follette, *La Follette's Autobiography*, 5–7. See also Nye, *Midwestern Progressive Politics*, 193.

63. Steffens, *Struggle for Self-Government*, 80.

64. Maxwell, *La Follette*, 10–11.

65. Ibid., 56.

66. Margulies, *Decline of the Progressive Movement*, 36.

67. On the 1900 election see Lovejoy, *La Follette*, 51–54, and Maxwell, *La Follette*, 17–26.

68. La Follette, *La Follette's Autobiography*, 143.

69. Steffens, *Struggle for Self-Government*, 109.

70. La Follette, *La Follette's Autobiography*, 31.

71. Margulies, *Decline of the Progressive Movement*, 22.

72. La Follette, *La Follette's Autobiography*, 144.

73. Maxwell, *La Follette*, 76.

74. La Follette, *La Follette's Autobiography*, 31.

75. Ibid.

76. Fenton, *Midwest Politics*, 47.

77. La Follette, *La Follette's Autobiography*, 147–48; Maxwell, *La Follette*, 65; Coletta, *William Jennings Bryan*, 381.

78. La Follette, *La Follette's Autobiography*, 143.

79. "Claiming Our Privilege to Serve," *La Follette's Weekly Magazine* 1, no. 1 (January 9, 1909): 3.

80. Goebel, *A Government by the People*, 104–5.

81. Southern, *Malignant Heritage*, 24; Nye, *Midwestern Progressive Politics*, 207–8.

82. Nye, *Midwestern Progressive Politics*, 208; Amos Parker Wilder, "Governor La Follette and What He Stands For," *The Outlook*, March 8, 1902, 631–33.

83. Maxwell, *La Follette*, 57.

84. Unger, *Fighting Bob La Follette*.

85. Maxwell, *La Follette*, 83–84.

86. Ibid., 84–85, See also "Bitter State Fights from Coast to Coast," *New York Times*, November 4, 1906, 3.

4

MORE FROM THE MIDWEST

Cummins, Johnson, Folk, Harmon, Cox, and Marshall

Altgeld, Pingree, and La Follette were far from the only prominent reform-minded governors in the Midwest during the Progressive era. In Iowa we find insurgent Republican Albert Cummins, who well articulated the case against large corporations and whose career was much like that of La Follette, whom he followed into the US Senate. In Minnesota we find a strong Populist influence, a place where it paid to be a Scandinavian candidate and a place where John Johnson, a Swede, rose from humble beginnings to become a mildly Progressive governor and seriously considered as the Democratic Party's nominee for president.

The Missouri story is largely one of Democrat Joseph Folk, a local prosecutor who turned on the searchlight and built his political career by exposing and attacking corruption. Folk's story also illustrates how quickly recognition can fade. As a biographer noted in the foreword to his 1953 study: "Seldom if ever is the fact mentioned that Folk was once one of the most famous of all the Progressive reformers, that for a brief period his fame was probably greater than that of even La Follette or any of the others whose names are the household words of progressivism."[1]

Much of the attention on Progressivism in Ohio has focused on the meaningful reform activity that occurred on the local level. The state level has been relatively ignored. Still, as the following indicates, Progressivism bubbled up to the state level with considerable force in the administrations of Democrat governors Judson Harmon and James Cox, the latter becoming the Democratic nominee for president and the former making a serious bid for that honor. In Indiana too there was considerable action through a succession of governors, both Republican and Democratic, who followed a moderately Progressive course. One of them, Thomas Marshall, became vice-president under Woodrow Wilson.

INSURGENCY IN IOWA: ALBERT CUMMINS

The insurgent faction in the Iowa Republican Party first made itself felt under governor William Larrabee, a wealthy banker and landowner who had served several years in the state senate where he was known to favor improved rail regulation but was considered by the railroad interests as a relatively safe Republican. He, however, fell out with the railroad leaders who had supported him and, following his reelection in 1887, this time with the support of the antirailroad forces, set out to curtail the power of the railroads. Eagerly working in the same direction, a Republican legislature filled with angry farmers produced a strongly empowered elected board of railroad commissioners, which proceeded to police the companies and cut freight rates 20 percent.[2]

Railroad leaders, shocked by what they saw as radical action aimed at them, poured their money and energy into a campaign to replace the Republicans with more railroad-friendly Democratic officeholders. They did not do well in this regard in the 1888 election, giving some credence to a prediction made by a Republican congressman several years earlier that Iowa "would go Democratic when hell went Methodist." In 1889, though, a miracle took place, at least above ground, and Iowa went Democratic when that party's candidate, Horace Boise, won the office of governor with the strong support of railroad leaders, who were still angry about what the Republicans had done, and by drawing upon the antiprohibition vote (Republicans were split over the issue).[3]

Insurgent Republicans were not done, but their success at the gubernatorial level was not to be realized until the turn of the century with the election Albert B. Cummins, who served three successive terms between the years 1902 and 1908. He had to take on not only the Democrats but the Republican old guard political machine closely tied to the railroads and other corporate interests headed by US senator William Boyd Allison.

Cummins was born in Pennsylvania, the son of a carpenter, studied law in Chicago, and set up legal practice with his brother in Des Moines, Iowa, in 1878. He frequently represented the interests of businessmen or corporations and in 1881 for a time represented the Grangers in a lawsuit to break the control of an eastern syndicate over the production of barbed wire. This helped make him something of a hero in rural areas, though in fact, as historian Leland Sage had noted, to Cummins "it was no crusade on behalf of embattled farmers; his client, the Grange, was a business organization, engaged in manufacturing farm equipment, not farmers as a downtrodden minority group."⁴ Cummins, though, did show an anticorporate disposition during his single term in the state legislature in 1887 when he served as Governor Larrabee's chief lieutenant on railroad control legislation.

An ambitious young man, Cummins set his sights on gaining a seat in the US Senate but was rebuffed in 1894 and 1900 by Republican Party regulars who saw him or at least depicted him as an anticorporate, antirailroad left-winger with Populist sympathies. Like La Follette, Cummins was not easily discouraged. Immediately after being turned down for the US Senate seat in 1900, he ignored the bosses and warnings of big business opponents and launched a successful campaign, using a strategy of attacking railroads, to secure the gubernatorial nomination of the Republican Party in 1901. He went on to win with general election with over 58 percent of the vote.

Cummins came to the governor's office as a severe critic of rich and powerful corporations. He saw them as a threat to democracy. He became well known for the "Iowa Idea" of denying tariff protection to any industry in the country that was controlled by a monopolizing trust. Along with denouncing tariff policies for furthering the concentration of economic power, he lambasted the political activities of corporations in Iowa and elsewhere. Speaking to the legislature, he declared: "Wealth, and especially corporate wealth, has many rights; but it should always be remembered that among them is not the right to vote. Corporations have, and ought to have, many privileges; but among them is not the privilege to sit in political conventions or occupy seats in legislative chambers."⁵

Shortly after his first election as governor he effectively declared his independence from the party establishment and the powers that be by vetoing a measure that would have facilitated a merger between the Burlington and Great Northern Railroads. Reflecting the Republican insurgency that was building in the Midwest, his reform package featured calls for more corporate and railroad regulation and taxation, controls on insurance companies, primary elections, corruption practices legislation, and improvements in public health, prisons, and working conditions. As a contemporary observer noted, during Cummins's reign and thanks largely to Cummins's efforts, "Iowa was rampant with 'progressive politics,' almost everybody wanted nearly everything reformed."⁶

Cummins was responsible for much legislation, including a railroad commission bill, a pure food law, an outlawing of the free pass system, and a direct primary. He also contributed to the development of the innovative city government commission plan, which the legislature approved for use in Des Moines, though he made only a lukewarm endorsement of the plan when it was put before the voters.⁷

Historian Sage saw Cummins as "a rather aloof, fastidious man of elegant tastes and patrician manner" who had considerable support from "urban, middle-class fairly well-to-do businessmen, lawyers, and reform-minded editors" but "no special appeal for or contact with small farmers and the working classes."⁸

Similarly, a contemporary evaluation of him in *The Nation* magazine concluded that Cummins is "the kind of public man who can always be relied upon to do the well-considered thing" but not the kind who would be found "leading forlorn hopes to make a record for a cause..."[9]

He was, though, a widely respected anticorporate reformer, more low-key, more patient, less dramatic, and less colorful than La Follette but a highly influential leader of the insurgent Republicans in the Midwest.[10] Following Allison's death in 1908, the legislature chose Cummins to fill the unexpired term of his longtime opponent in the US Senate. As a senator he joined La Follette and other insurgents challenging the Taft administration and the eastern establishment Republicans. Cummins went on to be reelected to the Senate in 1914 and 1920.

BURSTS OF REFORM IN MINNESOTA: SCANDINAVIANS, TRUSTS, POPULISTS, AND JOHN JOHNSON

Knute Nelson, as Russell Nye noted several years ago, was "a free-wheeling Republican who was both a farmer and a Scandinavian, a practically unbeatable combination in Minnesota."[11] The attorney, born in Norway, started his political career in Wisconsin, where he became a member of the state legislature. Moving to Minnesota, he continued on as a state legislator and won a seat in Congress. He defeated his Democratic challenger, Daniel Lawler, and nationally known Populist Ignatius Donnelly in the 1892 contest for governor. Nelson picked up 43 percent of the vote compared with Lawler's 37 percent and Donnelly's 16 percent. Sensing the rise of Populist sentiment in the state, Nelson moved to champion reform causes and, as governor, was quite willing to work with Donnelly, for example, in an investigation of land claim frauds by the "timber ring" operating in the state.[12] Nelson also invited Donnelly to join him in representing Minnesota at an interstate antitrust conference in Chicago. that Nelson had organized. He was especially concerned with monopolistic conditions in the local coal industry, linked, in part, to the activities of out-of-state railroads. In welcoming delegates from thirty-four states who assembled for the conference in June 1893, Nelson argued that the national Sherman Antitrust Act was an experiment that "will do as an entering wedge" in the battle against the trusts but it was up to the states to join in and "devise a plan to fight this worst form of the modern Antichrist."[13]

Running for reelection in 1894, Nelson virtually ignored the Democratic candidate and focused on the Populist Party candidate. To attract Populist support he pointed to his record in the antitrust conference and the land fraud investigations and his support of the free-silver cause. Nelson also stressed his friendship with labor as evidenced in his willingness to sign off on factory inspection legislation.[14] This time he got 57 percent of the vote, while the Populist got 30 percent and the Democrat finished last with 18 percent.

In 1896 Minnesota Populists, Democrats, and Silver Republicans saw the virtue of joining forces and rallying behind Swedish-born Democrat John Lind for governor. Lind had been elected to Congress as a Republican but by the mid-1890s had identified as a Silver Republican and, after corresponding with Bryan and others in the silver movement, became a Democrat.[15] Opponents in 1896 charged that electing a Populist was dangerous because it would have a disastrous effect on business. Minnesota, they argued, would become as bad as Populist Oregon and Colorado in the eyes of investors.[16] Lind lost a close election to a Republican candidate for governor, considered by some to be aligned with a corrupt political machine, who appeared to have greatly benefited by McKinley's popularity at the head of the Republican ticket.[17]

Two years later Lind again accepted the triple nomination and this time came out on top against the Republican candidate for governor—becoming the first non-Republican to win that office in forty years. As governor, he proposed a variety of new laws regarding railroads and other corporations, direct legislation, and the care of the unfortunate.[18] He worked particularly hard for a measure that would have increased taxes on railway property, but this, like most other measures he sponsored, failed in the legislature, where the Republicans held large majorities in both houses.[19] Lind felt that the railroad companies had bribed members of the legislature to vote against the bill.[20]

Lind served as governor for just one two-year term, going down to defeat in 1900 in another close election to Samuel Van Sant, who had started off as a state legislator and made two attempts at the Republican nomination for the governorship before finally succeeding. His trust-busting efforts as governor helped him get reelected in 1902. He got some reforms, including a primary election law, increases in railroad taxes, and some labor legislation, but he could not get the legislature to go along with his proposals for railroad regulation or tax reform and several other measures he suggested. His antimerger lawsuit against the Northern Securities Company eventually led to the dissolution of the railroad trust that had a monopoly on travel to the Pacific Northwest.[21] In terms of character and style, historian Carl H. Chrislock noted that Van Sant demonstrated a "flair for flamboyant patriotic oratory," an "eloquent defense of values which no one disputed," and a tone of righteousness, taking a stand on policy issues in highly moral terms. While having some success, he showed only limited talent as an administrator and struggled to control the Republican Party.[22]

The next burst of reform came after the election of Democrat John A. Johnson in 1904. He became nationally known as a reformer, though a relatively moderate one, and was frequently talked about as a presidential nominee on the Democratic ticket. He was reelected in 1906 and 1908. He died in office on September 21, 1909. Born in St. Peter, Minnesota, in 1861, one of six children of Swedish immigrant parents, Johnson overcame a harsh childhood, being raised in abject poverty by his mother, a washerwoman, and a drunken father, a blacksmith who died in the poorhouse. Johnson had limited education. He had to drop out of school at age twelve and take menial jobs to help support his mother, who had been deserted by his father. Still he was able to become editor and part owner of a weekly Democratic newspaper, the *St. Peter Herald*.[23] In 1896 Johnson's paper endorsed John Lind in his unsuccessful bid for governor.

Johnson had ups and downs in running for office. He lost a race for the state senate in 1894, won in 1898, and lost again in 1902, but was able to rebound in 1904 when, with some Republican support, he successfully ran for governor. In recounting the story of his quest for elective office, Johnson told reporters: "There is nothing like not knowing when to quit."[24] As a legislator he voted for the bill supported by Governor Lind seeking to increase railway property taxes, but it went down to defeat.[25] He became the virtual leader of the Democratic Party when Lind retired in 1900. Still, as a reporter for the *New York Times* noted: "There was little about him or his record to suggest that he was gubernatorial material beyond the fact that he was a Swede, and that the only man whom in forty years the Democrats had succeeded in electing Governor had been a Swede—John Lind."[26]

In running for governor in 1904, Johnson benefited from a split in the Republican Party between railroad and antirailroad factions over who should be the party's gubernatorial nominee. The pro-railroad candidate won, and Johnson picked up the support of antirailroad, anticorporate Republicans. Johnson also drew support from his Swedish extraction (he enjoyed the endorsement of all Swedish newspapers) and his close ties to fellow newspaper editors, some of whom were Republicans who, if not endorsing him, refused to attack him.[27] Johnson's opponents circulated scurrilous stories about his upbringing, vilifying his father as a "drunken loafer" and describing his mother as a lowly woman who took in washing. All this, however, appears to have prompted sympathy for the candidate.[28] After a successful first term, Johnson was reelected in 1906, running with the slogan "one good term deserves another." Once again a Republican pro- and anticorporate split worked in Johnson's favor.

Nye described Johnson as "a big, slow-moving man with a quick mind" who, working without a staff of experts, "began with no definite or carefully worked-out pattern of reform but worked piece by piece and month to month, tinkering here and there with progressive ideas."[29] Another author credited Johnson with the "capacity for establishing friendly relations with all kinds of people without, apparently, arousing serious suspicions of his sincerity."[30] Somewhat along the same lines, a contemporary observer concluded: "the real key to John A. Johnson's success is personal charm, which gets and holds for him the regard of everybody. It is significant that men never turn upon him and blame him for their political wrongs. They have a grievance against some of his lieutenants, but they want it understood that Johnson is all right. They want to like him, and it is because he likes people."[31]

As governor, Johnson demonstrated the ability to work with legislators from both parties. He had generally pleasant relations with a legislature that was three-fourths Republican during his tenure and wisely refrained from attempting to force legislative attention on various matters. Much of what he was able to accomplish came with the support of Progressive Republican legislators.[32] Johnson's administration brought reduced passenger and freight rail rates, an end to railroad passes, a strengthening of the ability of the state's power to tax corporations, and a host of labor measures and other reforms. Johnson, though, his critics charged, often demonstrated his talent for "masterly inactivity"—of seeming to be on the side of reform but not really following through. As an example they contended that while the state under Johnson adopted a two-cent-per-mile passenger rate maximum, Johnson did little to enforce the railroad rate regulations.[33] Still, some of his actual anticorporate accomplishments were noteworthy. His board of equalization and tax commission, for example, raised the valuation of iron mines owned by US Steel and other corporations nearly fourfold, dramatically raising its tax load.[34]

Considered by many as a centrist, Johnson moved up rapidly in politics. His remarkable success with the voters in 1904 and 1906 in heavily Republican Minnesota drew nationwide attention to him as a possible Democratic candidate for the presidency. Toying with the idea, he began to speak out on national issues. By supporting labor and opposing trusts and high tariffs he came off as a moderate Progressive, though not everyone saw him that way. A story in the *Los Angeles Times*, for example, described him as a strong but very dangerous radical: "It will be no child's play to put the son of the Vikings down and out. His doctrines are as dangerous as Bryan's; his personality is more dangerous. Look out for him!"[35]

In 1908 a group of eastern and southern Democrats, however, advanced his name as a "safe and sane" alternative to Bryan as the Democratic Party nominee for president. Johnson had supported Cleveland in 1892, and Cleveland joined those who endorsed Johnson for the presidency.[36]

Johnson also had the backing of party bosses like Thomas Taggart of Indiana, Roger Sullivan of Illinois, and leaders of the Tammany organization in New York. He appeared to have ample campaign funds.[37]

Johnson realized his chances were slim but decided to take the plunge. He seemed to enjoy the publicity he was receiving as a possible nominee and, some suspected, was hoping to cash in on the lecture circuit later on.[38] He hired a campaign manager, established campaign offices in various cities, and lined up some delegates to support him at the Democratic convention in Denver, doing particularly well with the New York delegation. While he was overwhelmed by the Bryan forces in 1903, he may well have been a serious contender for the presidency in 1912 had not his life been cut short at the age of forty-eight when he died in office.

Adolph Eberhart, a Republican born in Sweden and a former state legislator, moved up from lieutenant governor to governor following Johnson's death and was subsequently elected to the office in 1910 and 1912. Though generally conservative, he moved to head off protest activity with various reforms including a corrupt-practices act and legislation providing for a direct primary for all state officials. Protest activity, however, did not die out and fed the growth of the Nonpartisan League, especially among Scandinavian wheat farmers in the western part of the state. In 1918 the NPL offered a full slate of candidates in the Republican primary. The Republican candidate for governor, Joseph Burnquist, who was seeking reelection, departed from the established practice of the party of co-opting reform parties by adopting many of their programs, and went on the war path, waging a viscous attack on the NPL as a party of treason.[39] He won and went on to another term.

MISSOURI'S JOSEPH FOLK: "THE LONE WARRIOR FOR RIGHTEOUSNESS"

In Missouri we find back-to-back reform governors from competing parties, Democrat Joseph Folk and Republican Herbert Hadley, leading the Progressive cause, which died out quietly after Hadley's administration.[40]

Folk was born in Tennessee, one of ten children, of strict Baptists parents. From his religious upbringing he may well have acquired a strong sense of what was proper moral behavior, which became evident in his career.[41] He graduated from Vanderbilt University in 1890. Three years later, at the age of twenty-four, he came to St. Louis to practice law with politics as a side. In 1900 voters elected him circuit (district or state) attorney of St. Louis, and he went on to make a name for himself by exposing corruption at the state and local levels involving corporations and political bosses such as St. Louis boss Ed Butler.

Butler, a blacksmith by trade, built up his profitable political machine in St. Louis by providing services to those in need of help, be it for food, jobs, health care, legal aid, or something else in exchange for their votes. A number of wealthy, well-respected people did business with the Butler machine. Butler, officially a Democrat, also lent support to Republican candidates when he deemed it necessary or useful to do so. He could also make a quick reversal in support when necessary.[42]

The year 1900 brought a public uprising against a corrupt Republican regime headed by St. Louis mayor Henry Ziegenhein. Butler had helped elect Ziegenhein three years earlier. When trouble broke out, Butler did the logical thing. He decided to lead a campaign that would turn the city over to the Democrats—ostensibly in the interest of reform but in reality as way of allowing him to retain power and reboot the corrupt activity. Folk was selected as one of the reform candidates. He had the support of several prominent business leaders and met with Butler's approval as a candidate for circuit attorney.

Figure 4.1. Joseph Folk. Courtesy of the Library of Congress, Prints & Photographs Division, photograph by Harris & Ewing, LC-DIG-hec-00584.

Folk had gained much favorable publicity for his involvement as an attorney in a recent transit strike, representing the striking streetcar workers. Responding to the refusal of transit company officials to accept a settlement proposal, he declared that they "seem to forget that the transit company is not a private organization, but a quasi-public corporation in which the public has an interest. The public demands that some settlement be made."[43] By the time the settlement was reached, Folk had become a public hero, popular not only with the workers but many businesspeople.

At the time Folk agreed to be a candidate, he made it clear to those who recruited him that, if elected, he would take his duties seriously. They ignored this warning, likely feeling that he could be handled. After his election he indicted Butler and nineteen municipal assembly people associated with him for accepting bribes from street railway corporations in exchange for franchises and other favors. He followed up with probes into bribery involving state legislators.[44]

In 1902 Lincoln Steffens wrote a glowing report of Folk's activities. Steffens described Folk as "a thin-lipped, firm-mouthed, dark little man, who never raises his voice" and who is "doing his duty." The noted muckraker reported that all this had come as a shock to some of the politicians who had supported Folk. Some of these people were now on their way to the penitentiary; others were hiding out in Mexico.[45] To observer William Allen White, Missouri politicians were learning that, for the time being at least, it paid to be honest.[46]

Folk's investigations put him in the limelight, giving him a powerful base of public support that enabled him to take on party professionals and make them go along with him in his bid for the governorship in 1904. Even though his exposures had hurt the Democratic Party, party leaders realized that the only way the Democrats could avoid losing the governorship and possibly the legislature as well was to back Folk.[47]

Following his nomination, Folk had an interview with a writer for the *Atlanta Constitution*, in which the gubernatorial candidate was described as the "young Tennessee Hercules" who came to St. Louis only a few years ago and "is trying to clean the Augean stables of this boodling municipality and boodling state." In the interview Folk declared he would end bribery in the legislature and purify party politics, including in his own Democratic Party. He told the press: "I don't believe in closing our eyes to corruption for fear it will hurt the party. No party can be hurt by getting rid of bad men, nor by cutting off its rotten limbs." He felt he would have the support of the "better elements" of the Democratic Party in his battle against corruption.[48] In November the editor of same paper declared: "Folk stands clearly and unmistakably for good government. His fight has been against the corrupt in both parties, and against all sorts of odds, and the entire nation should welcome his election."[49]

During the 1904 campaign for governor, Folk presented himself as a "lone warrior for righteousness" and called on those who opposed the political machines to back him in his fight against corruption and special privilege. This imagery appears to have helped get him elected.[50] By then he had received endorsements not only from William Jennings Bryan but from prominent out-of-state Progressive Republicans, including La Follette, and William Allen White, editor of the *Emporia Gazette* in Kansas. President Theodore Roosevelt also apparently favored Folk, though this caused him some embarrassment.[51] In Missouri Folk's efforts received the support of the influential *St. Louis Post-Dispatch*, owned by Joseph Pulitzer. In the 1904 election the votes of Progressive Republicans for Folk more than compensated for the loss of his support with Democrats who were angered by his investigations.[52] Bryan campaigned for Folk and spoke at his inaugural, declaring that Folk's victory had been a victory for good government.[53]

Governor Folk drew upon public support to force through several reforms over the opposition of members of his own party. He had just turned thirty-five when he was elected. Veteran lawmakers, accustomed to doing things their own way, resented being rolled over by a young whippersnapper who knew nothing about the ways of the legislature.⁵⁴ In the short run, Folk won out. Party leaders, however, survived and did not forget. Later on, they blocked his initial attempt to secure the party's nomination to the US Senate and worked against his presidential bid.

Folk launched successful antitrust prosecutions and secured laws ending the ability of state officials to get free railroad passes, requiring the registration of lobbyists, and banning racetrack gambling as well as a constitutional amendment establishing the initiative and referendum. Folk's term in office also brought a direct primary. On this issue he had the support of some Democratic Party bosses who saw it in the party's interest in building public confidence.⁵⁵ He also used his executive authority to direct the St. Louis Police Department to close gambling houses and enforce Sunday closing laws. On race Folk did go along with segregation, at least as it applied to schools.⁵⁶ He did, however, act swiftly and sternly early in April 1906 after a mob in Springfield lynched three black men who were being held in jail. Folk sent militia troops to patrol the streets and restore order, offered a reward for the arrest and conviction of mob members, and instructed the assistant attorney general to help in the fact-finding and prosecution of those involved.

Folk set out to get the Democratic nomination for the presidency in 1912. He borrowed much from Bryan's platform and hoped to win over Bryan and his supporters. He received some encouragement from Bryan but did not gain much ground.⁵⁷ After dropping out, he supported Champ Clark, a leading political figure in Missouri, for the nomination. He became a strong supporter of Woodrow Wilson after he received the nomination and campaigned for him across the country. Wilson later appointed Folk to a position in the State Department, and he moved on from there to do legal work for the Interstate Commerce Commission. Folk, like many other Progressive governors, later sought a seat in the US Senate. He secured the Democratic nomination in 1918 but lost the election. He did not run again for anything.

Like Pingree, Dunne, and others, his Progressivism initially reflected his experiences in local politics. Like Cummins, he received support in rural areas but was not agrarian in outlook. To the contrary, both were essentially spokespeople for middle-class, professional, business-minded urbanites.⁵⁸ He did, though, strongly support and share certain outlooks and values with the rural-based William Jennings Bryan, including a "fervent evangelical Protestantism," the notion that government was there to protect the weak from the strong, and a commitment to democracy.⁵⁹

Biographer Louis Geiger wrote that Folk did much for the cause of good government and viewed him as a crusader who "lived and breathed politics, and was never completely happy out of it." He also noted Folk's failures: being poor at making alliances and bargaining, being too rigid and too cold to develop a strong following. To Geiger, Folk came across as something of an opportunist, shallow, and vague in advocating "clean government" with no deep understanding of issues.⁶⁰

He was very much a lone wolf who had few close friends or close followers: "The Folk movement always remained something of a one-man affair, as was painfully apparent when no strong successors or running mates appeared to hold the progressive Democrats together in 1908."[61]

Folk, though, did get along relatively well with Republican Herbert Spencer Hadley, who followed Folk as governor. Hadley had begun his political career in Kansas City as an energetic county attorney engaged not only in ordinary criminal cases but also in investigations into jury-bribing accusations against large corporations and in violations involving public gambling.[62] He had been attorney general while Folk was in office and gained considerable attention for successfully prosecuting Standard Oil and other giant corporations doing business in Missouri for violating the state's antitrust law. Like Folk, Hadley's record as a prosecutor helped him secure his party's nomination for governor. Folk did not endorse Hadley in the general election of 1908, but he refused to endorse his opponent, a conservative, machine-backed Democrat.[63]

Hadley promoted Progressive ideas and programs, but his legislative success as governor was minimal because he faced a legislature controlled by conservative Democrats.[64] Like Folk, he made a direct attack on a political boss, in his case the machine led by Thomas Pendergast of Kansas City. Hadley appointed his own man as the city's police commissioner, who immediately set out to purge the voter registration rolls of nonexistent people registered as Democrats. This hurt the machine, though only temporarily, as the registration list was later repadded with new names.[65] Hadley supported Roosevelt in his battle with Taft at the 1912 Republican national convention but refused to bolt the convention when it went Taft's way and ultimately endorsed Taft. Roosevelt considered Hadley "a Progressive with the bridle on."[66]

OHIO: FROM THE LOCAL LEVEL TO HARMON AND COX

In Ohio reform got off the ground largely on the local level in the administrations of Sam Jones, mayor of Toledo (1897–1904), and Tom Johnson, mayor of Cleveland (1901–9), both of whom made unsuccessful runs for governor. The reform spirit they introduced gained some momentum on the state level in the administrations of Democratic governor Judson Harmon (1909–13) and reached its peak in the Ohio Constitutional Convention of 1912, which attracted national attention to Ohio as a leader in the Progressive movement, and in the first administration of Governor James M. Cox (1913–15) when the constitutional changes were implemented and various other reforms were adopted.[67]

Ohio-born Judson Harmon had begun his career as a follower of Grover Cleveland and had served as Cleveland's last attorney general. In 1908 Ohio Bryanites, including Tom Johnson, initially objected to Harmon as a Democratic candidate for governor. However, they decided to go along with him after he agreed to accept a highly Progressive state party platform. Two years later, when Harmon ran for reelection, his running mates and platform were drawn from the Tom Johnson faction of the party.[68] Harmon won reelection in 1910, defeating future president Warren G. Harding, and with this election gained considerable prominence as a candidate for his party's presidential nomination in 1912.[69]

Running for the nomination Harmon encountered the wrath of William Jennings Bryan who was supporting Woodrow Wilson. Bryan called Harmon a reactionary. An article printed in Bryan's *The Commoner* charged that Harmon was backed by a "band of mugwump commercial criminals who know no party but the one which permits them to pillage the helpless and who profess or practice no creed but the divine right to rule for their own selfishness."[70] In rebuttal, though, Harmon could point to a record of Progressive accomplishments as governor. These included measures calling for the direct election of US senators, nonpartisan judicial elections, worker's compensation, public utility regulation, a corrupt-practices act, a limited direct legislation system for cities, short-ballot reform, and increases in corporate taxes.[71] One scholar has suggested that Harmon's basic motivations were essentially opportunistic—he had seen the rising Progressive tide, the political gains being made by Hiram Johnson and others, and, overall, the value of moving leftward.[72] Still, the results were positive as far as Progressivism was concerned.

Democrat James M. Cox, who served as governor in 1913–15 and 1917–21, had stronger standing than Harmon as an out-and-out Progressive, though some were suspicious of his sincerity, based in part on his close association with reactionary Democratic Party boss Edward Hanley and his sudden jump from the Hanley camp to the Progressive one.[73] Eager to pursue the Progressive path, Cox borrowed ideas from both Mayors Jones and Johnson as well as from reformers in Wisconsin and elsewhere. He earnestly set out to implement the Progressive constitution and sought the assistance of leading experts on various areas of policy.[74]

Cox, a successful publisher and businessman, noted in his autobiography: "Despite my record as a rather advanced political progressive, the fact that I had achieved some measure of success in the business conduct of a newspaper inspired conservative Ohioans with a certain confidence in me. They regarded me as a 'safe' kind of liberal."[75] A contemporary observer saw him as "an aggressive, active man" who was also "able to use the arts of diplomacy or politics."[76] Another looked on him as "a downright and decisive character" for which "there is no neutrality of thought which paralyzes action. There is black and white."[77]

Cox was born on an Ohio farm. He started out as a high school teacher but became attracted to journalism and eventually spent much of his career as the owner and editor of several newspapers in Ohio and other states. In 1903 the *Dayton Daily News*, published by Cox, endorsed Tom Johnson in his unsuccessful bid for the office of governor. Voters elected Cox to the House of Representatives in 1908 and 1910. He won the governor's race in 1912, lost it in 1914, and won it again in 1916 and 1918. In 1920, while governor, his national reputation as a reform governor helped get him the Democratic Party nomination for the presidency. He lost to fellow Ohioan and newspaperman Warren G. Harding, who was serving as US senator. While running for the presidency he made a special effort in several states to promote the adoption of woman suffrage on a national basis.[78]

In his 1913 message to the legislature Cox made fifty-six proposals, some of which were needed to implement the new constitution. Many came straight from the party's Progressive platform.[79] His time as governor brought reforms involving the direct primary, the initiative and referendum, lobbying control, bill drafting, civil service, the state court system, penal reform, the improvement of rural schools, worker's compensation, and other matters. On practical side, he "wielded the club of patronage to hold recalcitrant party members in line, refusing to commit himself on appointments until the end of the regular session."[80]

To improve the status of the governor as chief administrator, Cox called for the short ballot, eliminating some elective offices, putting more agencies under gubernatorial control, and an executing budgeting system giving the governor greater control over state agency spending.[81] In 1913 he successfully pushed for the adoption of a legislative reference service along the lines of that established in Wisconsin to help implement the package of progressive reforms he had called for in his 1912 campaign.[82] Like La Follette, he was a believer in using commissions headed by policy experts. He spent much time in managing the prison system, making frequent contact with prisoners. Cox felt his major accomplishments as governor were in the areas of penal reform, worker's compensation, and improvement of rural schools.[83]

INDIANA: PROGRESSIVES WITH THE BRAKES ON, GOING THEIR INDIVIDUAL WAYS

During the first two decades of the twentieth century Indiana had a series of governors, Republicans and Democrats, whose Progressive inclinations took them in various directions. The first of these, Republican Winfield Taylor Durbin, was elected governor in 1900 and proceeded to push for antitrust protections, honest elections, and juvenile courts. He also enforced the law against lynching and the related activities of "Whitecap" vigilante organizations active in the southern part of the state.

The election of Republican James Franklin Hanly as governor in 1904 brought a change in focus. Hanly, a former state legislator and congressman, might best be considered a party maverick with his own agenda. He had the reputation of "a speaker of force and eloquence" but also as being "a cunning politician, a master of intrigue" who, with a history of poverty as a child, touted himself as "the poor man's candidate."[84] Much of the passion of this teetotaling Methodist was directed against political corruption, gambling, and drinking. In 1908 he secured the passage of a local-option law that led to the banning of liquor sales in over half of the state's counties. After leaving office, Hanly became a leader in the drive for prohibition. He was the presidential nominee of the Prohibition Party in 1916.

Soon after taking office, Hanly found widespread disregard for the laws: "I found liquor sold at illegal hours; I found wine rooms open all night, where men, women and beardless boys congregated; I found gambling machines, poolrooms, and betting on races everywhere." He said he decided to enforce the law even though some of his party associates said that if he did, he would destroy the Republican Party in Indiana.[85] He worked with a Republican legislature to produce a law restricting gambling on horse races. He also ordered the state police to raid a resort hotel partially owned by Thomas Taggart, chair of the Democratic National Committee, where illegal gambling was taking place. The police seized a great deal of gaming equipment, but proceedings against Taggart were dropped after Democrat Thomas Marshall succeeded Hanly in 1909.

In 1907 Hanly signed eugenics legislation requiring the sterilization of criminals, imbeciles, idiots, and rapists in state custody when recommended by a board of medical experts. Indiana was the first state to adopt this type of legislation. Dr. Harry Sharp, a prison doctor, led the drive for the legislation. A similar bill had failed in Pennsylvania in 1905, thanks to a veto by Governor Pennypacker. Indiana sponsors took care to ensure that they had Hanly's support as well as sufficient legislative support before they introduced the legislation. Sharp was able to catch Hanly's ear. The governor had no qualms about doing what could be done to improving human purity and righteousness or in using a medical approach to moral problems.[86]

Democrat Thomas R. Marshall, who won the Indiana governor's office in 1908, was a small-town Indiana lawyer who had been very active as a loyal party worker stumping the state for other Democrats. He did not hold any public office until elected governor. He described himself as a "progressive with the brakes on" but pursued a substantial number of reforms.[87] Marshall, like Hanly, favored prohibition. Being dry put him on the wrong side of the issue as far as party boss Taggart was concerned, but the prohibitionists and anti-Taggart factions plus the support of organized labor got Marshall the party nomination over Taggart's opposition. Marshall financed his own campaign, offered a broad Progressive program, and narrowly edged out his Republican opponent (49 percent to 47 percent). Once in office, Marshall moved to make peace with Taggart by giving him considerable influence over the distribution of patronage and, as noted earlier, dropping proceedings against him initiated by Hanly. He also opposed the eugenics and sterilization laws adopted under Hanly and refused to allow state agencies to implement them.

As governor he sought several reforms, many of which were in a proposed new state constitution he had written. The proposed constitution was designed to strengthen the state's regulatory powers regarding corporations, give greater protections to unions, and bring direct legislation, among other reforms. Although the state courts blocked the adoption of his proposed constitution, he did get child labor protection and anticorruption measures through the legislature. Anticorporate in orientation, he used antitrust laws to break up large businesses and sponsored a measure giving the railroad commission the power to set rates.

Marshall stood against capital punishment and regularly either issued pardons to those on death row or commuted their sentences. No executions took place during his term. In one case involving the death penalty, he was alarmed by the trial of a black man who was sentenced to be hanged. He later noted: "They were so anxious to hang him that they set the date before he could even get his case to the Supreme Court." Marshall granted the prisoner a stay of proceedings so the court would have time to review the conviction. After going through court records, Marshall concluded it was a case of self defense. The attorney general agreed with him, got a new trial, and the man, with the help of a far better lawyer than the first time around, was acquitted.[88]

Marshall also issued more than his share of pardons. He noted in his autobiography that "critics made a good deal of sport of me, as they called me the 'Pardoning Governor.' They even cartooned me, having a man jostling me in a crowd, saying: 'Pardon me, Governor,' and my response being: 'Certainly! What crime have you committed?'"[89]

Democrat Samuel Ralston followed Marshall in office. The former teacher became a lawyer and an active Democrat, often using his own funds to campaign for party members around the state. Over the years he developed a close personal relationship with Taggart.[90] In 1908 he had Taggart's support for governor as an antiprohibition candidate but lost the Democratic nomination to Marshall. Four years later, with Taggart's support, he won the gubernatorial nomination and defeated former governor Durbin running as a Republican and Albert Beveridge running on the Progressive Party ticket. Ralston later appointed Taggart to the US Senate.

In his augural address Ralston called for a variety measures contained in the party's platform, including a public utilities commission and a worker's compensation act. When it came to the accumulation of wealth and corporations, he took what might be considered "a Progressive within boundaries approach" in declaring: "I believe in the accumulation of property, but the acquisition of riches by the special interests, through the perversion of the functions of government, tends to divide the people into classes and weakens their confidence in the government. Nor am I hostile to corporations. On the contrary I recognize their worth. The business of the country could not be carried on without them. But I insist that when they dominate legislatures and control the people's government in their own interests, they violate the law of their creation, become wrongdoers against the public and should be dealt with accordingly."[91]

During his term (1913–17) Ralston earned the reputation of "a middle-of-the-road progressive and a champion of governmental economy."[92] He secured the enactment of a public utilities law, a revised corrupt-practices act, an inheritance tax, and, reaching into the social realm, a tenement housing act and a child labor law. Two years later came more accomplishments, including worker's compensation, lobbying control, and statewide primaries.[93]

NOTES

1. Geiger, *Joseph W. Folk of Missouri*.
2. Sage, *A History of Iowa*, 204–8; Jensen, *Winning of the Midwest*, 100–101; Hahn, *Urban-Rural Conflict*, 51–52.
3. Merrill, *Bourbon Democracy*, 194–95, 203–5.
4. Sage, *A History of Iowa*, 226.
5. Iowa Documents, 1902, 1:2, quoted in De Witt, *Progressive Movement*, 61. See also "Gov. Cummins' Plain Words," *The Commoner*, February 7, 1902, 2; and "Lobby Legislation Not Probable," *Evening-Times Herald*, January, 5, 1907, 2.
6. Rice, *Progressive Cities*, 57.
7. On the politics surrounding the plan see Rice, *Progressive Cities*; and Hamilton, *Dethronement of the City Boss*.
8. Sage, *A History of Iowa*, 226.
9. "Notes from the Capital," *Nation*, May 18, 1916, 538.
10. Nye, *Midwestern Progressive Politics*, 213.
11. Ibid., 81.
12. Ridge, *Ignatius Donnelly*, 316.
13. "Antitrust Convention," *New York Times*, June 6, 1893, 5.
14. Ridge, *Ignatius Donnelly*, 336, 338.
15. Ibid., 357–59.
16. Stephenson, *John Lind*, 112–13.
17. "The New Governors," 35.
18. "Lind's Message," *Little Falls Weekly Transcript*, January 6, 1899, 8.
19. Stephenson, *John Lind*, 161, 171.
20. Helms, *John A. Johnson*, 97.
21. Fenton, *Midwest Politics*, 78; Nye, *Midwestern Progressive Politics*, 214.
22. Chrislock, *Progressive Era in Minnesota*, 14, 15.
23. On his background see generally Helms, *John A. Johnson*.
24. "From Pauper's Son to Governor of a State," *New York Times*, July 1907, SM5.
25. Helms, *John A. Johnson*, 97.
26. "Governor Johnson and His Record in Public Life," *New York Times*, June 7, 1908, SM1.
27. Helms, *John A. Johnson*, 164–65.
28. Commentary on these attacks and other aspects of his background are found in "From Pauper's Son to Governor of a State"; "Johnson May Be Re-elected," *New York Times*, November 3, 1906, 1; "Governor Johnson and His Record in Public Life"; and "Bitter State Fights from Coast to Coast."

29. Nye, *Midwestern Progressive Politics*, 215.
30. Chrislock, *Progressive Era in Minnesota*, 19.
31. Charles B. Cheney, "Johnson of Minnesota," *The Outlook*, January 25, 1908, 173.
32. Ibid., 171.
33. "Masterly Inactivity Is Johnson's Policy," *Worthington Advance*, August 17, 1906, 9.
34. "U.S. Steel as Chaperone," *Willmar Tribune*, September 30, 1908, 6.
35. "A Strong Dangerous Man", *Los Angeles Times*, November 8, 1908, II-4.
36. Helms, *John A. Johnson*, 70, 254–55.
37. Coletta, *William Jennings Bryan*, 397.
38. Helms, *John A. Johnson*, 254.
39. Fenton, *Midwest Politics*, 79.
40. Burckel, "Progressive Governors in the Border States," 519.
41. Piott, *Holy Joe*, 7.
42. Geiger, *Folk of Missouri*, 20; Wetmore, *Battle against Bribery*, 6.
43. Piott, *Holy Joe*, 24.
44. "Nomination of Folk Now Seems Assured," *New York Times*, April 18, 1904, 9.
45. Steffens, *Shame of the Cities*, 19–20. This chapter (19–41) originated as an article in October 1902 under the title "Tweed Days in St. Louis."
46. White, "Political Signs of Promise," 668.
47. Burckel, "Progressive Governors in the Border States," 161.
48. Folk interview with Frank G. Carpenter, "Joe Folk, The Boodle Fighter, On Corruption in Public Life," *Atlanta Constitution*, August 28, 1904, 2.
49. "Governorship Fights Sharp in Many States," *Atlanta Constitution*, November 6, 1904, B1.
50. Geiger, *Folk of Missouri*, 63, 64.
51. Burckel, "Progressive Governors in the Border States," 67.
52. Ibid.
53. "Governor Folk's Inaugural," *The Outlook*, January 21, 1905, 152–53; "Governor Folk and the Lobby," *The Outlook*, February 11, 1905, 359; Geiger, *Folk of Missouri*, 91.
54. Burckel, "Progressive Governors in the Border States," 533, 540.
55. Ware, *American Direct Primary*, 148.
56. Piott, *Holy Joe*, 110.
57. Geiger, *Folk of Missouri*, 143.
58. Ibid., 15.
59. Piott, *Holy Joe*, 153.
60. Geiger, *Folk of Missouri*, 172.
61. Ibid., 96. See also Piott, *Holy Joe*, 52–53.
62. L. C. Dyer, "Governor Hadley of Missouri," *Mumsey's Magazine*, April 1909, 94–95.
63. Burckel, "Progressive Governors in the Border States," 164.
64. See ibid., 131–59.
65. A more devastating blow came from Hadley's Democratic successor, Elliot W. Major, who hurt the Pendergast machine by limiting its ability to make patronage appointments. See Steinberg, *Bosses*, 316, 317.
66. Martin, *Ballots and Bandwagons*, 63.
67. See generally Warner, *Progressivism in Ohio*.
68. Sarasohn, *Party of Reform*, 47–48, 88.
69. "The Elections," *The Outlook*, November 19, 1910, 607–9.
70. Article reprinted in "Who Pays the Freight," *The Commoner*, June 16, 1911, 3.
71. "Harmon to Fight for the Presidency," *New York Times*, June 4, 1911, 1. See also the glowing account of his record in "How Judson Harmon Looks as Presidential Timber," *New York Times*, December 3, 1911, SM1; and his list of accomplishments in Sarasohn, *Party of Reform*, 112–13.

72. Warner, *Progressivism in Ohio*, 262, 273.
73. Ibid., 367. Warner also suggests on page 366 that Cox wrote his autobiography, in part, to document his development as a Progressive.
74. Ibid., 386–87.
75. Cox, *Journey through My Years*, 117.
76. "Cox and Harding Both Ohioans and Printers," *Evening Missourian*, July 6, 1920, 1.
77. "Jimmy Cox, Before and After Nomination," *Literary Digest*, July 24, 1920, 42.
78. See Harper, *History of Woman Suffrage*, 6:234, 499, 620–21.
79. Warner, *Progressivism in Ohio*, 391.
80. Ibid., 389.
81. Ibid., 433.
82. Burns, "The Legislative Reference Movement in Ohio."
83. "Jimmy Cox, Before and After Nomination," 42–49.
84. Bowers, *Beveridge and the Progressive Era*, 81.
85. Speech quoted in "I'd Pay the Price," *New York Times*, October 9, 1905, 2.
86. Pieces of the story are found in Haller, *Eugenics*; Lombardo, *Century of Eugenics in America*; and Pickens, *Eugenics and the Progressives*.
87. Among other sources, the quote of Marshall as a "progressive with the brakes on" is found in Gable, *Bull Moose Years*, 23.
88. Marshall, *Recollections*, 193–94.
89. Ibid., 190.
90. Hoy, "Samuel M. Ralston," 233–34.
91. "Ralston Is Now Indiana's Governor," *Lake County Times*, January 13, 1913, 1.
92. Hoy, "Samuel M. Ralston," 236.
93. Ibid., 236–39.

5

RAISING HELL ON THE PLAINS

Lewelling, Hoch, Stubbs, Sheldon, Burke, and Norbeck

On a speaking tour in May 1911, Woodrow Wilson called Kansas and Nebraska "the pacemakers for the nation" when it came to reform.[1] Kansas farmers had followed Populist Mary Ellen Lease's advice to "raise less corn and more hell" and along the way had put two Populists in the office of governor in the 1890s. Though backing away from the Populist surge somewhat, insurgent Republicans and Progressive Democrats in Kansas were to usher in a series of reforms in the first two decades of the twentieth century. Similar developments took place in Nebraska, where William Jennings Bryan played a leading role. In the Dakotas there was a backing away from the leftward farm-based protest of the Populist movement, but it was to reemerge in a somewhat radical form, especially in North Dakota.

Differences between North and South Dakota have long captured the attention of political observers, with North Dakota on the liberal side and South Dakota on the conservative side, but the differences were less pronounced in the period under review: both were Progressive, even radical in some respects, though the governor of South Dakota took pains to distinguish his reforms from similar reforms in North Dakota. Indeed, contemporary observers of state politics may well be struck by how liberal or progressive all the states considered in this chapter were during the period under review.

The discussion of Populist governors in Kansas, Nebraska, North Dakota, and South Dakota in this chapter illustrates the types of electoral and governing problems generally encountered by this group. We also see the rise, thoughts, and activities of several Progressive Republican governors, including Edward Hoch and W. R. Stubbs in Kansas and Peter Norbeck in South Dakota. Along with this comes Democrat John Burke of North Dakota, who, with the help of Progressive Republicans, had a productive tenure as governor of North Dakota and in the same state Governor Lynn Frazier, who initially, at least, was not much more than a front man for a radical group that had captured the Republican Party.

KANSAS POPULISTS AND BOSS BUSTERS

Kansas Populists did well in 1890 with the dramatic election of William A. Peffer to the US Senate but had some anxiety about continuing to do so because of relatively poor showings in municipal elections in 1891. Hoping to increase their chances in 1892, they sought an alliance with the Democrats and nominated Lorenzo Dow Lewelling, a merchant from Wichita who was willing to work with "honorable allies" in the Democratic Party in his quest for governor. The tactic worked; Democrats helped Lewelling win election as governor in 1892, narrowly edging out his Republican opponent with 50 percent of the vote compared to 49 percent.[2]

Lewelling went out of his way immediately after his election to let the public know he was not the radical his opponents had made him out to be during the campaign.[3] His inaugural address on January 9, 1893, however, alarmed conservatives. A *New York Times* writer, for one, took note of "its peculiar tone" and expressed strong opposition to the views expressed.[4] In this speech Lewelling declared that government had an obligation to come to the rescue of farmers, laborers, businesspeople, and others in need. He made a call for action:

> "Government is not a failure, and the State has not been constructed in vain. This is the generation which has come to the rescue ... Conscience is in the saddle; we have leaped the bloody chasm, and entered a contest for the protection of home, humanity, and the dignity of labor. The grandeur of civilization shall be emphasized by the dawn of a new era, in which the people shall reign; and, if found necessary, they will 'expand the powers of government to solve the enigmas of the times."[5]

In his first message to the legislature Lewelling returned to a moderate tone and emphasized his willingness to compromise.[6] Early on, however, he was caught up in a furious battle between Populists and Republicans over who should control the statehouse. At one point Populist lawmakers locked the Republican legislators out of the house chamber. Republicans gained entry by breaking down a door and proceeded to set up a barricade in expectation of a counterattack by the Populists. Only intervention by the governor and the state supreme court prevented armed warfare between the two sides.

Lewelling later approved of a compromise settlement favorable to the Republicans on the control issue. His failure to stand up for a Populist house as the legal body angered many in his own party. Populist legislators were also put off by the governor's support of a Democrat over a pure Populist for a US senator seat. Still another area of tension was that Populists and Democrats in the legislature differed over enforcement of the state's prohibition law, the Populists being far more favorable to the cause than the Democrats.[7] Given all the turmoil, the Populists did not even come close to implementing their platform through legislation.[8] Lewelling, though, continued to defend causes he felt were important. For example, in an interview he offered the thought that the "Coxey movement is a spontaneous uprising of the people. It is more than a petition, it is an earnest and vigorous protest against the injustice and tyranny of the age."[9]

Lewelling ran on a Democratic-Populist ticket in 1894 but failed in his bid for reelection. The Populists, however, regained the governor's office in 1896 with the election of John W. Leedy, a farmer who had been serving in the state legislature. Leedy had started off as a Republican, became a Democrat, and in 1892 switched to the Populists. He focused his attack on the railroads and corporations. He served one relatively uneventful term. He made an effort to secure the adoption of a bank deposit guarantee law, but the measure failed in the house by four votes in a special session he called.

Following the decline of the Populists, the drive for reform reemerged, though in a far milder form in the early 1900s under the leadership of insurgent Republicans known as the "Boss Busters," who took aim at a group of politicians backed by the railways, insurance companies, packing houses, and brewers.[10] Edward Hoch, a newspaper owner and publisher in Marion, Kansas, was an early leader of the Boss Buster reform faction. He had started his political career in the Kansas house where he also served as speaker. He ran for and won the office of governor as an antimachine candidate in 1904 and was reelected in 1906.

Under Hoch came a slew of reforms, including a statewide direct primary law, an anti-free-pass measure, maximum railroad rate legislation, a tax commission that made it more difficult for the railroads to avoid paying their share of the load, a child labor law, and an improved pure food law. Hock appointed an attorney who took his duty seriously in regard to the enforcement of prohibition laws. He successfully opposed Jim Crow legislation, declaring that such laws were intended to humiliate African Americans and served no legitimate purpose. On the criminal justice side, Hoch opposed the death penalty—he swore never to sign an order for execution and did not do so.[11]

To also curb chicanery Hoch and the Boss Busters put the state printer on a fixed salary (no longer allowing the holder of that office to make as much as possible by charging fees), put some agencies under a merit system where they were no longer exposed to political pressure, cut down on the number of "useless" people hired by legislators, and reformed the state treasurer's office so that the interest made on public funds would be returned to the state rather than go, as it customarily had, to a state party machine.[12]

Insurgent Republicans had further success with the election of wealthy businessman Walter Roscoe Stubbs as governor in 1908. He had been a leading Boss Buster while serving in the state legislature in the early 1900s. He was the first governor to win nomination under the state's direct primary law. Three weeks after winning the primary he played a prominent role in drafting the Republican platform and making it a highly Progressive one. It called for such measures as those regulating lobbying and campaign expenditures and guaranteeing bank deposits. He felt by putting these in the platform, he would be helping to insure their adoption if he and other Republicans were elected.[13]

Stubbs sailed through the 1908 general election campaign, which he won with close to a 10 percent lead over his Democratic opponent. He had, however, done nothing to encourage the nomination of legislative supporters in his own party and after the election came into office without giving much consideration to what he had to do to line up Republican votes for his legislative program. He assumed Republican legislators would go along with what the party had promised in its platform and this would be all he needed. The legislature passed several measures but fell far short in 1909 of honoring all the pledges in the platform and approving all the measures requested by Stubbs. He was especially upset about his failure to get a valuation of railroad property and a public utilities law such as that passed in New York and Wisconsin.[14]

Stubbs won renomination in the 1910 primaries while campaigning this time against those legislators who had opposed his agenda. The primaries turned out to be a victory not only for Stubbs but for insurgents running for nearly all the other offices on the ticket. The party council, under the control of reformers, again wrote a highly Progressive platform. In the general election Stubbs faced Democrat George Hodges, another successful businessperson and newspaper owner who, as state senator, had become the most influential Democrat in the state and a leading Progressive. In challenging Stubbs he created considerable confusion over who was the most Progressive. They had very similar platforms and debated over who was the most sincere. Voters sided with Stubbs. Coming back into office, Stubbs once again demanded that the Republican legislators implement the party's highly Progressive platform.[15]

Stubbs has been viewed as something of a crank but also someone who was able to "secure important reforms and further the cause of honest government." He had a lot of opposition in both political parties. According to one assessment, "He was never able to master the intricacies of the legislative process, but he salvaged much of his program by taking advantage of the popularity of reform. In this way he forced reluctant legislators to support his goals."[16]

During his tenure much was accomplished: a public utilities commission was created that put not just railroads but a variety of public-serving "natural monopolies" under greater control; restrictions were tightened on insurance companies; railroad rates were regulated; and lobbying restrictions, a campaign expense law, and a voluntary bank guarantee law were approved. The state also adopted a blue sky law under his watch to put an end to the selling of worthless stocks and bonds by dishonest promoters. This law, the first in the nation, had been promoted by Joseph Dolley, the state's banking commissioner appointed by Stubbs.

Stubbs was also intent on enforcing anti-liquor laws. Employing the authority given to him by the legislature, he removed local officials who refused to enforce state laws against illegal distillers, bootlegging, and saloons. Stubbs was especially concerned about such activity in the "Little Balkans" area in Crawford County; with its large immigrant population, immigrants working in strip mines supplemented their incomes by making whiskey and illegal saloons were common. Stubbs put pressure on sheriffs to enforce the law or lose their job and threatened to send in the state militia if necessary. He made some progress in closing down illegal saloons, though illegal sales continued on a clandestine basis.[17]

Stubbs, a businessman, had no problem taking on the railroads. Opening up an interstate conference on freight rates in September 1910, he charged: "The principle railroad systems of the United States have combined for the purpose of advancing freight rates on a scale never before known in the history of this country."[18] The same year, while testifying before the Interstate Commerce Commission against a proposal by the railroad executives to raise freight rates, he maintained that increases would not be needed if the companies were not so badly managed and "ran their business honestly and decently and sanely." On this occasion, though, he softened his tone a bit and went on suggest that, in being critical of the railroads, he was simply doing his job as governor. He paid his respects to President Edward Ripley of the Santa Fe as a railway man and added: "We don't agree, that's all. Mr. Ripley works for the railroads and I work for the people of my state. He has no more right to complain of me than I have of him. If we fail to work for our employers we ought to be fired."[19]

Contrary to expectations about a man with a business background, Stubbs did not turn out to be antiunion or antilabor. During one labor dispute he told coal operators that the demands made by workers for an increase in wages was fully justified and advised them to make a speedy settlement.[20] He supported a variety of labor legislation and took particular pleasure in reporting on a worker's compensation measure he had sponsored at a governors' conference meeting.[21] He, along with his wife Stella, also actively supported the woman suffrage cause. He signed the measure sent to the voters in 1912 that brought this about in Kansas.

Democrat George Hodges, who had lost to Stubbs in 1910, won the office of governor in 1912 by beating out Republican Arthur Capper, the owner and publisher of several newspapers, by just twenty-nine votes—the decision of the canvassing board came twenty-five days after the election; at first count, he led by thirty-one votes. Hodges had played a large role in the passage of several Progressive measures while in the state legislature when Stubbs was governor and continued on the path of reform as governor in his single term from 1913 to 1915. He was just the second Democrat in the state's history to win the gubernatorial office.

During his career, Hodges made the headlines regarding his involvement in some real or alleged physical confrontations. During the 1911 session he got involved in a fistfight on the floor of the legislature during debate over a bill. He came out on top and was able to knock a Republican senator who attacked him senseless.[22] While governor, he had an alleged altercation in his office with a woman who claimed she struggled with him over some letters written by a prisoner seeking parole. The woman said the governor struck her on the shoulder and wrenched her wrists trying to get some of the letters out of her hand. A jury, though, did not go along with her charge that Hodges was guilty of assault and battery.[23]

Though he put considerable emphasis on economy in government, Hodges had a large reform package that included direct democracy, corporation taxation, antitrust laws, woman suffrage, and prohibition.[24] He gained some national attention in his call for unicamerialism. Feeling that the legislature as structured was costly, clumsy, and inefficient, in 1913 he called for replacing the existing two-house legislature with a small single legislative body. His plan, the particulars of which changed over time, also made the governor an ex-officio member of the legislature.[25]

During the 1914 campaign, Bryan's newspaper, *The Commoner*, gave Hodges high marks for bringing the state through a budget crisis he inherited without raising taxes, being able to increase spending on education by increasing the efficiency of state government, and giving newly enfranchised women places on important boards and in the running of public institutions.[26] Voters, however, on a rematch preferred the Republican candidate, Arthur Capper, who won again in 1916. Capper, known as "the meek and mild governor," worked to improve the administrative and budgeting process, the blue sky law, and the establishment of a civil service commission.[27] He, like Hodges, also saw the need for structural change, in his case a massive reorganization of the state government. To the governor, the state government had become an "antiquated, cumbersome, wasteful, inefficient" patchwork of "boards, commissions, bureaus, and departments."[28] He went on to the US Senate for several terms.

NEBRASKA: FUSION, INSURGENCY, RAILROADS, AND LIQUOR

Led by William Jennings Bryan, the Nebraska Democratic Party in the 1890s became more reform-minded, abandoned the Cleveland types, and joined forces with the Populists. In 1894 Bryan enthusiastically endorsed the decision of the Nebraska Populists to nominate Judge Silas A. Holcomb for governor and was able to get the Democrats to also nominate Holcomb, a move that prompted the Cleveland Democrats to bolt from the party convention in protest. With Nebraska Populists, Democrats, and independent Republicans working together and enjoying the support of pro-silver organizations such as the Free Coinage League, Holcomb got elected, though only narrowly edging out his Republican opponent by about 3,000 votes, 48 percent to 46 percent. The fusion worked again in 1896 when Holcomb was reelected along with the entire Populist-Democratic state ticket and a Populist-Democratic legislature.

To offset charges that putting a Populist in office would scare off investors, the fusionists presented Holcomb in 1894 as a conservative candidate who would cut spending and maintain the state's full faith and credit.[29] In office, though, he mixed fiscal conservativism with a number of demands as far as the railroads were concerned. In his first inaugural message he called for keeping spending low to relieve the burden on taxpayers, a call that was consistent with his campaign, but, as a critic of the railroads, he also asked for an abolition of the free pass system and an increase in railroad taxes and regulations.[30] In his second inaugural address Holcomb declared: "Railroad companies should be restrained by wholesome legislation from active participation in party politics."[31]

Holcomb was the most active governor the state had experienced up to that time, breaking with the tradition of governors deferring to the legislature.[32] His accomplishments were limited in his first term by the opposition of Republicans who dominated the legislature. Republican legislators had greatly benefited by the election support given them by agents of the Union Pacific Railroad, whose leaders had hoped the legislature would appoint a US senator who would be favorable to the railroad's interests The legislature promptly chose a railroad man for the Senate.[33] Holcomb's call for nonpartisanship was largely ignored, and his role was largely confined to using his veto power to keep expenditures low.

The 1896 election put the fusion forces in control of both houses. Some legislation got through, including a measure to protect school lands from further sales—a major scandal had broken out when it was discovered that more than a half million dollars made from the sale of land set aside for schools was lost or stolen. Further progress was limited, though, by conflict within the coalition that brought Holcomb to power. He found it difficult to hold on to the support of the Democrats. They claimed they had been severely shortchanged by how the Populist governor dispensed state jobs.

Democrats continued to see the value of fusion, however, and did so again by joining forces in 1898 and electing William A. Poynter governor along with the rest of the fusion ticket. Poynter, a farmer who had helped organize the Farmers' Alliance, had been a state senator. Poynter took the Populist view that when it came to the giant transportation and communications corporations, the only real solution was national regulation if not ownership. Until that time, he declared, "state legislatures are obliged to afford all possible relief to the citizens of the State from unjust freight, passenger, telegraph, telephone, and sleeping-car charges."[34] His efforts at reform, however, were frustrated because the Republicans had come back to control the legislature. Only a few generally weak reform measures sponsored by Republicans became law. One regulated the use of money in campaigns and another limited the hours of railroad workers—to a maximum of eighteen consecutive hours! Both passed without a dissenting vote. Under Poynter, Democrats continued to complain about being kept on a "starvation diet" of patronage.[35]

Poynter went down to defeat in 1900. The fusionists continued to lose gubernatorial races in 1902 and 1904, though in close elections. Populist leader George Berge, one of the fusionist candidates, contended that the victorious Republicans had sold out to the "free pass machine" operated by the managers of the Burlington Railroad. As Berge saw it, "Corporate mastery over the politics and government of Nebraska people commenced with the beginning of railroad construction on Nebraska soil."[36] The Republicans, though, as well as the Democrats, were beginning to feel a Progressive surge, even if it was somewhat different in direction than that sought by the Populists, being less intent on the redistribution of economic power and wealth.[37]

John H. Mickey, a Roosevelt Republican, was elected governor in 1904 and reflected the spirit of times in calling for the state to act in the areas of food protection, lobbying regulation, and antitrust legislation, much of which he got, but he had little luck against the railroads. He pushed without success to get a state board to increase the property assessment of the Union Pacific and Northwestern Railroads. He banned those who served in his administration from taking railroad passes, but reports surfaced that many took them anyway.[38]

Reform reached a peak with the election of another Republican governor, former state legislator George Sheldon in 1906. Like several reform candidates elsewhere, he broke the tradition of confining preconvention campaigning to courting party politicians by taking his campaign for the nomination directly to the people. His campaign was one in which he, picking up where the Populists had left off, spent much of his energy lambasting the railroads. The party platform he ran on drew from those put together by insurgents in Wisconsin and Iowa, which called for a wide range of reforms.[39]

Under Sheldon's leadership, the 1907 session of the Nebraska legislature, controlled by insurgent Republicans, produced a historic body of reform legislation that included the establishment of a statewide direct primary, a child labor law, a measure ending free railroad passes for politicians, a law limiting railroad passenger fares to two cents a mile, and increased railroad taxation. Sheldon felt that while it was not in the state's interest to put the railroads and other great corporations out of business; it was in the state's interest to get them out of Nebraska politics.[40] He gained considerable attention for standing up to President Roosevelt in a face-to-face encounter in which he declared that he was going to continue criticizing federal court decisions interfering with the right of the states to control railroad rates no matter what the president said.[41]

Sheldon alienated both the railroads and the liquor interests—the latter by standing for the right of counties to prohibit drinking. In 1908 he lost to a fusion candidate who was supported by the brewers and saloon keepers. Another issue that seemed to work against him was his opponent's support of a popular proposal for a bank deposit guarantee system, something Sheldon also favored but could not get into his party's platform because of the opposition of leading Republicans and bankers.[42] Following Sheldon's defeat, an editor sympathetic to him wrote that Sheldon "had met every demand made upon him for reform legislation, and as a reward was kicked out of office for doing just what the people demanded of him. . . . The defeat of Governor Sheldon is the basest political ingratitude ever heaped upon a candidate."[43]

Liquor control was also a major issue in 1910 when a "dry" Republican Progressive, Chester Aldrich, won the office of governor with the backing of the Anti-Saloon League and Bryan himself, who by this time had become an ardent prohibitionist. Prohibition would continue on as an issue until the state went dry in 1917. In the meantime, the state, no matter who was governor, remained tough on the railroads and continued to go into new areas of regulation, including the adoption of a bank deposit guarantee act.

Some newspapers considered Aldrich a "radical"; others preferred designating him an "aggressive Republican."[44] In 1911 the Ohio native and graduate of Ohio State University told a gathering of the university alumni association: "In college I was known as an insurgent and revolutionist. I had such a definite view of how things should be run there that I had 39 demerits before I even knew it, and it took only 40 to expel me." He went on to tell the audience that when he got into public life, "I suddenly began to realize that some corporations because they were big and mighty, thought they owned everything."[45] His attitude on railroads, the corporations he had in mind, helped get him in the state legislature, even though he was a Republican in a Democratic district. Aldrich as a member of the Nebraska senate gained considerable prominence by pushing for legislation that brought down freight rates. As governor he continued to push for reform, but his agenda was not well received by the Democrats who controlled the legislature. During his term, though, the voters approved the initiative and referendum.

A follower of Teddy Roosevelt, Aldrich wound up backing the Progressive Party in 1912. By running as both a Republican and a Progressive for governor that year, he hoped to surmount the division among Republicans. He lost, however, in a close election to Democrat John H. Morehead, who had held local offices and served in the state legislature and as lieutenant governor. Like Democrats around the country, Morehead benefited from the split in the Republican ranks between Taft and Roosevelt in 1912. He was reelected in 1914. Under Morehead came a worker's compensation law and a blue sky law to prevent fraud in selling stock. Also coming was the first state budget law, giving the governor an important role in shaping state revenue and expenditure patterns. Looking for an improvement in the operation of state government, he called for a reduction in the number of legislators in both the senate and the house, arguing that "fewer men would be a move in the right direction."[46]

NORTH DAKOTA: ANGRY FARMERS, POPULISTS, INSURGENTS, AND RADICALS

Much of the focus of reformers in both North Dakota parties from the 1890s to the early 1900s was on longtime political boss Alexander McKenzie, who dominated Republican Party and state politics as a behind-the-scenes manipulator who could dictate the choice of candidates and control the legislature in the interests of the railroads, principally the Union Pacific, and other corporations he represented.[47]

In 1892 a short-term revolt of farmers against McKenzie and railroad control in North Dakota produced a gubernatorial victory for Populist Eli Shortridge, who ran on a fusion ticket as the candidate of the Democratic-Independent Party, which was put together by Populists, Democrats, and Farmers' Alliance members. The fusion ticket came together largely in response to Republican governor Andrew Burke's decision to veto a bill favored by the Farmers' Alliance to require railroads to lease sites for grain elevators and warehouses. Shortridge, a farmer who had led the alliance, condemned corporate control of the state and called for state-owned terminal elevators. The Republican National Committee poured money into North Dakota to save it from the Populists, but both the Populist Party candidate for president, James Weaver, and Shortridge, sixty-three at the time, carried the state.

Shortridge did not accomplish a great deal in his single term, 1893–95.[48] One problem was that a long fight over who would be chosen to go to the US Senate tied up the legislature in 1893, preventing it from doing much of anything else. The governor was able to secure an appropriation for a state-owned elevator to be built in Minnesota or Wisconsin, but the project did not get off the ground because officials in these states would not go along with a requirement that the elevator would accept grain only from farmers in North Dakota.[49] He had some anticorporate victories, for example, in regard to freight rates on coal mined in the state, but he was disappointed with the overall performance of the legislature. In a letter to a friend he noted the fundamental problem: "It is a well known fact that every bill intended to benefit the people, was either sidetracked or crippled in some way by the tools of the Railroads and other Corporations."⁵⁰

While at war with the railroads, Shortridge, like many other officials in the state, frequently sought free railroad passes for his own use or for friends, associates, and others whose friendships he was eager to cultivate. Sometimes the railroad officials were put in the embarrassing position of having to turn down the governor. For example, writing in response to a request from the governor for free tickets to send someone from Bismarck, North Dakota, to St. Paul, Minnesota, a railroad official sent the following to the governor's private secretary on March 14, 1893: "I want to assure the Governor (which I think he already knows) that we desire to extend to his friends and to the employees of the State every possible (courtesy) and favor which we consistently can, and certainly will do, but free transportation from points within one State to points within another State is absolutely prohibited by the provisions of the Interstate Commerce Law." He went on to write that special agents of the ICC might well investigate and that this would be bad for the company and "might place the governor in an embarrassing position." He concluded: "Again permit me to say that I hope the Governor will not understand this as showing a desire not to grant anything that he may want, but that is merely to place the matter in proper light for his own sake as well as ours." Doing what he could to help out and hopefully stay on the governor's good side, he sent Shortridge passes for in-state travel from Morehead, Minnesota, to St. Paul.⁵¹

His accomplishments were limited, but Shortridge helped pave the way for a later wave of reform in the state. Much of this came in the administration of John Burke, who, like John Johnson of Minnesota, was a reform-minded Democrat who got enough support from reform-minded Republicans in a traditionally Republican state to get elected governor. In Burke's case this happened in 1906 when voters also gave him a supportive legislature with which to work. Burke was reelected in 1908 and 1910.

Burke had been a conservative while serving in the North Dakota state legislature in the early 1890s. He opposed improving the powers of the railroad commission, ignored agrarian demands for a terminal elevator, and came out against prohibition and woman suffrage. He was hostile to the agrarian reform movement in 1893 that produced Populist governor Shortridge, but in a marriage of convenience rather than principle he ran on a fusion ticket with the Populists in 1896 for a seat in the US House, a race that he lost.⁵²

In the late 1890s Burke's political views began to undergo a definite transformation, and by the early 1900s he was most sympathetic to the cause of reform. The country had changed and he changed. To some extent, changing his views was also a matter of party loyalty. The Democratic Party under Bryan had become a party of reform, and Burke, a loyal Democrat, was impressed by the new leader and his message and joined the cause.⁵³ Burke moved from being a conservative,

Cleveland-type Democrat to a leadership position among those who took issue with the railroads, banks, and other corporations. He put greater emphasis, however, on political reform.[54]

North Dakota politics in 1906 was influenced by the publication in January of Rex Beach's "The Looting of Alaska" in *Appleton's Booklovers Magazine*. This muckraking piece told of a conspiracy on the part of Boss McKenzie to control gold mines in Alaska. Beach described McKenzie as a "hidden" politician who was in fact the Republican Party of North Dakota. He also quoted McKenzie as saying, "Give me a bunch of Swedes and I'll drive them like sheep."[55] The publication gave North Dakota Democrats lots of ammunition.

Insurgent North Dakota Republicans had already been protesting the control of railroads over the state under McKenzie. They were also unhappy about lack of enforcement of the prohibition law and scandals in Bismarck. They demanded anti-free-pass laws and primary elections. Burke jumped on these issues. He put together a platform attacking railroads and did well with anticorporate Republican voters. Burke, benefiting from lots of Republican votes, was the first Democrat to be elected governor of the state. He was, however, the only Democrat on the state ticket to win office in 1906. Prior to Burke's election, eight Republicans served as governors, and seven of them were linked to the McKenzie machine and, through him, the corporate interests.[56] Burke's brand of reform, however, had little to do with the Populist-agrarian surge that made Shortridge governor or, later on, brought the Nonpartisan League (NPL) and its candidate for governor, Lynn Frazier, into office as a Republican.

Burke had a legislature when he first came into office that, while not Democratic, was insurgent, and because of this, he was able to deliver the goods. He got the direct primary and other bills through the legislature. He won again in 1908 and in 1910—though by 1910 there was much less unity in Democratic ranks because of disputes over the disposition of patronage.[57]

Still, with Burke in control of the legislature in 1911, a whole boatload of Progressive reform legislation sailed through with virtually no opposition. Lawmakers put limits on campaign finances and lobbying, outlawed free railroad passes ("the McKenzie pass"), established a presidential primary, and provided for worker's compensation and juvenile courts.[58] He also took the enforcement of prohibition laws seriously.

One of his political friends described Burke as "an everyday sort of man, who associates with a common people, dresses like them, and when he is with them is one of them."[59]

He appeared to be more concerned with the political than economic aspects of Progressive reform and, like several other Progressives, had a legalistic mind that put considerable emphasis on "the need for obedience to and respect for the law."[60] Much of the movement for reform occurring during Burke's time in office came from the insurgent surge in the Republican Party and had little to do with the problems facing the farmers of the state or its Populist past.[61] The NPL episode that followed him though represented a return to these earlier concerns and impulses plus experimentation in state socialism.

The NPL came to life in North Dakota in 1915 under the leadership of Arthur Townley with the aim of organizing small farmers into a political movement to establish a number of state-owned enterprises, terminal elevators, packing plants, and flour mills. Rather than form a third party, NPL leaders sought to nominate a slate of candidates in the Republican Party who, if successful, would run as the nominees of the Republican Party. With some 40,000 members the NPL represented a considerable political force. In 1916 NPL leaders debated among themselves over whether it was wiser to look for a well-known candidate for governor to represent the league or to draft a genuine "on-the-land farmer" to run and demonstrate the strength of the organization by getting him elected. Proponents of the genuine-farmer option, led by Townley, won out.[62] The NPL leaders decided on Lynn Joseph Frazier as their candidate for governor.

Frazier, a forty-one-year-old farmer who lived near a little town named Hoople, was virtually unknown outside his small rural community. One newspaper writer asked: "Who is Frazier, and is Hoople a place or a disease?"[63] William Lemke, who was among the NPL leaders, recommended Frazier, with whom he had attended the University of North Dakota. Frazier, a lifelong Republican, was willing to take up the cause of reform.[64] He drew well with the farmers and won the 1916 Republican Party primary for governor as the NPL candidate. He went on to win the general election with close to 80 percent of the vote.

A contemporary observer who sat on the state supreme court during this period viewed Frazier as a "stolid, unemotional, full-blooded and kindly-hearted farmer" who "relied implicitly on the judgment of Townley and Lemke" and did "everything that they dictated or suggested."[65] Along similar lines, another author years later simply noted: "Frazier, trusting his old friend from university days, constantly looked to Lemke for counsel."[66] Throughout his tenure as governor, it seems, Townley and other NPL leaders controlled the NPL legislative caucus meetings where important legislative decisions were made and clued in Frazier as needed.[67]

In 1917 the NPL had considerable difficulty because it did not have a majority in the legislature. An attempt by the NPL to have the legislature implement its platform by acting as a constitutional convention was thwarted in the senate.[68] Progress was furthered in 1918, however, by the NPL's success in both the primary and general elections, which gave it control over both statehouses, brought Frazier's reelection, and, along with these, voter approval of various constitutional amendments that further facilitated the ability of the NPL to implement its legislative program.[69] In 1919 the "farmers' legislature" under the control of Townley and Lemke enacted much of the NPL program. It established state-owned banks, grain elevators, mills, and hail insurance agencies and an industrial commission to manage and operate them.

The session also brought a great deal for labor. A labor official noted: "We asked them for nothing. They exacted no pledges or promises from us. All they did was to inquire what laws organized labor in North Dakota wanted passed. We submitted eight measures. Every one is now on the statute books of the state, and it cost organized labor just $110."[70]

Frazier was reelected in 1920. His years in office saw the creation of several state-owned and -operated enterprises, a Progressive tax system, increased worker protections, and a constitutional amendment providing for the recall that, ironically, was used by NPL opponents in 1921 to remove him and other members of the state's industrial commission from office. Frazier, however, went on to serve in the US Senate from 1923 to 1941.

SOUTH DAKOTA POPULISTS AND PROGRESSIVES: NORBECK IN CHARGE

South Dakota, like North Dakota, experienced a late-nineteenth-century reform surge that resulted in the election of a Populist governor, Andrew Lee, a successful merchant and reform mayor in Vermillion. He won in 1896 with the support of the Farmers' Alliance on a Populist Party ticket and again in 1898 on a Fusion Party ticket based on an alliance of Populists, Democrats, and Free Silver Republicans. The fusionists saw their campaign as "a struggle of the masses against the entrenched privilege, a choice between free institutions of a democratic society and domination by corporate interests."[71] Lee narrowly won in this strong Republican state, the first time by 308 votes, the second time by 339 votes. Governor "Andy" Lee took office "without any flourish of trumpets" in a simple ceremony. He took aim at the railroads and was able to help subject them to the rate-making authority of the railroad commission and to a reassessment of the value of their properties by another state board. He also made direct legislation one of his chief issues and was instrumental in securing voter adoption of a statewide initiative and referendum law in 1898.[72]

Lee was an example of a successful Populist governor. Still, he had problems. He was in competition with Democrats and Republicans for the allegiance of various ethnic groups, including Norwegians, Germans, Irish, and Czechs. In an effort to accommodate the competing demands of the ethnic groups for patronage, he wound up wishing he had more jobs to hand out. Relatively inexperienced in such matters, he made some very poor appointments. Some of his appointees were just as corrupt as those who had been working for the previous Republican governor whom he had condemned while campaigning.[73] Lee lost a bid for a seat in Congress as a Populist in 1900 and lost again in 1908 as candidate of the Democratic Party for governor.

The reform effort was renewed with the election of a series of Republican governors. The first of these was Coe Crawford, who in 1903 resigned from his position as attorney for the Chicago and Northwestern Railroad in South Dakota and left the Republican Party, which was under the control of a political machine led by US senator Alfred Beard Kittredge, to run as an independent Progressive candidate for governor focusing on curbing railroad abuses. He lost in 1904 but came out on top two years later.

Crawford opened his campaign with a vigorous speech in which he pledged: "The time has come when the corporation and its special attorneys and lobbyists, and the political boss and political broker shall be prevented from controlling political organizations and manipulating the selection of candidates for public office and from exercising an undue influence over the making, as well as enforcement, of law." He concluded by offering a long list of reforms for the state: controlling railroads by abolishing free passes, requiring that all lobbying be open and public, establishing a primary law, and requiring the disclosure of campaign spending—all of which were in the party platform. "No man," he said, "who is elected to office as a republican can be honest with his party and play false to these propositions."[74]

Once in office, Crawford proceeded to push through a program that had the standard set of political reforms, including a direct primary law, lobbying and corrupt-practices regulations, and several measures affecting the railroads, such as those lowering rates, increasing railroad taxes, and prohibiting free passes. He went on to the US Senate in 1908.

When Crawford decided to run for the US Senate, he backed Robert Vessey, a Progressive leader in the state senate and a close supporter of Crawford, for the office of governor. Vessey won the office in 1908 and for a second term in 1910. He continued to push a reform agenda regarding railroad rates and taxation, adding a drive for a revision of banking and insurance laws and laws restricting gambling and drinking. He was also a strong supporter of woman suffrage.[75] He joined the insurgent Republicans who rallied behind La Follette and, later, Teddy Roosevelt in their challenge to President Taft.

The tradition begun by Crawford and carried on by Vessey was continued by Republican governor Frank Byrne, who followed Vessey as governor in 1913. Byrne had also served in the state legislature where he was an active Progressive leader, introducing and securing the passage of several laws imposing controls on railroads, insurance companies, and lobbying activity.[76] As governor from 1913 to 1917, he got a tax commission and bank deposit guarantee act through the legislature. He also took a special interest in conducting anti-liquor campaigns, sometimes taking his attack to other states. He charged that the liquor forces were among those special interests that made up the "invisible government, existing outside of the constitution and law, and in no way responsible to the people ... that seeks to pervert the constitutional government to its own use."[77] He failed in a later bid for the US Senate.

The movement for reform reached its height under Peter Norbeck, who followed Byrne in office. Norbeck, the first of six children born to a Scandinavian preacher, was raised in poverty and had limited formal education but went on to make a fortune drilling deepwater wells. A devoted Progressive, he began his political career in 1908 by winning election to the South Dakota senate. In the first of what turned out to be three two-year terms in that body, he joined Governor Coe Crawford's inner circle of Progressives.[78]

In 1912 his work in the legislature and on behalf of Theodore Roosevelt's presidential campaign established him as one of the most powerful Progressives in the state. Party leaders, however, did not view him as a diehard Progressive. Rather, they saw him as a mediator who could bring the Progressive and moderate factions of the party together. Seeing him in that role, leaders urged him to accept an invitation from Governor Byrne to join him on the party ticket in 1914 as the candidate for lieutenant governor. Norbeck joined the ticket and wound up winning. Two years later voters elected Norbeck governor, an office he held from 1917 to 1921. Following this, he went on to the US Senate.

Norbeck felt the government had a role to play in alleviating basic social and economic problems and was especially concerned with those of the farming population. He favored a rural credit system as far back as 1912 and made it part of his campaign plank in 1916. He was elected with considerable support from discontented farmers. Coming into office in 1917, he made a set of recommendations to the legislature that closely resembled those being proposed by the NPL, which was making considerable progress in South Dakota.[79] Following through, he led in the creation of numerous state-owned and -operated agencies intended to help farmers and others in rural areas. These included agencies administering a rural credits law providing low-interest state loans to farmers having financial problems and a hail insurance program. Other enterprises included a state coal mine and cement plant and state-controlled terminal grain elevators.

Norbeck did not so much borrow ideas from the NPL—he had thought along the same lines long before the NPL had come into existence—as he used the promise of adopting similar programs to steal the thunder from the NPL, which had signed up some 20,000 members in South Dakota, particularly in the eastern region of the state, and dampen its support. Running for reelection in 1918, he branded the NPL as being led by a bunch of radical socialists, disloyal to American ideals. At the same time, he tried, with limited success, to explain why his advocacy of much of the NPL platform did not make him or South Dakota radical.[80]

Writing early in 1920, Norbeck acknowledged that South Dakota had adopted much of what North Dakota had adopted, and in many cases before North Dakota had acted. As he saw it, however, conditions were far different in North Dakota than in South Dakota. North Dakota had been a corporation-ridden state, farmer demands were being ignored, and socialists had taken advantage of the situation. In South Dakota progress had been made without the help of radicals. To the governor it was wrong to think South Dakota was as radical as North Dakota. On the other hand, he claimed "we are more progressive than North Dakota."[81]

To the governor, the state had the right to "use its credit to help its people . . . in their attempts toward greater comfort and prosperity." Too, as he saw it, there was nothing wrong about the state going into business in competition with private enterprises, though only when the state could provide a greater service than the private business and operate with sound management. Norbeck declared that in South Dakota "we have been trying to go just as far in the direction of helping one another as we can go with safety. We like to look upon the people of our state as one great family with common interests. We believe in extending the credit of the whole family to assist worthy members in safe enterprises, for we know that by doing this the wealth of the family as a whole will be increased. This is not socialism nor is it paternalism in any objectionable sense of the word. It is good sound business practice."[82]

NOTES

1. "A News Report of a Day in Lincoln, Nebraska," *Nebraska State Journal*, May 27, 1911, in Link, *Papers of Woodrow Wilson*, 23:96–102.
2. Goodwin, *Populist Moment*, 183, 184.
3. "A Program Outlined," *New York Times*, November 19, 1892, 1.
4. "The New Kansas Rule," *New York Times*, January 10, 1893, 1.
5. Clanton, *Kansas Populism*, 130.
6. "Gov. Lewelling's Message," *New York Times*, January 18, 1893, 3.
7. Argersinger, *Limits of Agrarian Radicalism*, 24.
8. Argersinger, *Populism and Politics*, 155–56.
9. "Governor Lewelling Talks," *Advocate*, April 25, 1894, 8.
10. For an early account see White, "Free Kansas."
11. "No Stain on the Fair Name of Kansas," *Broad Ax*, February 8, 1913, 2; "Bitter State Fights from Coast to Coast"; White, "Free Kansas."
12. White, "Free Kansas."
13. La Forte, *Leaders of Reform*, 109, 112.
14. Ibid., 123–27. For a slightly different account see "State News Notes, Railway Valuations Remain Same," *Chanute Times*, April 2, 1909, 2; and "Topeka Correspondence," *Chanute Times*, March 12, 1909, 1.
15. La Forte, *Leaders of Reform*, 127–28, 179–80.
16. Ibid., 111.
17. Ibid., 113–15.
18. "Stubbs Charges R.R. Combine to Increase Rates," *Los Angeles Herald*, September 23, 1910, 1.

19. "Hearing Ends," *Topeka State Journal*, October 29, 1910, 3.
20. "Appeal to Governor," *Topeka State Journal*, May 13, 1910, 10.
21. "Stubbs at Conference of Governors," *Chanute Times*, September 15, 1911, 6.
22. La Forte, *Leaders of Reform*, 130.
23. "She Sues Gov. Hodges," *Washington Post*, April 12, 1914, 32; "Big Suit Opened," *Topeka State Journal*, June 1, 1914, 1; "Jury Clears Gov. Hodges," *Washington Post*, June 7, 1914, 11.
24. La Forte, *Leaders of Reform*, 206.
25. Aspects of the proposals that he made at various times are mentioned in Childs, *Civic Victories*, 11; "25 Governors Race Down a Mountain," *New York Times*, August 29, 1913, 8; "The Latest Kansas Idea," *Hartford Courant*, May 30, 1913, 8; "To Abolish Legislature," *Los Angeles Times*, March 11, 1913, 17; "Hodge's New Plan," *Topeka State Journal*, April 5, 1913, 13; and "Governor Hodges's Novel Plan for Kansas," *The Commoner*, March 21, 1913, 5.
26. "Hodges of Kansas" *The Commoner*, October 1, 1914, 7.
27. See generally Socolofsky, *Arthur Capper*.
28. Robinson, "The Governors in 1917," 127.
29. Cherny, *Populism*, 46.
30. Olson, Naugle, and Montag, *History of Nebraska*, 217.
31. Gilson Gardner, "Nebraska Politics," *Los Angeles Times*, November, 18, 1899, 5; "The New Governors."
32. Cherny, *Populism*, 72, 73.
33. "Governors, 1890–1917," *Who's NEGenWeb Project—Adams County: Who in Nebraska, 1940*, http://www.usgennet.org/usa/ne/topic/resources/OLLibrary/who1940/hist/wwnhistb.html.
34. "Governors on Current Problems," *Literary Digest*, January 21, 1899, 61–65.
35. Koenig, *Bryan*, 281.
36. Berge, *Free Pass Bribery System*, 1, 10.
37. Cherny, *Populism*, 158–59.
38. "Friction in State House," *Omaha Daily Bee*, June 18, 1906, 2.
39. Cherny, *Populism*, 111.
40. Olson, Naugle, and Montag, *History of Nebraska*, 229.
41. "Roosevelt Scolded State Executives," *New York Times*, October 22, 1907, 5; "Severe Curtain Lecture," *Idaho Recorder*, October 31, 1907, 2.
42. Cherny, *Populism*, 112.
43. Item, *North Platte Semi-Weekly Tribune*, November 6, 190, 8.
44. "The Governors and the Judge, A Poll of the Press," *The Outlook*, September 30, 1911, 268.
45. "Tells How Nebraska Curbs the Railroads," *New York Times*, September 17, 1911, C12.
46. "Governor Morehead's Speech," *The Commoner*, March 16, 1913, 4.
47. See generally Wilkins, "Alexander McKenzie."
48. Robinson, *History of North Dakota*, 223–25.
49. Johnson, *Governors of North Dakota*.
50. Governor Shortridge to Friend Burke, May 4, 1893, Outgoing Letters, Governor Eli Shortridge Papers, State Historical Society of North Dakota, Box 2, Folder 3. See also Burdick, *History of Farmers' Political Action*.
51. G. S. Fernald, Northern Pacific Railroad, to Orr Sanders, Governor Shortridge's private secretary, March 14, 1893, Governor Eli Shortridge Papers, State Historical Society of North Dakota, Box 2, Folder 2.
52. Glaab, "John Burke and the North Dakota Progressive Movement," 23, 25, 29, 30, 32, 33.
53. Ibid., 70.
54. See Glaab, "John Burke and the Progressive Revolt."
55. Glaab, "John Burke and the North Dakota Progressive Movement," 54, 57.
56. See generally Wilkins, "Alexander McKenzie."

57. "Honest John Burke of Fargo Gains Supreme Court Seat" *Saint Paul Pioneer* November 9, 1924; found in John Burke Papers, State Historical Society of North Dakota.

58. Robinson, *History of North Dakota*, 268.

59. "Sketch of John Burke The New Governor," *Weekly Times*, November 16, 1906, n.p., found in Biographies of the Governors of North Dakota, State Historical Society of North Dakota.

60. Glaab, "John Burke and the North Dakota Progressive Movement," 71.

61. Ibid., 184.

62. Morlan, *Political Prairie Fire*, 58n.

63. Ibid., 54.

64. Ibid., 58.

65. Bruce, *Nonpartisan League*, 70.

66. Robinson, *History of North Dakota*, 338.

67. Ibid.; Erickson, *Gentleman from North Dakota*, 13–14.

68. Robinson, *History of North Dakota*, 338; Erickson, *Gentleman from North Dakota*, 13–14; John Spargo, "Report of the Nonpartisan League of North Dakota and Various Other States," 6, found in Socialist Party of America Papers, Duke University.

69. Remele, "Power to the People."

70. Quoted by John W. Gunn, "Awakening of Farmers Is Shown in Growth of Nonpartisan League," *Appeal to Reason*, September 6, 1919, n.p.

71. Piott, *Giving Voters a Voice*, 28.

72. "Gov. Lee's Message," *Black Hills Union*, January 15, 1897, 4; Piott, *Giving Voters a Voice*, 29.

73. Argersinger, *Limits of Agrarian Radicalism*, 6–7, 22–24.

74. "Coe I. Crawford on the Trusts," *Black Hills Union and Western Stock Review*, October 26, 1906, 2.

75. See remarks of Dr. Anna Howard at 1909 convention of the National American Woman Suffrage Association, in Harper, *History of Woman Suffrage*, 5:261.

76. Coursey, *Who's Who in South Dakota*.

77. "Address by Governor Byrne of South Dakota," *The Commoner*, October 1, 1915, 11.

78. Fite, *Peter Norbeck*.

79. Morlan, *Political Prairie Fire*, 124.

80. Biographical file on Peter Norbeck, State of South Dakota Archives.

81. Peter Norbeck, "For the Whole Family, South Dakota's Sane Legislation Helps Ambitious Farmers to Succeed," *Country Gentleman*, February 14, 1920, 4, 34, 36, found in biographical file on Peter Norbeck, State of South Dakota Archives.

82. Ibid., 4, 34, 36.

6

MIXING RACE AND REFORM IN THE SOUTH

The Deep South, with Tillman, Blease, Vardaman, Bilbo, Hoke Smith, and Comer

The Progressive movement in the South was an unusual mixture. It was deeply tainted by racism but also had strong strands of humanitarian and social justice concerns. Nearly all southern governors serving from 1890 to 1900 were white supremacists. At the same time, several governors, even some of the most virulent racists, fervently pursued various Progressive goals and programs.

In much of the South the 1880s and 1890s brought a drive for reform that found expression in Republican, Populist, and other third-party challenges, drawing in part on black votes, which sometimes brought victory but even if not, were strong enough to prompt reform activity in the dominant Democratic Party. This produced significant political, economic, and social welfare changes, but these gains also helped give life to a white supremacy movement. We find outrageous black-baiting demagogues rising to champion the interests of common white people, cultivating hatred of blacks, demanding black disfranchisement and segregation, and defending violence directed at blacks. We also find lower-class whites in farming areas venting their anger with the well-off planters and conservative Bourbon politicians and expressing contempt for railroads and other corporations.

By the early 1900s the Progressive movement in the South was becoming more urban and middle-class in nature and white Progressives had gone considerably far in establishing a political system largely free of black voters and a segregated society—changes that in their minds "settled" the race problem. With this done, Southern politicians, governors included, moved on to a campaign of modernization. Working to secure outside capital for economic development in order to catch up with the industrial North, they became far more business-friendly. The "New South" or "business progressive" governors were also more accepting of the notion that state government should play a more positive role in providing a large set of services and programs. In the "New South" paradigm business regulation mattered less than good roads and universities and other basic programs to fulfill the service role of the state. This focus, however, did not include much of anything in direct relief for those in economic distress.[1]

Throughout much of the Progressive period we find one-party Democratic politics in much of the South. Whoever won the nomination of the Democratic Party, be it through the convention system or the direct primary, was likely to win the general election. The vast majority of governors were Democrats, and the opposition that mattered the most to them generally came from within the Democratic Party. Differences among political opponents often were largely personal in nature rather than issue based. Southern politics seems not only more personal but more violent than elsewhere—with the course of political events being influenced by riots, beatings, shootings, lynchings, and political assignations.

The South had urban political machines in New Orleans, Baltimore, Memphis, and elsewhere that had considerable influence on the state level, but these types of operations were less common in the South than in the East. What passed for a "machine" in much of the South was far from a highly disciplined organization headed by a single "boss" and was, as illustrated in Florida, more of a loosely organized club of party leaders who set informal rules regarding political philosophy, socioeconomic status, political connections, and party loyalty in determining what type of person could qualify as a party candidate for office (see chapter 7).

This chapter examines gubernatorial leadership in the Deep South states of South Carolina, Mississippi, Louisiana, Alabama, and Georgia. Here we find a particularly heavy strain of overt racism accompanied by class politics and anti-corporate themes. We start off with Bill Tillman of South Carolina, who borrowed much of the Populist reform program but who also paved the path in the early 1890s for other demagogic race-baiting leaders championing the cause of poor whites. Coleman Blease, who followed in his footsteps, was an even more extreme racist than Tillman, using the prejudices of poor whites to gain office in 1910 and 1912. He is also an example of a purely "rhetorical Progressive" who gave very little to the people who voted for him. South Carolina came out of the period with a more humanitarian and businesslike governor in Richard Manning.

Tillman and Blease had much in common with Governors James K. Vardaman and Theodore Bilbo in Mississippi in terms of race-baiting. Vardaman's story also illustrates the importance of the direct primary in opening up the political process and changing the politics of a state. In Louisiana we find a largely urban, middle-class reform effort, struggling to break the hold of an alliance of rural interests and an urban political machine. We do not find any particular governor with a highly productive administration, just a few gains during several administrations that eventually added up to a fairly long list of significant accomplishments.

Hoke Smith of Georgia, though hardly a moral crusader, has to be considered among the more prominent of the Progressive governors in the South with wide-ranging accomplishments.

In Braxton Comer of Alabama we find a successful businessman, being sparked into action by seeing the need for railroad regulation and going on to develop a broad Progressive program, though having little sympathy with striking workers and, being an employer of children, having a tough time going along with child labor legislation. Following him, Emmet O'Neal also had a mixed Progressive package, strong on regulating railroads and insurance companies, campaign finance measures, and primary reform but opposed to woman suffrage, prohibition, and the initiative and referendum.

TILLMAN, BLEASE, AND MANNING

"Though he was blind in one eye, unattractive in appearance, irascible in disposition, careless in manners, and rasping in speech, the people of South Carolina loved him."[2] The person thus described, Ben Tillman, was a pioneer reformer who mixed Populism with racism to become governor in 1890. He was reelected in 1892 without any opposition in the general election and, following the expiration of his second term, was sent by the legislature to the United States Senate. He served in the Senate from 1895 to 1918.

He was known as "Pitchfork Ben" because he often used the imagery of a pitchfork, reflecting his ties to the farmers and his advocacy of their cause. He furthered this image on his way to the Senate when he called President Cleveland, whom he opposed on the silver issue, a "scoundrel" and "an old bag of beef" and declared that he was "going to Washington with a pitchfork and prod him in his old fat ribs."[3]

Tillman set the pace as a brutal black-baiting white supremacist, paving the way for a host of similar demagogues seeking public office in the South, some of whom turned out to be even more extreme.[4] He was among the Democrats hoping to end Reconstruction by preventing black Republicans from voting and among those "Red-shirts" (a forerunner of the Ku Klux Klan) who stirred up a mob in 1876 in a voter intimidation effort that led to the murder of several blacks in Hamburg, South Carolina, an event known as the "Hamburg Massacre."

Tillman in 1890 revolted against the conservatives who had been running the Democratic Party. He led poor white farmers, known as the "wool hat boys," and rural residents in their battle with the old regime of do-nothing Bourdon Democrats who represented the interests of the states' traditional (pre–Civil War) economic and social elite. He set out in his own words "to organize the common people against the aristocracy."[5] The common people he had in mind were the common white people of the state whom he led in a war against not only the aristocrats but black people. He used Populist themes and white supremacy to build up his personal following.

Tillman was a relatively prosperous farmer. Other than a simple ambition for office, his principal motive appears to have had less to do with personal economic self-interest than with building and maintaining the power position of people like himself and the Democratic Party. He felt that giving political rights to blacks threatened both the social order and the rule of the Democrats.[6]

When he ran for governor in 1890, he dressed in the clothing of the successful South Carolina farmer that he was, and was always on the attack, saying, as he admitted, "some hard things" but adding that this was necessary in the reform effort he was leading as "the exponent of the principles represented by the farmers' movement." One paper noted: "To the casual observer" Tillman "appears to be very ascetic in habit and decidedly of an unsociable nature"; he is "capable of the most bitter and uncivil sarcasm and denunciation."[7]

Tillman spent much of his time during his career stirring up common white farmers and workers against the aristocrats and black people.[8] He included an attack on the University of South Carolina in his campaign against the state's privileged class.[9] Though he was not governor at the time, he headed the committee on suffrage at the convention that framed the South Carolina 1895 constitution, which, in effect, disfranchised most black voters and, not unintentionally, crippled the Republican Party. As governor, he spoke in favor of lynch mobs—declaring while governor that he would proudly lead one to bring to justice a black man who raped a white woman.[10] Eighteen blacks were lynched in the state during his four years in office.

Tillman was a skillful, demagogic, race-baiting politician who nevertheless was not without accomplishments, though about the only thing he directly did for his farmer constituents was improve rural education. Beyond this, he established new colleges, created a rail commission with power to make rates, got increases in railroad and other corporation taxes, and limited working hours in mills. On the innovative side, Tillman created a dispensary system, headed by a commissioner appointed by the governor, through which the state bottled and sold all the liquor purchased in the state. This, no doubt to the relief of many South Carolinians, headed off a drive for prohibition. It also produced a great deal of revenue for the state.

After the 1892 election, Tillman began to think about seeking another office and started speaking out on national issues as a spokesperson for the pro-silver, anti-Cleveland wing of the Democratic Party. Tillman attacked Cleveland on the silver issue and voted against his nomination at the 1892 Democratic national convention. He campaigned for Cleveland in the general election, but Cleveland did not forget the earlier attack and cut Tillman out of the process of deciding who would get what federal jobs in South Carolina. This made it more difficult for him to hold his coalition together.

Coleman Livingston Blease, lawyer and former state legislator, even outdid Tillman, his old mentor, in playing on the prejudices of poor whites to gain their votes. Running as a candidate for governor in 1906 on an anti-black platform, he was reported as saying: "God never intended that the negro should be anything else but the servant of the white man."[11] He opposed black education and encouraged black lynching. He did not win that year but managed to win the office in 1910 and 1912.

Blease had four stormy years as governor. There was much controversy over his pro-lynching, anti-black policies and his use of the pardoning power. While he presented himself as an anticorporate, antirailroad reformer, he did not accomplish much in these areas or much at all of a positive nature as governor.[12] At best, he had only a rhetorical attachment to reform. Putting it bluntly, historian James Temple Kirby concluded: "Blease, purporting to be the champion of poor whites, was an utter fraud. He hated blacks, harangued the upcountry 'wool hat boys,' and rallied against the 'aristocrats' and the 'trusts'; in power, he covertly opposed most so-called progressive reforms."[13]

Political scientist V. O. Key once noted that Blease's "original contribution is found in his ability to make a class appeal without offering a class program."[14] Blease "mesmerized the mill workers, the tenant farmers, and the poor whites, while at the same time opposing governmental programs to benefit them . . . Perhaps so nonrational a politics can be practiced only when some diversionary issue, such as race, lies handy for use."[15] In opposing some reforms, such as compulsory education and child labor laws, he played upon the strong suspicion among his mill worker and rural followers that Progressivism meant creeping state centralization and control and an invasive big government that threatened the independence of poor whites.[16]

Like Tillman, Blease had some quarrels with the universities, especially the University of South Carolina. While governor he attacked Samuel Mitchell, president of the university, for diverting funds intended for the education of white women to the education of black men. The attack in part reflected a grudge he carried over having been expelled from the university for plagiarism years earlier. More broadly, it reflected his hostility to universities in general and what he viewed as meddlesome academics aligned with the urban middle- and upper-class reform movement in the state.[17]

In December of 1912 Blease drew considerable fire from his fellow governors for defending the lynching of blacks by vigilantes. When Governor Carey of Wyoming asked him if it was not true that the state constitution he had sworn to uphold protected blacks as well as whites, Blease yelled: "To hell with the Constitution."[18] A dozen governors, including four from the South, criticize Blease for his remarks. He responded: "You can expel me for all I care.... Long after many of you gentlemen here today are resting in the shades of private life I will be reaping the awards of public sentiment. Long after you Governors are no longer Governors, the white women of South Carolina will pray for me with their arms around their girls, and will arise from their knees to kiss their husbands and beg them to go to the ballot box and vote for Blease to protect them from their daily terror."[19]

While Blease refused to back down from his position regarding the lynching of blacks, he did point out that he had pardoned more blacks than all the previous governors of South Carolina since 1876.[20] Indeed, he had excelled in issuing pardons to whites as well as blacks. Coming into office in 1911, he declared: "I love the pardoning power. I want to give the poor devils a chance. I hope to make the number (pardoned) an even thousand before I go out of office."[21] He apparently exceeded his hopes. Described in the *New York Times* in January 1915 as "famous as pardoner of criminals," Blease was thought to have pardoned more criminals than any other governor in history—some 1,671 in four years, an average of more than one convict for every day he held office. The article also noted that Blease had been a well-known criminal lawyer before becoming governor and that some if not many of the people he pardoned were his former clients.[22] His political enemies suggested that Blease received payments to pardon criminals. On December 12, 1912, he pardoned seventy-six convicts, giving some of them (presumably the most dangerous) twenty-four hours to leave the state—if they were going to be a problem, best that it be for some other state.

At one time Blease and Tillman were personal friends, but they had a falling out, largely on a personal level. They did, though, have different support groups—Tillman had drawn closer to the more successful white farmers and planters while Blease drew his strength from less prosperous white tenant farmers (sharecroppers) and textile mill workers. Conflict between the Tillman and Blease wings of the Democratic Party characterized South Carolina politics for several years. Tillman and the upper classes that supported him tried but could not defeat Blease's bid for reelection in 1912.

The state, however, moved in more a Progressive direction in 1914 when Richard Irving Manning III, from the anti-Blease faction, won the office of governor. Manning turned back a primary challenge from Blease himself in 1916 in going on to another term. Out of spite, Blease had resigned five days before the end of his term to avoid attending Manning's inauguration in 1915. Manning was born in South Carolina to a prominent family—his grandfather, Richard Irving Manning I had served as governor in the 1820s. Political opponents cursed him as an aristocrat. Manning's political career started in the statehouse when Ben

Tillman was governor. A Bourbon conservative, he generally opposed Tillman. Though a conservative, he worked for the secret ballot. His effort came up short, in part, because some thought it would endanger white supremacy. He also supported a measure that passed limiting hours of work in cotton mills, a measure later supported by Tillman.[23]

As governor he proposed a program, described by his biographer, as one of "humanitarian progressivism," intended to improve the lot of citizens in distress and enable the state to enter into the current of Progressive thought and catch up with other states.[24] In his 1915 inaugural address he declared: "The time has come when we have to meet new conditions; we are living in a time of change and progress ... We are progressive Democrats and we must have the courage to do justly to each and every class of our citizens, even if it requires legislation hitherto untried by us."[25]

Manning quickly went to work—there was a guarantee of only two years in office—meeting with legislators who shared his views and would push for them in their respective chambers.[26] During the session he held daily morning conferences with legislative leaders to set the legislative program of the day. If the leaders approved, a measure would be introduced; if there was considerable opposition, a measure would be tabled for further discussion or abandoned.[27] Manning's time in office brought a doubling of educational expenditures, a tax commission, prohibition of alcohol, compulsory education, and, in a reversal of Blease, a child labor law and compulsory education. Manning also strongly condemned the lynching of a black farmer in Abbeville, South Carolina, in 1916.[28] Moving from Blease to Manning was like going into another world.

VARDAMAN AND BILBO

While Tillman was making waves in South Carolina, James K. Vardaman was making a profound impact on Mississippi politics. Vardaman had a fondness for Tillman, shared his views concerning race and corporations, and, like Tillman, rose to power as a friend of poor white farmer and by focusing on race.[29]

Following his inability to secure the Democratic nomination for governor through the convention system in 1895 and 1899, this longtime state legislator changed his position and became a leading supporter of the idea of replacing this nominating method with a direct primary. This was accomplished in 1902, and Vardaman became the first statewide candidate to benefit from the new system when he ran for governor the following year.[30] In the bitter 1903 primary campaign for governor Vardaman successfully challenged the delta planters and other conservative interests that had been running the Mississippi Democratic Party by attacking blacks and appealing to white workers and small farmers with a package of reforms that included corporate regulation, public education, and prohibition.

His election shifted political power away from the conservatives aligned with the dominant economic interests and into the hands of "redneck" white farmers and nonfarm workers.

During his campaign Vardaman made it clear that if elected governor he would stop spending taxpayer money on the education of African American children. Education, he felt, would make them ambitious and dangerous. Moreover: "The negro is not permitted to advance, and his education simply spoils a good field hand and makes a shyster lawyer or fourth-rate teacher.... It is futile to attempt to elevate the negro."[31] As governor he continued on with the basic themes in vetoing a bill providing funds for an African American school. A writer for an African American newspaper declared that to the governor "an ideal Negro is one that is both ignorant and humble."[32]

Vardaman fostered an exceptionally offensive brand of racism in the politics of the state but seemed to draw the line when it came to violence directed against blacks—as evidenced in his opposing the vigilante activity of a group called the Whitecappers. He also mixed in with racism calls for effective corporate regulation, tax reform increasing the burden on the wealthy, free tax-supported schools (though for whites only), better credit for farmers, restrictions on child labor, and even a graduated income tax.[33] Known as the "Great White Chief," he served as governor from 1904 to 1908, with some accomplishments in the areas of business regulation, public education, prison leasing, and penitentiary management.[34]

Lawyer, planter, and poet William Alexander Percy—who grew up in Mississippi and followed the political career of his father, Le Roy Percy, in that state—described Vardaman as "a kindly, vain demagogue unable to think, and given to emotions he considered noble. He was a handsome, flamboyant figure of a man, immaculately overdressed, wearing his black hair long to the shoulders, and crowned with a wide cowboy's hat. He looked like a top-notch medicine man."[35] Percy felt Vardaman "craved public office because the spotlight was his passion and because, eternally in need of money, he abhorred work.... He stood for the poor white man against the 'nigger'—those were his qualifications as a statesman.... [H]e was such a splendid ham actor, his inability to reason was so contagious, it was so impossible to determine where his idealism ended and his demagoguery began."[36] All in all, Vardaman coupled his contempt for the corporations and the rich with concern for the common white person and added in race baiting and the theatrics of a ham actor.[37] Pennsylvania governor Pennypacker, who met Vardaman in Mississippi while on official business, described him as "a long-haired, black-eyed, noisy swashbuckler."[38]

Democrat Theodore Bilbo, also an out-and-out white supremacist, followed in Vardaman's footsteps. A short man who liked flashy clothing and who was known as "The Man" because he referred to himself in the third person became governor of Mississippi in 1916. He served in the state senate from 1908 to 1912 and held the office of lieutenant governor from 1912 to 1916 before becoming governor. In building his career he somehow survived two bribery scandals and an encounter in which a state senator broke a cane over his head.

William Percy had some less than complementary thoughts about Bilbo, especially since Bilbo as a state legislator helped do in Percy's father's bid for a US Senate seat by accepting a bribe to vote for his opponent, James K. Vardaman. Percy saw Bilbo as "a pert little monster, glib and shameless, with the sort of cunning common to criminals which passes for intelligence. The people loved him not because they were deceived in him, but because they understood him thoroughly; they said of him proudly, 'He's a slick little bastard.' He was one of them and he had risen from obscurity to the fame of glittering infamy—it was as if they themselves had crashed the headlines. Vardaman's glamour waned and this man rode to power."[39]

In his campaign for the governorship Bilbo ran as "the Progressive and Constructive Statesman" the state needed.[40] As governor he was not a washout as a Progressive. He offered a reform program regarding improvements in schools, highways, and health care.[41] Under him came a state tax commission with the primary job of equalizing taxes in the state, prohibition, and an expanded school system. Much of his agenda faced considerable opposition. Opponents, in particular, were bent on strict economy and complained about the cost of new programs.[42]

LOUISIANA GOVERNORS, REFORM IN BITS AND PIECES

For a brief period, Populists and their Republican allies threatened the Bourbon oligarchy in Louisiana. In 1896 a Populist-Republican faction nominated John Newton Pharr as its candidate for governor. Populists welcomed Pharr, a wealthy sugar planter, because he accepted most of the Populist platform and, as an added attraction, could afford to bear the expense of a statewide campaign and was willing to do so. Pharr lost in 1896 to Democrat Murphy J. Foster, a result widely attributed to vote fraud by the Democratic Party machine in New Orleans and the use of violence or the threat of violence to suppress the voting turnout of black Republicans. The Democratic oligarchy, unsettled by the shaky victory, came to the conclusion that a much safer and subtler way to avoid such threats was to do it under the guise of "reform." In the late 1890s and early 1900s reform took the shape of a variety of laws and new constitutional provisions that dramatically reduced the number of blacks who could vote and greatly diminished the size of the Republican vote.[43]

Starting in the first decade of the twentieth century, political power in the state began to shift toward an alliance of cotton planters and rural courthouse politicians with a political machine in New Orleans known as the Regular Democratic Organization (RDO), which was somewhat comparable to Tammany Hall in New

York. The RDO was headed by the city's longtime mayor, Martin Behrman. His organization depended greatly on the patronage provided by governors he helped put in office. From 1908 to 1920 the only successful gubernatorial candidate who was not affiliated with this alliance was longtime judge Luther Hall. Hall ran at the urging of the New Orleans Good Government League.[44] Hall came out on top in a three-person Democratic primary contest and went on to win in 1912. But seeking peace with Behrman, Governor Hall disappointed his supporters by scaling back his Progressive demands, settling for little more than a weak worker's compensation law. Behrman combined some elements of Progressivism with machine politics but regularly stood in the way of effective business regulation and labor protection.[45]

In 1916 John Parker, a successful businessman and cotton planter who had been an active reformer since the 1890s with the Good Government League, ran for governor under the banner of the Progressive Party. This supporter of Teddy Roosevelt picked up 37 percent of the vote against the Democratic candidate. During the campaign Democrats pointed out that Parker was born in Mississippi "of rich parents" and "never had a want he couldn't satisfy," while his opponent, Ruffin Pleasant, was born in Louisiana, was "poor but clean as a hound's tooth," and someone who "knows what it is to work for a dollar." They added other important contrasts: while Parker had jumped around from party to party, Pleasant had always been a Democrat and always voted that way; and while Parker opposed the white primary (one in which only whites could vote), Pleasant believed in the system and would as governor do what he could to keep it in force. Democrats also criticized Parker for favoring the short ballot, while Pleasant wanted to continue to elect all state officials.[46]

Parker ran as a Democrat in 1920, won the primary, and was unopposed in the general election. He pushed Progressive causes on a wide variety of issues—child labor, woman suffrage, income taxation, conservation, to mention a few—and focused as governor on fighting governmental corruption. In 1920 he helped bring down Behrman in his attempt to be reelected mayor of New Orleans.[47] Parker operated in an aloof and very businesslike manner. One scholar considered him the "perfect embodiment of a 'good' reformer—dignified, systematic, and moderate."[48] He mixed his Progressivism with fiscal conservatism. He is also remembered for a feud with future governor Huey Long. Parker had reportedly begged Long, at the time a popular crusading railroad commissioner, to campaign on his behalf in 1919–20. Long did so enthusiastically. As the story goes, the war between the two was set off after Parker, responding to pressure from Standard Oil lobbyists, dropped further association with Long. Parker was branded by Long as a "bought" Standard Oil man.[49]

While the struggle for reform in Louisiana over the Progressive years was prolonged and difficult, as author Dewey W. Grantham discovered, "a surprising amount of progressive legislation emerged from Baton Rouge during the first two decades" of the twentieth century, including that providing a direct primary, corrupt-practices regulations, restrictions on lobbying, a shorter ballot, child labor protection, pure food and drug safety laws, utility regulation, and protections against monopolies.[50] The major movement for reform had an urban, middle-class flavor. From 1890 to 1920, the state lacked a significant champion of poor rural whites such as Tillman and Blease of South Carolina, Vardaman of Mississippi, or Jeff Davis of Arkansas.[51]

HOKE SMITH OF GEORGIA

In the early 1890s reform in Georgia was advanced by the election of Democrat William Northen, who defeated the president of the Georgia Farmers' Alliance for the Democratic Party nomination for governor in 1890 and ran unopposed. He won again over a Populist candidate supported by Populist leader Thomas Watson in 1892 by a 2-to-1 vote margin. Northen, a reformer in his own right, was encouraged to move even more in that direction by Watson's challenge. He was an advocate of rail regulation, prohibition, penal reform, and increased educational funding and a strong opponent of lynching.[52] Stirrings of reform and some Progressive accomplishments also came under Joseph Terrell (1902-7), who was known as the "education governor" for his leadership in this area, but the first gubernatorial proponent of a broad range of Progressive reforms was Hoke Smith, who held the office from 1907 to 1909 and in 1911 before moving on to the US Senate.[53]

Smith, born in Newton, North Carolina, moved with his family to Atlanta, Georgia, where he later made a fortune and exercised considerable political influence as an anticorporation lawyer and owner of the *Atlanta Journal*. He worked for Grover Cleveland in his presidential election campaigns of 1888 and 1892. In 1892 Smith seems to have taken particular delight in printing nasty things about Populist presidential candidate James Weaver. Populists accused him of hiring ruffians to break up Weaver's meetings in Georgia wherever they could.[54] His strong support for Cleveland in the *Journal* led to his appointment as Cleveland's secretary of interior.

Loyal to Cleveland, Smith abandoned his support of free silver. He was embarrassed by Bryan's nomination in 1896 but wound up backing him—though, complicating matters, not the free-silver cause that stood at the heart of Bryan's platform. His stand against free silver was something that did not go over well with the Democrats of Georgia. Yet, after ten years of political exile for deserting silver in favor of a single gold standard, he came back to be elected governor. The endorsement of former Populist leader and agrarian rebel Tom Watson, whose views had much weight with farmers in the state, greatly helped Smith's campaign

Figure 6.1. Hoke Smith. Courtesy of the Library of Congress, Prints & Photographs Division, photograph by Harris & Ewing, LC-DIG-hec-01345.

in 1906. Smith and Watson shared the goal of excluding blacks from the electorate as a way, as they explained it, of bringing social stability, eliminating political corruption, and allowing Georgians to focus on their "real problems."[55] Smith's platform mixed the call for black disfranchisement with calls for rail regulation, improved public schools, and a variety of other Progressive changes. He hoped to build on an antirailroad and anticorporate movement that was already strong in the state.

During the primary in 1906, Smith focused on one of the four other candidates in the race, Clark Howell, conservative editor of the *Atlanta Constitution*. Howell's paper was a longtime rival of Smith's paper, and Smith and Howell were personal enemies. Smith claimed Howell was the candidate of the Southern Railroad, which, he further charged, had controlled Georgia politics for many years. He promised, if elected, to tax the railroad so heavily that stockholders would be forced to sell it to the state. While Smith said he was fighting railroad domination of the Georgia Democratic Party, Howell said he was fighting Populism and the fusion element backing Smith.[56] In the 1906 campaign both candidates played to white fears of black economic and political advancement and called for putting blacks "in their place" by taking away their voting rights. These calls likely helped inflame the passions that led to the Atlanta race riot in September 1906 in which white mobs killed dozens of blacks.[57]

At his inaugural Smith urged abolition of railroad passes, taking the vote away from blacks, and protecting dry counties through local option. As in the case of several other governors, Smith enjoyed considerable success in securing a large package of reforms in a relatively short period. From 1907 to 1909 his accomplishments included a stronger railroad commission, modeled after one put together by Governor Hughes in New York with broader powers over not only railroads but power companies; gas lines and street railways; a reduction in passenger rates on railroads; greater spending on education that furthered the expansion of facilities; a state pure food law; the ending of the convict lease system; the creation of a system of juvenile courts; corrupt-practices legislation; and the abolition of free railway passes.[58]

Smith also fully supported the prohibition cause and happily signed off on a statewide prohibition law passed by the legislature in 1907, the first measure of this nature to pass in the South. This helped get the ball rolling for the prohibition cause elsewhere in the region. A major accomplishment, as he saw it, was the virtual disfranchisement of blacks that came during his term when the voters adopted a constitutional amendment establishing a literacy test that grandfathered in most whites and was designed so that few blacks would qualify to vote.[59] In October 1910 only 12,000 blacks out of a possible 200,000 were registered to vote.[60]

However, 1908 turned out to be a bad year for Smith. In a battle of opposites, Progressive Smith, who was six feet two and weighed over 200 pounds, lost the governorship to "Little Joe" Brown, a conservative who was just a few inches over five feet and weighed less than 100 pounds. A year earlier Smith had fired Brown, officially known as Joseph M. Brown, the son of former governor Joseph E. Brown, from his position on the state railway commission. Brown, friendly to the railroads, had opposed Smith's reform policies. Smith's enemies recruited Brown to run for Smith's office in 1908. Brown won out at the party convention.

Smith appears to have suffered because of his support for the prohibition law. This turned out to be unpopular with many in the business community. Critics complained that the law was intended "to abolish the black man's saloon," not to prevent "the white man from getting liquor," but had the latter effect and businesses had lost a lot of money. Brown took up the businessmen's cause.[61] Another, perhaps more crucial problem for Smith in 1908 was a breakup with Watson. Smith was never really trusted by some old-time Populists, and they set out to split the two by complaining that Smith was not giving enough credit to Watson for various reforms made and was not really a true reformer. The precipitating factor in their split was Smith's turning down Watson's request that he help out in the case of a prisoner, an old political supporter of Watson, who had been convicted of murder. He wanted Smith to spare the prisoner's life, but Smith refused to do so.[62]

The broader problem, according to one source who knew Watson well, was that Watson expected Smith to pay him back for his support in 1906. He had worked hard for Smith, and he felt he was largely responsible for Smith's victory. He expected to be brought in on major decisions and to hold a strategic position in state politics, but found that Smith did not feel that way. Watson regarded himself the real political boss of Georgia and deeply resented Smith's "better than thou" indifference to him.[63] Watson said he would help Little Joe Brown in 1908 and did so.[64] Brown, though, did not do much as governor. He was a fiscal conservative who lowered taxes, cut expenses, and avoided new laws or innovations.[65] He lost in his bid for renomination to Smith, even though Watson continued to support him.[66]

In September of 1910 the state Democratic Convention in Georgia, reflecting primary elections in the various counties, not only nominated Smith for governor, rejecting Brown's bid for another term, but endorsed Smith for the presidency of the United States. An editorial in Bryan's publication, *The Commoner*, congratulated Smith on securing the nomination over Brown, whom it described as the candidate of "the corporations and liquor interests," and welcomed Smith, viewed as an enemy of the special interests, back to office.[67] Showing the anticorporate Progressive streak in his thinking, Smith declared in his acceptance speech: "The great corporations in Georgia must keep out of politics. They must not be allowed, by political agents, to dominate or control legislation or administration."[68] In one last shot, Watson was able to get Brown to make a run against Smith as an independent candidate in the general election. Smith, though, easily coasted to victory.

In his second term Smith worked to increase education funding and secure an antilobbying law, a measure that reduced the working hours for mill workers, and a law creating a Department of Commerce and Labor.[69] This term, though, was cut short. He resigned after a few months to take a seat in the US Senate. Watson, in an act of vengeance, tried to prevent the legislature from sending Smith to the Senate but failed, again forcing him to reexamine his status: "Watson returned home with a readjusted view of this power—what went with the masses did not necessarily go with the politicians, men themselves in politics."[70]

Smith is generally considered to be the state's "most outstanding Progressive" and, except in matters of race, "a genuine reform governor."[71] He was politically flexible—like so many others, a conservative Cleveland Democrat who became a reformer pursuing railroad regulation, increased corporate taxation, an improved educational system while attacking the convict lease system and liquor traffic. At the same time, like other politicians "of the people" who sprang up in the South during the same period, Smith "saw the advantage and the necessity of appealing to the passions of the people, whether to denounce the abuses of corporations or to urge the threat of Negro domination."[72]

Jack Slaton of Georgia, one of the most courageous of Southern governors in the 1890–1920 period, moved up from his position as president of the state senate to assume the duties of governor when Smith resigned that position in 1911 to become a US senator. Slaton went on to win the office in 1912. Though a conservative when it came to fiscal matters, he supported reforms regarding such matters as child labor, railroad regulation, the convict leasing system, and prohibition.

He is best remembered, however, for commuting the death sentence of Leo Frank to a life sentence. Frank had been convicted of murdering a young girl. Slaton felt that Frank's conviction had rested on questionable evidence and that there had been a miscarriage of justice. He was aware that commuting Frank's death sentence would be unpopular and might well end his political career, but decided to do so shortly before he left office in June 1915.

His decision to commute, which was encouraged by several governors, including Dunne of Illinois and Hunt of Arizona, provoked public outrage in Georgia. Newspaper coverage by Tom Watson and others, some of which was anti-Semitic (Frank was Jewish) called for the lynching of Slaton as well as Frank. Some contended that Slayton had a conflict of interest because of his connection as a law partner to Frank's defense attorney. Slayton was threatened with mob violence—over a thousand protesters marched on his home, but local police and National Guard troops came to his rescue and dispersed the mob. Slayton and his wife left the state at the conclusion of his term and did not return for more than ten years. In August 1915 several armed men kidnapped Frank from prison and hanged him.[73]

ALABAMA'S BRUSH WITH REFORM: BRAXTON BRAGG COMER

"Come to my house, (where) you will find the door open. Take a chair, put your feet on the mantelpiece and spit on the floor."[74] This invitation to his constituents from Alabama governor Joseph H. Johnston was a bit unusual even in his time, but then Johnston was also unusual in other ways.

Democrat Joseph Johnston came to power in 1896, defeating a Populist candidate with 59 percent of the vote by bringing many Populists into the Democratic Party with a call for free silver and programs favoring farmers and workers. He was reelected in 1898, again defeating a Populist candidate in a two-person race, with 67 percent of the vote. In his two terms he pioneered in calling for rail rate regulation, increased taxes on railroads and large landowners, an investigation of the convict lease system, and more spending on roads and education. His accomplishments were limited, though, because of opposition, especially from the railroads, and Johnston's inability to hold his coalition together. His refusal to call for a constitutional convention that would disfranchise black voters was used against him.[75]

Alabama had its next brush with reform in the administration of Democrat Braxton Bragg Comer, who became governor in 1907 for a single four-year term. Comer was a successful planter, banker, and president of the Birmingham

Cotton Mills, the state's leading cotton manufacturer. He had a long, continuing fight with Milton Smith, president of the Louisville and Nashville Railroad over rail regulation.

Comer began his political career determined to bring down railroad rates. Overcoming railroad opposition, he won a seat on the three-member state railroad commission in 1904. As president of the commission, he conducted a series of spectacular hearings on the railroads but was not able to accomplish much because the other two commissioners regularly lined up with the railroads and outvoted him. He then decided to run for governor in 1906 at the age of fifty-eight using the railroad issue. He began to organize for the race in the early part of 1906 and easily defeated a candidate supported by the railroads in the Democratic primary by drawing support from a coalition of urban, middle-class, professional, and business interests with planters and others in rural areas.[76] He had no trouble at all winning the general election in the one party Democratic state. Unlike many reform-minded Progressive governors, Comer did not opt for simplicity for his inauguration. His included a parade of 2,000 guardsmen, a speech before 10,000 citizens, and an elaborate ball.[77]

A majority of the legislators coming into office with him were also committed to rate reform. He had been well aware that he would need legislative support and had spent much energy during the campaign getting legislative candidates to align with him and doing what he could to get them elected. The legislature approved twenty bills he proposed relating to the railroads, including ones calling for the reduction of passenger and freight rates.[78] Though Comer focused on rail regulation, he was not a one-issue governor. He had a broad program, which brought greater education and transportation spending, health services, a tax commission, and a statewide prohibition bill. Working with the Roosevelt administration, he was also active in the area of conservation.

Comer and the legislature partially financed the cost of new programs through reforms that shifted more of the tax load to businesses and large property owners, including railroads, much to their displeasure. Lawmakers, however, also financed a good part of the bill for the greater funding for education and other programs by increasing the charges to private enterprises using the convict leasing system. Most of the convicts leased out were black. In effect, the state used revenue from selling black slave labor to help support educational programs for white students only.[79]

An employer of children in his mills, mines, and plantations, Comer long opposed legislation that would restrict the use of child labor, but after considerable pressure he agreed to go along with some modest reforms. He also took the side of organized labor in opposing efforts to adopt a program aimed at bringing cheap labor from various parts of Europe into the state.[80] Comer, however, was not inclined to line up on the side of striking workers. In 1908 he led the effort to break a strike of 18,000 coal miners called by the United Mine Workers Union. Miners complained about pay, working conditions, and having to compete with convict labor. Comer was not disposed to listen to these complaints. He sent the National Guard into the coal fields to escort and protect "scabs" that the companies were bringing in to replace the striking workers. Workers and their families were forced off company property and out of their company-owned housing. They lived in tents just outside the company property. Comer ordered guardsmen to cut down the tents, claiming their existence violated health regulations. This helped break the strike.[81] Comer could not run again in 1910 because of a restriction on successive terms and had to wait until 1914 to make another bid for the gubernatorial office. That year opponents of statewide prohibition and supporters of organized labor joined his usual corporate enemies in helping to defeat him in the primary election.

Following Comer, Governors Emmet O'Neal and Charles Henderson, though both from the conservative wing of the party, continued on supporting various Progressive measures.

O'Neal, whose father, Edward O'Neal, had served as Alabama governor in the 1880s, decided to take a shot at the office in 1910 and won. He was no stranger to politics. He had worked on his father's campaigns, received an appointment from President Cleveland as a US attorney in Alabama, got elected as delegate to the state's constitutional convention, and, in 1906, was an unsuccessful candidate for lieutenant governor. He had a very mixed package of ideas and programs. He was a believer in white supremacy and immigrant restrictions, especially of the Chinese, and an opponent of woman suffrage, statewide prohibition, and the initiative and referendum (seeing it as a threat to executive authority), but on the Progressive side he was someone who wanted to regulate railroads and insurance companies, bring campaign finance and primary reform, and spend more on education and highways. O'Neal was another white supremacist who stood for law and order in condemning mob violence against blacks. He felt he had the duty to enforce the laws equally, regardless of skin color.[82]

Henderson, who won the office in 1914, became known as the state's "business governor" for his skill in managing the budget and his efforts to stimulate the economy. Prior to his election, he had been the longtime mayor of Troy, Alabama, and a member of the state railroad commission, which served as a stepping-stone to the gubernatorial office. He defeated former governor Comer, who was trying to make a comeback in a Democratic Party runoff for governor in 1914. Along with fiscal conservatism, Henderson brought more reform, including a primary system, tax equalization, and a public service commission. Henderson also pushed for improvements in state prison conditions. He did not support statewide prohibition, but the legislature voted to override his veto of a measure bringing this change.[83]

NOTES

1. This general shift is discussed by Tindall, *Emergence of the New South*, 224, 232–33, 248; Lisenby, *Charles Hillman Brough*, 24, 25, 28, 29; Ledbetter, *Carpenter from Conway*, 10, 175.
2. Hollingsworth, *Whirligig of Politics*, 8.
3. Simkins, *Pitchfork Ben Tillman*, 315. According to another source, Tillman said in regard to his race for a seat in the US Senate: "If I go there, I promise I will use that pitch fork in his old fat ribs." "South Carolina Campaign," *Roanoke Times*, June 23, 1894, 1.
4. Tillman is viewed this way by Cash, *Mind of the South*, 253.
5. Koenig, *Bryan*, 141.
6. Kantrowitz, *Ben Tillman*.
7. "At Anderson, the Second Speech of Captain Tillman's Canvas," *Fairfield News and Herald*, May 21, 1890, 1; "The Next Governor," *Fairfield News and Herald*, September 17, 1890, 1.
8. Southern, *Malignant Heritage*, 10.
9. Dennis, *Lessons in Progress*, 163.
10. Southern, *Malignant Heritage*, 10.
11. "The Campaign," *Manning Times*, June 27, 1906, 1.
12. Grantham, *Southern Progressivism*, 58.
13. Kirby, *Darkness at the Dawning*, 27.
14. Key, *Southern Politics*, 144, quoting Rupert B. Vance.
15. Ibid.
16. Dennis, *Lessons in Progress*, 192–95.
17. Ibid., 192.
18. "Blease Says 'To Hell with Constitution,'" *New York Times*, December 6, 1912, 1.
19. "Blease's Utterances Stir Up Conference," *Herald and News*, December 10, 1912, 6. See also "Fellow Governors Do Not Follow Him," *Herald and News*, December 10, 1912; "A 'Lynch-Law' Governor," *Literary Digest*, November 25, 1911, 964–65; and "Governors Discuss the Granting of Pardons," *New York Times*, January 19, 1913, SM11.
20. "Blease Says 'To Hell with Constitution.'"
21. Quoted in Glashan, *American Governors*, 94.
22. "Fiery 'Cooley' Blease No Longer Governor," *New York Times*, January 17, 1915, SM5.
23. Burts, *Richard Irvine Manning*, 14–18.
24. Ibid., viii.
25. "Inaugural Address of Gov. R. I. Manning," *Herald and News*, January 22, 1915, 1.
26. Burts, *Richard Irvine Manning*, 85.
27. Ransone, *Office of Governor in the South*, 101.
28. "To Lynch or Not to Lynch," *The Outlook*, January 24, 1917, 137–38.
29. Holmes, *White Chief*, 86.
30. Grantham, *Southern Progressivism*, 41–42.
31. "The Personal Platform of Major Vardaman," *Hartford Courant*, July 10, 1899, 8. These and related comments also appear in "Democratic Doctrine," *Afro-American*, August 12, 1899, 1.
32. "The 'Jim Crow' Governor," *Afro-American*, March 19, 1904, 4. Vardaman's views are also covered in "Education a Curse," *Washington Post*, January 20, 1904, 1.
33. Kirby, *Darkness at the Dawning*; Holmes, *White Chief*. On his stand opposing using tax money to support black education see "Two Pleas for Negro Rights in Mississippi," *The Outlook*, May 16, 1903, 152–53.
34. Grantham, *Southern Progressivism*, 130; Fortenberry and Abney, "Mississippi, Unreconstructed and Unredeemed." See generally Holmes, *White Chief*.
35. Percy, *Lanterns on the Levee*, 143.
36. Ibid., 143, 144.

37. Key, *Southern Politics*, 238.
38. Pennypacker, *Autobiography*, 418.
39. Percy, *Lanterns on the Levee*, 148.
40. Quote from caption under Bilbo's picture in supplement to *Neshoba Democrat*, July 22, 1915, 5.
41. See Grantham, *Southern Progressivism*, 37–45.
42. "Bilbo Program of Legislation Are in Danger," *Hattiesburg News*, February 17, 1916, 1, 4; "Hard Sailing for Gov. Bilbo," *Hummer*, March 24, 1916, 2.
43. Haas, "Bourbonism." See also Grantham, *Southern Progressivism*, 94–95.
44. Schott, "Luther Hall."
45. Grantham, *Southern Progressivism*, 95, 97.
46. "Are You, Mr. Voter, a Democrat?" *St. Landry Clarion*, April 15, 1916, 5.
47. Schott, "John Parker."
48. Haas, "Bourbonism," 278.
49. Steinberg, *Bosses*, 211–12.
50. Grantham, *Southern Progressivism*, 97–98.
51. Ibid., 95; Key, *Southern Politics*, 160.
52. Zainaldin and Inscoe, "Progressive Era."
53. See generally Grantham, *Hoke Smith*. On Terrell's accomplishments see Jones, "The Administration of Governor Joseph M. Terrell."
54. "Mr. Hoke Smith," *Virginia Sun*, reprinted in *Kansas Agitator*, March 16, 1893, 5.
55. Zainaldin and Inscoe, "Progressive Era."
56. These observations of the 1906 contest are based on a survey of items in Atlanta newspapers and a discussion of the contest by Dittmer, *Black Georgia*, 97–101.
57. See generally Godshalk, *1906 Atlanta Race Riot*.
58. See generally Grantham, *Southern Progressivism*; Zainaldin and Inscoe, "Progressive Era"; and A. J. McKelway, "Hoke Smith: A Progressive Democrat," *The Outlook*, October 1, 1910, 267–72.
59. Grantham, *Hoke Smith*, 54, 179.
60. McKelway, "Hoke Smith."
61. "Why Hoke Smith Was Defeated," *Valentine Democrat*, November 19, 1908, 4.
62. Grantham, *Hoke Smith*, 183–87.
63. Benton, *Life of Thomas E. Watson*, 348. Benton corresponded and talked with Watson and had access to his private papers following his death.
64. Ibid., 316.
65. See generally Cook, *Governors of Georgia*.
66. Watson made his views known in "Says Hoke Smith Will Be Opposed," *Atlanta Constitution*, September 3, 1910, 1; and "Thomas Watson Finishes Speech," *Atlanta Constitution*, September 22, 1910, 1.
67. "Good for Hoke Smith," *The Commoner*, September 2, 1910, 1.
68. "Hoke Smith Nominated." *New York Times*, September 2, 1914, 4.
69. Grantham, *Southern Progressivism*, 54.
70. Benton, *Life of Thomas E. Watson*, 349.
71. Cook, *Governors of Georgia*, 179.
72. Grantham, *Hoke Smith*, 178.
73. Cook, *Governors of Georgia*, 207–9. See also Goldfarb, "The Slaton Memorandum."
74. Quoted in Glashan, *American Governors*, 258.
75. Perman, "Joseph F. Johnston," 152.
76. Grantham, *Southern Progressivism*, 150.
77. "Governor Comer Takes Up Reins," *Atlanta Constitution*, January 15, 1907, 5.
78. Grantham, *Southern Progressivism*, 150.
79. Ibid., 48–49.

80. "Alabama's New Chief Opposes Cheap Labor," *Labor World*, February 16, 1907, 1.

81. Harris, "Braxton Bragg Comer," 180.

82. Rosenburg, "Emmet O'Neal." On his stand on the initiative see his statement made while attending the Conference of Governors and after debating with Wilson on the issue, as found in "Montana's Chief Believes in Strengthening the Gubernatorial Powers," *Daily Missoulian*, September 13, 1911, 1.

83. Grantham, *Southern Progressivism*, 50; "Two Dry Bills Passed over Henderson's Veto," *Atlanta Constitution*, January 23, 1915, 1. See also Allen, "Charles Henderson."

7

THE SOUTHERN PERIPHERY

Broward, Davis, Hogg, and Haskell

Turning to the states in what is generally considered the southern periphery—Florida, Arkansas, Texas, and Oklahoma—we find a continuation of the basic Progressive economic, social, and political drives we found in the Deep South. We also find a continuation of issues involving race, though, with the exception of Arkansas during the Jeff Davis years, race-baiting seems less intense and less of a factor in the building of gubernatorial careers than it was in most of the Deep South. We find, however, an example in the career of Florida governor Sidney Catts of a candidate adding the extra punch of anti-Catholic rhetoric to serve his purposes.

The careers of Florida governors—Catts and, before him, William Sherman Jennings and Napoleon Broward—illustrate the ability of politicians who were in several respects "outsiders" or unconventional candidates to build successful careers bucking the establishment. The accounts of Davis and James Hogg of Texas illustrate the usefulness in the 1890s of being a prosecutor and pursing antitrust activity in the fight against the new industrial order. The careers of George W. Donaghey and Charles H. Brough in Arkansas illustrate the emergence of business Progressives. At the other extreme are Davis and Pa Ferguson of Texas, who played the role of hillbilly folk heroes. In Oklahoma the Progressive governor story is largely that of Charles Haskell—a radical-sounding business entrepreneur who, like George Hunt of Arizona, played a leading role in producing a Progressive state constitution, an activity that led to the governorship.

JENNINGS, BROWARD, CATTS: OUTSIDERS, DRAINING THE EVERGLADES, COMING ON LIKE A CYCLONE

In the 1880s down to the early 1900s the dominant Democratic Party in Florida was highly fragmented statewide with members divided along ideological lines or competing personalities. Still, as historian Wayne Flynt has noted, "the party leadership did constitute a loosely organized club whose members informally set demanding rules for participation."[1] Getting a green light to the party's nomination for governor was greatly facilitated if the candidate came from a prominent family, was a highly regarded lawyer, or was someone who had shown loyalty to the Democratic Party by years of service.[2] It was also extremely helpful to adhere to an acceptable level of philosophical conservatism and align oneself with the corporate interests that had come to prominence in the state.

Florida's economic development had been greatly facilitated by entrepreneurs. One of the most prominent of these was Henry Flagler, a leading industrialist and railroad and land developer and one of the founders of Standard Oil. Following Reconstruction, Flagler and other developers established close ties with conservative Democrats. The developers received generous subsidies, including tax exemptions and more than 11 million acres of state land.[3] A small clique, headed by Flagler, controlled the convention system used to nominate Democratic Party candidates, selecting those from the conservative wing of the party. Governors and legislators had to deal with a powerful Flagler-led railroad and developer lobby.

By the early 1900s, a counter force had developed on the state level leading to a succession of reform-minded governors, starting with William Sherman Jennings, a cousin of William Jennings Bryan. He was followed by Napoleon Bonaparte Broward, who broke through in his quest for the governor's office even though he lacked orthodox conservative political views and important political connections. He did so by going to the voters directly and focusing on political and economic issues of importance to them. In 1916 Sidney Catts, even more of an outsider, was also able to reach the gubernatorial office by taking his case directly to the "plain people of the panhandle," though in a far more demagogic fashion than Broward by mixing racism with religious bigotry and the promise of Progressive reform.[4]

Prior to becoming governor, Jennings, trained as lawyer, had served as a county judge in 1888 and a state representative from 1893 to 1895, becoming speaker of the house in 1895. The fact that he was related to William Jennings Bryan was a political asset because of growing sentiment for anticorporate, antirailroad reform.[5] At the same time, Jennings was something of an outsider. An ex-Yankee from Illinois, he had proposed Progressive reforms ranging from free textbooks for children to railroad and corporate regulation as a member of the state legislature. At the Democratic Party convention in 1900 some delegates opposed his nomination as governor because he was too much of a Yankee and too Progressive.[6] On the other hand, this young, under-forty-years-old candidate was said to have scored well with many others in terms of ideology, temperament, and, perhaps more than anything else, his judicial-like impartiality: "He is known to the people as a conservative and thoughtful man, unusually well posted on state affairs, and absolutely independent. In the latter quality lies the secret of most of his strength. He is not backed by any particular influence, and is neither a corporation man nor an anti-corporation man."[7]

Jennings took the lead in securing the adoption of a statewide primary election system, replacing the practice of nominating candidates at party conventions. He and others saw the convention system for nominations to have generally worked in favor of conservative candidates and hoped that the new system would bring better outcomes. He also led in pushing for a plan to drain and reclaim for development more than 3 million acres of land, mostly in the Everglades. Along with this, he sought to recover large amounts of public land controlled by railroad companies.[8]

The most controversial measure that Jennings signed off on made insanity a ground for divorce. This measure, speedily adopted by the legislature, was widely criticized for being for the special benefit of Henry Flagler, the political powerhouse, whose second wife had been determined incurably insane and was living in a sanatorium. Flagler had wanted a divorce, but Florida did not recognize insanity as a legal cause for such action. Jennings had taken a swipe at Flagler with the direct primary and other proposals but, being politically savvy, likely saw no reason in this instance to further upset Flagler and went along with the divorce legislation.

Future governor Napoleon Bonaparte Broward started out in his early thirties as sheriff of Duval County (Jacksonville)—an office he first secured by appointment in 1887 and to which he was elected several times up to 1900. Following this, he went on to serve as a state legislator. He gained considerable public attention and name recognition in the late 1890s because of his daring as a riverboat captain who, evading Spanish guns and US authorities, ran ammunition on his steam tug, named, *The Three Friends*, to Cuban freedom fighters. In 1904 he won the office of governor of Florida for a single four-year term. Broward also became one of the most prominent Progressives of his time.[9]

Early in his career Broward sided with the Populist and farmer faction of the Democratic Party known as the "Straightouts." This anticorporate reform group battled with a conservative pro-business faction called the "Antis" who were close to the railroads and other corporate interests. As part of the fight, Broward supported Jennings in his successful campaign for governor in 1900, stumping the state for him.

Serving as a legislator while Jennings was governor, Broward generally lined up on the Progressive side. He pushed hard for a direct primary bill in 1901 but opposed the particular plan proposed by Jennings and adopted by the legislature on the grounds that it was too weak. He, like Jennings, was willing to go along with what the newspapers called "Flagler's Divorce Bill," saying he did so because he felt it was the right thing to do. Following the lead of Ben Tillman of South Carolina, Broward proposed a measure calling for state-owned and -operated liquor dispensaries, seeing this as wise move in the direction of temperance, but it was defeated by an attack led by the wholesale and retail liquor interests.

In 1904, at the age of forty-seven, Broward surprised many by challenging, with Governor Jennings's endorsement, popular congressman Robert W. Davis in the Democratic primary for governor, the only contest that really mattered, since the winner was virtually assured of being elected. Davis, a conservative, had the support of Flagler and was affectionately known around the state as "Our Bob." Broward drew largely on Populist ideas to rally the support of the "crackers"—poor white farmers in rural areas and small towns. He did not do well in urban areas and won the primary by only 600 votes out of 45,000 cast. Following his nomination a writer for the *Atlanta Constitution* noted that Broward was not simply some adventurer, as might be suggested by his exploits in Cuba, but an "unusually serious-minded, well-informed, and clear-headed man."[10]

In office Broward adopted and built upon many of Jennings's ideas, though he offered a much broader Progressive agenda. He focused, as had Jennings, on draining and developing the Everglades to recover millions of acres of land for agricultural purposes.[11] Faced with objections to the land tax he instituted to pay for the drainage, he lessened the burden by securing, with the enthusiastic support of Theodore Roosevelt, federal funds for the project.

Beyond the Everglades project Broward offered an expansive, anticorporate, common-man Progressive program. He was strong on railroad regulation, education, and conservation and successfully promoted reforms in such areas as child labor and pure food and drug protections.[12] The legislature gave him much but ignored his proposal that the state get into the business of providing life insurance for Floridians.[13] Angry with the newspapers, especially those owned by or sympathetic to the corporations, he tried but failed to get legislative approval of a strong libel law.[14] Broward, as governor, was also a strong spokesperson for prohibition. Even Cary Nation, the temperance leader who attacked saloons with a hatchet, had something good to say about him on this score.[15]

On race, Broward's thinking was in line with those who regarded blacks as inferior. His solution was sending the black population to some territory purchased by Congress where they could govern themselves. Florida legislators, seeing black workers essential to the state's economy, which was already suffering from a shortage of labor, were more interested in segregation of the races than in reducing the size of the black population. The legislature, with Broward's support, enacted several Jim Crow laws during his years in office.[16]

The more central Progressive drive established by Jennings and Broward continued on in the administrations of Democrats Albert W. Gilchrist and Park

Trammell, the former being especially active in regard to health protection and the latter being productive in a large number of areas, including putting controls on campaign spending, strengthening rail regulation, equalizing property taxes, and promoting conservation.[17] Through all of this, though, white supremacy was still the norm, bringing racial segregation and lynching.

In an unlikely journey Alabama-born Sidney J. Catts started out as a lawyer, became an ordained Baptist minister, switched to going on the road selling insurance, and wound up governor of Florida. He had been in Florida but three years when, in 1914, he decided that he wanted to be governor of the state. He reached that office in 1917. Catts liked to refer to himself as the Ben Tillman of Florida. Others compared him to Blease and Vardaman. Like Vardaman, he took a stand against black education. Following his death, a Florida newspaper noted: "He came to us like a cyclone."[18]

In his position as an insurance salesman, one he took in 1915, Catts traveled all over Florida, met lots of people, and built up a political following. He ignored the existing power structure and took his case to the masses, mixing insurance and religion with talking politics in trying to stir up the people.[19] In 1916 he entered the Democratic primary as a candidate for governor. Explaining his decision, he reportedly told an audience: "The Catholics were about to take Florida and I told the people about it wherever I went. I was tramping on their toes and raising the devil to such an extent that many of the Catholics wanted to kill 'Old Catts.'" He decided to run when he could not get any of the other candidates "to stand on a platform of 'America First'" and take on "those holding allegiance to a foreign potentate."[20]

The Democratic organization was not pleased with this challenge from a novice and "outsider" and gave him stiff opposition. At first count Catts won the party's nomination. Democratic Party leaders, however, responded by getting the state supreme court to order a recount, which went against the outsider. Following this, an infuriated Catts went to the leaders of the Florida Prohibition Party, received their endorsement for governor, and went on to win the general election as the Prohibition Party's candidate. He trounced the regular Democratic candidate, basing his campaign on a call for prohibition, various Progressive measures, and, more than anything else, the need to combat Catholics, corporations, and blacks, roughly in that order.[21]

Shortly after taking office, Catts became a Democrat again, though he used patronage appointments to build his own power base rather than to accommodate party leaders, many of whom had opposed him, or to promote the interest of the party.[22] He served as governor from 1917 to 1921 but lost badly in a run for the US Senate in 1920. While governor, he regularly fought with the Democratic legislature and the press. Still, he secured passage of a statewide prohibition act and made some advances in the areas of tax and labor reform, road building, and programs improving the treatment of convicts and the mentally ill.[23] He built a strong record of labor support.²⁴ He also endorsed woman suffrage and appointed a woman to his staff, one of the first governors to do so. In terms of policy, about the only product of his anti-Catholic viewpoint was an unenforced convent inspection law, which was picked up by several other southern states.²⁵

Catts first became politically active on the issue of prohibition. As a Baptist minister in Alabama, he condemned "demon rum" and fought efforts to legalize liquor in the county where he was residing. As governor, he once publicly criticized a judge's decision on a liquor control matter and warned him that he had better "get right" on the liquor question if he wanted to stay a judge. The bar association condemned him for trying to intimidate a judge. Still, his rigid stand on the evils of liquor played well with the rural and evangelical voters. Hypocrisy was no problem: He took a strong public stand against the consumption of liquor even though he personally was not committed to total abstinence and drank privately.²⁶

During his administration a disaster brought attention to the evils of the system of leasing out convicts to private businesses. A fire broke out in a turpentine camp where black convicts were chained to their beds in a long barrack, the chains being barely long enough to reach the window that served as their toilet. Unable to flee, they all burned to death. Catts did not eliminate the leasing system but greatly reduced its use by launching a good roads program, supported in part by federal highway funds, under which convicts, working under much better conditions, were used to build badly needed roads.²⁷

ARKANSAS: JEFF DAVIS AND THE BUSINESS GOVERNORS

Stirrings of reform in Arkansas during the 1880s came in the protest of workers and small farmers who, joined by Republicans, rallied behind the candidacy of C. P. Norwood for governor. Running on the Labor Party ticket, Norwood lost (54 percent to 46 percent) to the Democratic candidate, James P. Eagle, in 1888, but the showing was strong enough to prompt Eagle into backing spending more on education and road improvements and to support proposals to equalize tax rates, humanize the penal system, and impose railroad regulations. As political scientist Diane Blair noted, most of these proposals failed in the legislature, but the effort was "the entering wedge of populism as opposed to patricianism; and the populist impulse periodically surfaced from that time on in gubernatorial elections"²⁸ Unfortunately, it also brought fear and a series of Jim Crow laws imposing segregation and electoral changes to establish the rule of an all-white Democratic Party.²⁹

As conservative Democrats lost their hold in the mid-1890s, Jeff Davis began to build a political career that ultimately brought him to the governor's office. Born in Arkansas, the son of a Baptist preacher, lawyer, and judge, he was not related to Jefferson Davis, president of the Confederacy, but he was perfectly willing to allow others to think that this was the case. Like Hoke Smith of Georgia and many other Southerners, he began the 1890s campaigning for Cleveland for president. By 1896 he had switched to Bryan and the free-silver cause.

In the early 1890s the young lawyer became prosecuting attorney in the Fifth Judicial District, pledging to go after liquor dealers and to "fill the penitentiary so full of negroes that their feet would be sticking out the windows."[30] In 1898 he became state attorney general. Shortly after being elected to that office, Davis was quoted as saying: "I am going to run for governor of Arkansas and be elected. Then I am going to run for the United States senate and be elected."[31] He did both of these things.

Attorney General Davis gained considerable favorable attention by instituting court suits charging out-of-state insurance companies and other corporations with violating the state's antitrust laws. Though he did not have much success in the courts, his crusade against the "Yankee trusts" helped get him elected governor in 1900. He was reelected twice, holding office from 1901 to 1907. In 1906 he was elected to the US Senate. Along the way, he campaigned as a champion of the interests of the common people against the rich and powerful "money interests," of the plebeians against the patricians, of the rednecks from the hills against the city types, and of poor whites against blacks. He functioned, in part, as a sort of "Karl Marx for Hillbillies."[32] He was a well-educated, solidly middle-class attorney who played the role of a hillbilly folk hero.[33]

Davis played a leading role in democratizing political campaigning in the state by setting the practice, a highly successful one copied by others, of drumming up support by going directly to the voters at the grassroots level rather than simply going around the state courting local leaders or courthouse cliques.[34] As Diane Blair noted, he also represented a sharp departure from the traditional model of a dignified but largely passive chief executive. He stirred things up by appealing to emotions and mass prejudices. He saw the possibilities that "the office offered for dramatizing if not achieving reform" and in building or sustaining a political career.[35]

Throughout his career Davis waged a long war on the corporations, resisting the new industrial order. This battle paid off in votes but was one that he, like other governors of his time, eventually lost.

Other than seeing government playing a legitimate role in controlling railroads and other corporations, he took a generally negative view of government, being as suspicious of it as many of his followers were, and saw the governors' job largely as being a watchdog to prevent others from doing something dangerous or wasteful.[36] Still, he often faced considerable opposition, including a powerful business lobby, old-time legislators who resented his attempts at domination, and Baptist Church leaders who charged him with public drunkenness and immoral behavior. Davis responded to the church leaders by denouncing the "morality crowd," becoming a friend of the liquor industry, vetoing temperance legislation, and pardoning hundreds of people who had been convicted of violating liquor laws.[37] He was able to survive an effort to impeach him. He did not accomplish much meaningful legislation. He was also one of the most virulent racists in the South. He defended the disfranchisement and lynching of blacks.

Following Davis, the reform banner was taken up in a much more businesslike and business-friendly way, reflecting the views and values of the urban middle class, by Governor George W. Donaghey, though problems remained in terms of gubernatorial behavior and race relations. Born in Louisiana, Donaghey spent several years in Texas and Oklahoma as a building contractor and came out of this as a wealthy man. Arkansas Democrats saw him as someone who might be willing to spend money on campaigns and cultivated his interest in politics and running for office. Donaghey did not speak well in public and had a temper, which made him a bit difficult to get along with.[38] Still, running on a Progressive platform in 1908, he defeated a candidate supported by Jeff Davis to win the Democratic Party's nomination for governor.

Donaghey served two terms, from 1909 to 1913, in which he introduced a broad range of Progressive measures, especially in the areas of public health, education, and penal reform.[39] He was disposed to do more but had to make drastic budget cuts because of a fiscal crisis. He was unable to get the legislature to reform the tax structure but successfully promoted a constitutional amendment providing for the initiative and referendum.

Donaghey saw direct legislation as the cure for a variety of legislative ills, including corruption. Worried about getting public approval of an amendment providing for this reform in the 1910 election, he used his own money to bring in William Jennings Bryan to campaign for its adoption. He and Bryan had formed a friendship at the 1908 Democratic national convention. Bryan, accompanied by Donaghey, made a five-day blitz of the state on a special train, talking to an estimated 125,000 people about the value of the initiative and referendum. The voters approved the amendment, making Arkansas the only Southern state with these direct democracy mechanisms.[40]

Unlike Jeff Davis, Donaghey believed governors should be strong legislative leaders and, in attempting to do this, met regularly in his office with legislators to line up support and sent a series of special messages on various topics to the legislature. His eagerness to push his agenda got him into some fistfights and a shoving match with the speaker of the house, who resented what he considered the governor's overly intensive lobbying of house members.[41] Donaghey also had some trouble on the racial front. Speaking to some 3,000 African Americans at a Baptist convention in December 1910, he declared: "It is not for any political purpose I come to talk to you. It is not for the purpose of getting your votes, this you know as well as I do, because your people do not vote much. This perhaps is best for you. . . . The greatest man of your race [an apparent reference to

Booker T. Washington] has told you to stay out of politics and I agree with him on that."[42]

Rejecting the notion that blacks were best off not voting, a writer in an African American paper shot back: "The thing which makes a man a citizen is the vote, and without that you are not a citizen. . . . It is the ballot with which my people must protect themselves and if they fail to get it into their hands then they are not men. . . . Let every Negro get a ballot in his hand and walk up to the ballot box and use it."[43] Later on, at a meeting accompanied by Booker T. Washington, he advised a black audience: "Don't waste your time running around begging for social equality; be contented with the progress you are making industrially."[44] Once again the governor's comments were roasted in the black press. This press, however, did back Donaghey's effort to abolish the convict lease system.[45]

During his four years in office the legislature repeatedly rejected Donaghey's request that it abolish the convict leasing system used by the state. He characterized the system as one in which the prisoners were kept in "burning, seething Hells."[46] Toward the end of his term, on December 17, 1912, the governor made one last attack on convict leasing in a spectacular fashion. Inspired by a similar move made in South Carolina by Governor Blease, he abruptly pardoned 360 convicts at one time, most of whom were serving short sentences. The spectacular mass pardoning wiped out three work camps.[47]

Donaghey ran for another term in 1912, calling for tax reform and prohibition and taking aim at the state legislature, which he charged was full of bribe-takers and completely subservient to the liquor interests.[48] He was defeated in the Democratic Party primary by Joseph T. Robinson.

In September 1912 voters elected Robinson to the office and, at the same time, rejected statewide prohibition and an amendment, supported by Donaghey, that would have disqualified as many as three-quarters of the black voters. Coming into office, Robinson repeated the request to abolish the convict leasing system, and this time the legislature agreed. Robinson served only fifty-five days before, with the blessing of the legislature, heading off to join the US Senate, replacing Jeff Davis, who had died in office. Still, he was able to push through a strong Progressive agenda regarding such matters as banking, public health, and transportation along with a corrupt-practices act and bringing an end to the convict leasing system.

Arkansas experienced another period of reform under Democratic governor Charles H. Brough, whom voters put in office in 1916 and, for a second term, in 1918. Born in Mississippi, Brough had earned a PhD from Johns Hopkins University and left his position at the University of Arkansas at Fayetteville in 1915 to campaign as a Progressive for governor. Brough and his followers were encouraged by the example set by Woodrow Wilson, also a Johns Hopkins PhD, showing that a southern-born academic could succeed in running for political office, even the highest office in the land, and that in this Progressive age voters might well favor an erudite, articulate leader of unquestioned integrity, a statesman, over a professional politician.[49]

As governor Brough brought greater funding for education, more and better roads, medical care and limited financial assistance for people in need, a corporation commission to regulate public utilities, and a prohibition law. Though he was not in the forefront of the suffrage drive, with the encouragement of his wife, who was active in the cause, he signed legislation allowing women to vote in primary elections, making Arkansas the first southern state to allow woman suffrage.[50]

On race, he was a white supremacist but paternalistic toward blacks and eager to protect their rights when it came to mob violence. In handling what is considered one of the worst race riots in the nation's history, one that occurred in Phillips County in 1919 and took the lives of twenty-five blacks and five whites, Brough got the federal government to send in 500 troops to restore order. Later, however, he accepted a highly questionable report that put the blame for the riot on a radical union for organizing black sharecroppers with the purpose of massacring white men in the area.[51]

HOGG, CAMPBELL, FERGUSON

Writing in 1914, a Texas newspaperman claimed: "Texas is the original progressive state." This was true, the writer declared, because its governor during the 1890s, James Stephen Hogg, "was the pioneer progressive of all governors. It was he who blazed the way, who fought the first hard battles."[52] Many would disagree with much of this, but Hogg was well known around the country in the 1890s as a reformer, at least close to being up there with Tillman and Altgeld in recognition. Hogg, a Democrat, preempted the message and much of the following of the Populists, took control of the Democratic Party in Texas away from the conservatives, and helped lay the basis for Progressivism in the state. He focused much of his attention on extending greater control over the railroads and other large, often out-of-state corporations.

Texas-born, he had a variety of occupations, including farm worker, typesetter, and newspaperman, before finding his true calling as a lawyer and politician. In private law practice he worked with farmers and businesspeople who had complaints about railroad rates and services. Turning to public office, he moved up the ladder from justice of the peace to county attorney, to district attorney, and to state attorney general, the last coming in 1886, all the time demonstrating his commitment to the enforcement of all the laws. As a justice of the peace, this even included enforcing previously widely ignored laws requiring the closing of saloons on Sunday.[53]

As state attorney general in 1886, he attacked out-of-state insurance companies and battled the railroads. He filed suit against various non-Texas corporations for violating Texas antitrust laws and avoiding Texas taxes. His most prominent

Figure 7.1. James Hogg. Courtesy of the Library of Congress, Prints & Photographs Division, photograph by Carol M. Highsmith, LC-DIG-highsm-27902.

action was taken against the Texas Traffic Association, a railroad pool, organized in 1885 by the heads of major railroad lines operating in the state to limit competition and, more specifically, stop rate wars among the various railroads. He followed up on a successful court suit against the association in 1887 by helping design a new and far more stringent state antitrust statute that became law in 1889. Hoping to draw upon his performance as attorney general, he decided to run for governor, pushing the idea that a railroad commission would be a more effective way than lawsuits to control the railroads.[54]

Voters put Hogg in the governor's office in 1890 and reelected him in 1892. He represented the influence of rural communities and small farmers in a crusade against out-of-state railroads, especially the Southern Pacific, and other corporations. He sought policies to foster native industries and help create a self-sustaining state economy. Like other Progressives, Hogg "wanted to redistribute the benefits of political capitalism, not to exterminate them."[55]

His efforts as governor from 1891 to 1895 led to the creation of an appointed railroad commission, which served as a model for other states, and legislation restricting railroad rates and the selling of "watered" railroad stock. Hogg took special pride in the creation of a railroad commission, considering the well-organized lobby working against it.[56] Another measure successfully pushed by Hogg was tailored to reduce corporate land ownership by requiring railroads and other corporations to sell land they were holding for speculative purposes within fifteen years—legislation that proved difficult to implement because of loopholes. He also signed off on a measure requiring railways in Texas to have separate coaches for black and white passengers.

He did, though, take a firm stand against lynching and other acts of violence directed at blacks. One of the most horrific of these was the lynching of a black man, Henry Smith, in Paris, Texas, in 1893. Smith, accused of killing a three-year-old girl, the daughter of a Paris policeman, was publicly tortured by the policeman and his family using iron brands and later doused with oil and set on fire, burning him alive. Hogg showed considerable courage in seeking murder charges against the mob.[57]

On the administrative level, Hogg was also involved in a series of successful antitrust suits against out-of-state corporations. One of these was against J. D. Rockefeller's Standard Oil Company and its subsidiary in Texas for price-fixing and other violations of state law. The subsidiary had its charter revoked. Hogg was unsuccessful in getting Rockefeller extradited from New York to stand trial in Texas but did manage to try others associated with him, some of whom were found guilty.

In national politics Hogg campaigned for Cleveland in 1884 but later sided with the anti-Cleveland faction of the party. A states' righter, he stood with Governor Altgeld of Illinois in the condemnation of President Cleveland for sending troops into Illinois during the Pullman Strike. He too defended the Coxey Army movement, coming to the defense of unemployed men demanding free transportation on the Southern Pacific who had been left stranded in Texas in the middle of nowhere without food in an uncoupled boxcar. He blasted the railroads for leaving the men to starve to death. To Hogg, "Food not fines will be the treatment of the law-loving, law-abiding element in this state when men commit no greater crime than travelling as tramps for lack of work."[58]

Overall, like Ben Tillman in South Carolina, Hogg successfully took on conservative party leaders and blunted the appeal of the Populists by addressing farmer discontent. Like Tillman, he represented the agrarian wing of the Democratic Party and initially received the support of the Farmers' Alliance even though he was not a Populist. In Hogg's case, the alliance broke with him over the proper method of selecting the railroad commission—he favored an appointive body whereas the alliance favored an elected one. Under Hogg, the Democratic Party "found a middle ground between its conservative, pro-railroad wing and the more radical demands of the Populists."[59] He may be best considered "an embattled Democratic" trying to steer "a course between the Populists and the conservative

Democrats" rather than "a convinced progressive."[60] As historian Lewis Gould once pointed out, Hogg was no Robert La Follette.[61]

Though initially a strong corporate critic, to the dismay of reformers he drifted over time into a more comfortable relation with his former corporate adversaries.[62]

Democrat Charles Culberson, who followed Hogg as governor, had been attorney general of Texas while Hogg was governor and worked with Hogg on antitrust cases, including the one against Rockefeller. Hogg picked him as his successor. Culberson was elected in 1894 and 1896, being pressed in both contests by Populist candidates. As governor he was frequently at odds with the legislature. He set a new record in using the veto weapon thirty-three times; none of his vetoes were overridden.[63] Culberson focused most of his attention on managing the state's budget, which was in deep trouble. Out of principle and his concern for law and order, however, he led the successful effort to prohibit prizefighting in the state, even though this led to loss of a considerable amount of state revenue at a time when it was needed.[64] Culberson later went on to the US Senate.

Following the Hogg-Culberson era, Texas had eight years of conservative rule. Corporations were in control under the political leadership of Joseph Bailey, US representative and senator from 1891 to 1913, and a couple of conservative governors who held office from 1899 to 1907. The reform effort bounced back with the election of Thomas M. Campbell in 1906.

Campbell, born in Texas, opened a law practice in 1878. He took a position with the Great Northern Railroad but, becoming distrustful of big business and siding with labor, resigned his position in 1897.

Campbell had a strong link to Hogg. The two grew up as neighbors in East Texas. They were longtime friends and on the same page philosophically. Hogg eagerly backed Campbell for the governorship in 1906, hoping to end the long dry spell for Progressive reform that had set in after Culberson. Unlike his opponents in the 1906 campaign, Campbell did not travel around the state on a free pass while running for governor.[65] Running for reelection in 1908, Campbell defeated a candidate who called for justice to the corporations. Though having a productive reign as governor, he ran unsuccessfully for a US Senate seat in 1916.

With a legislature sympathetic to Progressivism, Campbell's two terms brought a slew of reforms, including more effective regulation of railroads and other businesses, more equitable taxation, lobbying restrictions, ending the giving of railroad passes, bank deposit guarantees, pure food regulations, and more money for schools. Campbell also frequently used his power to pardon. In two terms he issued 783 pardons.[66] Reports from journalists and legislative staffers of brutality and violence in the operation of the convict leasing program had also prompted Campbell to call a special session of the legislature in 1910 in an attempt to end the practice by 1914. This was done in 1912 by Governor Oscar Colquitt, but general abuses in the prison system at large continued.[67]

In 1915 what is considered the "Ferguson era" began when James Edward "Pa" Ferguson took office as governor. Ferguson, a Texas-born lawyer, had been active in Democratic Party politics but had not held public office prior to becoming governor. While running in the 1914 primary as a "businessman's candidate," he also tried to appeal to rural voters by focusing on the evils of farm tenancy, calling for rent control for sharecroppers. He also pledged to veto all prohibition legislation: "I will strike it where the chicken got the axe."[68]

He faced an opponent named Thomas Ball, who had the backing of the prohibitionists and the railroads and other corporations. Ball supporters turned to the Wilson administration to stave off defeat. They sought an endorsement of the dry cause and told the president that Ferguson was an agent of reaction. Wilson and Secretary of State William Jennings Bryan issued public statements for Ball in mid-July, a tactic that moved Ferguson to denounce federal interference in state affairs. Despite the presidential action, Ferguson combined the wet vote with the ballots of North Texas farmers concerned about tenancy and achieved a 45,000-vote majority. The voters gave him another term in 1916.[69]

Ferguson had a strong following in rural areas. He was attentive to their problems and could count on their vote. When rallying tenant farmers he would criticize "city-slickers" and the "educated fools" in urban areas. He would also purposely use bad grammar and expressions he felt would go over well with a rural crowd. During the 1914 campaign against Ball, for example, "In a typical speech in Galveston he said he 'warn't no college dude, and durned glad of it' and that he didn't have to have 'no edgecashun to be smarter than the durned fool Ball crowd.'"[70]

The Ferguson regime is perhaps best described as "demagogic government with overtones of liberalism."[71] As governor he brought some educational accomplishments—for example, increasing aid to rural schools and creating three teacher colleges. He also used the pardoning power 2,253 times between 1915 and 1917, so frequently that critics accused him of having an open door policy at the state penitentiary.[72] He also made some unusual announcements and offers, such as the one in January 1915: "In 1915 I want to see the stork visit more Texas homes than in the past. To encourage more frequent visits of this big bird I offer a personal prize of $10 in cash for the first twins and a cash prize of $50 for the first triplets born in Texas in 1915."[73]

Ferguson's downfall came when accusations of misconduct involving the misuse of state funds and a battle with administrators at the University of Texas resulted in impeachment proceedings against him.[74] Having angered woman suffrage leaders with his opposition to extending the vote to women and, as one suffrage group declared, being against "every great moral issue for which women stood," he became targeted by members of the movement, who actively participated in the drive to have him impeached.[75]

He resigned in 1917 before the proceedings were completed, but the legislative action prohibited him from holding any future public office in Texas. Undaunted, he kept running for office, including the governorship, a US Senate seat, and the presidency. His most productive step came from managing the gubernatorial campaign of his wife, Miriam "Ma" Ferguson, who was elected in 1924. "Pa" maintained a desk in her office and was consulted on most decisions. Working through various boards and commissions, he influenced the awarding of jobs and contracts.[76] Overall, he seemed impressed by the prestige and power he felt the office of governor gave him. He once expressed the view that "I am Governor of Texas. I don't have to give reasons."[77]

OKLAHOMA: THE ENTREPRENEUR IN CHARGE

The Progressive story in Oklahoma is largely one of Democrat Charles Haskell, its first governor. A railroad promoter and entrepreneur in Ohio, Haskell came to Muskogee, Oklahoma, in 1901 to make money. He bought and sold townsite lots, built a hotel to lure trade, and tried to stimulate growth, becoming an untiring civic booster and an aspiring politician.[78]

In 1907 he was a leader in a constitutional convention dominated by Democrats that framed what was widely considered a highly Progressive state constitution, one that conservative President Taft described as "a zoological garden of cranks" filled with dangerous ideas such as direct democracy and, most threatening, the recall of judges. Convention delegates made a strong effort to curb monopolies and control corporations, especially the railroads. A contemporary journalist noted that when it came to "dealing with the corporation problem," the final product in Oklahoma "may be taken as the latest word in constitutions."[79] At the convention Haskell led a successful effort to include a prohibition provision but also blocked an effort to include woman suffrage in the basic document. Suffragists later described him as "among the bitterest" opponents of suffrage.[80]

In 1906 both the Democratic and Republican Parties adopted platforms favoring segregated schools and transportation facilities. For Republicans this came as a reversal of policy. Their decision to abandon blacks was based on the belief that their party was going to continue to lose to Democrats unless they became as lily white as Democrats and adopted similar racial policies. At the convention delegates put a provision for school segregation into the constitution. They backed off on adding a provision regarding segregated transportation facilities because of the opposition of President Roosevelt, but Democrats made this the first order of business in the first legislature, a step that provoked some protest from black Republicans and small-scale black riots.[81] Later, to the amusement of passengers around him, Haskell was caught violating the Jim Crow law by accidentally sitting in the "Negroes Only" section of a train. When informed, he made a speedy exit.[82] The first term produced not only Jim Crow laws but laws excluding blacks from voting.

Haskell, enjoying the support of traditional party leaders, farm and labor groups, and prohibitionists and benefiting from his association with a highly popular constitution, had little problem securing the Democratic Party's nomination for governor, turning back a conservative banker named Lee Cruce, whom he labeled an "insincere friend of the constitution."[83] He won the general election by ten percentage points over his Republican opponent.

The Republicans, though, did make some trouble by raising questions about Haskell's suspicious connections to various corporations, including Standard Oil, before coming to Oklahoma.[84] Haskell brushed off the charges and went on the attack against big business.[85] Employing a labor theory of value, he praised the productive efforts of those in what he called the producer class, be they farmers, workers, or merchants. He saw the big business elite as belonging to a class of parasites who were living the good life off the work of others and rubbing it in by engaging in "conspicuous consumption."[86]

Voters swept Haskell into office on September 17, 1907, the same day Oklahomans ratified the constitution. He proposed several measures of a Progressive nature and got a great deal from the legislature—antitrust legislation, public utility laws, and legislation establishing corporate and individual income taxes. Haskell also got a bank deposit guarantee law through the legislature in 1907, the first such law in the nation. This encouraged similar action in other states, including Kansas after the governor in that state discovered that depositors in Kansas had started to put their money in Oklahoma banks. Haskell had favored the idea at the state's constitutional convention, and William Jennings Bryan had recommended it in an address to the first Oklahoma legislature.[87]

During Haskell's term the legislature produced several laws benefiting labor, including safety inspections of factory and mining conditions and an eight-hour day for workers on public projects. Haskell also asked for a child labor law in the first legislature but, having second thoughts, vetoed the child labor measure sent to him. He was thoroughly roasted for his veto, being inundated by more than 3,000 angry letters and receiving criticism in the national press. He quickly signed off on a child labor measure sent to him in the next legislative session.[88]

According to contemporary accounts, Haskell had been drawn into vetoing the child labor law by legislative leader Alfalfa Bill Murray, who was angry with the bill's chief sponsor, Kate Barnard, the commissioner of charities who had successfully gotten through several pieces of legislation over his opposition.[89] Murray, too, did not think much of women as officeholders. Still, as author Keith L. Bryant noted, Murray had to acknowledge: "Though small of stature, the lady carried a large political stick."[90]

Barnard had managed to win election as Oklahoma's commissioner of charities and corrections, even though women were not allowed to vote. Along with pushing for labor measures, she helped goad Haskell into the area of prison reform. Taking her job seriously, she blew the whistle on the abuse being suffered by individuals convicted of crimes in Oklahoma who were imprisoned in Kansas. Following her disclosures, Haskell felt compelled to do something and got a bill through the legislature that brought fifty prisoners back to McAlester, Oklahoma, where, under the watchful eye of state militia guards, they were housed in tents and undertook the task of building a penitentiary where they and others could be confined.[91]

When it came to the enforcement of the prohibition law, Haskell, like governors in other states, was more proactive and cracked down on the illegal sale of intoxicating liquor by forcing the resignation or removal of local officials who were suspected of taking money to allow the bootleggers and saloons to operate or who simply refused to enforce the law.[92]

In 1908 Haskell worked for the Democratic Party on Bryan's presidential campaign, but during the campaign the Hearst newspapers dug up the charges accusing him of having engaged in some corrupt activity on behalf of the Standard Oil Company earlier in his business career. Haskell vehemently denied the changes, but the constant attack on him was hurting the campaign and forced Bryan to severe his ties with the governor.

Haskell finished his term in 1911 and made a bid for the US Senate but lost the primary to incumbent senator Robert Latham Owen. Meanwhile, the state turned in a conservative direction with the gubernatorial election of Democrat Lee Cruce, the banker who had lost to Haskell in 1907 for the party's nomination.

NOTES

1. Flynt, *Cracker Messiah*, 29.
2. Ibid., 30.
3. Grantham, *Southern Progressivism*, 61.
4. Flynt, *Cracker Messiah*, 33.
5. Proctor, *Napoleon Bonaparte Broward*, 160.
6. Colburn and Scher, *Florida's Gubernatorial Politics*, 61.
7. "Governorship of Florida," *Atlanta Constitution*, February 10, 1900, 6.
8. Grantham, *Southern Progressivism*, 61.
9. For material drawn here on Broward's background see Proctor, *Napoleon Bonaparte Broward*, 55–61, 165–69.
10. "New Florida Governor a Man of the People," *Atlanta Constitution*, June 12, 1904, A7.
11. Colburn and Scher, *Florida's Gubernatorial Politics*, 63, 84.
12. Ibid., 63; Proctor, *Napoleon Bonaparte Broward*, 149, 255.
13. Proctor, *Napoleon Bonaparte Broward*, 229.
14. Ibid., 252–55.

15. Ibid., 35, 280.
16. Colburn and Scher, *Florida's Gubernatorial Politics*, 220–21.
17. Grantham, *Southern Progressivism*, 62–64.
18. Flynt, *Cracker Messiah* 46–47, 266, 274.
19. Ibid., 28–29.
20. Item in *Ocala Evening Star*, December 19, 1916, 2.
21. Colburn and Scher, *Florida's Gubernatorial Politics*, 67.
22. Ibid., 137.
23. Grantham, *Southern Progressivism*, 63.
24. Colburn and Scher, *Florida's Gubernatorial Politics*, 202–4.
25. Flynt, *Cracker Messiah*, 140.
26. Ibid., 9, 117–19, 130.
27. Ibid., 137–39.
28. Blair, *Arkansas Politics*, 34.
29. Ibid., 33–34.
30. Arsenault, "Jeff Davis," 117.
31. Quoted in "Jefferson Davis, Who Will Be Chosen Senator," *Evening Times*, December 13, 1906, 1.
32. Grantham, *Southern Progressivism*, 91.
33. Arsenault, "Jeff Davis," 130.
34. Grantham, *Southern Progressivism*, 92.
35. Blair, *Arkansas Politics*, 153.
36. Ledbetter, *Carpenter from Conway*, 10, citing Richard L. Niswonger, "Arkansas Democratic Politics," PhD diss., University of Texas at Austin, 1974.
37. Arsenault, "Jeff Davis," 124.
38. Ledbetter, *Carpenter from Conway*, 52.
39. Grantham, *Southern Progressivism*, 92.
40. Piott, *Giving Voters a Voice*, 127, 131; Moore, "George Washington Donaghey."
41. Ledbetter, *Carpenter from Conway*, 157.
42. Quotes found in "The Governor of Arkansas Addresses Baptist Convention," *Afro-American*, December 3, 1910, 1; and J. O. Midnight, "Not Pleased with the Governor's Way of Thinking," *Afro-American*, December 10, 1910, 1.
43. Midnight, "Not Pleased with Governor's Way of Thinking."
44. "Quit Begging for Social Equality," *Chicago Defender*, September 2, 1911, 1.
45. "Convict Lease System," *Afro-American*, February 3, 1912, 2.
46. Moore, "George Washington Donaghey," 137.
47. "Governors Discuss the Granting of Pardons," *New York Times*, January 19, 1913, SM11.
48. Ledbetter, *Carpenter from Conway*, 6.
49. Lisenby *Charles Hillman Brough*, 27.
50. Ibid., 40.
51. Ibid., 47–48. See also Lisenby, "Charles Hillman Brough"; "Negro Fostered Elaine Uprising Says Committee," *Arizona Republican*, October 7, 1919, 1; and "Says Negro Union Plotted Uprising," *New York Times*, October 7, 1919, 2.
52. Zach Lamar Cobb, "'Nubbins' by Cobb," *El Paso Herald*, February 21, 1914, 6.
53. Childs, *Texas Railroad Commission*, 57.
54. Ibid., 58–59.
55. Gould, *Progressives and Prohibitionists*, 10.
56. Gantt, *Chief Executive in Texas*, 197.
57. "Gov. Hogg Aroused," *New York Times*, February 3, 1893, 2; "Gov. Hogg Proposes Remedies," *New York Times*, February 8, 1893, 6.

58. Quoted by Schwantes, *Coxey's Army*, 94.
59. Gould, *Progressives and Prohibitionists*, 6.
60. Ibid., 8–9.
61. Ibid., 113.
62. Kirby, *Darkness at the Dawning*, 30–31.
63. Gantt, *Chief Executive in Texas*, 189.
64. Robert T. Hill, "Texas Past and Present," *Forum*, August 1900, 744; "The New Governors"; Wagner, "Charles A. Culberson."
65. Item in *Palestine Daily Herald*, May 15, 1906, 4.
66. Gantt, *Chief Executive in Texas*, 151. For an overview see Schmelzer, *Our Fighting Governor*.
67. Gould, *Progressives and Prohibitionists*, 41.
68. Gould, "Progressive Era."
69. Gould, *Progressives and Prohibitionists*, 141–43.
70. Gantt, *Chief Executive in Texas*, 294.
71. Schlesinger, *How They Became Governor*, 86. One study classifies both Fergusons as liberals. See Gantt, *Chief Executive in Texas*, 324.
72. Gantt, *Chief Executive in Texas*, 151.
73. "Texas Getting Progressive," *Cut Bank Pioneer Press*, January 29, 1915, 3.
74. On his financial dealings see Wilson, *In the Governor's Shadow*.
75. Harper, *History of Woman Suffrage*, 6:634.
76. Gantt, *Chief Executive in Texas*, 45, 128.
77. Ibid., 42.
78. Goble, *Progressive Oklahoma*, 140.
79. "Oklahoma and Statehood," *The Outlook*, March 30, 1907, 727–28.
80. Harper, *History of Woman Suffrage*, 6:523–24.
81. "To Meet Urgent Demand," *Guthrie Daily Leader*, November 6, 1907, 8; Scales and Goble, *Oklahoma Politics*, 36.
82. "Governor Jim Crow," *Daily Ardmoreite*, July 28, 1909, 1.
83. Scales and Goble, *Oklahoma Politics*, 27.
84. Ibid., 27, 30–31.
85. Ibid., 179.
86. Goble, *Progressive Oklahoma*, 181, 182.
87. McCulley, *Banks and Politics*, 136; T Robb, *Guaranty of Bank Deposits*, 23; and La Forte, *Leaders of Reform*, 123–26. See also Harlow and Gibson, *Harlow's Oklahoma History*, 266.
88. Musslewhite and Crawford, *One Woman's Political Journey*, 57–59, 95–96.
89. "The Week," *The Outlook*, October 3, 1908, 236.
90. Bryant, *Alfalfa Bill Murray*, 81.
91. See generally Musslewhite and Crawford, *One Woman's Political Journey*.
92. Harlow and Gibson, *Harlow's Oklahoma History*, 273.

8

THE UPPER SOUTH

Not So Southern, a Succession of Progressive Governors

The politics of the Upper South states—North Carolina, Kentucky, West Virginia, Maryland, Virginia, and Tennessee—were, in some respects, less "southern" than elsewhere in the South. Race was still important but, with a few exceptions, more subtle. We also often find more party competition, with Republicans doing relatively well and enjoying breakthroughs in the 1890s, an era of Republican rule in West Virginia and, under exceptional conditions, a Republican breakthrough in Tennessee. Also, while the Upper South had its share of Progressive governors, fewer of them stand out on their own because reform commonly took place through a prolonged effort that spanned several chief executives and several administrations.

The following account includes a couple of political murders and finds several governors caught up in difficult and explosive situations: Governor Russell of North Carolina confronted by mob violence, Governor Stanley of Kentucky standing up against a lynching, and several West Virginia governors trying to cope with or avert labor violence. Along with this we find "New South" education governors in North Carolina and Virginia. In Maryland and Virginia we come across governors considered Progressives largely because they were antimachine rather than because of what they stood for or were able to accomplish or even because they were more Progressive and productive than the machine candidates they opposed. In Tennessee we find Democratic governor Patterson done in by the prohibition issue and how he used his pardoning power, and Republican governor Hopper benefiting from all this but trying to survive being a Republican in a Democratic state and facing the opposition of a big-city boss.

NORTH CAROLINA: RUSSELL, AYCOCK, AND MODERATE REFORMERS

North Carolina has the distinction of being the southern state in which the Populists and Republicans, working together on biracial fusion tickets, had their greatest success. In 1894 a highly fragile coalition of the two parties, drawing support from blacks and poor white farmers, captured several state and local offices. They took control of the state legislature in 1894. In 1896 they not only held on to the legislature but also won the governorship behind Daniel Lindsay Russell.

Russell was born on a plantation near Wilmington, the son of a wealthy North Carolina planter. He joined the Confederate Army but withdrew after quarreling with his superiors. Like his father, he was a Union sympathizer and after the Civil War became one of the few affiliated with the planter class to join the Republican Party. He went on to serve in the state legislature, study law, accept an appointment as a Superior Court judge, and get elected to Congress as a fusion candidate of the Republican and Greenback Parties. After this he helped bring Republicans and Populists together in the coalition that offered an alternative to Democratic Bourbon rule in the state and won election as governor in 1896.

Russell was the first Republican to be elected to that office since Reconstruction ended in 1877. Republicans and Populists, acting in an alliance, also took control of the legislature. The Russell administration proceeded to push for reforms to increase the regulation of corporations, especially the railroads, and the level of educational benefits. When it came to the promotion of black participation in the political process, Russell saw the need to be cautious and conservative, feeling that whites would not accept too much. Still, the fusionists acted to expand the voting rights of black as well as white men. They passed laws restoring the right to vote for local officials, prohibiting employers from threatening or firing employees for political reasons, and furthering the goal of an honest count. Election reform increased black voting by close to 30 percent.[1]

The last two years of his administration, however, were filled with frustration. His political base weakened because the conservative Republicans in the legislature would have nothing to do with his attempts to rein in the railroads and his Populist allies in the legislature found it difficult to agree with each other on much of anything. Russell himself had his limitations. As his biographers noted: "Russell was not quite a Populist, but then he was not quite a Republican either. Too much the nonconformist and maverick, Russell plotted his own independent course in the face of Republican censure and Populist suspicions as to his actual motives."[2]

To make everything even worse, the state was rocked by racial conflict. Aiming to regain power in the legislature and other offices, Democratic Party leaders conducted a vicious campaign of fear and white supremacy in 1898. Toward the end of their campaign they went beyond editorials and speeches to threaten violence against blacks, who usually voted Republican, to keep them away from the polls. Large groups of white men wearing red shirts rode through black neighborhoods openly brandishing weapons and issuing the warning against voting. Ben Tillman from South Carolina, who had developed the "Red Shirt" strategy (see chapter 6), appeared at several rallies being staged by North Carolina Democrats during this period.

Two days after the 1898 election the white supremacy campaign led to a race riot, massacre, and coup d'état in the city of Wilmington.[3]

Governor Russell attempted to stem the mounting violence. He issued a proclamation on October 26 calling for an end to unlawful conduct and worked behind the scene with Democratic businessmen to ease the tension. He even went along with the takeover of Wilmington's city government by white supremacists, hoping this would bring peace. At one point he ordered out the state militia, but this was largely ineffective and even counterproductive, as many of the guardsmen and other law enforcement officials in the area sided with the rioters and joined in with them. Meanwhile, the 1898 Red Shirt campaign had put the Democrats back in control of the state legislature, where in 1899 they proceeded to adopt a new constitution over Russell's objections and without securing voter approval. The document disfranchised most blacks and many poor whites for decades to come. Republicans did not elect another governor until 1973.

Democrats, however, did see the need to become more reform-minded in some areas and adopted the views of the Republicans and Populists in regard to business regulation and the funding of education. They regained the office of governor in 1900 with Charles Aycock, who became known as his state's "Education Governor." He did, indeed, give strong support to public schools. As governor he often pardoned prisoners for humanitarian reasons and did what he could to prevent lynching but was often unsuccessful in doing so. Eleven people were lynched while he was governor.[4]

Like several other governors in the South, Aycock had been a Cleveland Democrat. Like others, too, he was a believer in white supremacy. He felt that Russell had failed "because he had behind him the negroes of the State and not the white men."[5] Aycock played a prominent role in the white supremacist campaigns in 1898 and 1900 and in the framing of a constitutional amendment to disfranchise black voters. He argued that eliminating black voters was the first step on the road to progress, be it better schools, clean government, or more effective regulation of big business. Aycock, described as "a simple, unassuming figure," was politically tied to the business-friendly and powerful machine of US senator Furnifold M.

Simmons, a white supremacist who had managed Aycock's 1900 campaign and who ran the state from Washington, keeping up on developments in the state through political lieutenants.⁶

Four relatively Progressive governors followed Aycock. One of these was Robert Glenn, an anti-organization candidate who served from 1905 to 1909. Glenn had been in the state legislature just prior to securing the Democratic gubernatorial nomination in 1904 and, as governor, led a prohibition effort that culminated in 1908 with a statewide ban. Though once employed by the Southern Railway, he supported a measure reducing passenger rates and stood behind it in defiance of a federal court decision. On the issue of corporate control he took the position that while the state should do all it could to encourage corporations, it should also do all it could to break up combinations and agreements that destroy competition. Turning to the legislature, he urged action on a variety of Progressive measures in the party platform so that "we may go before the people of the state and say we have kept faith"; the legislature generally responded in a positive fashion.⁷ Though a white supremacist, he took forceful action against those involved in a 1906 lynching of five black men accused of murdering a white family in Salisbury and put county sheriffs and the state militia on guard to prevent further lynching.⁸

It took sixty-one ballots at the state party convention for former US House member William Kitchin, a Progressive, to defeat a candidate of the Simmons machine for the Democratic Party nominee for governor in 1908. Running on an antitrust platform, pledging to take down the tobacco trusts and railroad combines, he sailed through the general election. His administration, lasting from 1909 to 1913, brought increases in public health as well as education spending, labor protections, and, though not to the extent he had recommended, a strengthened antitrust law. His opponents had condemned him during the gubernatorial campaign as a wild-eyed radical who would bring disaster to the state. After his years in office they condemned him for not having lived up to his campaign promises and, in effect, doing nothing. His supporters contended that both charges were false—he was never an extremists and he accomplished much of a reasonable Progressive nature.⁹ Kitchin supported white supremacy, as did his successor, Locke Craig, who as a state legislator had helped craft the constitutional amendment that disfranchised blacks. Unlike Kitchin, Craig was tied to the Simmons machine. Yet the Simmons machine was not altogether opposed to change, and reform did as well as if not better under Craig than it did under Kitchin. Under Craig came educational improvements, factory inspection, and the direct primary.¹⁰

The last of the four governors, Democrat Thomas Bickett, won the office in 1916. Bickett, a lawyer with a degree from the University of North Carolina, started his political career as a member of the statehouse, where his efforts led to the construction of a facility to care for the mentally handicapped. He went on to serve two terms as attorney general. As governor he placed emphasis on improving schools, reforming the penal system, modernizing the tax system toward a more equitable distribution of the tax burden, increased spending on charitable institutions, and a variety of measures to improve the quality of life in rural areas. Bickett had considerable success with the legislature—during his term it approved forty of the forty-eight proposals he made.[11] One biographer concluded: "Bickett's oft-expressed concern for the lot of the oppressed and disadvantaged among the state's population, the tenant farmers, blacks, and prison inmates, marked him as a man of humane disposition."[12] On the other hand, this deeply religious man discouraged blacks from becoming active in politics and favored Jim Crow laws, telling a black audience: "It is not for your good, the good of your people or the good of mine, that they should ride in the same coaches. I am opposed to that."[13]

By the end of his term, though, North Carolina was well on its way toward developing its reputation as the South's most Progressive state—which would be furthered by a succession of governors in the 1920s.

KENTUCKY: FROM BRADLEY AND GOEBEL TO STANLEY

Kentucky, like North Carolina, had a Republican governor in the late 1890s who was a strong supporter of blacks. The governor, William O'Connell Bradley, had taken advantage of a split among Democrats over the silver issue to become the first Republican governor in the state following his election in 1895, when he edged out the Democratic candidate with 48.3 percent of the vote—a third candidate, a Populist candidate, also drew a few thousand votes. Bradley benefited from a division among Democrats between the conservative Bourbons and those who wanted to go off in the direction of a "New South."[14]

As governor Bradley tried to work with a house controlled by Republicans and a senate controlled by the Democrats. The two houses had a very difficult time agreeing on anything. Here, as in several other states of the period, the legislature spent most of its time in a fierce battle over who should be sent to the US Senate. The legislature was deadlocked. After 112 ballots, tempers began to flare, and Bradley called the state militia into the capitol at Frankfort and declared martial law to maintain order. Bradley himself spent considerable time maneuvering for the position.[15]

Bradley gave state jobs to many blacks, including some important positions, and in a special session of the legislature in 1897 secured the adoption of an anti-lynching law. He failed, however, to get legislative support for the repeal of the state's "Separate Coach Law," requiring the separation of blacks and whites on trains and streetcars. Most of his other proposals also went nowhere.

Bradley decided not to run for reelection. Democrat William Goebel was among those who sought to replace him as governor in 1899. Goebel had championed antirailroad and pro-labor policies as a member of the state senate while Bradley was governor. His support of these causes and free silver prompted a break with many leaders of the Democratic Party. Touring the state in 1899, accompanied for several weeks by the highly popular William Jennings Bryan, and enjoying the support of several Populist leaders, Goebel took on the Democratic Party establishment, which was closely aligned with the Louisville and Nashville Railroad. He called for greater railroad and corporate control through regulatory and antitrust action and more labor protection. With the farmers in mind, he also targeted the monopolistic American Tobacco Company.

After a bitter, hotly contested election in 1899 Goebel was declared the winner by a vote of the legislature, but an assassin shot him the day before he was sworn in as governor as he was walking to the state capitol; he died three days later. Among those indicted for their involvement in the murder of Goebel was Caleb Powers, the secretary of state—the shots that killed Goebel were thought to have been fired from a window in the secretary's office. Powers served nearly eight years in prison for his complicity in the assassination before being pardoned. He went on to be elected to Congress.

Historian C. Vann Woodward once offered the following evaluation of Goebel: "A man of remorseless determination, Goebel fought ruthlessly against equally ruthless foes and inspired hatred as well as devotion."[16] Goebel's critics have seen him as "a cold, power-hungry man who catered to the masses publicly, while behaving like a dictator privately."[17] Some also have wondered if he was a fake reformer. Illinois governor John Altgeld thought so. He warned Bryan that Goebel was actually very close to the corporations and the gold men that the two of them were fighting and urged him not to endorse Goebel's candidacy.[18] Historians, however, generally have concurred with the more positive view that Goebel should be viewed as "a rare reformer in a conservative state, a caring man who dared attack the old guard and the old ways."[19]

The reform movement lost its momentum with Goebel's death and did not get cranked up again until Democrat James B. McCreary won the gubernatorial office in 1911. McCreary, who had first been elected governor in 1875, was seventy-three in 1911 but very much caught up in the Progressive wave. The Democratic platform on which he ran contained several proposals made by Goebel twelve years earlier. McCreary, however, was only modestly successful in getting reform measures through the legislature.[20] Among those that made it were a state-funded direct primary system (the Democratic Party had been financing its own primaries) and a state tax commission that proceeded to raise corporate taxes.[21]

The floodgates of reform finally opened following the election of Democrat A. O. Stanley in 1915. Stanley, the son of a Kentucky preacher, had been a teacher and a lawyer and had served six terms in Congress representing a district in Western Kentucky prior to being elected governor. In Congress he gained recognition as a trust-buster, focusing on giant corporations, including the American Tobacco Company, whose practices were of particular concern to tobacco growers in his district, and J. P. Morgan's US Steel. He lost in his bid for the US Senate in 1914. Hoping to keep his career alive and strengthen his position for another shot at the Senate, he decided to run for governor the following year. He energetically stumped the state and turned back two primary challengers, using the question of the local option on liquor as an issue, and nosed out Republican Edwin Morrow by 487 votes, Morrow later became governor. In 1919 Stanley resigned the governorship to fill a vacancy in the US Senate, fulfilling a longtime ambition.[22]

Coming into office, Stanley sent a brief message to the legislature, stressing the need to keep expenditures as low as possible but to also to implement the several reforms recommended in the party's platform.[23] Working with a Democratic majority in both legislative chambers, he had considerable success in getting his legislative program adopted. This included antitrust legislation, a worker's compensation law, a corrupt-practices act, anti-lobbying legislation, and tax reform in the interest of the state's farmers. Stanley is regarded by one scholar as having "established the best record of any Kentucky governor of the period for progressive legislation."[24]

Showing courage, in 1917 he vetoed a popular wartime measure that banned the teaching of German in schools. In January 1917 he also showed considerable courage and oratorical skill in facing down an angry mob and thereby preventing the lynching of a black prisoner, a judge and public prosecutor in the town of Murray, by the sheer force of his personality. Standing in front of the mob, by himself and without a weapon or a bodyguard, the governor said: "I have come here to plead with you to allow the law to take its orderly course, and to declare that I am here to uphold the law and to protect this court with my own body if necessary."[25] Stanley also stood as an opponent of prohibition and the Ku Klux Klan and as a supporter of women's rights.

WEST VIRGINIA: THE REPUBLICAN COMBINATION, LABOR PROBLEMS

In West Virginia Progressive reform unfolded slowly over a sixteen-year period, 1901–17, in which a series of Republican governors held office for four-year terms. Included among the reforms made were increased taxes on corporations, a primary system, worker's compensation, improved mine safety, strong public health laws, and woman suffrage. The first of the Republican governors was Albert B. White, who took office in 1901. He was followed by William O. Dawson in 1905, William Glasscock in 1909, and Harry D. Hatfield in 1913.

Over much of this period reformers had the good fortune to have an easy boss in US senator Stephen Elkins, who died in 1911. His machine had considerable influence in the West Virginia Republican Party, but he either did not get in the way or was willing to compromise and work out agreements when it came to change. As historian Nicholas C. Burckel noted, Elkins "did not seek progressive gubernatorial candidates, but both Dawson and Glasscock had served as his lawyers before becoming governor and neither aired their differences in public. In that kind of atmosphere compromise came more easily since neither person lost face in a public battle of wills."[26]

White initiated the reform drive. The former newspaper owner and editor had been a campaign manager for Elkins. As governor he led an effort that, in spite of industry opposition, gave birth to a state tax commission. The commission proceeded to develop plans to shift more of the tax burden to corporations. White was also supportive of rail regulation, election reform, environmental measures, and pure food and drug protections. Dawson had been a schoolteacher, editor-owner of a weekly newspaper, state legislator, state party organizer, and the secretary of state. As a state legislator he had been a strong advocate of railroad rate regulation and taxation. Coming into office, he proposed a wide variety of Progressive reforms but faced conservative-business opponents in both parties, and only a few made it through. Many problems were left unaddressed. One of these, as the governor made clear in a 1906 letter to the state senate, was that a railway trust, the Pennsylvania Railway Company, in effect controlled all the trunk lines in the state. The governor wrote: "West Virginia today is in the grasp of a railroad trust which practically says what part of the state shall be developed, how much coal shall be shipped out of the state, to what points or ports it shall be shipped and when it shall be shipped. Of course it makes its own rates and we are helpless."[27]

Glasscock had a background as a school superintendent, circuit court clerk, chair of a state Republican committee, and an attorney for Senator Elkins. He was an ardent Progressive when it came to business taxation and regulation, election reform, lobbying restrictions, environmental protection, and labor reforms such as worker's compensation.[28] However, he did no favor for himself in cultivating labor support during labor unrest in the Paint and Cabin Creek coal-mining areas by declaring martial law, sending in 1,200 militia men to put down strike activity, and allowing the militia officers to come to the aid of coal operators in organizing mine guards and openly align themselves with the operators.[29] In national Republican politics Glasscock moved from his support of Taft in 1908 to urging Roosevelt to run against Taft in 1912, but refused to bolt the 1912 Republican convention with others who supported Roosevelt and would not endorse the Bull Moose Party in West Virginia out of fear that it would damage Republicans' chances of carrying the state.[30]

Harry D. Hatfield, who followed Glasscock as governor, was related to the Hatfield clan of the famous Hatfield-McCoy feud. He missed much of the action, being in college while the feud was underway. Graduating college, he went on to receive medical training in what is now the University of Louisville and New York University and to practice medicine as a coal-camp physician for a West Virginia coal company. Appalled by the health conditions he found while on this job, he worked with a state legislator to raise funds for three new miners' hospitals.

In 1908 he won a seat as a Republican in the state senate where he pushed for Progressive reforms, including a public utilities commission and a worker's compensation law. Drawing on his background in medicine and his experience as a practitioner in southern coal fields, he also proposed several health protection measures, though he was not very successful in securing the support of his colleagues for his proposals. In the 1910 general election voters created havoc by putting an even number of Democrats and Republicans in the state senate. After a protracted struggle for control of the body, one in which several Republican legislators hid out in Governor Glasscock's office and later fled to Cincinnati to prevent a voting quorum, Hatfield was settled upon as a compromise candidate and was elected president of that body in 1911.[31]

In 1912 Hatfield decided to make a run for the office of governor. Glasscock, in ill health and frustrated by the ongoing coal mining strike, was more than willing to leave office and felt Hatfield would be a good pick for the job because of his ties with the miners and operators in the strike area. Showing his Progressive inclinations, Hatfield broke with William Howard Taft, with whom he had had a friendship, and supported Theodore Roosevelt for the presidency. He won the office of governor at the age of thirty-seven on a highly Progressive platform that called for a long list of political and economic reforms, featuring measures such as worker's compensation and putting restrictions on the use of private mine guards, which were design to appeal to labor. He vowed to end the violent Paint and Cabin Creek labor war involving the right of miners to join the United Mine Workers union.[32]

One day after his inauguration he visited the strike area, using his medical skills to treat wounded miners. Legendary labor activist Mary Harris "Mother" Jones and 125 other union leaders and protestors had been arrested and imprisoned in a bullpen (detention cell) awaiting trial in a military court. They hoped that Hatfield would come to their rescue. Many of the prisoners were released, but in an effort to put pressure on the union to cooperate in ending the strike, the governor pushed to have the strike leaders, including Jones, put on trial in the military court, despite cries that it was unconstitutional to try civilians in such courts during peacetime. Hatfield abandoned the middle ground in the dispute and chose to put pressure on the weaker contenders—those on the side of the labor unions.[33]

Jones and several other strike leaders were tried, convicted, and sentenced to prison terms by military tribunals, but Hatfield, under considerable pressure, later pardoned them. Meanwhile, he proceeded to create a board of arbitration with himself at its head, which essentially ended the strike—the striking miners were forced into choosing his terms, many of which improved working conditions, or face deportation out of the state.

Hatfield was also successful during his term in securing the passage of a long list of proposals, many of which went back to Governor White's time in office. The list included measures relating to public utility regulation, mine inspection, the use of "company thugs" by coal companies, woman suffrage, corrupt practices, the direct election of US senators, and worker's compensation. Passage of the inspection legislation was facilitated by a mine explosion killing 180 miners in Eccles, West Virginia. The governorship went to conservative Democrat John J. Cornwell in 1916, in large part because corporate leaders had turned against Hatfield due to his reform efforts.

THE MARYLAND COMBINATION, OVERCOMING, SURPRISING THE BOSSES

Another combination of governors dominated reform activity in Maryland, though unlike in West Virginia, they were Democrats. From 1900 to 1908 John Walter Smith, Edwin Warfield, and Austin L. Crothers pushed for an assortment of reforms, sometimes finding themselves locked in combat with Democratic Party bosses, especially US senator Arthur Pue Gorman and, working with him, Baltimore boss Isaac Freeman Rasin, who also was influential on the state level through his control of the city's delegates in the state legislature.[34]

Smith, a businessman, bank president, and former state legislator, was serving in Congress when Democrats nominated him for governor in 1899. He went on to defeat incumbent Republican Lloyd Lowndes with 51 percent of the vote, compared to 46 percent for Lowndes, who had been elected four years earlier representing a biracial coalition. Some were highly skeptical that Smith, an Eastern Shore lieutenant of Pue Gorman, was going to deliver on his campaign promise to provide good government. But Smith surprised them and stood by his promises.[35] Though allied with Gorman, he sought and secured reforms in the areas of health care, education, and labor protection.

Warfield—a banker, newspaper editor, and gentleman farmer—made his first bid for governor in 1899, the year Smith emerged the winner, but was opposed by Gorman and Rasin, who led the Baltimore party organization. Both bosses continued to oppose him in 1903, but Warfield was better organized and was able to secure the nomination.[36] The major event in Warfield's term was his opposition to a proposed amendment to the state constitution supported by Senator Gorman, known as the "Poe Amendment," which would have taken the vote away from black men. Gorman had once lost his seat in the US Senate when Republicans captured the state senate with the crucial help of black voters. He was determined to prevent this from ever happening again through the adoption of a constitutional amendment that would disfranchise blacks.[37]

Gorman invited several southern governors, including Vardaman of Mississippi, to tour the state on behalf of this amendment. This "invasion of the state," however, apparently prompted considerable protest.[38]

Warfield, while Progressive in some respects, was no supporter of African American rights. In March 1904, for example, he signed on to Jim Crow bills bringing segregated travel on trains and streamboats.[39] He was also among those who favored the elimination of the black vote to, as he and others explained it, purify the election system, the claim being that having black voters brought corruption. Warfield felt, however, that the Poe Amendment went too far and was so vaguely worded that it also threatened the voting rights of many whites. His opposition provoked the wrath of Gorman's party organization, but it helped bring the amendment's defeat at the polls by a majority of some 30,000 votes.[40]

Warfield gained fame and something of a reputation as a reformer, not so much because he favored Progressive policies (though he did stand for primary nominations for all state offices and the US Senate) or what he accomplished as governor but because he was willing to stand up to the party bosses. As the editor of a Maryland paper put it:

> As Governor of the State, Mr. Warfield will be remembered not so much for concrete things—though he accomplished not a little—as for his brave defiance of dictation, his honest and unswerving devotion to public interests, his demonstration of the fact that a Marylander need not beg the consent of anyone to serve his State, if he have any real Maryland manhood in him. He reinvested the office of Governor with the dignity and independence which belonged to it in the old days. He converted it from the satrapy of a powerful machine into an unfettered agency of the people, a public trust responsible only to the public. For this, had he done nothing else, he would richly deserve to be held in grateful memory. He was one of our "pioneers" in this as in business and his vision, faith, and courage still remain as moral guidons in struggles for cleaner and freer government.[41]

In 1907 Democrat Party affairs were quite fluid because the party was without leadership—both party bosses Gorman and Rasin had passed away.[42] With these bosses gone, reform-minded Democrats were able to make an impact on the state platform, inserting a call for a corrupt-practices act—a reform that became highly salient because of the disclosure of bribery and vote-buying irregularities in the 1906 election—along with other Progressive measures. The party nominated Austin Crothers for governor. Crothers, a party leader in a small rural county, was relatively unknown on the state level. Initially he looked like a safe, conservative candidate from the county courthouse clique. He, however, surprised everyone by providing a Progressive administration.[43] Indeed, he was credited with accomplishing more in terms of Progressive legislation than any previous governor.[44]

Crothers was able to secure the adoption of a corrupt-practices act, something Lowndes had proposed in 1898. Under his watch the state also adopted a statewide direct primary, something that Warfield had proposed in 1906 and had been in the Democratic Party platform in 1907—even though rural politicians feared this would give too much influence to Baltimore over nominations.[45]

Crothers further successfully worked for the creation of a public service commission to regulate public utilities and, in the interest of development, steered a considerable amount of money into road building. On the other hand, he lost out in a determined effort to remove some Baltimore commissioners whom he felt were guilty of improper conduct. The members simply refused to be ousted, and the courts eventually supported their position.

Like Warfield, he favored taking the vote away from "illiterate and irresponsible" black men, but he opposed a proposed constitutional amendment that would have disfranchised black voters. He felt the measure was unconstitutional, and the voters sided with his position.[46] On a broader political level Crothers hoped to steer his party away from reliance on the race issue by becoming a party of reform, giving the voters what they wanted and needed. In an interview in 1908 he described himself as a party man who wanted what was best for the Democratic Party. He felt the party could possibly continue to draw upon the race issue to keep it in control and keep Maryland a one-party Democratic state, but he wanted "to get the party away from a reliance on this issue" and "make the party stand for something so wholesome clean and good that we can win without this issue." He praised adoption of the corrupt-practices act; he felt it was good not only for the state but for strengthening public confidence in the political system and the Democratic Party and called for more reform along the same line. He wanted his party "to place itself squarely back of the reforms and measures which the State needs and which the public has a right to expect." This, he argued, would bring success, keeping it in control for many years without relying on race.[47]

VIRGINIA: MONTAGUE, SWANSON, AND THE MACHINE

Like several southern states for a time, white Populists and black Republicans in Virginia were joined in coalition bent on reform. In Virginia, though, this movement never took root statewide and by the mid-1890s had fallen apart. Much of what change occurred represented the impact of mild white middle-class reform efforts in the state that began to develop in the early 1900s and shifted the direction of the Democratic Party.[48] Progressives took considerable delight in 1901 when Andrew Jackson Montague, running for governor as an independent Democrat, defeated Congressman Claude Swanson, a candidate backed by a political machine headed by US senator Thomas Staples Martin in the Democratic primary and went on to win the general election over his Republican opponent.

Montague, a lawyer, had worked on Cleveland's presidential campaign in 1892 and was rewarded afterward with an appointment as a US attorney in Virginia. He served in that capacity from 1893 to 1898, when voters made him the state's attorney general. At that time he began to identify as a Progressive, though this included, in his view, the need to eliminate blacks from the electorate. Montague was especially concerned about the corrupting influence of railroads in state politics. Martin, he charged, had won his senate seat by using railroad money to purchase the necessary votes in the legislature. He further angered Martin by calling for the direct election of US senators, though the idea had little support.

During the gubernatorial campaign against Swanson, Montague offered a broad-ranging Progressive platform but made the political control and corruption of the Martin organization the key issues. It had long been the custom in state politics to refrain from preconvention campaigning. Montague, however, decided to break this tradition and tour the state in search of votes, using his considerable oratorical skills to drum up public and delegate support at the convention. He wound up with nearly 60 percent of the vote.[49]

Much like Warfield of Maryland, Montague achieved the status of his state's most famous Progressive governor by taking on machine rule and corrupt politics in his campaign for governor rather than for what he did in terms of policy as governor. Overall, his greatest achievement may have been in promoting political dissent and, with this, pushing the Martin machine toward Progressivism in an effort to stem his appeal.[50] In 1901 there were few differences in the basic philosophical and policy views of Montague and Swanson, Martin's candidate for governor.[51] Nor did the opponents differ in their acceptance of white supremacy, the notion that the "best people" should rule, and the principle of states' rights.[52]

Montague, one historian has written, was "well known for his scholarly bent and kindly demeanor" and as "more of a patrician than a populist."[53] Another historian has noted that he was "sincere, idealistic, calm, and reserved. In effect, he resembled a statesman of the old school, a gentleman."[54] As the chief executive Montague spent most of his time talking about problems in the educational system but gave little attention to working with the legislature on specific measures. He had a restricted view of the role of the governor when it came to legislation. He once remarked: "My position as governor prevents my interceding with members of the legislature in behalf of any measure . . . I do not think I should undertake to favor in advance bills which are likely to come before me for approval or disapproval."[55] Beyond this, he appeared reluctant by temperament to get into the rough-and-tumble of legislative politics.

He may also have shied away because he faced strong opposition in the legislature. Most of the few requests he made were turned down. A new state constitution adopted in 1902, which he supported, included a variety of standard Progressive reforms, such as a commission to regulate railroads and a primary requirement for candidates to the US Senate. It also, however, included "settlement" provisions that all but eliminated the black vote through poll taxes and a literacy test and required segregation in public schools.

In 1905 Montague lost a primary challenge to Martin for Martin's seat in the US Senate. Bowing to popular sentiment and aiming to take away an issue from Montague, Martin had gotten the party convention to adopt a primary system for this and other offices. He also moved to drain support away from his opponent by becoming a strong supporter of spending more on roads and schools. Following his defeat, there was little more for Montague to do as governor except to turn power over to his political opponent, Claude Swanson, who won the office in 1905 and, ironically, went on to expand on Montague's Progressive agenda.

In 1905 Swanson became the first gubernatorial candidate to get the Democratic Party nomination through the primary process. The primary system worked to his advantage. He had been unable to get the nomination through the convention system in 1901, but the primary gave him the opportunity to use the campaigning skills he had developed in running for Congress.[56] Swanson went on to win the office in the general election. With the backing of regular Democrats, he was far more successful than Montague with the legislature. He worked with great success to lower railroad rates, increase corporate taxes, put more money into education and road building, and generally promote the cause of Progressive reform. His biographer, Henry Ferrell, gives Swanson considerable credit for his political and administrative skills and for his understanding of legislative folkways, which helped enable him to get approval of his policies. To Ferrell, Swanson "conducted one of the most effective terms of executive leadership in the history of the commonwealth."[57] Observers too gave him high marks on his stand against lynching.[58] Swanson went on serve in the US Senate from 1910 to 1933.

From 1900 to 1910 the state had followed a path of reform consistent with the "New South" objectives centering on upgrades in education and transportation. Over the next decade a trio of governors continued a mild path of Progressivism, bringing some tax reform, but the primary issue became prohibition. Liquor control was central to the career of William Mann, another Progressive aligned with the Martin machine who won election as governor in 1909. As a member of the state legislature he had led in the adoption of legislation that closed down saloons in many of the state's counties. As governor he pushed for statewide prohibition, but his effort to put a proposal of this nature on the ballot failed in the senate. After an intense struggle, Virginia finally went dry in 1916. In 1917 voters put Progressive-minded Westmoreland Davis in the governor's office—someone who had no love for the party organization. With Davis came an emphasis on improved management, including an executive budgeting system, and various reforms in regard to prison management and labor protection.

TENNESSEE: LIQUOR, PARDONS, FUSION, AND MR. CRUMP

Democrat Malcolm Patterson, born in Alabama, moved to Tennessee as a child, became a lawyer in Memphis, got elected to Congress, and won election as governor in 1906 and 1908. He pushed for improved education, fought off vigilante groups, and helped bring about reforms, including food and drug regulations and bans on public executions and horse-race gambling. He also became one of the state's most controversial governors whose career was wrapped up in the prohibition issue and disputes over his use of the pardoning power.

In his 1908 campaign for reelection, Patterson ran as an opponent of statewide prohibition. He defeated a challenge for the Democratic nomination by Edward Carmack, a newspaper editor and former US senator who had the backing of the pro-prohibition Anti-Saloon League. Carmack called for a statewide ban on the sale of liquor while Patterson stood for exempting cites from the ban. On this issue Patterson had the full-hearted support of Edward Crump, Democratic Party boss in Memphis who, a few years later, became its mayor.[59]

Patterson got the vote of just over half of the delegates to the state convention to win the nomination and went on to defeat his Republican opponent in the general election with 54 percent of the vote.

Following the election one of Patterson's advisors, Duncan Cooper, and his son were convicted of murdering Carmack. The fatal shot was fired by the son after the two encountered Carmack on the street. Carmack had recently written an article attacking the father. In 1910 Patterson pardoned Duncan Cooper, provoking a widespread outrage. Observers had frequently accused Patterson of using the pardoning power to help out his political allies. Now he had issued a pardon to one of his top advisors who had been convicted of murdering a longtime political opponent. One result of this action was legislation that restricted the ability of governors to issue pardons. The murder of Carmack also helped to prompt the legislature into passing two prohibition measures in 1909—one prohibiting the sale of liquor within four miles of any schoolhouse in the state and another prohibiting the manufacture of liquor in the state. Patterson vetoed them both, but his vetoes were overridden by the legislature.

With the Democratic Party divided over the issue of prohibition, Republican Ben Hooper, an opponent of the liquor interests, was able to attract enough like-minded Democrats on this issue to secure election as governor in 1910 and again in 1912. He was one of the few Republicans to hold that office since the end of Reconstruction.[60] Hooper, a Tennessee native, born out of wedlock, moved around as boy from his mother's custody to an orphanage to his father's custody.

He earned a law degree and started his political career by being elected to the Tennessee House of Representatives in 1893, where he spent several years. In 1910 he was serving in Tennessee as an assistant attorney general when Republican leaders encouraged him to run for governor.

Hooper got much of his program through legislative sessions of 1911 and 1913, though only after some bitter fights. Accomplishments in 1911 included laws limiting child labor and requiring the direct payment of wages to the women who earned them (rather than to someone else, such as their husbands) as well as pure food and drug legislation. In his second term came mandatory school attendance, banking inspection, indeterminate sentencing, and a change from hanging to electrocution for executions. His two years in office also brought laws and new departments to deal with banking, workplace, public utilities, mining, and insurance regulations.

At various times during his administration Hooper had the backing of an alliance that included not only Republicans and Independents (pro-prohibition Democrats) but Boss Crump. Crump, however, dropped out soon after the 1912 election and returned to the regular (anti-prohibition) Democrats because of his differences with Hooper over the enforcement of the prohibition laws, a cause Hooper coupled with the need to fight corruption in city politics.[61] Hooper had not tried to hide anything. During the 1912 campaign he had made prohibition his major talking point. With Boss Crump in mind, he declared: "When I am elected governor... I will with the help of an honest legislature and a good God, clean out every saloon and every low-down dive in Memphis."[62]

To strengthen the fight against Crump and others who wanted to keep cities open to liquor, even though the state had officially gone dry in 1909, Hooper signed the "Jug Bill," banning the shipment of liquor within the state, and a "Nuisance Bill," making it easier for citizens to shut down saloons and gambling houses in their communities. In his drive against corruption Hooper also sought to eliminate free railroad passes. He later noted: "At that time, practically all legislators and all judges in the state used railroad passes. It was a rather anomalous situation, to use a very mild term, for a judge to sit on the trial of a damage suit against a railroad, with his pockets full of railroad passes."[63]

While he had several legislative successes, Hooper, in looking back, complained about how difficult it was trying to get anything meaningful out of the legislature. Tension was especially pronounced after Crump withdrew his support in 1913. The Democratic majority in the legislature not only rejected his proposals but came after him, attempting to take away his power to make appointments and launching investigations directed at his administration.[64]

Partly because of the difficulty of dealing with the legislature, Hooper spent considerable time on administrative matters, hoping to make significant changes in the agencies and institutions that he supervised.[65] Prison reform was high among his priorities. Hooper subscribed to Progressive ideas about how to treat prisoners. He felt Tennessee was "woefully backward in penology."[66] Hooper frequently visited the state prison and received considerable national attention for spending two nights there to learn about conditions and, in response to charges that he had been too generous in granting pardons, to collect information on cases worthy of this action.[67]

Hooper during this period is somewhat of an enigma when it comes to his political philosophy. Many in the South may well have thought of him as a moderate Progressive, even though, after being heavily pressured by both Roosevelt and Taft, he decided to go with Taft in 1912, making an enemy out of Roosevelt.[68] Unfazed by all of this, Republicans adopted a 1914 resolution at a Republican Party convention that praised Hooper as "one of the most firm and progressive governors that Tennessee has ever had."[69]

Hopper's problem in 1914 was that the Democrats had managed to unite on a platform calling for statewide prohibition. No longer able to draw Democratic support on this issue, Hooper lost to the Democratic candidate for governor, Thomas Clark Rye. Hooper blamed his loss in 1914 on voter fraud in Shelby County under the direction of his political enemy, E. H. Crump. About Crump it was said: "His personal honesty was unquestioned; he would not steal a nickel, just an election."[70] Hooper lost a bid for the US Senate in 1916.

Rye, a local public attorney, ran on a platform defending prohibition and opposing its repeal. He served two terms, from 1915 to 1919. Rye, like Hooper, came after Crump for his continued resistance to prohibition. Responding to Rye's request, the legislature passed the "Ouster Law," which, aimed at Crump, gave the courts greater power to remove incompetent or corrupt public officials or those who were unwilling to enforce state laws. Crump resigned as mayor of Memphis just ahead of court action to have him ousted.[71] Under Rye, the state also moved from the convention system to a primary system for nominating candidates for state office.

In a notable and well-received speech to members of the National Negro Business League in 1917 Rye remarked: "I have tried and am determined to be the governor of all the people . . . regardless of race, creed, or other affiliation."[72]

NOTES

1. Beckel, *Radical Reform*, 178–80.
2. Crow and Durden, *Maverick Republican*, 119.
3. Southern, *Malignant Heritage*, 11.
4. Orr, *Charles Brantley Aycock*, 272–78.
5. Crow and Durden, *Maverick Republican*, 150, quoting the *Charlotte Observer*, April 12, 1900.
6. Kirby, *Darkness at the Dawning*, 14–15, 36, 40; Woodward, *Origins of the New South*, 376.
7. "The N.C. Legislature," *Caucasian*, March 7, 1907, 1.

8. Hill, "Robert Brodnax Glenn"; Woodward, *Origins of the New South*, 381–82.
9. Hunter, "Governor Kitchin"; Hill, "William Walton Kitchen."
10. Kirby, *Darkness at the Dawning*, 43.
11. Hill, "Thomas Walter Bickett."
12. Magruder, "Thomas Walter Bickett."
13. "Governor Talks to the Negroes," *Daily Times*, January 2, 1920, 1, 6.
14. Burckel, "From Beckham to McCreary," 285.
15. Ibid., 286.
16. Woodward, *Origins of the New South*, 377.
17. Klotter, "William Goebel," 134.
18. Coletta, *William Jennings Bryan*, 241–42; Koenig, *Bryan*, 306–7.
19. Klotter, "William Goebel," 134–35.
20. Grantham, *Southern Progressivism*, 85.
21. Burckel, "From Beckham to McCreary."
22. "Stanley Is Named in State Primary," *Central Record*, August 12, 1915, 3; Appleton, "Augustus Owsley Stanley," 146.
23. "Administration in Control of Assembly Organization," *Hopkinsville Kentuckian*, January 6, 1916, 1; "Steps to Probe State Expenses," *Breckenridge News*, January 12, 1916, 7.
24. Burckel, "Progressive Governors in the Border States," 521.
25. "The Week," *Nation*, January 18, 1917, 63. See also "To Lynch or Not to Lynch," *The Outlook*, January 24, 1917, 137–38.
26. Burckel, "Progressive Governors in the Border States," 536, 541.
27. "No Show Given in the Senate," *Atlanta Constitution*, February 9, 1906, 2. See also "In Grasp of Trust," *Washington Post*, March 14, 1906, 2.
28. See generally Tucker, *Governor William E. Glasscock*.
29. Cooper, *Rise of the National Guard*, 151.
30. Burckel, "Progressive Governors in the Border States," 353; Gable, *Bull Moose Years*, 17, 29.
31. Karr, "Henry D. Hatfield."
32. Green, *Devil Is Here in These Hills*, 120–21.
33. Ibid., 138.
34. Crooks, *Politics and Progress*, 11.
35. Ibid., 54–55.
36. See generally White, "Edward Warfield."
37. Crooks, *Politics and Progress*, 55. See also discussion on the Poe Amendment in "Fight of Three States," *The Outlook*, September 23, 1905, 154–56.
38. "Negro Suffrage or Gormanism Are the Issues in Maryland," *Minneapolis Journal*, October 22, 1905, 2.
39. "Jim Crow Bills," *Ottumwa Tri-Weekly Courier*, March 19, 1904, 1; "Maryland 'Jim Crow' Law," *Omaha Daily Bee*, March 19, 1904, 6; "The Week," *Nation*, March 24, 1904, 221.
40. White, "Edward Warfield."
41. Ibid., quoting the *Baltimore Sun*, April 1, 1920.
42. See generally "Crothers" in White, *Governors of Maryland*, 239–42.
43. Crooks, *Politics and Progress*, 52.
44. "Death of Austin L. Crothers," *Newark Post*, May 29, 1912, 1.
45. Crooks, *Politics and Progress*, 51, 74.
46. Ibid., 65, 69.
47. "The Governor's Views," *Democratic Advocate*, December 18, 1908, 1.
48. Pulley, *Old Virginia Restored*.
49. Heinemann, "Andrew Jackson Montague."
50. Larsen, "Andrew Jackson Montague," 168.

51. Pulley, *Old Virginia Restored*, 120–23.
52. Kirby, *Darkness at the Dawning*, 40.
53. Heinemann, "Andrew Jackson Montague." See also Larsen, *Montague of Virginia*, 123–24.
54. Ferrell, *Claude A. Swanson*, 50.
55. Larsen, "Andrew Jackson Montague," 165.
56. Ferrell, *Claude A. Swanson*, 52.
57. Ibid., 70.
58. "A 'Lynch-Law Governor,'" *Literary Digest*, November 25, 1911, 964–65.
59. Crump was a successful businessman in Memphis with a passion for politics who began his political career a bit like Pingree as a mugwumpian upper-class conservative but wound up in 1911 building a biracial, multiethnic coalition; he became something of a municipal reformer on transportation and utility regulation, working-class issues, and public health protection, though he did not favor prohibition, especially as far as his city was concerned. See generally Dowdy, *Mayor Crump Don't Like It*.
60. See generally Boyce, *Unwanted Boy*.
61. Isaac, "The Problems of a Republican Governor," 234.
62. Miller, *Mr. Crump of Memphis*, 109–10, citing *Commercial Appeal*, October 8, 1912.
63. Boyce, *Unwanted Boy*, 105.
64. Isaac, "The Problems of a Republican Governor," 246.
65. Boyce, *Unwanted Boy*, 86, 101.
66. Ibid., 101.
67. "Governor Hooper Goes to Jail," *New York Times*, December 21, 1911, 1; "Gov. Hooper Tells of Life in Prison," *New York Times*, December, 24, 1911, 3.
68. Casdorph, *Republicans, Negroes, and Progressivism in the South*, 37, 140.
69. "Harmonious Republican Convention," *Dresden Enterprise and Sharon Tribune*, April 3, 1914, 3.
70. Crandlemere, "Edward Hull Crump."
71. On these developments see Miller, *Mr. Crump of Memphis*, 111–13.
72. Quoted by William M. Davis, "Governor Rye's Notable Speech," *Denver Star*, October 27, 1917, 7.

9

GOING EAST

Roosevelt, Hughes, Al Smith, Governing and Dealing with the Bosses

Turning to the East in this and the following two chapters, we discover a general tendency, especially in the 1890s and early 1900s, among private groups and politicians to tilt toward a relatively mild "honesty and efficiency" approach to reform. With less of a base in Populism, eastern reformers were more likely to be of the limited-government, Mugwump variety. There was far less enthusiasm in the East about anticorporate or direct democracy reforms than found in other parts of the country, especially the western region.

In the East we also often find well-organized political machines, some of the most notorious in the nation. Bosses were not always opposed to reform but were more than willing to fight back against proposed changes that threatened to diminish their power or the interests of their important business clients and were often able to do so successfully. At the same time the problems of a large and growing immigrant urban population were especially salient and generated pressure for social causes and demands for change that were reflected in the voting behavior of the state legislators representing these people.[1]

Overall, we find a practical politics approach to reform in the East—policy changes that might be best viewed as the result of political party leaders in power, usually Republicans, doing what they felt was necessary to stay in power.[2] This does not mean, however, that the region lacked true Progressive leadership at the gubernatorial level. Some were "educated up" from their Mugwump dispositions by events and exposure to ideas. Though somewhat offset by a counter streak of negativism, it is possible to discern in the political culture of eastern states, some more than others, an attachment to the Progressive-like notion called "positive liberalism," which, simply put, refers to the belief that "the state should promote the welfare and protect the rights of as many of its people as possible."[3]

In New York positive liberalism found a home not only in the thoughts of politically active people from the upper classes, perhaps in part, as a matter of noblesse oblige, but sometimes also in the views of those who rose from poverty and well remembered what that meant. Beyond social status, one might argue that New York governors in the period under review and perhaps since then have been bent in the direction of reform, especially greater social justice, because of the unusually high degree of their involvement with and exposure to politically active reformers and reform groups.[4]

In New York we find Governors Theodore Roosevelt, Charles Evans Hughes, Al Smith (whose service extended only a few years into the period under review), and William Sulzer taking varying attitudes toward the party organization or bosses. We also find differing temperaments and styles, represented by Roosevelt and Hughes, when it comes to flexibility and compromise. Hughes emerges as a central figure in the drive for Progressive reform, but note is made of the contributions of relatively unknown governors such as Benjamin Odell.

THE ROOSEVELT WAY

In the early 1900s Elihu Root, longtime observer of New York politics who later served under President Theodore Roosevelt, asked an audience: "Who runs New York?" Over the last twenty years, Root said in reply to his own question: "It was not the governor; it was not the legislature; it was not any elected officers; it was Mr. Platt."[5]

Root was referring to Thomas Collier Platt, three-term US senator from New York who headed the state's unofficial government as "Boss" of the Republican Party in the 1890s and early 1900s. He controlled the nomination of several governors, including Roosevelt in 1898.

Platt followed the lead of Richard Crocker of the rival New York Democratic Party's Tammany Hall machine in relying not so much on patronage, though this was important, as on providing services to powerful political corporations to finance operations. He was, in effect, their political agent.[6] New York's period of Progressive reform, developing out of resistance to the machine system, lasted from Theodore Roosevelt's election to the office of governor in New York in 1898 to Al Smith's election to the same office in 1918. In between came Charles Evans Hughes, the most prominent New York Progressive of the period.[7]

Roosevelt began his political career in the New York state legislature in the early 1880s. Here he took a leading role in investigating the possibility of judicial corruption in a matter involving an effort by financier Jay Gould to avoid taxation. He also voted for a bill that would force Gould to reduce fares on the elevated trains in New York City but, showing the flexibility that would characterize his later career, reversed himself after Governor Grover Cleveland vetoed the bill. On second thought, Roosevelt and several other legislators concluded, as Cleveland had argued, that in order to restore the system, Gould actually needed the revenue he would lose by reducing fares. Roosevelt also stood with Cleveland in supporting a merit-based civil service law.

Roosevelt's focus as a legislator on corruption and civil service reform marked him as a Mugwump, but, much to the surprise and distress of his Mugwump friends in New York, he did not join them in 1884 in backing Cleveland for president. Being practical, he felt he would be better off as far as his long-term political career was concerned by staying with the Republican Party and backing the Republican nominee, James G. Blaine, even though he had been among those strenuously opposing his nomination.[8]

Roosevelt lost a race for mayor of New York City in 1886, coming in third as the Republican nominee behind the winner, Democrat Abram Hewitt, and independent candidate Henry George, a highly influential reform-driven political economist. Out of fear that George might win, many Republicans reportedly voted for the Democrat. Two years later Roosevelt campaigned mostly in the Midwest for Republican presidential candidate Benjamin Harrison, who went on to defeat Cleveland. In reward for his help, Harrison appointed Roosevelt to the US Civil Service Commission.

In 1892 Cleveland came back and won the presidency, defeating Harrison. In spite of the fact that Roosevelt had supported Harrison, Cleveland reappointed Roosevelt to the commission. The two had had an amiable past in New York and were in friendly contact during the 1892 campaign, even though Roosevelt was saying unflattering things about Cleveland. Roosevelt enlisted the aid of well-respected civil service reformer Carl Schurz in his effort to convince Cleveland that he should be reappointed. Cleveland found Roosevelt acceptable, and it also solved a problem for him: by law he had to appoint one Republican to the three-member commission.[9] Roosevelt served on the commission until 1895, enthusiastically doing battle with those who defended the spoils system.

Following this, he spent two years as New York City's police commissioner, working to clean up corruption in the police department but angering many by trying to enforce the previously unenforced blue law prohibiting the sale of alcohol on Sundays. He took time in 1896 to campaign for Republican Party presidential nominee William McKinley and against the Democrat-Populist Bryan, though much of his attention was directed toward Illinois governor John Altgeld, a much better known figure than Bryan and one that conservatives loved to vilify. Roosevelt enthusiastically joined the attack on Altgeld, pulling no punches (see chapter 3). After the election President McKinley appointed him assistant secretary of the navy. A year later, in 1898, when war broke out with Spain, Roosevelt resigned his position and helped to form a volunteer unit known as the Rough Riders to fight in the war.

After leaving the army, Roosevelt received the cautious and somewhat reluctant support of Boss Platt in his bid for governor of New York. Platt did not get along well with Roosevelt, who was a member of the antimachine wing of the party. Platt too had some reason to worry about whether he could control a Governor Roosevelt, a popular figure in his own right who could appeal directly to the public.[10] On the other hand, he had little choice but to go along with Roosevelt in his bid for the nomination. The party needed a good candidate. The party's current governor, Frank S. Black, tainted by scandal, seemed destined to lose should he run again. Beyond this, there was a threat that Roosevelt, who had risen to fame because of his leadership of the Rough Riders, would run for governor as an independent—a move that was likely to be disastrous for Republicans. With Platt's endorsement, Roosevelt secured the nomination and proceeded to win the 1898 gubernatorial election, though by a very thin margin (49.0 percent to 47.7 percent) over a well-respected Democratic candidate, Augustus Van Wyck, a judge on the state supreme court.

As governor, Roosevelt came under conflicting demands—on one side stood Boss Platt and on the other side reformers and independent Republicans who opposed Platt and had not been altogether happy about Roosevelt's willingness to go along with the machine.[11] Platt gave Roosevelt some freedom but drew the line on matters affecting important corporate clients or the direct welfare of the party organization. Reformers and independent Republicans called on him to oppose the corporations and the bosses. It was impossible for Roosevelt to escape criticism, but he did hope to rise above the conflict by compromise and by trying to gain as much support as possible from diverse groups. He "inevitably sought a position that was above party or special group, a stand that he could defend as in the broad public interest."[12]

As far as Boss Platt was concerned, Roosevelt adopted an approach that was midpoint between compliance and defiance. He regularly consulted Platt on appointments but reserved the right to make the final decisions. The major conflict between the two occurred when, over Platt's opposition, Roosevelt supported a measure, the Ford Franchise Tax Bill, levying a tax on corporations holding public franchises. Platt regarded the measure as "radical legislation" aimed at the business community and "an extreme concession to Bryanism."[13] Platt felt that Roosevelt's approval of the legislation put him "in the public mind in the Pingree and Mayor-Jones-of-Toledo class of statesmen"[14] A New York newspaper editor warned that if Roosevelt signed the bill, New York would be up there "with Kansas, Nebraska and Missouri in the scale of communistic and social legislation, as a state for capital to shun, for investments to abandon and for enterprise and confidence to desert."[15]

Roosevelt had been planning to run for another term for governor, preparing himself for a run at the presidency in 1904, but Platt refused to endorse his reelection. Platt felt it would be a good idea to find Roosevelt another job and replace him with someone more compliant. Working with political insiders at the 1900 Republican national convention, Platt was able to shelve Roosevelt by putting him on the ballot as the national party's candidate for vice-president. From McKinley's point of view, Roosevelt was an attractive running mate because of his popularity in the West.[16] Roosevelt wrote his friend US senator Henry Cabot Lodge on February 3, 1900, that one reason Platt wanted him to be nominated for the vice-presidency was pressure from the "big moneyed men" and corporations affected by the franchise tax who wanted to get him out of the state.[17] On a tour of the state in October 1900 Roosevelt told a crowd that his position on the franchise tax bill cost him "the friendship of very powerful men."[18]

Platt may have felt good in the closing weeks of the year 1900. By maneuvering Roosevelt into the vice-presidential position, he had gotten rid of a pest and avoided the possibility of Roosevelt running for governor as an independent candidate. Roosevelt's replacement, Benjamin Odell, an organization man, won the governorship with 52 percent of the vote. All of a sudden things fell apart. Odell declared his independence from the machine, and in September 1901 Theodore Roosevelt, only forty-two at the time, became president following the assassination of McKinley. Roosevelt went on to assert control over federal patronage and other matters regarding the state, depriving Platt of much of his influence.[19]

Coming to the end of his term as the chief executive of the state of New York, Roosevelt said: "I have thoroughly enjoyed being governor."[20] Being governor was just one of the positions he held in a long career, and one suspects that, if asked, he would have said he thoroughly enjoyed every one of them. He was that way. Still, being governor was something special. It was a great learning experience for Roosevelt, one in which he honed his skills and learned much about the techniques of governing and the issues of the day. While governor, he developed and attempted to implement his views about the role of government. To him, governing amounted to giving people a square deal through a neutral state—a system in which favoritism would be eliminated and officials would mediate conflicting demands in an open and even-handed manner in the public interest.[21]

Roosevelt had come into office still very much inclined toward the negativism of his Mugwump or good-government supporters, but by the time he went off to Washington to become vice-president, he had moved in a more positive Progressive direction as an "honest broker" for reform, including effective corporate taxation.[22] Still, Roosevelt also demonstrated a practical side—as a politician thinking long range about his career and, viewing politics as the art of the possible, being willing to compromise and accommodate various interests.

A contemporary of Roosevelt, prominent journalist and academic Albert Shaw, later wrote: "In the ideals of good government, Mr. Roosevelt stood with the reformers; in the methods to be pursued, he took leaves from the book of the politicians."[23] Roosevelt, Shaw noted, carried a grudge against a certain type of reformers, the pure theorists or detached students "who could not or would not understand his more practical views regarding methods by which desirable changes might be brought about."[24] In Roosevelt's own words:

> ... a man who goes into the actual battles of the political world must prepare himself much as he would for the struggle in any other branch of our life. He must be prepared to meet men of far lower ideas than his own, and to face things, not as he would wish them, but as they are. He must not lose his own high ideal, and yet he must face the fact that the majority of the men with whom he must work have lower ideals. He must stand firmly for what he believes, and yet he must realize that political action, to be effective, must be the joint action of many men, and that he must sacrifice somewhat of his own opinions to those of his associates if he ever hopes to see his desires take practical shape.[25]

Roosevelt was a more committed Progressive in his presidency, though still highly flexible. He became the uncompromising Progressive reformer in 1912 only when he was out of office during his quest for the presidency as the head of the Progressive Party.[26]

GOVERNOR HUGHES

Mildly Progressive Republicans Benjamin Odell, who turned against Platt, and Francis Higgins followed Roosevelt in office. Odell, a successful businessman, set out to apply business principles to government, seeking efficiency and economy by streamlining state government where he could and by cutting unnecessary costs. He also brought about a new revenue system for the state by replacing the state property tax with a personal property tax and new business taxes. The series of tax levies he ushered through the legislature shifted much of the tax burden away from real estate to large corporations. Overall, as historian Richard L. McCormick has noted: "In actual achievements, Odell's record as governor surpassed Roosevelt's."[27]

Odell was "a brusque and overbearing man" who, McCormick concluded, "did not win his authority through personal pleasantries." His ability to win over most leading Republicans and legislators may have well rested on the status and powers of his office, his concern for the welfare of the Republican Party, and his identification with highly popular issues, especially the economy and tax reform.[28] While still governor, he reassumed the position of state party chairman. He was considered by some a more powerful and worse boss than Platt, whom he had largely replaced.[29] Regular Republicans in the party organization were willing to give him much of what he wanted.[30]

Higgins began his political career in the state legislature and became lieutenant governor on a ticket with Odell in 1902. He received the gubernatorial nomination in 1904 with the backing of Roosevelt and Odell. The strength of Roosevelt's presidential reelection campaign in the state that year helped elect Higgins governor. Higgins had been a close supporter of Odell and continued on the same policy path. During his administration the legislature launched two dramatic investigations that altered state politics, producing much legislation regarding business regulation and corrupt practices and bringing Charles Evans Hughes to power.

Hughes, born in New York, the son of a reverend, graduated from Columbia Law School and then taught and practiced law. He became a prominent figure in New York and around the nation in 1905 because of his leading role as a counsel to the New York legislature in the investigations of corruption involving the Consolidated Gas Company, which had a monopoly on the sale of gas in New York City, and insurance companies based in New York. A highlight of the insurance investigation were accounts of state lawmakers interacting with lobbyists and being royally entertained at a resort in Albany known as "The House of Mirth." Along with this came accounts about how a group of state legislators, known as the Black Horse Cavalry, extorted money from corporations by threatening to introduce legislation detrimental to their interests.[31]

Hughes's efforts, uncovering a wide range of corrupt relations between business leaders and politicians, transformed state politics. Changes made directly as a result of the 1905 investigations while Higgins was governor included laws prohibiting corporations from making campaign contributions, requiring greater publicity for what contributions and expenditures were made, and clarifying what types of expenditures were allowable. Investigations also led to laws making corporate lobbying more difficult, new regulations on gas and electric monopolies, and insurance legislation widely copied in other states.[32]

While his investigation of insurance companies was going on, Hughes turned down an offer from the bosses to be named the Republican nominee for mayor of New York. He quickly discouraged such talk. He later wrote that the offer came not as sign of respect and admiration but as part of an effort to pull him out of the insurance investigation that had already angered party leaders and caused the Republican Party considerable damage.[33] Newspaper publisher and leading Democrat William Randolph Hearst also urged Hughes to run for mayor, but he had another reason. Hearst figured that this would be an excellent way to reduce the possibility that Hughes would end up challenging him in the 1906 contest for

Figure 9.1. Charles Evans Hughes. Courtesy of the Library of Congress, Prints & Photographs Division, photograph by Harris & Ewing, LC-DIG-hec-02423.

governor. Hughes, he reasoned, would be unlikely to run after spending only a few months as mayor.

Though thinking little of Hughes, Republican Party bosses came to the conclusion that he offered the best chance of the party's holding on to the governor's office in 1906. Their support and an endorsement from President Theodore Roosevelt was all that Hughes really needed to receive the nomination for governor at the Republican state convention.[34] The general election campaign against Hearst was more difficult. Toward the end Republicans panicked a bit. President Roosevelt, greatly concerned about the possible outcome, sent his secretary of state, Elihu Root, to New York to help out Hughes, primarily by attacking Hearst.

On November 1, 1906, speaking at Utica, New York, Root threw everything he could think of at the newspaper publisher. He lit into him as a demagogue, a wily capitalist posing as a friend of labor, a tax evader, a specialist in hate mongering who was partly responsible for the murder of McKinley, a tool of Tammany Hall, a former congressman who excelled only at not showing up for roll calls, someone who could not find anyone who knew him who was willing to testify to his private virtues, and, topping it off with little left to cover, a poor citizen.[35]

In accepting the nomination Hughes did nothing to make the organizational Republicans comfortable. He emphasized his intent "to give the state a sane, efficient and honorable administration, free from taint of bossism or of servitude to any private interests."[36] The bosses apparently dismissed this as campaign oratory, expecting that he would come around should he win and be a regular Republican.[37] Looking back, Hughes noted that party leaders regarded his 1906 vow to clean up the state as just campaign talk and that after his election "my noble sentiments could be conveniently and profitably laid aside." But he soon showed them he intended to keep his word.[38]

Coming into office in 1907, Hughes asked the legislature to adopt a wide range of reforms. Hughes's biographer, Merlo Pusey, noted: "It was a sweeping program that was about as palatable to the Old Guard as earthworm soup."[39] Hughes, for his part, may have misjudged the temper of the party leaders. He thought they would give a certain level of support to a newly elected governor of their own party, in spite of their disagreements. He was surprised when they went straight for his jugular.[40] Hughes had to deal with several party leaders because Platt had, by this time, become too ill to provide leadership. The party pros had been only annoyed with Theodore Roosevelt. They hated Hughes.[41]

Hughes managed to get renominated in 1908, again with the support of Roosevelt and rank-and-file Republicans and over the objections of party leaders who condemned him for not being a party man or having any respect for the party organization. To them Hughes was the type of politician who expects the support of organizational leaders at party conventions and the polls but goes his or her own way once in office, doing nothing in return for the organization.[42]

Hughes was initially disposed toward the view that the governor should have only a limited role when it came to legislation, but, as an observer noted, he "soon discovered that this was an unworkable theory" and attempted to steer the course of legislative activity through personal contact with individual legislators, messages to the both houses, and direct appeals to the public for support for particular causes.[43]

In pushing for reform Hughes often received the support of Democrats in the legislature. This support was necessary because of the resistance of many legislators in his party to his policies and to him personally.[44] When all was said and done, Hughes accomplished a great deal. His accomplishments included a commission to control public utilities that became a model for other states. Hughes set out to win the vote of working people in his campaign against Hearst and by the end of his two terms received the praise of social reformers.[45] Historian

Pusey argued that labor legislation was "a specialty of the Hughes régime" and that Hughes's two terms in office brought fifty-six statutes for the benefit of labor.[46]

Progressives, though, criticized him for vetoing a two-cent-per-mile maximum passenger rate bill and for fighting and defeating New York ratification of the income tax amendment to the US Constitution. Some suspected he had vetoed the rail measure to get corporate support for his presidential bid. His ground for opposing the income tax amendment was that it would have led to federal taxation of state and local bonds, thus infringing upon states' rights.[47]

Hughes, after a long fight, won the repeal of a law that, in effect, allowed racetrack gambling. Hughes saw this as a clear and deliberate violation of the state constitution and a simple matter of right and wrong. He was determined to win. During the intense debate over the issue he received some threatening letters, including a death threat and a warning that his daughter might be kidnapped. He also received one reporting that gamblers were prepared to dole out $200,000 to legislators to defeat the repeal effort. Fake letters from constituents opposing the repeal measure flooded the mail of legislators.[48]

In showing his appreciation for the support he received from a vast number of people who were behind him on this cause, he declared: "In the solitude of the Executive Chamber it makes you feel that there is a great army outside at your back, and that this army will stand by you in your effort to accomplish that which it is right to accomplish." He also said the battle against the bookmakers and pool sellers at racetracks presented "questions which test the consciences of legislators."[49] Hughes promoted the cause with a torrent of speeches, backing up his legislative supporters and hoping to put pressure on others. In the end he won out.

Hughes saw little value in the wide-open direct primary systems being advanced in the West—in his estimation they only took power away from unscrupulous bosses and gave it to dangerous demagogues. He wanted to keep party organizations at the heart of the nomination process but also to place party leaders under greater control with a plan that would increase the role played by regular party members.[50] His direct primary proposal calling for a system of nominations of candidates by elected party committees, however, met the determined opposition of party bosses of both major parties and went down to defeat in the legislature. This failure, to Hughes, constituted his "most severe and bitter defeat."[51]

Hughes saw himself as a strong party man but thought his party was weak. It had been tainted by its ties to business interests and had not been doing as well with the electorate as it should have. He wanted to get the party away from bossism and give state government a general housecleaning. He desired to operate independently of the party leaders and establish an antimachine administration. He felt that Republicans could win back public favor by simply providing honest and efficient government and by relying on experts and impartial administrators rather than partisan legislation. He had a tough time selling any of this to the party professionals, however.[52]

Hughes raised the level of conflict by setting out to end the hold that party bosses and corporations had over the operation of various service and regulatory agencies by removing administrators he disapproved of and replacing them with those he felt would be more independent of the bosses and more competent. He successfully pushed for the Moreland Act of 1907, which gave him the power as governor to review the operation of state agencies and remove administrators who were corrupt or not up to the job.[53]

On the administrative side, he also took steps toward establishing an executive budgeting system, giving the governor greater control over departmental spending, and sought the adoption of a state administrative reorganization plan that would put more of the state agencies headed by elected officials under the supervision of the governor. His reorganization plan, submitted to the legislature in 1909 and 1910, went nowhere—not surprising, given the tension already existing between Hughes and the Republican legislators and the further reluctance of many legislators to increase the powers of the gubernatorial office—but did help build the case for reform.[54]

When it comes to Hughes's temperament, biographer Pusey noted: "No greater mistake could be made about Hughes than to assume that he was merely a thinking machine. On the contrary, he was a bundle of nerves. Having inherited a mercurial temperament from his Welsh-Irish-Scottish forebears, he shifted easily from elation to depression and back again. At the office he was called 'the ship,' and his associates would say 'the ship' was 'plowing along steadily' or sometimes that it was 'in stormy seas' and 'pitching heavily.'"[55] Pusey noted that Hughes appeared to many to be cold and aloof—no one ever slapped him on the shoulder and called him Charlie—but he inspired loyalty from those who worked for him and was far from being an icicle; one newspaper described him as "a remarkable example of the live, glowing wire."[56]

Hughes, though, was far less flexible than Roosevelt, with whom he had on-again, off-again relations. When it came to campaigning, Hughes was unwilling to sacrifice what he saw as principles in the interest of winning, while Roosevelt was far more willing to play the game of politics as conventional politicians played the game. Hughes sometimes rejected or ignored Roosevelt's advice when it came to governing, insisting on being the governor in his own right. Roosevelt was especially irritated by Hughes's uncompromising attitude toward the party organization, feeling he had needlessly insulted party workers, and urged him to bend at least a little, as Roosevelt had done, in the interest of party unity.[57] In 1910 Hughes resigned the governorship after President Taft appointed him associate justice of the US Supreme Court. He left the court in 1916 to run for president on the Republican ticket and lost to Woodrow Wilson, who was seeking reelection.

SULZER, SMITH, AND THE BOSSES

John Dix won election as governor in 1910, the first Democratic governor in New York in sixteen years, as part of a Progressive surge. Dix, a "clean" upstate businessman, ran on what was generally conceded to be a strong Progressive platform free from corporate influence.[58] The Democrats also captured control of both statehouses. During Dix's administration, the tragic fire at the Triangle Shirtwaist Company in 1911—which killed 146 workers, mostly women and young girls, some of whom could not get out of the building because of locked doors—led to the creation of a commission chaired by state senator Robert F. Wagner to look into working conditions. The commission's work led to a slew of new labor protection laws covering topics from fire safety and building codes to hour limitations, though most of these secured passage under the regime of Dix's successor, William Sulzer. Dix achieved little in office other than some limited reform in regard to conservation.

In 1912 Dix lost the party's nomination to Sulzer, who was serving in Congress at the time. He had been there since 1894, establishing a liberal voting record. Sulzer went on to win the governorship with the strong endorsement of both the Tammany and reform factions of the state Democratic Party and prominent outsiders such as Woodrow Wilson, William Jennings Bryan, and William Randolph Hearst. He won in a three-way contest that included a Progressive Party candidate.

Not long after taking office, however, Sulzer angered Tammany leader Charles Murphy by pushing for a direct primary system and for an investigation into charges of corruption in the legislature and various state institutions and for not allowing Tammany to make the decision as to who should have what state jobs. Summing up the situation, Sulzer wrote to a friend in July of 1913: "When the bosses found out they could not control me, and make a rubber stamp of me, they threatened to destroy me politically, and have been doing everything in their power to that end."[59]

The bosses' effort culminated when Murphy, working with a most cooperative Republican majority in the state legislature, impeached Sulzer on the grounds that he had misused campaign funds for personal use; a special court removed him from office on October 17, 1913. The charges were not altogether baseless. Many believed, however, that his primary "crime" was being a reformer. Following Sulzer's removal, a series of election laws were passed, including one relating to direct primaries, while Democrat Martin H. Glynn held the governor's office. Glynn had moved up from lieutenant governor when Sulzer was ousted.[60]

Al Smith was one of Sulzer's opponents in the legislature. Coming out of a rough ethnic neighborhood on Manhattan's Lower East Side, the son of working-class parents, Smith got the backing of Tammany Hall, won an election to the state assembly in 1903, and stayed there until 1915, becoming speaker of that body in 1913. He began his career in opposition to Tammany Hall but was won over by the organization and wound up having nothing but good things to say about "Boss" Murphy, whom he commonly referred to as "Mr. Murphy." He noted that Murphy had also fought his way up from lowly surroundings and took a keen interest in social legislation, and declared that Murphy was not a "boss" but a "good adviser" who let people he had confidence in make their own decisions.[61] Siding with the bosses, Smith opposed Sulzer's nomination for governor and, as speaker of the house, supported Sulzer's impeachment, feeling that the charges against him were true.[62]

In his autobiography Smith noted that in his first few terms in the legislature he attended all the meetings but really didn't know what was going on. He was seated in the last row and had been appointed to the Committees on Banks and Public Lands and Forestry, even though "I knew nothing about banking laws and had never been in a bank except to serve a jury notice, and I had never seen a forest."[63] Matters improved in 1906 when he got appointed to some important committees, including one handling the insurance industry investigation that Hughes was leading. He became a legislative leader after the Democratic victory in 1910.

With the encouragement of labor activist Frances Perkins, Smith began to take an interest in the problems of working people and was further encouraged in that direction by serving as vice-chair of the state commission looking into factory conditions following the Triangle Shirtwaist Factory fire. Deeply disturbed by this event, he became an outspoken leader in a campaign for the improvement of working conditions. As a delegate to the state's constitutional convention in 1915 he picked up on several other reform ideas. That same year, with Tammany Hall's support, voters elected him sheriff of New York County, a patronage-rich position, and two years later he won election as president of the Board of Aldermen of New York City.

In 1918 the well-known reformer made a bid for the governorship. Though he was a Tammany man, he also had friends among Tammany's opponents. The *New York Times* endorsed him, saying it was only natural that he began his political career with Tammany and that he had "grown in a way Tammany has not. He has fitted himself to be Governor. He understands the business."[64] Smith won the election by a narrow margin, and this victory may have had less to do with any issue he championed or his personal appeal than an upstate influenza epidemic that reduced Republican turnout.[65] He lost the gubernatorial position in 1920, in part because of a national landslide for Republicans that year, but came back to win the office several times in the 1920s and eventually became the Democratic Party's nominee for president in 1928.

Governor Smith brought Progressive reforms in the areas of worker protection, housing, and public education. On the labor front he appointed Frances Perkins to the state industrial commission and named her his representative in a serious labor strike in Rome, New York. He later noted: "The heads of the business were shocked to find that I had selected a woman to negotiate a treaty of peace between the workers and their employers"; but they found she was, as he had expected, more than up to the task.[66] Smith also led a successful effort, picking up where Hughes left off, to increase the governor's control over state administrative agencies. He was attracted to the idea of administrative reorganization while a delegate to the state's constitutional convention in 1915 and decided to make this a central theme in his gubernatorial campaign in 1918 and a top priority following his election. He viewed gaining greater control over the spending and activities of state agencies as important in helping him to serve the needs of his urban immigrant constituency.[67]

All in all, it can be said that if "Theodore Roosevelt and Hughes had been educated up from 'googooism,' Al Smith was educated up from Tammany." It is also fair to say, though, that Tammany itself had changed under Smith's mentor, Charles Murphy, who, like Smith, appreciated the fact that backing social reform was a good way to get votes. Smith had a far better relation with the party organization leaders than Roosevelt and, especially, Hughes. Working with Tammany leaders as well as social reformers in New York, Smith was able to bring the "triumph of positive liberalism" to the state.[68]

NOTES

1. Buenker, *Urban Liberalism*.
2. See, for example, McCormick, *From Realignment to Reform*.
3. Roper, "The Governorship in History," 16.
4. Ibid.
5. Quoted by Gosnell, *Boss Platt*, 71.
6. Chessman, *Governor Theodore Roosevelt*, 10.
7. Roper, "The Governorship in History."
8. Tucker, *Mugwumps*, 80.
9. White, *Roosevelt the Reformer*, 97–100.
10. "Rising Tide for Roosevelt," *New York Times*, September 3, 1898, 1.
11. See account in Shaw, "Theodore Roosevelt as Political Leader."
12. Chessman, *Governor Theodore Roosevelt*, 4.
13. Ibid., 138.
14. Ibid., 149.
15. Ibid., 147, 148.
16. Ibid., 282.
17. Gosnell, *Boss Platt*, 117–18.
18. "Roosevelt's State Tour," *New York Times*, October 24, 1900, 3.
19. Gosnell, *Boss Platt*, 291.
20. Quoted in Glashan, *American Governors*, 90.
21. See generally Chessman, *Governor Theodore Roosevelt*.
22. Roper, "The Governorship in History."
23. Shaw, "Theodore Roosevelt as Political Leader," xv.
24. Ibid., xix.

25. Roosevelt, "The Manly Virtues and Practical Politics," 551–52.
26. On Roosevelt as a Progressive see Noble, *Progressive Mind*, 168–80; Gable, *Bull Moose Years*; and comments by La Follette in La Follette, *La Follette's Autobiography*, 205–8, 272.
27. McCormick, *From Realignment to Reform*, 166.
28. Ibid., 173.
29. Ibid., 189.
30. Ibid., 169.
31. Smith, *Up to Now*, 113.
32. McCormick, *From Realignment to Reform*, 212, 213; Pusey, *Charles Evans Hughes*, 166–68.
33. Danelski and Tulchin, *Autobiographical Notes*, 128.
34. Gosnell, *Boss Platt*, 304; Pusey, *Charles Evans Hughes*, 172.
35. Swanberg, *Citizen Hearst*, 299.
36. Pusey, *Charles Evans Hughes*, 173, quoting the *New York Daily Tribune*, September 27, 1906.
37. Ibid., 18.
38. Danelski and Tulchin, *Autobiographical Notes*, 135.
39. Pusey, *Charles Evans Hughes*, 225.
40. Ibid., 184.
41. McCormick, *From Realignment to Reform*, 227.
42. "Battle on Hughes," *Washington Post*, August 31, 1908, 3.
43. "What Is a Governor?" *The Outlook*, December 24, 1910, 893–94; Rowland, "Hughes—Governor," *The Outlook*, February 8, 1908, 303–9.
44. Buenker, *Urban Liberalism*, 93, 111, 112.
45. Roper, "The Governorship in History," 27.
46. Pusey, *Charles Evans Hughes*, 212.
47. "Mr. Justice Hughes," *The Commoner*, May 20, 1910, 1; "A Big Surprise," *Vinita Daily Chieftain*, June 12, 1907, 3; "The Income Tax under the Hughes Microscope," *Literary Digest*, January 15, 1910, 88.
48. Pusey, *Charles Evans Hughes*, 226, 227.
49. "Governor Replies to Black's Plea," *New York Times*, March 6, 1908, 2.
50. Pusey, *Charles Evans Hughes*, 260–61; Feldman, "The Direct Primary in New York State."
51. McCormick, *From Realignment to Reform*, 246.
52. Ibid., 197–222, 229, 230.
53. Pusey, *Charles Evans Hughes*, 191, 210–11.
54. Stonecash et al., "Politics."
55. Pusey, *Charles Evans Hughes*, 118.
56. Ibid., 221.
57. Ibid., 178, 188, 196, 234, 242.
58. Sarasohn, *Party of Reform*, 88.
59. Sulzer to Everett P. Wheeler, July 7, 1913, William Sulzur Letters, Special Collections Research Center, Syracuse University Libraries.
60. Feldman, "The Direct Primary in New York State."
61. Smith, *Up to Now*, 55, 121–22.
62. Ibid., 123, 132.
63. Ibid., 74–75.
64. Finan, *Alfred E. Smith*, 112.
65. Roper, "The Governorship in History," 28.
66. Smith, *Up to Now*, 177–78.
67. Stonecash et al., "Politics."
68. Roper, "The Governorship in History," 18, 27.

10

WILSON OF NEW JERSEY, SCHOLAR AND TACTICIAN, CONFRONTING THE BOSSES

Few governors have received as much praise as Woodrow Wilson. In June 1911, for example, one observer wrote of the accomplishment of this "able, responsible, and fearless" governor as bringing a new era in executive leadership and ushering in a new era in state government.[1] His accomplishments as governor were impressive but came at the end of a drive for reform that began long before he took office. Wilson was a latecomer to reform. He somewhat abruptly moved from a conservative Cleveland Democrat to a Progressive Democrat and initially had a hard time convincing other Progressives of his sincerity. He got elected with the encouragement and help of Democratic bosses who later claimed he had turned on them. In both winning office and governing, this scholar demonstrated considerable skill as a politician. This was especially well demonstrated in his dealings with the bosses.

THE SETTING

In the early 1900s Democratic and Republican Party bosses who were aligned with railroad, utility, and other corporate interests exercised considerable influence in New Jersey politics. Not surprisingly, the bosses looked for gubernatorial candidates who supported the machine and who would further the interest of the machine once elected. Starting in the late eighteenth century nearly all the governors of New Jersey were essentially party machine men, be they Republicans or

Democrats, though most were Republicans, who heavily relied upon or, in effect, worked as part of a political machine for party bosses.[2]

Along with having great influence over governors, the machine leaders had great influence over legislators. They simplified the work of legislators—all they had to do was follow directions. Ray Stannard Baker, a noted muckraking journalist who later wrote a biography of Woodrow Wilson, described how it worked in New Jersey: "The Big Boss and his satellites haunted the capitol, often sitting in the lobbies or on the floor of the houses, sometimes actually directing legislation at the elbow of the speaker. The really important bills originated in the offices of corporation lawyers, and the Big Boss of one party or the other had them introduced by certain dependable members. Debate was usually farcical and when the moment for voting came the Boss and his lieutenants would assume command."[3]

Both parties during this period had Progressives, but they were especially strong in the Republican Party as the "New Idea" men. Their efforts help set the stage for Democrat Woodrow Wilson, a latecomer to Progressivism.[4] Among the New Idea leaders was George L. Record, a lawyer by trade who had began working for reforms in the 1890s and who functioned as the movement's chief theoretician.[5] Mark Fagan, reform mayor of Jersey City, and Everett Colby, Progressive leader in the legislature, were also prominent in the New Idea Progressive movement. Republican John Franklin Fort, a former judge, who held the office of governor in New Jersey just prior to Wilson, from 1908 to 1911, was generally aligned with the movement for reform in his party. He received political machine support in securing the Republican nomination in 1907 but broke away from the party professionals a year and half after his election, denouncing boss rule and embracing the New Idea principles.[6] Sometimes, though, he distressed Republican reformers by his willingness to deal with the conservative Republicans.[7]

Fort patterned his administration along the lines of the Hughes administration in New York. He sought some much-needed reform, but, given his tiff with the bosses, he had little support in the legislature.[8] The legislature in 1910 changed the name of the Railroad Commission to the Board of Public Utilities Commissioners and extended its jurisdiction to other public utilities but gave it only slight authority. Progressive Democratic legislators called it a "public futility bill" for "the relief of the Public Service Corporation." It was later rewritten in the Wilson administration to give the commission some power.[9] Fort tried but failed to extend the primary requirement to congressional and gubernatorial elections. Over the objections of machine leaders, however, he secured the adoption of a civil service law that extended civil service to a large number of state employees.[10]

Fort was under fire by the corporations, which, he felt, were largely responsible for the machines in both parties. He was very conscious of their influence in state politics. Yet he felt there was considerable support in New Jersey for political and economic reform and that history was on the side of the reformers.[11] Wilson, who followed him in office, was to carry out the revolution Fort had in mind.

GETTING THERE

Wilson, born in Staunton, Virginia, earned a PhD in political science from Johns Hopkins University and became president of Princeton University in New Jersey in 1902. He received the initial push for public office from wealthy journalist George Harvey, president of Harper and Brothers and editor of *Harper's Weekly*, a conservative publication. Harvey was impressed when he first heard Wilson speak in 1902 in his inaugural address as president of Princeton. He was among the first to see Wilson as a potential candidate for the presidency and later told Wilson he would do what he could to bring this about.[12] In March 1906 Wilson noted to a friend that he was not taking Harvey's suggestion that he run for president seriously.[13]

Harvey, though, continued on and touched bases with his friend Democratic Party boss James Smith, who later also came on board behind Wilson. Smith, a former US senator and a wealthy banker, businessperson, and publisher headquartered in Newark in Essex County, had influence throughout the state. Harvey and Smith settled on a strategy of first getting Wilson elected governor of New Jersey in 1910 and using this as a stepping-stone to get him elected president. The Democratic Party in 1910, to say the least, needed a strong gubernatorial candidate. The party had not won that office since 1892. Both Harvey and Smith thought Wilson would do well with Republican and independent voters as well as with Democrats of the Cleveland variety. They also felt that with some adjustments in his policy stands, he might also be able to ride into office on the crest of the Progressive wave sweeping the nation and the state.[14]

Smith said he would endorse Wilson if he accepted the party organization. Wilson agreed that he would not try to break down the party organization and replace it with one of his own should he be elected governor: "The last thing I should think of would be building up a machine of my own." Wilson also said he would expect the existing organization to work with him on policies that were good for the party and the state and that he would be free in regard to the choice of "measures and men." Consulting with a friend in a letter dated June 27, 1910, Wilson noted that the plan to nominate him as governor was part of a broader plan to make him president, that he had been in a meeting with Smith on the matter, and that "I have promised nothing."[15]

Wilson had a decidedly unprogressive background. A Cleveland Democrat, he had been critical of Altgeld, Bryan, and organized labor. Progressive reformers were aware of these stands and his close association with the bosses. Among the reformers was Joseph P. Tumulty, who later served President Wilson as his private secretary. At the time Wilson was considering a run for governor, Tumulty was among the Progressive Democrats in the New Jersey legislature. He attacked Wilson bitterly as a tool of the bosses and the big interests that the Progressives were fighting.[16] Tumulty later wrote: "We suspected that the 'Old Gang' was up to its old trick of foisting upon the Democrats of the state a tool which they could use for their own advantage, who, under the name of the Democratic party, would do the bidding of the corporate interests . . ."[17] Hoping to get some idea of what the bosses were thinking, he contacted Bob Davis, known as the Boss of Hudson County, who had lined up behind Wilson. Tumulty somewhat naively asked Davis if he thought Wilson would make a good governor. Davis turned to Tumulty and shouted: "How the hell do I know whether he'll make a good governor . . . he will make a good candidate, and that is the only thing that interests me."[18]

Wilson frequently expressed his hostility to labor unions in writings and speeches during the early 1900s. He once claimed unions were out to keep production as low as possible.[19]

In 1910 the New Jersey Federation of Labor opposed his candidacy for governor and denounced him as a foe of labor.[20] Wilson was ready and willing to change his views regarding labor, but he backpedaled only a bit, being fearful of alienating Smith or Harvey just before the nominating convention.[21]

With the bosses' support, Democrats chose Wilson as their gubernatorial nominee on the first ballot at the party convention in September 1910. Wilson in accepting the nomination called for corporate control, equal taxation, and economy in governmental operations. He also noted that he had not sought the office and, in accepting the nomination, had made no pledge of any kind that would prevent him from doing what he felt was right.[22] Following the convention, though, Wilson conferred with party leaders and, no doubt to their satisfaction, became convinced that he was not going to emerge victorious without the help of the state Democratic committee, headed by James Nugent, who was also the chief lieutenant of James Smith. Wilson went on to place a lot of reliance on the Democratic machine to run his campaign. He told an interviewer in response to a question about the speaking tour: "I shall place myself in the hands of the Democratic State Committee. I shall do whatever that committee thinks best and wise." Nugent took care of campaign arrangements, publicity, and fund-raising. Publisher George Harvey functioned as an advisor on media matters.[23] Wilson, though, made the final decision as to what went into the campaign message.

Throughout much of the ensuing campaign, Progressives continued to express their concern about Wilson's commitment to Progressive ideas and his ties to the party bosses. The situation was cleared up for many of them by Wilson's response to a series of questions posed to him by George Record. In his response Wilson went on record as strongly favoring a long list of Progressive reforms. As for the boss system, Wilson declared: "Its existence is notorious. I have made it my

Figure 10.1. Woodrow Wilson campaigning. Courtesy of the Library of Congress, Prints & Photographs Division, LC-DIG-ds-09981.

business for many years to observe and understand that system, and I hate it as thoroughly as I understand it." Wilson declared he wanted to abolish the system. He added that, if he were to be elected, he would not "either in the matter of appointments to office or assent to legislation, or in shaping of any part of the policy of my administration, submit to the dictation of any person or persons, special interest or organization." During the campaign Wilson repeatedly made it clear that he was his own man and would stay that way.[24]

Wilson showed his independence from the bosses by sticking to his position in favor of local option on the prohibition question. This was acceptable to reformers but conflicted with the stand that Democratic Party bosses, aligned with the brewers and saloon keepers, and those in the urban-industrial wing of the party had taken for years. He also pledged transparency, telling an audience that while he could not promise them what he would be able to accomplish as governor, he could promise them this: "Only let me inside and I will tell you everything that is going on in there."[25]

In the general election of 1910 Wilson faced Republican gubernatorial candidate Vivian Lewis, who, although he had the support of the conservatives, pledged he would pursue Progressive reforms if elected. Republican leaders hoped to pull both sides of the party together by nominating Lewis.²⁶ Lewis advocated a program as fully Progressive as Wilson's, but he lacked Wilson's personal and dramatic appeal and picked up only 43 percent of the vote compared to 54 percent for Wilson.²⁷ Wilson had pulled together both genuine reformers and political bosses who did not care one way or another about reform but only wanted power and the rewards that came with winning office. Observers commented on the quality of his campaign—an educational one based on "calm, sane, and clear speeches"—and his ability to draw votes from Republicans as well as Democrats.²⁸ According to one estimate, he won over about one out of every three Republican voters, doing far better in this regard than anyone else on the Democratic ticket.²⁹

CONFRONTATION WITH SMITH

Wilson, like Roosevelt and Hughes, owed his nomination for governor to the party bosses.

Yet, though he ran with their backing, he also campaigned as a Progressive who rejected machine politics and declared that he would not only be independent of the machine if elected but would work against it. The bosses brushed all this talk aside as campaign rhetoric. They just did not believe Wilson meant what he said. They felt he was just wisely looking for votes. They also felt that in Wilson they had a candidate who would be a good vote-getter but who, being a greenhorn when it came to practical politics, could easily be handled after the election should he win, no matter what he was now saying to the voters.³⁰

The situation was very much like that in which Charles Evans Hughes found himself in New York, and, as in the case of Hughes, the bosses found that Wilson could not be handled. A major confrontation took place between Wilson and party boss Jim Smith, who had played a major role in recruiting Wilson and giving him his start. Smith had assured Wilson that he would not make any effort after the election to go to the state legislature and gather the votes he needed to return to the US Senate. Smith had stayed out of a senatorial preference primary held in 1910 and won by James Edgar Martine, a less than impressive figure who had run unsuccessfully for various offices over a forty-year period without winning any of them.³¹

Under the primary election system in effect, those seeking a senate seat did not have to enter the primary, and the voters' first choice among those who did enter was not binding on state legislators—legislators still made the final decision. Many top-flight Democrats saw the primary as a waste of time because they expected that Republicans would be in control of the legislature and would choose a Republican senator no matter what the preference primary indicated.³² As it turned out, however, while the Republicans controlled the Senate by three votes, the Democrats had a majority in the joint session that would choose the US senator.

Seeing this after the election, Smith decided he wanted to go back to the US Senate and announced he was going to ask the legislature to send him there. Wilson did not think much of either Martine or Smith as US senators. He initially asked Smith to step back and support a compromise candidate they could agree on. When Smith refused, Wilson turned to Martine. Though Wilson did not think much of Martine and hoped to get someone more qualified for the position, Progressives pressured him to stand behind the person who got the most votes in the preference primary. In December 1910 Wilson declared that Smith was not "the people's choice" and every Democratic legislator had the duty to vote for Martine, whom the voters had favored. Wilson was applauded in some quarters for getting involved in the selection of a US senator—unlike Governor Dix of New York, who refused to intervene in a similar situation in his state, saying, in effect, it was none of his business—and to act in respect of the popular vote.[33]

Smith responded with charges that Wilson was guilty of foul play and making "a gratuitous attack upon one who has befriended him"; James Nugent, state Democratic chairman and an ally of Smith, said Wilson's action was not well advised.[34] Around this time, Oregon reformer William U'Ren wrote Wilson: "It hurts the politicians to play your game and their squeals are audible through the Associated Press even so far away as Oregon. Smith's whine that you are ungrateful is a very old story in Oregon, though we have not heard it since our Direct Primary Law was adopted."[35]

Wilson went on to lobby the legislature for Martine. In the first vote at the start of the legislature on January 10, Martine got forty votes, one shy of what he needed, and Smith received only ten votes. Smith, seeing no hope, released his delegates and left the city. This amounted to a huge victory for Wilson. Wilson wrote a friend:

> The whole country is marveling at it, and I am getting more credit than I deserve. I pitied Smith at the last. It was so plain that he had few real friends—that he held men by fear and power and the benefits he could bestow, not by love or loyalty or any genuine devotion. The minute it was seen that he was defeated his adherents began to desert him like rats leaving a sinking ship. He left Trenton (where his headquarters had at first been crowded) attended, I am told, only by his sons, and looking old and broken. He wept, they say, as he admitted himself utterly beaten. Such is the end of political power—particularly when selfishly obtained and heartlessly used. It is a pitiless game, in which, it would seem, one takes one's life in one's hands,—and for me it has only begun![36]

EXECUTIVE LEADERSHIP AND LEGISLATING

During the 1910 campaign, his Republican opponent Lewis championed the idea of a "constitutional governor"—who honored the separation of powers and kept out of the activities of the legislature. Wilson objected, saying that if this actually was a valid definition of a constitutional governor, he intended to be an unconstitutional one. He rejected the idea that he, as governor, should do no more than offer advice and use the veto if necessary. Rather, he argued, that he as governor should take a leadership role when it came to legislation. He contended that in New Jersey and elsewhere the failure of governors to take charge had created a power vacuum that the bosses and machines had been filling.[37]

Speaking in Trenton on October, 3, 1910, he went on to point out: "You will notice that the Governor of this State is the only officer of the State government elected by all the people of New Jersey. Every member of the legislature is elected by some portion of the people of New Jersey. If the Governor does not talk, therefore, the people of New Jersey, as a whole, have no spokesman."[38]

By breaking Smith's power Wilson had become undisputed head of the New Jersey Democratic Party. With the bosses in retreat, he was free to become the executive leader he had called for during the campaign and in many other speeches prior to his inauguration. Beating the bosses also gave him national acclaim, boosting his visibility as a presidential candidate. What he needed to further advance his political career was a record of legislative achievement.

After meeting with advisors, including George Record and Progressive leaders from both major parties in the legislature and some practical politicians from the old school, Wilson decided to focus on four priorities in the upcoming legislature: a campaign practices act that would impose campaign spending limits and require disclosure; a more effective public utilities bill; a worker's compensation measure, and a direct primary bill.[39]

Following a meeting with U'Ren after his election as governor in 1910, Wilson came away with a more favorable impression of the initiative and referendum. The longtime critic of these devices of direct democracy now said he was impressed by how well they had turned out in Oregon. He felt they were no sure cure-all, but contrary to what he had expected, they had proven to be useful tools in bringing reform. At the same time, he decided not to make direct democracy one of his priorities, at least for the time being, and concentrated on the four areas agreed upon by the group he met with prior to his inaugural. Among these people only Record had been enthusiastic about the instruments of direct democracy.[40]

Wilson led the legislative charge for his priorities much as he had done in the contest against Smith, showing his skills in political maneuvering and infighting. This time he took the unprecedented step of attending the caucus of Democratic assemblymen. This turned out to be a three-hour, sometimes heated meeting in which he argued his position that the Democrats had an obligation to stand behind the historic measures as a matter of party policy for the good of the people.[41] He was able to get his program adopted in 1911, even though the senate was controlled by Republicans and Regular (non-Progressive) Democrats and the bosses of both parties opposed him. To the governor the passage of Progressive legislation during his first term was "just a bit of natural history. I came to the office in the fullness of time, when opinion was ripe on all these matters, when both parties were committed to these reforms, and by merely standing fast, by never losing sight of the business for an hour, but keeping up all sorts of (legitimate) pressure *all the time*, kept the mighty forces from being diverted or blocked at any point."[42]

The bosses were especially upset by the corrupt-practices act and the law extending the primary requirement for the nomination of candidates to several offices, including the governor and members of Congress. These measures were aimed directly at the bosses and the machine system they operated. The reaction of legislators tied to Democratic and Republican Party bosses to the Wilson-sponsored bill calling for the primary election of virtually all candidates is best described as "violent."[43]

Wilson had a particularly heated run-in with Nugent, who led the effort in the legislature to "line up the boys" against "Wilson's crazy laws."[44] Wilson attempted to persuade him to back off, but to no avail.[45] In July 1911 Nugent publicly toasted Wilson as "a liar and an ingrate."[46] Not long after this outburst Nugent lost his position as state party chair to someone more acceptable to the governor. Nugent and others accused Wilson of using his patronage to win over legislative votes, in effect of bribing legislators.[47] The first time Nugent suggested this, Wilson became furious and ordered him out of his office.[48] Wilson later stated: "My record will show that never have I bestowed or promised to bestow a political office in the state of New Jersey for the purpose of affecting the enactment of a law or for any political advantage whatever."[49]

After the election Wilson found himself besieged with applications for state jobs. He complained that "the question of appointments drives me nearly distracted, it is so nearly impossible to get true information or disinterested advice about persons—and so many persons are trying to impose upon me. I shall get used to it, but am not yet, and it goes hard."[50] By his own estimation, he spent nine-tenths of his time considering applications for jobs with the state.[51] He made eighty-one appointments, all Democrats, but, he claimed, all were well qualified for their positions.[52] He did not, however, as his biographer Baker pointed out, appear to have "the remotest idea of building up an organization of his own by the familiar method of placing his strong supporters in the best offices."[53]

Overall, Wilson disliked the patronage system and took little interest in using it to exert influence on legislators or to build up Progressive influence in the Democratic Party. Like most Progressives of the times, he expressed a dislike of spoils and a commitment to civil service.[54] In December 1910 he received a letter informing him that he had been unanimously elected vice-president of the National Civil Service Reform League. In an earlier message to the organization, Wilson had declared that he regarded civil service reform "fundamental to all good government."[55]

FOLLOWING UP

Wilson had been governor for only five months when he began his campaign for the presidency by taking a speaking tour around the country in the spring and summer of 1911. He campaigned as a full-fledged Progressive. In some places, though, he was viewed by some in the press as not that much different in his basic political outlook from the late John Johnson of Minnesota, who was considered a moderate.[56]

As might be expected, he started off with praise for Bryan in a speaking engagement in Lincoln, Nebraska.[57] Later, while in Texas, he received tremendous applause when he paid tribute to the late Governor Hogg for playing a leading part in bringing Progressivism to the state.[58] Shortly after his visit to South Carolina, the notorious racist demagogue Governor Coleman Blease came out against him. One of his advisors, however, told Wilson not to worry: by making an enemy of this "contemptible ass," he had made 20,000 friends in the state.[59] Stopping in Kentucky, he set off rumors that James McCreary, who was running for governor in that state, might wind up as Wilson's running mate.[60] Along the trail Wilson picked up the support of former Minnesota governor John Lind and frequently communicated with Virginia governor Andrew Jackson Montague, another supporter.[61]

Speaking in Nebraska on May 27, 1911, he noted that many in the East, including himself, had been slow to accept the devices of direct democracy but that he now accepted the fact that they worked in practice.[62] He went on to make a strong defense of the initiative and referendum at the Conference of Governors in September of 1911 in a spirited dispute with Governor Emmet O'Neal of Alabama.[63] In a private letter a few days later, however, he noted he had only tepid support for the initiative and referendum and had long opposed the recall as it applied to judges.[64] A newspaper interview indicated that he saw the principal value of these devices as shotguns behind the door promoting "righteousness among public officials."[65]

Wilson received considerable criticism from his opponents in state politics and those opposing his bid for the presidency for neglecting his duties as governor while traveling around the country in search of delegates.[66] This was one of the lines of attack by the New Jersey bosses who set out to both derail Wilson's run for the presidency and hurt Wilson in the 1911 state legislative elections. He campaigned in 1911 for all the Democratic legislative nominees with the exception of those supported by Smith's machine in Essex County. Smith and Nugent, in return, decided to throw the election so that the governor would face a Republican legislature, look bad, and lose momentum in his bid for the presidential nomination. Smith sat out the election, doing nothing to get Democratic candidates elected. A bitter man after his loss, he also used his *Newark Star* to do what damage he could to Wilson.[67]

New Jersey Republicans took over both statehouses in 1911. With a hostile legislature Wilson did not accomplish much in 1912 other than to use his veto power to prevent the undoing of reforms he had made in the previous session. Writing to a friend in the closing week of the 1912 session, Wilson noted: "This has been a petty and barren legislature. It has done nothing worth mentioning except try to amend and mar the wonderful things we accomplished last year."[68] He provoked a Republican outrage by vetoing forty-two bills in one bunch.[69] Wilson was happy when the session was over: "Now I must rush out again in search of delegates,—shy birds more difficult to find in genuine species than the snark itself!"[70]

Prior to taking office as president in March 1913, Wilson, acting in his capacity as governor, addressed the New Jersey legislature and called upon it to enact several reforms. The most significant of these to secure passage was a set of regulatory bills, known as the "Seven Sisters," intended to curb mergers leading to monopolies, price fixing, and other restraints of trade. In putting together this legislation, he acted on the principle that "guilt is personal" and the directors of corporations who violated the law should be liable to fine and imprisonment.[71]

LEGACY

Wilson had a short, dramatic, and productive gubernatorial administration, intended to propel him into the presidency. He showed himself as a versatile political strategist, adapting to changes in public opinion, furthering his goals by working with those who could advance his interests, and breaking those ties as expediency dictated.[72] He had set an example of "purposeful gubernatorial leadership" when it came to combating the bosses and steering through legislative reform.[73]

On several occasions Wilson built the case for gubernatorial leadership. Speaking before a group of businesspeople in Portland, Oregon, in 1911, for example, he declared: "The whole country . . . is clamoring for leadership; and a new role, which to many persons seems a little less than unconstitutional, is thrust upon our executives. The people are impatient of a President or a governor who will not formulate a policy and insist upon its adoption. They are impatient of a governor who will not exercise energetic leadership, who will not make his appeals directly to public opinion and insist that the dictates of public opinion be carried out in definite legal reforms of his own suggestion."[74] Wilson not only built the case for executive leadership but provided an example of how leadership could be exercised.

Like other governors, he was also aware of the need to improve the ability of legislators to do their work. The legislature he knew in New Jersey was one in which 90 percent of the measures introduced "came out of cubbyholes all over the state," written by an unknown lawyer hired by a constituent or private group. Much better, he thought, was a system of common counsel and one where measures came out of "public places where men had got together and compared views."[75]

While he might not have been a deeply full-fledged Progressive, he did effectively express Progressive ideas, especially when it came to corporations. In the spring of 1910, for example, he declared that "the individual, not the corporation, the single living person, not the artificial group of persons existing merely by permission of the law, is the only rightful possessor alike of rights and of privileges. The corporation is a convenience, not a natural member of society. Society must be organized so that the individual will not be crushed, will not be unnecessarily hampered. Every legal instrument created for his convenience, like the corporation, must be created only for his convenience and never for his government or suppression..."[76]

The reform package he was willing to pursue was far from comprehensive. He was a latecomer as a supporter of direct democracy He was no fan of woman suffrage or prohibition. When it came to race, in the words of his biographer Arthur Link, he "inherited and retained the upper-class southern affection for the Negro and the belief that the black man should remain segregated and not aspire toward so-called equality with the whites."[77] In New Jersey he built on the work of others, especially the "New Idea" men, and his behavior in running for governor and as governor demonstrated his high capacity as a political strategist: "With great skill, by adjusting his views to conform with popular sentiment, by cultivating the favor of men who could advance his interests, by making and breaking commitments as expediency dictated, he maneuvered his way to his goal."[78] Wilson did not build for the future of Progressivism in New Jersey by strengthening the Democratic Party through use of patronage or any other means so that it could continue as an agency of reform. He always had his eye on the White House, and after he left New Jersey the state fell back into the hands of the conservatives.

NOTES

1. Mathews "The New Stateism."
2. See generally Lockard, *New Jersey Governor*.
3. Baker, *Woodrow Wilson*, 137.
4. Lockard, *New Jersey Governor*, 68.
5. Hirst, *Woodrow Wilson*, 33–34.
6. "Fort Has Gone to the Cobyites," *New York Times*, May 28, 1909, 7; "Jersey Republicans to War on Gov. Fort," *New York Times*, November 14, 1909, 10; "Gov. Fort Lashes All Party Bosses," *New York Times*, September 23, 1909, 7.
7. Noble, *New Jersey before Wilson*, 107.
8. "Woodrow Wilson Talks on Big Public Questions," *New York Times*, December 24, 1911, SM1.
9. Noble, *New Jersey before Wilson*, 112, 113.
10. Claim made by Fort in "Fort Has Gone to the Cobyites." See also Noble, *New Jersey before Wilson*, 142–45.
11. "Governor Fort on Bossism in Politics," *New York Times*, October 10, 1909, SM7.

12. See "Colonel Harvey's Speech Proposing Wilson for the Presidency," delivered at the Lotos Club, February 3, 1906, in Link, *Papers of Woodrow Wilson*, 16:299–301.
13. Wilson to A. W. Hazen, March 20, 1906, in ibid., 338.
14. Hirst, *Woodrow Wilson*, 5–7.
15. Ibid., 14–15, 25.
16. Ibid., 34.
17. Tumulty, *Woodrow Wilson As I Know Him*, 11, 14.
18. Ibid., 15.
19. Hirst, *Woodrow Wilson*, 36.
20. Baker, *Woodrow Wilson*, 70.
21. Hirst, *Woodrow Wilson*, 36.
22. "Wilson Named for Governor in Jersey," *New York Times*, September 16, 1910, 3.
23. Startt, *Woodrow Wilson and the Press*, 71–72.
24. Hirst, *Woodrow Wilson*, 103, 105.
25. Quoted in "Political Campaign," *The Outlook*, September 7, 1912, 5.
26. "Jersey Republicans Name Vivian Lewis," *New York Times*, September 21, 1910, 3.
27. Hirst, *Woodrow Wilson*, 62.
28. "The Elections," *The Outlook*, November 19, 1910, 607–9.
29. Reynolds, *Testing Democracy*, 138–39.
30. George and George, *Woodrow Wilson and Colonel House*, 57.
31. Baker, *Woodrow Wilson*, 110.
32. George and George, *Woodrow Wilson and Colonel House*, 60.
33. "Progress," *The Outlook*, January 21, 1911, 105–6; "What Is a Governor?" *The Outlook*, December 24, 1910, 893–4.
34. "Foul Play Retorts Smith to Wilson," *New York Times*, December 10, 1910, 12.
35. William U'Ren to Wilson, December 14, 1910, in Link, *Papers of Woodrow Wilson*, 22:197.
36. Hirst, *Woodrow Wilson*, 162.
37. Ibid., 83–84; Baker, *Woodrow Wilson*, 34.
38. Hirst, *Woodrow Wilson*, 86.
39. Baker, *Woodrow Wilson*, 131.
40. Ibid., 130–31.
41. Hirst, *Woodrow Wilson*, 189–93.
42. Wilson to Mary Hulbert, April 23, 1911, in Baker, *Woodrow Wilson*, 169–72.
43. Baker, *Woodrow Wilson*, 177.
44. Quoted by Baker, *Woodrow Wilson*, 139.
45. Story about the confrontation between Nugent and Wilson is from "Woodrow Wilson Talks on Big Public Questions."
46. "Chairman Nugent Insults Gov. Wilson," *New York Times*, July 27, 1911, 1.
47. "Woodrow Wilson Talks on Big Public Questions."
48. Baker, *Woodrow Wilson*, 143.
49. "Wilson Charges Deal to Beat Him," *Chicago Daily Tribune*, April 7, 1912, in Link, *Papers of Woodrow Wilson*, 24:300.
50. Baker, *Woodrow Wilson*, 152.
51. Campaign Address in Jersey City, New Jersey, May 25, 1912, in Link, *Papers of Woodrow Wilson*, 24:437.
52. Robert L. Norton, "Post Representative Meets Presidential Candidate in Princeton Home," *Boston Post*, January 27, 1912, in Link, *Papers of Woodrow Wilson*, 24:74–78.
53. Baker, *Woodrow Wilson*, 152.
54. Lockard, *New Jersey Governor*, 119.

55. See Elliot Hersey Goodwin to Wilson, December 23, 1910, and Wilson to Charles William Eliot, November 22, 1910, in Link, *Papers of Woodrow Wilson*, 22:256, 78.

56. Editorial, *Kansas City Star*, May 5, 1911, reprinted as "An Interview in Kansas City, Missouri," in Link, *Papers of Woodrow Wilson*, 23:4.

57. "A News Report of a Day in Lincoln, Nebraska."

58. "An Address in Dallas at the Texas State Fair," October 28, 1911, in Link, *Papers of Woodrow Wilson*, 23:499–500.

59. A. S. Colyar to Wilson, June 23, 1911, in Link, *Papers of Woodrow Wilson*, 23:173.

60. "Wilson-McCreary Boom," *New York Times*, July 13, 1911, 1.

61. "Minnesota Wilson Club," *New York Times*, January 21, 1912: 4, See also the series of letters from Montague in Link, *Papers of Woodrow Wilson*, 23: 133, 327, 359, 390.

62. "A News Report of a Day in Lincoln, Nebraska."

63. "Three News Reports about the Governor Conference at Spring Lake, New Jersey," September 12, 1911, in Link, *Papers of Woodrow Wilson*, 23:317–24.

64. Wilson to Andrew Jackson Montague, September 27, 1911, in Link, *Papers of Woodrow Wilson*, 23:390–91.

65. "Woodrow Wilson Talks on Big Public Questions."

66. See, for example: "Harmon to Fight for the Presidency," *New York Times*, June 4, 1911, 1.

67. George and George, *Woodrow Wilson and Colonel House*, 59. See also "The Elections: Their Significance, a Poll of the Press," *The Outlook*, November 25, 1911, 709.

68. Wilson to Mary Allen Hulbert Peck, April 1, 1912, in Link, *Papers of Woodrow Wilson*, 24:271.

69. "Forty Vetoes Start Fight," *Trenton True American*, April 12, 1912, in Link, *Papers of Woodrow Wilson*, 24:324–28.

70. Quoted in Baker, *Woodrow Wilson*, 292–93.

71. Ibid., 435; Hirst, *Woodrow Wilson*, 237–38.

72. George and George, *Woodrow Wilson and Colonel House*, 57.

73. Lockard, *New Jersey Governor*, 108.

74. Address before the Commercial Club of Portland, Oregon, May 18, 1911, quoted by Macmahon, "Woodrow Wilson," 100. See also McLean, "Early Modern Governor," 21; and Matthews, "The New Role of the Governor," 224.

75. Speech given in 1915 to US Chamber of Commerce, quoted by Graves, *American State Government*, 291–92.

76. Hirst, *Woodrow Wilson*, 11–12, quoting from "Living Principles of Democracy," published in *Harper's Weekly*, April 9, 1910, 9–10.

77. Link, "Portrait of the President," 9.

78. George and George, *Woodrow Wilson and Colonel House*, 57.

11

THE REST OF THE EAST

Republican and Conservative, Doing What Could Be Done with Boss and Corporate Control and Only Limited Power

Closing out the East with Pennsylvania, Delaware, and New England, we find states that, for most of the period under review, were heavily Republican and conservative. Gubernatorial leadership during the Progressive era is more difficult to find in these states than in New York and New Jersey. They had no Hugheses or Wilsons. Governors in Pennsylvania functioned in a political system in which political bosses, allied with powerful corporations, were a dominant force in state politics, constituting the real government. Still, a line of relatively unknown governors helped produce a set of moderate reforms through this boss-ridden governing system, working, for the most part, with the bosses. Delaware also was a state where business-oriented Republican governors helped usher in a modest set of reforms.

New England governors pursuing change had to contend with powerful bosses (the one established by Charles Brayton in Rhode Island was truly powerful) and powerful economic interests. Severe limits on the number of terms and the length of terms, one or two years in length, also worked against the ability of governors in this region to do much of anything. Voters in the six New England states elected seventy-six different governors from 1890 to 1920.[1]

In much of New England the conservatism of the states created a situation in which a push for reform was confined to those exceptional occasions when insurgent Republicans or progressive Democrats gained the gubernatorial office, but even then, conservative control of the legislature was so strong and the restrictions on the terms and power of the governors so severe that the potential for significant breakthroughs was severely limited.

WORKING WITH THE BOSSES IN PENNSYLVANIA

Manufacturers had much to do with the building of Pennsylvania and, in part because of Republican support for a high tariff that protected their industries, the building of the Republican Party in the state. As journalist John Gunther wrote, manufacturing made Pennsylvania "ferociously Republican."[2]

Simon Cameron, who served for a time as secretary of war under Abraham Lincoln, began to build a powerful state Republican machine shortly after the Civil War that was subsequently led by Matthew Quay and, following him, Boies Penrose. All three served in the US Senate and were immensely powerful political bosses in the state—and among the most powerful if not the most powerful in the nation. The Pennsylvania Manufacturers Association was closely allied with the organization, which rather steadily followed a conservative course for several decades.[3] From time to time, however, more Progressive Republicans representing urban centers, principally Pittsburgh and Philadelphia, challenged Quay and Penrose. At times, too, the bosses wound up supporting governors who turned out to be more Progressive than they had expected.

Republican Samuel Pennypacker noted in his autobiography that his gubernatorial victory in 1902 "came to me without the lifting of a finger, the expenditure of a dime, or the utterance of a sigh."[4] This longtime lower court judge was picked for the nomination by his distant relative, political boss Matthew Quay, who was anxious to head off another person he did not like who was making a bid for the nomination. Quay had someone approach Pennypacker with an offer of the nomination. Pennypacker was reluctant but agreed to meet with Quay, US senator Boies Penrose, and some other higher-ups in the party organization to further consider the matter. The party leaders won him over.

In running against former Democratic governor Robert Pattison, Pennypacker followed the itinerary prepared by the Republican campaign committee for two and half months, sometimes speaking three times a day. To him: "The crowds were pretty much alike, made up of the same kind of faces and shouting the same shouts."[5] Though he had the backing of the bosses, he was able to cultivate an image of an independent or nonmachine candidate. This was boosted when he received the endorsement of President Theodore Roosevelt, who announced from Washington that Pennypacker's defeat would be "a national calamity."[6] He also had the support of veterans and farm groups and an endorsement from popular former governor James Beaver. He won easily with over 54 percent of the vote.

In office, he sometimes showed his independence from Quay in the hiring and firing of officials, but he remained close to Quay, whom he greatly admired and to whom he felt a sense of loyalty. He later noted in his autobiography: "I recognized a subsidiary duty to the party which elected me and an obligation to those who had trusted me and given me support. If I had turned upon Quay, as Wilson turned upon Harvey and Smith in New Jersey, I should have given an exhibition of what I regard as doubtful ethics."[7] He went on to proudly add: "Mr. Quay not only had a fondness for me, but had confidence in my judgment."[8]

In his autobiography, written in 1918, Pennypacker was critical of the strong assertive role played by Presidents Roosevelt and Wilson in the legislative process. The former governor wrote: "It is one of the unwritten laws, never infringed upon, that the governor shall not appear before the legislature, and it is founded upon the correct theory that the legislative bodies shall be kept from undue influence."[9]

As governor he was far more assertive. Though he did say to legislators that he did not think it was appropriate for the governor to suggest legislation to them in person, he accepted the request of the legislature to address the body shortly after he took office. He also used his authority to call the legislature into special session after its members had refused to act on his recommendations.

Overall, he was a relatively active governor, often in the area of reform. Much reform activity took place in an extra session of the legislature in January 1906, which was called by Pennypacker to respond to what was widely seen as a repudiation of the Republican Party and its political bosses by the voters in the November 1905 elections. With the trouncing in mind, Pennypacker, as one account put it, became "eager to do anything to regain the favor of the people, and . . . seized the idea of calling the Legislature to meet and pass upon reform measures." Shortly after the November 1905 election Pennsylvania Railroad officials felt it wise to give up the practice of handing out free passes to politicians, and the legislators had to pay for their own transportation to Harrisburg to attend the session. Things were also different once they got there—there were no bosses around to greet them.[10]

During his term, lasting from 1903 to 1907, the legislature enacted voter registration legislation, increased penalties for election abuses, established requirements for civil service examinations for specific offices in Philadelphia, and restricted the use of child labor. During his reign the legislature also established the Pennsylvania State Police, the first statewide police force in the nation, to replace the use of private police forces by industrialists in disputes with labor or the use of the National Guard in such disputes. Organized labor at the time called the state policemen "Pennypacker's Cossacks," but the governor saw this as a step forward in handling industrial disputes.[11]

Pennypacker also gained a reputation as a conservationist by protecting wildlife and thousands of acres of forest land. On the revenue side, he did not hesitate to call for new taxes on out-of-state corporations engaged in mining activities in Pennsylvania. The legislature went along with this and, as he requested, used the funds to pay for new roads in the state. He was also active in securing pure food legislation. Although initially uncomfortable with the idea, Pennypacker became a champion of the direct primary, thinking that it would generally benefit the Republican Party in the state by helping to win over Progressive Republicans and restoring public trust in the party.[12] This reform, though, was not to come during his administration.

Early in his administration Pennypacker was smarting from criticism he had received during the campaign, especially from what he saw as the offensive way he was caricatured in newspaper cartoons. Being the butt of jest and drawings did not go down well with him: "He was portrayed as a perverse parrot and a flustered farmer. It was a new, surprising, and painful revelation to him. He had lived a tranquil and serene life on the bench and amid his musty volumes. To be held up day after day to criticism and ridicule was an unwanted and harrowing experience."[13] He struck back at the media in his inaugural address. He and a lot of legislators who shared his scorn for the media adopted a bill making it a crime to cartoon a public official in a negative way—a widely criticized measure that was repealed in 1907.

Pennypacker also gained some attention by demonstrating his discomfort with a scientific approach to the improvement of mankind when, in 1905, he vetoed an "Act for the Prevention of Idiocy," a measure prepared by eminent physicians and surgeons that gave medical experts the authority to sterilize "feebleminded" children in the state's several institutions. This was similar to legislation later adopted in Indiana (see chapter 4). In issuing the veto he declared: "To permit such an operation would be to inflict cruelty upon a helpless class . . . which the state has undertaken to protect." He expressed his reluctance to rely on the staff of scientific experts to make such decisions: "Scientists, like all other men whose experiences have been limited to one pursuit . . . sometimes need to be restrained. Men of high scientific attainments are prone . . . to lose sight of broad principles outside their domain . . ."[14]

After Quay's death in 1904, Senator Penrose took control of the Republican political machine. Penrose, born into a prominent and wealthy Philadelphia family, has been described as "burly in stature (6'4", 200 pounds)" and "blessed with a brilliant mind and great political talent" who "showed no interest in constructive legislation, good government, or attaining the status of statesman. As a party boss, to his credit, he never became a grafter, being independently wealthy. He craved only political power."[15] Still, he did not get in the way of reform or at least some reform. He backed Edward Stuart, former mayor of Philadelphia who became governor following Pennypacker and who proceeded to become active in many of the same areas as his predecessor. He led campaigns to combat tuberculosis and improve public schools and signed a bill creating a commission to regulate railroads. Another Republican governor chosen by Penrose, John Tener, a former professional baseball player, served from 1911 to 1915 and, though an early supporter of Taft for the Republican nomination in 1912, continued on the moderate Progressive path that produced the state's first direct primary law in 1913.[16]

In 1914, while seeking reelection to the US Senate, Penrose supported the nomination of Dr. Martin Brumbaugh as the Republican candidate for governor. Brumbaugh was a career educator, at the time superintendent of schools in Philadelphia, and well known around the state. Some looked at the recent election of Woodrow Wilson as an indicator that the times were good in politics for a scholar like Brumbaugh. Looking like a winner who could help the whole ticket, he received Penrose's support and went on to win the nomination and the general election, though he distanced himself from Penrose during the campaign.[17]

Brumbaugh generally followed a conservative path, doing little in terms of legislation and issuing a large number of vetoes (setting a record for the time of 409). Coming into office he declared that the state already had too many laws and a bloated bureaucracy, burdening the people and benefiting only self-serving politicians. He said he was going to work for only a "few vital" laws. One of these was the local option when it came to prohibition, but the legislature refused to go along with this. On the other hand, he took considerable pleasure in the passage of a child labor law in 1915. At the time, Pennsylvania led the nation in the employment of children under sixteen, most of whom worked in coal mines, glass factories, and textile mills.[18]

In no time at all Brumbaugh got on the wrong side of Penrose, control over appointments to office being a bone of contention, and the machine took off after him. Inspired by what had occurred in New York in the case of William Sulzer, party leaders for a time gave serious thought to impeaching and removing him from office but decided to back off. A biographer sympathetic to Brumbaugh argues that he was the victim of a terrible legislature: "Probably no other chief executive of the state ever had to cope with a legislature as recalcitrant, obstructionist, and rancorous as the Penrose-policed one of 1917."[19]

DELAWARE: ADDICKS, DU PONTS, AND THE BUSINESS GOVERNORS

Delaware was a Democratic state after the Civil War, but the Republican Party gained ground, being bolstered by the support of manufacturers that took root in the northern part of the state and the backing of black males who secured the vote through a constitution adopted in 1897. The result was almost complete control by the Republicans throughout the first two decades of the twentieth century—no Democrat was elected governor in this period.[20] Meanwhile, members of the illustrious du Pont family, whose gunpowder and chemical company made it one of the richest families in the nation, played a prominent role in the politics of the state. Nearly every cause that caught fire in the state had the support of one du Pont or another. The state existed as "a kind of caliphate of the family."[21]

The Republican buildup and the du Pont ascendancy in the state were complicated and somewhat frustrated in the late 1890s and early 1900s by a factional rift in the Republican Party instigated by the efforts of J. Edward Addicks, considered by his Delaware opponents as a "carpetbagger" from Philadelphia, to secure a US Senate seat representing Delaware. Addicks used his considerable wealth, made from financing and building gas works, to wage a series of campaigns, all of which were unsuccessful, for this position. He felt that the amount of money he had poured into party coffers, estimated to amount to $3 million over the years, entitled him to a Senate seat. As he once expressed it: "I've bought it, I've paid for it; and I'm going to have it."[22] Addicks's expenditures included the purchase of votes from ordinary citizens to get his supporters elected to the legislature.[23] Addicks's faction of the Republican Party, known as the "Union Republicans," fought with the "regular Republicans," led by Addicks's rival, Henry A. du Pont. One result of the struggle between two evenly matched sides was the difficulty in coming to a conclusion in the legislature over who should be chosen for the Senate. For a two-year period the state did not have any representation at all in the Senate because the lawmakers were deadlocked.

Over the Progressive period the state had a long line of Republican governors, most of whom had a business background. Some were more Progressive than others. Businessman John Hunn, elected in 1900, had mildly Progressive credentials. He encouraged the admission of women to the state college, the extension of the highway program, the provision of free public libraries, and the protection of wildlife. A loyal Republican and, some suspected, one sympathetic to the Addicks's faction, he refused to go along with an effort by reformers to repeal a law that allowed "voting assistants" to help people prepare their ballots. Republican Party leaders argued that without this help illiterate blacks would not be able to vote and, without this vote, the state might go Democratic. Addicks Republicans, outnumbered by regular Republicans and Democrats when it came to election officials, found it especially useful to have voting assistants looking out for their interests in the election booths.[24] Preston Lea, serving as governor from 1905 to 1909, earned some credit as a reformer by ending the payment of fees in order to vote and by promoting the initiative and referendum. Some progress in regard to the latter came after Francis I. du Pont, another member of the illustrious family, helped persuade the legislature to allow the voters to express their opinion on the subject in a statewide advisory referendum. In 1906 the voters overwhelmingly demonstrated their support for the initiative and referendum. The legislature, though, decided to allow their use only in the city of Wilmington.[25]

Republican Simeon Selby Pennewill, who held the office of governor from 1909 to 1913, was a supporter of Taft for the Republican nomination and a fiscal conservative who spent much of his time seeking efficiencies and budget cutting. He was more than willing to accept an offer from T. Coleman du Pont of a million dollars to construct a 103-mile road running between the state's northern and southern boundaries.[26] From his point of view one of the more unpleasant incidents of his time in office was getting a bad case of "ivy poisoning" after coming in contact with the plant while inspecting the state militia camping grounds.[27] Progressives may have taken some pleasure in this development. He had angered them by refusing to sign off on a factory inspection bill. According to one account, he was taken in by companies opposed to the law:

> The business interests of Wilmington, the only large manufacturing town in the little State, besieged Governor Pennewill with protests against the bill. They invited him to visit Wilmington, where he went through the farce of "examining" factory conditions carefully prepared for his coming. The United Tobacco Company, a large employer of women, declared that if the law went into effect it would have to close its Delaware factories. The laundries objected determinedly to the machinery provision, and so did the hosiery mills. Governor Pennewill, who is a farmer, residing in the southern part of the State, and has no personal knowledge of business conditions, had the additional disadvantage of being an organization Republican, and the organization took the side of the interests at once.[28]

On the more Progressive side, Charles Miller, who followed in 1913, promoted school reform, a pet project of one Pierre du Pont, and road improvements among other projects. He was another successful businessman, a director of several corporations across the nation, many of which were engaged in banking and mining. One source claimed: "Mr. Miller is perhaps more widely known than any previous governor of the state of Delaware. At the time of his election in 1912 he had a personal acquaintance with all but seven of the governors of the United States."[29] Investor-businessman John Gillis Townsend Jr. took over as governor from 1917 to 1921 and became the advocate of educational and labor reforms. He also stood for the ratification of the national woman suffrage constitutional amendment, telling state legislators in 1919: "Woman suffrage has been a subject of public discussion for over half a century. It is not an agitation of the moment, it is a worldwide question of right and wrong. Your supreme duty is to think and act for the good of your state and nation."[30] Suffrage leaders credited him with working hard to secure a positive vote—lining up the support of T. Coleman du Pont among others—but the legislature failed to go along. The Democrats were opposed, the Republicans, some of whom were very antagonistic to Townsend, were divided, and the liquor interests here, as elsewhere, opposed the amendment out of fear that women voters would bring prohibition.[31]

RHODE ISLAND: BOSS BRAYTON, GARVIN, HIGGINS

Rhode Island was one of the states where reform was particularly difficult to come by. Lincoln Steffens put it bluntly in 1905: "The political condition of Rhode Island is notorious, acknowledged, and it is shameful."[32] As Steffens saw it, the state was dominated by Republicans—US senator Nelson Aldrich and political boss General Charles R. Brayton, who organized and directed party affairs and, behind them, the leading business interests.[33] Steffens saw this system of boss control, corruption, and legal restraints on the state's chief executive producing "safe" governors who were basically powerless "administrative mummies."[34]

Brayton built his political machine in small towns and rural areas and through an alliance with railroads and other corporations. An influential lobbyist and chair of the Republican Party's Central Committee, he operated for thirty years out of room 2007 in the offices of the sheriff of Providence County in the Rhode Island statehouse. At the height of his power he would go into the house chamber, sit down next to the speaker, and hand him the bills he expected to be passed.[35] Taking a bribe or "being paid for their time" was a common practice of voters in several rural districts and resulted in sending reliable Brayton men to the legislature. Brayton also curried favor with legislators by getting them jobs with businesses he represented or appointments to offices, such as judgeships or party positions, and by steering clients their way if the legislators happened to be lawyers. At times legislators were paid to vote correctly.[36]

One of the few breakthroughs for the Democrats, who, being out of power, were pushing for reform, came with the election of Lucius Garvin as governor in 1902 and 1903 (governors in Rhode Island served a one-year term until 1912, when it was lengthened to two years). Garvin, born in Tennessee, the son of a college professor, became a physician and set up a private practice in Rhode Island. Switching from the Republican Party, he became involved in Democratic politics and Progressive causes.

Elected to the state legislature, he was, according to a newspaper account, initially seen as a radical or crank whose proposals were either ignored or ridiculed. Eventually, however, he won over public support for many of his ideas, and he played a leading role in securing the adoption of laws providing for factory inspection and reducing the workday of motormen and conductors to ten hours. He also led in the abolition of landholding property qualifications for voting. This doubled the size of the electorate.[37] Lincoln Steffens viewed Garvin as a "sweet-tempered radical" who showed considerable courage in promoting Progressive causes in this highly conservative state.[38]

Garvin ran on a highly Progressive platform in his campaign for governor. His victory in 1902 was described in the *Washington Post* as "a defeat for one of the most solidly constructed political machines to be found on this continent."[39] Independent Republicans, Socialists, and Prohibitionists joined Democrats in helping him get elected. He was thought to have also benefited from a strong labor vote growing out of worker resentment of the decision of the Republican governor to call out the militia to put down a strike in Providence.[40]

The problem was that Governor Garvin was virtually powerless. He had no veto power, and Brayton, seeing Garvin coming and branding him as a dangerous man, made it impossible for the new governor to make any appointments by securing legislation that transferred the appointive power to the state senate and, in effect, to Brayton and the Republican Party.[41] As a contemporary journalist concluded, he was "almost as helpless as his door keeper."[42]

With the support of the press Garvin made some progress in bringing the public into his crusade against bribery in state elections. His legislative efforts, however, were largely shot down by the Republican legislature. Garvin ran on a fusion ticket for governor in 1905, but the whole ticket was defeated. In 1912 he became a member of the Progressive Party but switched back to the Democrats in 1916.

Reform-minded Democrats had another success with the election of James Henry Higgins, who was born in Lincoln, Rhode Island. His father died when he was thirteen, and he helped support his mother and two younger brothers. He went on to graduate from Brown University and Georgetown University Law School, was admitted to the bar in 1900, and, at age twenty-six, was elected mayor of Pawtucket. He looked even younger than he was. At one early rally someone yelled: "Whose kid are you?"[43]

The "boy mayor of Pawtucket" went on win three more one-year terms as mayor and in 1906 defeated Republican George H. Utter, who had succeeded Garvin as governor. Higgins, at age thirty, became the state's youngest governor. He also became the first Catholic governor in New England. In his 1906 campaign Higgins made Brayton and the boss system a central issue and drew considerable support from anticorruption, anti-Brayton independents affiliated with the short-lived Lincoln Party, led by Robert Goddard, a prominent banker, industrialist, and political reformer. Voters reelected Higgins in 1907 with around a three percentage point lead over his Republican opponent. He chose not to run again in 1908. During his years in office the legislature was in Republican hands, and this limited his ability to bring changes. Criticism and pressure generated by Higgins, however, facilitated Brayton's decisions to give up his office at the capitol and to resign from a leadership position with the state Republican Party.[44]

After Higgins only limited reform activity came with the election of Republican Aram Jules Pothier, whose nomination and election was engineered by Brayton in 1908.[45] After 1908 voters reelected him to three more one-year terms (1909–12) and three two-year terms (1913–15 and 1925–28). As governor, he worked on budgetary matters to keep the fiscal affairs of the state in order and promoted economic development, receiving the endorsement of business groups such as the textile manufacturers.[46] He did, however, establish a record on morality issues.

In 1912 he waged a war on gambling places, bars where liquor was sold without a license, and houses of ill repute in Newport, closing establishments down despite the resistance of the police chief and mayor.[47] Pothier also crusaded against prize-fighting in his state and was able to get local authorities to call off scheduled bouts in Providence. He condemned boxing as a "disgrace to civilization" and for "attracting thugs, pickpockets and gamblers from all sections of New England."[48]

VERMONT CATCHES UP

The wave of Progressive reform that swept the nation from 1900 to 1917 arrived a bit later in Vermont than other states, but once it hit this small, agricultural, conservative, Republican, one-party state, it prompted considerable change.[49]

Up to the Progressive period, Vermont governors were generally tied to industrial interests rather than to the farmers. Several early governors were railroad presidents, and a succession of governors who followed them came from a wing of the Republican Party established by Redfield Proctor, founder of the Vermont Marble Company who promoted businesses interests by keeping the size and costs of government low and avoiding any type of labor legislation.[50]

Redfield's son Fletcher took over as governor in the period 1906–8 and departed from the fiscal conservatism of his father, declaring that the state had "a higher duty than to live cheaply."[51]

He pursued a highly ambitious legislative agenda, some of which was intended to apply up-to-date principles of business management, others to implement regulatory programs. Along with reorganizing the state court system, he worked to strengthen railroad regulation. Vermont had gotten into the business of regulating railroads back in 1855, but the commission established at that time was, thanks in part to court decisions, powerless when Fletcher Proctor took office. Showing his capacity for Progressive reform, he came to the commission's rescue by securing legislation that enabled it to issue and enforce orders.[52]

Another Republican, George Prouty, who followed Proctor in office, ran on a platform of extending railroad regulation to other utilities, and the legislature did so by changing the railroad commission to a commission with jurisdiction over all public service corporations. The Republican Party platform had called for this action. Prouty advised the New England Telephone Company not to send its lobbyists to the capitol because they were going to have to accept the measure and would be wise to do so gracefully.[53] In creating a public service commission, Vermont followed the lead of New York.

As the Progressive movement strengthened, observers got a fascinating view of the "internal acrobatics of the Republican Party" in Vermont as the old guard first resisted Progressive demands but, seeing the writing on the wall, eventually moved to the left in order to preserve what power they could.[54] The rise of the

Progressive Party provided the incentive for conservatives to do what they could to bring the insurgents who had drifted to the new party back into the Republican Party. Modifying the Republican Party platform in a Progressive fashion helped stem the loss.

In 1912 the Progressive Party as well as the Democratic Party and the Republican Party nominated a candidate for governor, and none of the three candidates won a popular vote majority as required by the state constitution. The final decision was made by the legislature, which chose Allen Fletcher, an independent who had run as the Republican candidate.

Seeing the need to appeal to the Progressives, the legislature started out on a program attractive to these people. They were able to do this with a relatively mild program.[55] Sitting longer than any previous legislature, the one that met in 1912 adopted several reforms found in the platforms of the three parties, including a great deal of labor legislation.[56] Meanwhile, Fletcher went to war with members of the public service commission, removing some of them, who, he concluded, were not doing enough to protect consumers from the unreasonable charges of a telephone company that had a monopoly on the service.[57]

More reform came under Republican governor Charles Gates, 1915–17, and included worker's compensation, various improvements in the educational system, and, after several years of struggle, the adoption of the direct primary system. Legislators had been debating direct primary bills since 1902 and finally decided to ask the voters in a 1914 referendum—the voters said yes, they wanted a direct primary. While the matter seemed settled, in March 1915 the house voted down a direct primary bill, reflecting the fears of lawmakers from small towns and rural areas that it would greatly reduce the ability of their constituents to influence nominations for statewide offices. The house vote prompted a scathing attack from the press.[58]

Taking charge, a distressed Governor Gates asked the house in a special message to "see fit to reconsider" its position, arguing that it was duty-bound to act because the people had spoken and the platforms of all the parties—Republican, Democratic, Progressive—had pledged support for the direct primary. As a face-saving compromise he suggested that legislators amend the primary legislation with a clause requiring voter approval of the measure before it could go into effect. The compromise was agreed to: "Like frightened rabbits the legislators scurried for cover, and the bill shot through 147-25. The Senate OK'd it promptly."[59] The electorate later approved the primary measure, though voters in smaller towns were generally in opposition.[60]

MR. BASS OF NEW HAMPSHIRE

The move toward Progressive reform in New Hampshire began in 1906 when a small group of Republican insurgents known as "Lincoln Republicans" organized behind novelist Winston Churchill's bid for the Republican gubernatorial nomination.[61] The reformers targeted the Republican Party machine allied with the Boston and Maine Railroad and put together a strong Progressive program, calling for an end to free railroad passes, the election of railroad commissioners, and increased taxation of railroad property along with new controls on campaign spending and lobbying and a direct primary system to combat corporate control. They added a call for the "stringent enforcement of anti-gambling and liquor laws."[62]

Churchill failed to get the nomination in 1906, but the effort helped prompt the legislature into some reform activity, such as banning free passes, and after a few more years of agitation the Lincoln Republicans came to power in 1910 behind the candidacy of state legislator Robert Bass, who ran for governor on the Republican ticket. Bass, a slender young man, was described by one contemporary writer as "an idealist who can be practical."[63]

In 1904, in a manner somewhat reminiscent of Robert La Follette, Bass, then thirty years old, ignored a local boss who tried to discourage him from running for the state legislature, rounded up supporters in the countryside, got his name put up as a candidate at a party meeting, won the nomination, won the election, and went off to the legislature where he tried to break the hold of the railroad machine on state politics. He and other young insurgents at the Republican state convention in 1908 managed to secure the adoption of a highly Progressive platform that they attempted to implement in the next legislative session. One of their mostly highly prized and most highly useful victories was the adoption of a direct primary system.[64]

Bass took advantage of the direct primary law he had helped write and get adopted to win the New Hampshire Republican Party nomination for governor, defeating a candidate supported by the old party organization. The eastern press viewed his campaign as significant because it was the first trial of the direct primary system in a New England state and, as it turned out, one that demonstrated that a system giving greater freedom to individual voters could bring down a powerful machine.[65] Bass went on to win the governorship by more than eight percentage points over his Democratic opposition.

Critics accused Bass, who was a wealthy man, of trying to buy the governorship. Bass, in defense, said that at least he was spending his own money, not that of the railroads.[66] His campaign was directed largely against the railroad's political influence. Bass promised to replace the railroad commission with a broader-ranged public utilities commission. He also called for worker's compensation, conservation, and, borrowing from Theodore Roosevelt, a Square Deal to New Hampshire citizens. He asked Roosevelt to campaign on his behalf in 1910. Roosevelt did so, touring the state in October with Bass, warmly endorsing him and attacking corporate intervention in politics.[67]

Several like-minded legislators, including Democrats, joined Bass in coming into office in 1910, and together they produced an impressive body of legislation, including a public service commission, a corrupt-practices act, a worker's compensation law, and a child labor measure.[68] Bass also helped out by using the veto power. Keeping a watchful eye on what the legislature was doing, on one occasion he took a second look at what appeared to be a Progressive tax measure sent on to him for his signature. He wanted to see the amendments. He became suspicious because the measure passed so swiftly. He was quoted as saying: "There's a joker in here somewhere ... The senate wouldn't have passed it so readily if there wasn't."[69] As written, it actually exempted corporation franchises from taxation. A labor journal commented on the episode as one in which the "attempt to exempt millions, tens of millions, of corporation franchises from taxation in New Hampshire, was done in the dark, as the burglar works."[70] In 1911 Woodrow Wilson noted Bass's general success, using it as an example of the people taking control of their government.[71]

Bass, though well respected as a Progressive, refused to join La Follette's Republican Progressive League. He said he did not want to get involved because it would interfere with his duties as governor, but, more importantly, he was, at the time, reluctant to take sides between Taft and La Follette. As his biographer James Wright noted, he also had philosophical reservations: "Bass was not comfortable with the western progressives who dominated the league, particularly with their emphasis on direct democracy. He had never participated fully in the New Hampshire Direct Legislation League and conceded his preference for representative government."[72]

He did, however, have no qualms about supporting Roosevelt for president and wound up backing him and the Progressive Party in 1912. Bass's support of Roosevelt over Taft, however, angered party regulars, and they retaliated by rejecting his attempt to secure a seat in the US Senate in 1913.

New Hampshire, meanwhile, had gone on to put another reformer in the office of governor by the name of Samuel Felker, a Democrat who had worked with Bass in drafting legislation in 1910 and in helping the governor secure its adoption in the legislature. With the vote split between him and candidates nominated by the Republican and Progressive parties in 1912, no one received a majority and the legislature made the final decision of who would be governor. Progressive Party legislators voted along with Democrats to make Felker the first Democratic governor since 1874. The legislature proceeded to approve much of his reform agenda, which included a large number of economic and social measures.[73]

REFORM IN MAINE

Maine received an injection of Progressivism with the election of Republican William Cobb in 1904 and his reelection in 1906. A Roosevelt Republican, he called for measures to stem the growing power of the railroads, ensure meat inspection, and provide food and drug protections. Being a moralist, he also insisted on the strict enforcement of the state's prohibition laws. In 1907 he vetoed a bill that would have limited his ability to enforce the liquor laws when a local sheriff refused to do so. That same year he pushed hard for a constitutional measure providing for a statewide initiative and referendum, which, in spite of considerable opposition in the press and from some political leaders, received voter approval in 1908 by a two-to-one margin.

Democrats enjoyed a surprising victory with the election of Frederick W. Plaisted as governor in 1910, a newspaper owner and editor who, at the time, was serving his fourth term as mayor of Augusta, Maine. The vigorous new governor declared: "I am going to make good."[74] Working with a Democratic legislature, he got a direct primary law and the ratification of the income tax amendment to the US Constitution. Plaisted, however, lost his bid for reelection to Republican William Haines, a relatively Progressive candidate, in 1912.

By 1912 both parties had agreed on the need for a public utilities law. In calling for such a measure in his inaugural address, Haines noted that the officers of the utilities "have practically a free hand to do as they please" when it comes to what rules they follow and the rates they charge, and, as far as they are concerned, "the public can take it or leave it." In 1914 voters came out in favor of the new regulatory system that lawmakers had put together. There was concern, however, about the quality or disposition of the people appointed to implement the law.[75] An antitrust measure also passed while Haines was governor. Haines was followed by Oakley Chester Curtis, a Democrat and mayor of Portland when elected, who brought improved labor laws. Curtis was defeated in 1916 by Republican Carl Milliken, who gave considerable attention to the enforcement of prohibition laws and was reelected in 1918.

BALDWIN OF CONNECTICUT

The first breakthrough in the strongly conservative Republican state of Connecticut came with the election of a seventy-year-old Democrat, Simeon Baldwin, in 1910. He was reelected in 1912. Baldwin, a lawyer, had been chief justice of Connecticut's supreme court just prior to his decision to run for governor. Like another judge, Pennypacker of Pennsylvania, Baldwin was unaccustomed to the demands and pressures of political life. Though his difficulties with the media were not as heightened as Pennypacker's, owners and managers had their complaints over his nonresponse to questions and lack of cooperation.[76]

Baldwin had started out as a Republican of the Mugwump variety but, rejecting the Republican James Blaine, became a Democrat in 1884. Much of his campaign for governor was directed against Republicans on national issues. He especially focused on the protective tariff, which he blamed for the high cost of living, hoping that this position would appeal to disaffected Republicans. His victory in 1910 may, indeed, have had much to do with the support he received from Progressive-minded Republicans in the electorate.[77] In 1910 Republicans still won most of the other top state offices and captured control of both houses of the legislature. Two years later, however, Republicans were even more divided because of the emergence of Roosevelt's Bull Moose Party, and Democrats were able to not only reelect Baldwin but capture several other important state offices.

Following his election in 1910 a Republican paper in Boston characterized him as a "man of the highest character and great learning," who might well turn out to be "conservative and safe."[78]

The editor was likely disappointed. In his inaugural address in 1911 Baldwin mixed a call for fiscal responsibility by reducing state expenditures and keeping them low with a call, viewed by some as a concession "to a growing public sentiment," for a wide set of reforms, including worker's compensation, public utility regulation, a stronger corrupt-practices act, direct primaries, direct election of US senators, and civil service. He did not think that the time had come for unrestricted woman suffrage, though he was willing to go along with extending suffrage to female taxpayers in local elections.[79] Some prominent Republicans applauded Baldwin's inaugural message.[80] As it turned out, however, Republicans were divided in their support for Baldwin's legislative program.

As governor, Baldwin received the backing of a new crop of Irish-Catholic Democrats in the legislature who had been elected along with him and whose election demonstrated the growing influence of this group in state politics. In getting any reform through the legislature, however, he also needed the support of the Progressive faction in the Republican majority. Concerned about corruption in state politics, the governor lobbied hard for and secured civil service reform and a corrupt-practices act. He got a relatively weak worker's compensation law and, over the determined opposition of Republican legislative leaders and lobbyists for the New Haven Railroad, a public utilities commission.[81] Baldwin in 1911 gave the direct primary idea a more positive endorsement than the two governors who preceded him, but while a direct primary plan made it through the senate, it failed in the house. Republicans backed away from the idea in part to avoid voter revolt in their party's small-town base, in which there was considerable concern that the new system would increase the influence of larger cities in state politics at their expense.[82]

FOSS AND WALSH OF MASSACHUSETTS

Looking at Massachusetts during the height of the Progressive movement, 1910–20, one finds very little going on in terms of reform—officials only tinkered with measures that the state had adopted decades earlier and that other states were now considering for the first time.[83]

Many viewed the state as under the control of upper-crust Republican "Brahmins"—a place where "the Cabots speak only to the Lodges and the Lodges only speak to God."[84] Massachusetts, though, did have some relatively strong Progressive governors in Eugene Foss and David Walsh. Making his assessment in May of 1911, Woodrow Wilson noted: "In Massachusetts the mistakes of early political life had been gradually corrected until on the statute books of that state are now many of the best laws to be found. A machine still exists there clothed with the odor of respectability, but the people are awakening and the delicate process of retirement is being practiced."[85]

Massachusetts had its moment under Foss, who was elected as the gubernatorial candidate of the Democratic and Progressive Parties in 1910 and 1911 and of the Democratic Party alone in 1912. He served from 1911 to 1914. A prominent manufacturer, Foss had run for several offices as a Republican, winning none of them. Throughout much of his career, Foss regularly attacked the oligarchy that ran the Republican Party, his chief target being Republican senator Henry Cabot Lodge. Foss had fallen out with the Republicans and Lodge on the tariff question, and Lodge had opposed his bid for Congress as a Republican. He became a Democrat in 1909. Well equipped with money, he used it to pick up a congressional seat as a Democrat in a Republican district in 1910. He resigned his seat in Congress following his election as governor in 1910.[86]

Foss was not much of reformer until he became governor, and much of what he was able to accomplish came during his first session. Under him came limitations on campaign finance expenditures, worker's compensation, minimum wage legislation, a reduced workweek for women, and direct primaries for state officials. According to historian Richard Abrams: "During Foss's three-year administration, considerable reform legislation passed which, in quantity and quality, compared favorably with anything achieved elsewhere in the country."[87] Looking at the process and results, historian David Sarasohn noted that he "was able to add enough Republicans from labor districts to his own alliance of Boston ward bosses, labor unions, and reformers to pass a substantial package of reform legislation, much of which had failed to pass earlier, more heavily Republican legislatures."[88] Foss failed, however, to get the initiative and referendum.[89]

Like other Progressive governors, he was considered liberal when it came to granting pardons on humanitarian grounds. He believed in giving prisoners another chance. He also was influenced by reports that conditions were deplorable in the state prison.[90] On the other hand, he did nothing to further his standing with organized labor when it came to strike activity. He fought the Brotherhood of Railway Trainmen over their threat to strike and sent in the state militia to Lawrence to put down a strike of some 15,000 striking textile workers.

In a message to the legislature regarding the textile strike he declared: "Not the slightest approach to anarchy can be tolerated in this commonwealth and I shall not hesitate to employ every means at my command to maintain law and order."[91] At one point he threatened to call the legislature into special session to adopt a law prohibiting strikes.[92]

Prior to becoming governor in 1914, Democrat David Walsh had served in the Massachusetts legislature, securing election in a largely Republican district, and as lieutenant governor. He was the state's first Irish American governor and first Catholic governor and, like Foss, a Progressive Democrat in a staunchly conservative Republican state. After serving two terms as governor, he went on to serve several terms in the US Senate.

Walsh was one of nine children born to immigrant parents. Though the family was relatively poor, Walsh managed, with the help of older siblings, to earn a law degree. He joined a law practice that had been established by an older brother and coupled this with political activity, first in the Massachusetts house, where he lost his seat for taking the unpopular stand in favor of limiting the employment of women and children to fifty-eight hours a week. In 1912 he won the position of lieutenant governor and used this as a springboard to the governorship.

As governor, Walsh took the Progressive stands in, for example, opposing machine politics, supporting the initiative and referendum, championing working people and labor causes like worker's compensation, favoring woman suffrage, and calling for the abolition of the death penalty. He did not hesitate to veto legislation favored by the railroads.[93] In arguing for the devices of direct democracy Walsh contended: "The strongest argument in favor of direct legislation lies in the fact that every dishonest politician, every selfish public utility corporation and every self-seeking interest is against it." The reform was not to come until after his time in office.[94]

NOTES

1. In the fifteen elections from 1890 to 1920 both New Hampshire and Vermont elected fifteen different governors who served two-year terms. In both Rhode Island and Massachusetts twelve governors served during this thirty-year period. They generally served only one-year terms. Rhode Island changed to two-year terms starting in 1914, but governors were allowed run for reelection. Connecticut and Maine allowed reelection to two-year terms and had eleven different governors during the same time span.
2. Gunther, *Inside U.S.A.*, 609.
3. Buenker, *Urban Liberalism*, 19.
4. Pennypacker, *Autobiography*, 263.
5. Ibid., 269.
6. Ibid., 271.
7. Ibid., 278.
8. Ibid., 475.

9. Ibid., 290–91.

10. "In Extra Session," *Fulton County News*, January 24, 1906, 1. See also "Reform Legislation for Pennsylvania," *New York Times*, November 12, 1905, 4; "Call by Pennypacker," *San Francisco Call*, November 12, 1905, 5; and "Current Topics," *The Commoner*, November 17, 1905, 6.

11. Pennypacker, *Autobiography*, 381.

12. Ware, *American Direct Primary*, 140–45, 151.

13. Charles Emory Smith, "On the Pennsylvania Libel Law," *Literary Digest*, June 20, 1903, 882.

14. Quoted by Black, *War against the Weak*, 66.

15. Kaylor, *Martin Grove Brumbaugh*, 239.

16. On support for Taft see "Nine Governors Join in Support of Taft," *New York Times*, February 28, 1912, 1.

17. Kaylor, *Martin Grove Brumbaugh*, 242–45, 249, 250.

18. Ibid., 280, 281.

19. Ibid., 336.

20. Boyer, *Governing Delaware*, 46.

21. Gunther, *Inside U.S.A.*, 630.

22. Munroe, *History of Delaware*, 177.

23. See, for example, some contemporary accounts in "The Latest Delaware Election," *The Outlook*, January 10, 1903, 93; George Kennan, "Holding Up a State: The True Story of Addicks and Delaware," *The Outlook*, February 7, 1903, 277–83; "Is Mr. Addicks Down and Out?" *New York Daily Tribune*, December 11, 1904, 4.

24. "Governor Hunn's Decision," *Hartford Courant*, April 20, 1903, 10.

25. "History of Direct Democracy in Delaware."

26. "Gives Delaware 103-Mile Road," *Republican News Item*, March 3, 1910, 4.

27. "Gov. Pennewill Has Ivy Poisoning," *Republican News Item*, June 23, 1911, 1.

28. "Delaware and Her Working Women," June 10, 1911, *The Outlook*, 275.

29. "Governor Charles R. Miller," *Newark Post*, April 14, 1915, 9.

30. Quoted by Mary R. de Vou, "Delaware," in Harper, *History of Woman Suffrage*, 6:95.

31. Ibid.; Boyer, *Governing Delaware*, 47.

32. Steffens, *Struggle for Self-Government*, 120.

33. Ibid., 126, 138, 139.

34. Ibid., 134.

35. "Little Rhody Full of Graft and Bribery," *Bisbee Daily Review*, December 16, 1908, 1.

36. Neal R. Peirce, *New England States*, 148; Luconi, *Italian-American Vote*, 32; "They Have Funny Ways of Bribing Men in Rhode Island, But Public Opinion Is about to Demand Reform," *New York Daily Tribune*, April 5, 1903, 2.

37. "The Defeat of a State Boss," *The Outlook*, January 10, 1903, 95.

38. Steffens, *Struggle for Self-Government*, 156.

39. Quoted in "The Rhode Island Victory," *The Commoner*, December 12, 1902, 5.

40. "Interesting Features of the State Elections," *Literary Digest*, November 25, 1902, 624–26; "Mr. Bryan's 'Boom' of Governor Garvin," *Literary Digest*, February 28, 1903, 295.

41. Steffens, *Struggle for Self-Government*, 157.

42. "They Have Funny Ways of Bribing Men in Rhode Island."

43. "Gossip about New Governors," *Coeur d'Alene Press*, December 19, 1906, 6.

44. "For Governor," *River Press*, November 6, 1907, 6; and "Gossip about New Governors," *McCook Tribune*, January 4, 1907, 4.

45. Peirce, *New England States*, 148.

46. "Lively Campaign in Rhode Island," *Norwich Bulletin*, November 6, 1911, 1.

47. "Tight Lid at Newport," *Bennington Evening Blade*, January 24, 1912, 1.

48. "Boxing Stopped in Rhode Island," *New York Times*, February 12, 1913, 13.

49. Flint, *Progressive Movement in Vermont.*
50. Peirce, *New England States,* 268.
51. Duffy, Hand, and Orth, *Vermont Encyclopedia,* 241.
52. Newton, *Vermont Story,* 53; Hand, *The Star That Set,* 81.
53. "Prouty on the Legislature," *Bennington Evening Banner,* January 4, 1909, 1.
54. Flint, *Progressive Movement in Vermont.*
55. See Schlesinger, *How They Became Governor,* 35.
56. Hand, *Star That Set,* 84, 85.
57. "Trouble Brewing," *Bennington Evening Banner,* July 29, 1913, 2; "Gov. Fletcher Has Removed Chas. D. Watson," *Barre Daily Times,* July 28, 1913, 1; "In Interest of Public Good," *Brattleboro Daily Reformer,* July 30, 1913, 1.
58. Newton, *Vermont Story,* 253.
59. Ibid.
60. Hand, Marshall, and Sanford, "Little Republics," 162–63.
61. See "Churchill May Beat New Hampshire Ring," *New York Times,* September 116, 1906, 2; "Novelist in Politics," *New York Times,* September 30, 1906, SM2. See generally Wright, *Progressive Yankees.*
62. Heffernan and Stecker, *New Hampshire,* 164–65.
63. Isaac F. Marcosson, "Bass of New Hampshire" *Munsey's Magazine,* February 1911, 631.
64. Ibid., 624–31.
65. "Insurgent Victories, East and West," *Literary Digest,* September 17, 1910, 428.
66. Peirce, *New England States,* 295.
67. Wright, *Progressive Yankees,* 105–6.
68. "Three Progressive States," *The Outlook,* May 13, 1911, 43–45; "Governor Bass a Real Governor," *The Outlook,* March 25, 1911, 610–11.
69. "A Typical Trick of Big Business," *San Francisco Star,* reprinted in *Labor World,* April 27, 1912, 5.
70. Ibid.
71. "A News Report of a Day in Lincoln, Nebraska."
72. Wright, *Progressive Yankees,* 128.
73. Ibid., 140, 143, 145–46.
74. "Maine Swept by Democrats," *United Opinion,* September 16, 1910, 7; "Plaisted Greatest Breaker of Political Records in Maine," *Rock Island Argus,* September 30, 1910, 8; "In the Political Fields: The Democratic Governor of Maine" *The Outlook,* October 22, 1910, 397–98.
75. Hormell, *Maine Public Utilities,* 40.
76. See, for example, "Judge Baldwin has 'Nothing to Say,'" *Hartford Courant,* December 3, 1910, 1.
77. Jackson, *Simon Eben Baldwin,* 165.
78. Quoted in "States That Saw a New Light," *Literary Digest,* November 19, 1910, 919.
79. "The Governor's Message," *Hartford Courant,* January 5, 1911, 8; "Venerable Governor Baldwin Takes Oath of Office in Presence of Notable Gathering of Public Men," *Bridgeport Evening Times,* January 4, 1911, 1; and "Progress," *The Outlook,* January 21, 1911, 105–6.
80. Jackson, *Simon Eben Baldwin,* 174.
81. Cesare, "Connecticut and the Progressive Era," 116.
82. Ware, *American Direct Primary,* 192–93.
83. Abrams, *Conservatism in a Progressive Era.*
84. John Colllins Bossidy, Toast, Holy Cross Alumni Dinner, 1910, in Bartlett, *Familiar Quotations,* 858a.
85. "A News Report of a Day in Lincoln, Nebraska."
86. Schlesinger, *How They Became Governor,* 39.

87. Abrams, *Conservatism in a Progressive Era*, 259.
88. Sarasohn, *Party of Reform*, 116.
89. Goebel, *A Government by the People*, 70.
90. "Governors Discuss the Granting of Pardons," *New York Times*, January 19, 1913, SM11.
91. "Foss Calls for Strike Inquiry," *Hartford Courant*, January 26, 1912, 1.
92. "Foss's Threat Called a Direct Attack on Fundamental Right of Workingmen," *Day Book*, October 6, 1913, 23.
93. "Governor Walsh on Railroad Legislation," *Norwich Bulletin*, January 2, 1915, 10.
94. Quoted by Piott, *Giving Voters a Voice*, 237.

12

WESTERN "RADICALISM"

Hiram Johnson, Curtailing the Railroads, Getting beyond Politics as Usual

Writing in 1912 a journalist noted: "In these days of political and social agitation many men and newspapers in the great centers along the Atlantic seaboard, like Boston, New York, and Philadelphia, regard the West as a hotbed of unintelligent and dangerous radicalism.... The Westerners should not whoop and hurrah so. It disturbs other people."[1]

While the "Wild West" of the Progressive era may, in the minds of some easterners, started somewhere west of Philadelphia, certainly taking in Kansas, Oklahoma, North Dakota, and Wisconsin, the discussion here and in the two following chapters starts farther west to cover gubernatorial activity in California and what are classified as the northwestern states of Oregon, Washington, Montana, Idaho, and Wyoming and the southwestern states of Colorado, Nevada, Utah, New Mexico, and Arizona—eleven states in all.

In the West governors bent on reform functioned in an environment in which political parties were relatively weak, corporations were relatively strong, and considerable emphasis was placed on new and experimental political reforms such as the initiative, referendum, and recall. Given the relative weakness of the parties in this region, we also find more split-ticket voting, more party-switching, and more new third parties popping up and finding it easier to catch on.[2] The Populists made a strong impact in several western states. Populist parties in Colorado, Montana, Nevada, Idaho, Washington, and Wyoming at one point or another replaced the Democrats as the second or opposition party to the Republicans.³ Populist governors emerged in Colorado, Montana, Oregon, and Washington.

The direct focus of reformers in this part of the country was not so much on powerful political machines aligned with one of the major parties—these were generally lacking—as it was on the big business interests: the railroads, mining companies, and leaders in the timber and other industries. It was much easier in the West to come up with measures crippling political parties but much more difficult to put reins on the influence of the dominant economic interests that had considerable control over state legislatures.

Politicians and people in western states were particularly attracted to devices of direct democracy (the initiative, referendum, and recall) as a way of circumventing the corporate control of legislative bodies. The image of the West as filled with wild-eyed radicals may have had much to do with the popularity of these "radical" innovations in the region and the general ferocity of the attack on corporations, many of which had their roots in the East. Direct democracy's unusual success in the West appears to be due in part to the relatively strong strength of the anticorporate movement in this region. Here too proponents of direct democracy had plenty of support from suffragettes, prohibitionists, farmers, workers, and others who were having a difficult time getting a positive response from state legislatures to their demands.⁴

Many of the characteristics of Progressivism are well illustrated in California, where our chief focus is on the career, personality, beliefs, and accomplishments on one man, Hiram Johnson, who rose to power pledging to kick the Southern Pacific out of politics and who wound up bringing a new or different way of governing—one of putting it in the hands of the governed through the adoption of the devices of direct democracy.

FIGHTING THE RAILROADS

California politics in the 1890s and first decade of the twentieth century demonstrated a growing concern with the railroads. The central focus of California reformers during this period was on ending what they saw as the control of the Southern Pacific Railroad, operating largely through its political bureau, over state politics.⁵ The California Populist Party pushed a strong antirailroad program but were partially drowned out by the Democrats, who took a similar stand.⁶

From 1898 to 1920, Democrats usually ran anti-railroad candidates for governor, but none of the Democratic candidates won the office.⁷

Progressive antirailroad forces first found a gubernatorial spokesperson in Republican George Pardee, a medical doctor and longtime party activist who won a four-person race for the office by fewer than 3,000 votes in 1902. Pardee had a run in with the Southern Pacific while he was mayor of Oakland in the mid-1890s, but this encounter appears to have been ignored in a somewhat frantic effort by party leaders to put together a ticket that had a chance of winning. They were embarrassed by the failure of the incumbent Republican governor to adequately respond to a bubonic plague outbreak in San Francisco and felt that Pardee, a medical doctor and former municipal official, would make an exceptional candidate.

Pardee proved to be a highly popular governor in large part because he put together an effective program that stamped out the plague, which killed 200 people and threatened an economically disastrous nationwide boycott of the city, and because he had responded efficiently and effectively to the 1906 earthquake in San Francisco. He also proved to be more Progressive than many expected. This was seen in his support of education and conservation policies and in his outspoken opposition to the monopolistic power and political influence of the Southern Pacific. At the 1906 state convention party leaders and Southern Pacific representatives were able to deny Pardee's bid for renomination and replaced him with a more railroad-friendly nominee named James Gillett, who was elected governor that year. Governor Gillette remained close to the Southern Pacific, though he showed some of the Progressive spirit in facilitating reform of the parole system and in opposing prizefighting. A eugenics law came during his time in office. Toward the end of his term his Republican supporters in the legislature honored him for "his unremitting efforts in the line of economy" and for lowering the state tax rate.[8]

Progressive reform in California took a giant step in 1907 when two California journalists, Chester H. Rowell and Edward A. Dickson, formed the Lincoln-Roosevelt League with the prime purpose of ending Southern Pacific's hold on the Republican Party and state politics. One of the league's earliest and most important victories came in 1909 with the passage of a direct primary law. The legislature rejected several Progressive proposals that year, including calls for the direct election of US senators and an initiative system, but a direct primary measure for various offices, including governor, slipped through.[9] It passed with virtually no debate in the legislature. Some observers noted that the legislation was complicated and that many legislators who supported it really did not have a clear idea of what was in it but felt they had to vote for the reform because of public pressure.[10]

With the direct primary Lincoln-Roosevelt leaders felt they had the means to wrest control of the nomination of political candidates from the Southern Pacific and quickly began a search for a candidate to support in the first Republican gubernatorial primary in 1910. They considered several people, including former governor George Pardee, but settled on Hiram Johnson and were eventually able to convince him to make the run.

JOHNSON: THE ROAD TO POWER

Hiram Johnson was born and raised in California. His father, Grove Johnson, a lawyer from New York, came west in 1863, switched from the Democratic Party to the Republican Party, and got elected to the California state legislature and to the US House of Representatives. He gave his son an inside view of politics.[11] There was, however, no love lost between father and son. Hiram, also a lawyer by profession, had long criticized his father's close ties with the Southern Pacific—he was the company's chief lobbyist—and rejected his stand on various policy matters involving the railroads. His father, who had served in the state legislature for twelve years as a railroad and corporation spokesman, was a short, belligerent man with a violent temper. According to Hiram Johnson's biographers, "Having Grove Johnson for a father was not easy."[12]

Hiram first gained public attention in 1906 for his performance as prosecutor in the graft trial of Abe Ruef, boss of the political machine in San Francisco with which his father was associated. Hiram began as an assistant to prosecutor and noted Progressive leader Francis J. Heney, but took over the case after gangsters shot and wounded Heney in the courtroom and incapacitated him. Hiram won the case and Ruef eventually went to prison. Hiram's role in the trials brought him into the inner circle of Progressive reformers in the state.[13] He joined the Lincoln-Roosevelt League in 1907. He had been fearful of entering the 1910 primary because he would be condemned for being the son of Grove Johnson but finally agreed to do so.[14]

On the day of the primary election, an editorial in the *Los Angeles Times* described Johnson as "the candidate dictated by a little clique of bosses and supported by as dangerous a political machine as ever existed in the state." As for Johnson himself: "He is simply a caricature, a bundle of abnormal characteristics. He is unreasonable, vindictive, unrestrained, abusive, tyrannical, unfair, unbalanced.... No person, no interest, no institution, is safe from his attacks. His political opponents are vilified, slandered and scandalized.... The man is unsafe. He will disgrace California if he is elected to office."[15] The writer saw the primary as "a legal device for stuffing Republican ballot boxes." In this contest, the editorial declared, Johnson was going to receive "much of his support from Democrats who lied about being Republicans in order to ruin the Republican Party."[16]

Johnson's campaign took on the character of a religious crusade against the Southern Pacific Railroad. He promised to "kick it out of politics." Opposition newspaper editors suggested that the son of Grove Johnson was, in reality, pro-railroad, but the charge appeared to have little effect.[17] The *New York Times* described his victory over four competitors in the Republican primary as a "severe blow to the railroad machine."[18] As Johnson's critics pointed out, his four opponents divided up the vote of the more conservative voters.[19] Still, Johnson won with a total of 101,666, votes, which was only 12,273 less than the combined vote for his opponents. He did relatively well in the southern part of the state and, research suggests, particularly well in rural areas and among native-born, Protestant, middle-class voters and voters supportive of prohibition.[20] Along with

Figure 12.1. Hiram Johnson. Courtesy of the Library of Congress, Prints & Photographs Division, LC-DIG-ggbain-07193.

his victory came a victory for nearly all other insurgent candidates in the primary. Hiram no doubt felt some relief that his father, a potentially strong and bitter opponent, had lost out in the 1910 Republican primary in his effort to secure the nomination from Sacramento for a seat in the legislature.[21]

GOVERNING

Following his primary victory Johnson remarked: "This fight has been made on progressive lines and it is a clearly-defined insurgent victory. We entered this fight with a serious purpose and with one great issue which we presented to the people of California for their determination. They have declared in favor of taking back the government which for more than a century has been an asset and chattel of the Southern Pacific political bureau."[22]

His Democratic opponent in the 1910 general election, Theodore Arlington Bell, was as Progressive as Johnson and campaigned equally hard against the railroads. Johnson, though, had the advantage of the large traditional Republican vote, especially in southern California. He also drew well with the large number of relatively unaffiliated voters in the state with his attack on political parties.[23] Johnson benefited from the support of the Hearst newspapers and also had the support of the California Anti-Saloon League. His running mate as a candidate for lieutenant governor, A. J. Wallace, was president of the league.[24] Johnson managed to come out on top with around a six percentage point lead. Wrapping up his quest for the governorship, Johnson told a reporter that during the campaign he had been "determined to see if the interests ... could be whipped by the people in a square, stand up fight." He found it could be done, but only by "hard, intelligent, and relentless war."[25]

Johnson, signaling the transfer of government from the wealthy special interests to the common people, refused the usual inaugural parade, walked to the capitol without a military escort, and canceled the traditional elaborate inaugural ball. Explaining his decision to cancel the ball, Johnson was quoted as saying: "My administration is going to be a direct one and one for business, and I couldn't see that a social affair would help particularly to make the laws of the land and to aid me in governing the state."[26]

In his inaugural address he asked: "How best can we arm the people to protect themselves hereafter?" His answer was the initiative, referendum, and recall, and he urged the legislature to take prompt action to propose these to the people as a constitutional amendment.[27] He also called for meaningful railroad regulations, reminding the lawmakers: "For many years in the past, shippers, and those generally dealing with the Southern Pacific Company, have been demanding protection against the rates fixed by that corporation. The demand has been answered by the corporation by the simple expedient of taking over the government of the State; and instead of regulation of the railroads, as the framers of the new Constitution fondly hoped, the railroad has regulated the State." Along with direct democracy and rail regulation, the governor called upon the legislature to take action on the short ballot and other ballot reforms, an advisory vote for US senators, nonpartisan judicial elections, county home rule, civil service, conservation, a reformatory for first offenders, and an employers' liability law.[28] These and several more came to pass.

Johnson came to office in a relatively good position because Lincoln-Roosevelt League candidates for the legislative offices had won a clear majority in the legislature.[29] He wasted no time in getting actively involved in the legislative process. He made it clear what he wanted and that he would rebuke publicly those legislators who did not follow his lead. He said he was adopting a policy of open dealing with the legislature as a whole rather than behind-the-scenes dealings with individual legislators and one in which every member would stand or fall on his or her own record, a record that the governor would make sure that his or her constituents would know about.[30]

Johnson replaced the regular party machine with a machine of his own making, taking legislative power from the railroads and other business interests.[31] He exerted considerable and unprecedented control over the state legislature, acting, in the eyes of some, as a dictator who rolled over both houses. He outlined proposed legislation through special messages, giving "energy and direction to the movement" of legislation.[32] He had effective control over the choice of legislative officers, appointments to legislative committees, the selection of chairs of important committees, and whatever legislation was produced. During the legislative session the lieutenant governor and the speaker would meet with Johnson every morning in his office and arrange the program for the day. Johnson too was active in reforming and staffing administrative agencies.[33]

The legislature in 1911 quickly passed several measures relating to railroads and public utilities, labor, and the election system. It adopted 800 of the 2,876 bills introduced and twenty-three proposed constitutional amendments for the consideration of the voters at a special election on October 10, 1911.[34] In one of the few setbacks, Johnson did not get all he wanted in terms of short-ballot reform. He tried but failed to get enough votes in the legislature to get a proposal on the ballot that would have confined the number of state elective offices to the governor, lieutenant governor, and state comptroller. He had to settle for legislative action that eliminated a few minor elected offices, including the state printer.[35] Though Johnson reportedly was not happy with all the provisions in a bill limiting working hours for women, which was supported by the Federation of Women's Clubs and other philanthropic groups, he went along with it at the urging of his wife Minne. After a lengthy debate the legislature turned down a proposal sponsored by labor unions recognizing the legality of the boycott.[36]

The voters did their share in October, approving twenty-two of the twenty-three proposed amendments. Among these were those providing for woman suffrage and the initiative, referendum, and recall (including the recall of judges) and extending the reach of the railroad commission to public utilities. Amendments also empowered the legislature to adopt a civil service system, worker's compensation laws, and regulations on weights and measures. The only measure that failed with the voters was one that prohibited railroad or other transportation companies from giving free passes to public officials. What appears to have been the objectionable feature made an exception for members of the railroad commission and peace officers. Many voters may have agreed with critics who felt that allowing railroads to do such favors for these people presented potential problems.[37]

Johnson campaigned for the many of the measures on the ballot, especially the devices of direct democracy and the stronger railroad commission, which he considered at the heart of his reform program. The recall of judges turned out to be a particularly heated issue, pitting the notion that an independent judiciary free from shifting public sentiment was vital to the protection of fundamental rights against the notion that judges, like all governmental officials, were not above the people. Though he supported woman suffrage Johnson did not join in the campaign for an amendment recognizing this right.[38]

THE FLING IN NATIONAL POLITICS

Following his initial success as governor, Johnson became a Progressive force in Republican politics on a national level. His first choice for the Progressive challenger to Taft in 1912 had always been Teddy Roosevelt, though he also considered Albert Cummins of Iowa, who had moved to the US Senate. When Roosevelt refused to run, Johnson pledged his support to the La Follette campaign. He thought highly of La Follette's Progressive record but was not convinced that La Follette could defeat Taft. When Roosevelt appeared to have changed his mind, Johnson visited him to get confirmation that he was indeed going after the nomination because, if so, he was going to have to make a strong fight against La Follette's people to swing California Progressives behind Roosevelt.[39]

In 1912 Johnson was a delegate to the national convention of the Republican Party held in Chicago. Like several others, he walked out in protest over the convention proceedings that resulted in Taft's nomination. He was irritated by the reluctance of some governors to bolt the convention, including Governors Stubbs of Kansas, Aldrich of Nebraska, Hadley of Missouri, and Glasscock of West Virginia. They argued that creating a new party presented too many difficulties and could hurt the Republican Party.[40] William Jennings Bryan, covering the proceedings as a reporter, noted with approval the manner in which Johnson denounced the Taft forces.[41]

Johnson later participated in the formation of the Bull Moose Party and accepted its nomination as vice-president. La Follette claimed that Roosevelt had won Johnson over to the new party by promising to put him on the ticket.[42] Johnson had been reluctant to serve as Roosevelt's running mate, seeing the contest as an uphill battle, which, indeed, it turned out to be; but he agreed do so, he claimed, out of admiration for and loyalty to Roosevelt.[43] During his campaign as the vice-presidential nominee, Johnson spent much of his time pointing out what the Progressive movement had accomplished in California.[44] Along the way he met with Bryan in Nebraska. Bryan announced that he liked Johnson better than Roosevelt for the presidency.[45]

His experience as an unsuccessful vice-presidential nominee did not discourage Johnson from considering another run for national office. By the end of 1913 Johnson was thinking seriously about doing so but was convinced by his closest associates to make another run for governor for the good of the cause. Running as a candidate of the Progressive Party, he repeated his 1910 stump speech, cited his accomplishments in his first term, and easily won again in 1914.[46]

He did not do much in his second term that resulted in new laws—most of his effort centered on refining and enforcing existing ones.[47] Johnson returned to the Republican Party in 1916 and was elected to the first of several terms in the US Senate that year. He served in the Senate from 1917 until his death in 1945.

EVALUATION OF JOHNSON

Political economist and author Raymond Moley once depicted Johnson as "emotion incarnate," someone who "hated and loved intensely" and operated as a flashy, flamboyant prosecutor who "gambled recklessly in politics," condemned those who stood in his way as "the enemies of God, corrupt, vicious" people. Johnson, he felt, was someone who "always walked alone."[48] In the preface to his fine study on Johnson, Richard Lower offered similar thoughts about the governor: "Thin-skinned and suspicious, forever on his guard, he could discover in any criticisms signs of a deeper malice."[49] Lower added: "Stubbornly independent, Johnson almost invariably brought an apocalyptic intensity to the battles he waged. For him politics was the art not of compromise but of confrontation."[50] Lower further noted that in certain respects Hiram was much like his father: "Johnson shared with his father not only a fighter's determination and an eagerness to personalize political contests and call into question the character of his foes, but also a jealous nature, a mercurial temperament, petulance, insensitivity to others, and self-absorption in any campaign he waged."[51]

An earlier biographer of Hiram Johnson, Spencer Olin, concluded that in political matters Johnson was "a suspicious and ungenerous individual. Several actions during his governorship testify to his selfishness and to his willingness to place his own political survival above that of any organization or party." Still, Olin concluded, Johnson was a "skillful tactician who fully comprehended the realities of political life. Hiram Johnson played the game of politics to win, and win he did; and because he won, California benefited from strong, vigorous leadership during the years 1911 to 1917."[52]

In the end Johnson did indeed accomplish a great deal as governor. He put controls on the Southern Pacific, expanded the ability of the public to participate in the political process, furthered the interest of labor, and pushed for various other causes. He made a crusade against corruption and injustice, the evil of big business, and the rule of special interests the focus of his campaigns. Much of what he supported, including corrupt-practices legislation and the initiative, referendum, and recall, were intended to open the political process and turn control over to the people.

In pushing for the recall, Johnson was pleased to have it extended to judges. He felt that the judiciary represented the "last stand of privilege and corporate aggression."[53] He further argued: "Judges are but men. They have the same blood, are actuated by the same impulses and by the same and bad spirits of action as the rest of us. The recall will make no weak judge weaker, and it will make no strong judge less strong. It menaces just one kind of a judge—the corrupt judge—and he ought to be menaced."[54]

With the support of business groups representing shippers and merchants, Johnson successfully pushed for the creation of a railroad commission with greater power over the railroads and extended its control to other public utilities. Business leaders, hoping for more order and stability in their operations, especially the practice of having to deal with a large number of local officials with differing ideas of what regulations were needed, supported this action.⁵⁵ The changes did not damage the economic position of the railroads or other corporations. The experience suggested that a state could have both strong democratic government and economically strong corporations. The two goals were compatible.⁵⁶

Johnson was one of many Progressives who had doubts about the value of labor unions—seeing them as a departure from individualism and inviting class conflict—but he also saw the need to build up his support among workers after his first election. The 1910 platform on which Johnson ran had little in it for labor, and he had not done well in San Francisco, a labor stronghold.

Once in office he moved to strengthen his ties with labor: thirty-nine of the forty-nine measures sought by the unions became law in the 1911 legislative session, and more were adopted in 1913.⁵⁷ He did well with the labor vote in 1914. He had pushed legislation and was rewarded for it as the working class became a significant part of his backing.⁵⁸

For whatever reason, Johnson wound up doing a great deal for labor. Between 1911 and 1915, with his leadership and support, over a hundred pieces of labor legislation became law. They included a breakthrough worker's compensation measure, an eight-hour day for women, the establishment of employment bureaus, and improved child labor laws.⁵⁹ Women did well under Johnson. He stood behind legislation intended to improve working conditions for women, and while he did not openly endorse woman suffrage, being at best ambivalent about it, he helped get the suffrage measure on the ballot that the voters approved.⁶⁰ Johnson also worked for prison reform, education, and conservation causes.⁶¹

Johnson and his followers attacked not only political machines but political parties and partisanship in general. The attack was particularly productive because California, like other western states, was a place where all three were relatively weak, making it easier to mount a significant attack. The reformers distrusted the formal party organizations of the major parties, seeing them as tied to special interests, and sought to turn power over to nonmachine voters acting through primaries and devices of direct democracy. They also sought to get away from partisan politics by turning over more authority to boards and commissions run by experts who, they argued, as did Governor Hughes of New York, could run the government much better than politicians. In the view of Johnson-led California reformers, the state could do well without political parties or partisanship—people could set policy goals directly and well-trained politically neutral experts, protected by strong civil service systems, could carry out their wishes.

To weaken the grip of parties, Johnson and his supporters worked for nonpartisan elections and were successful on this score when it came to judicial and local government offices, but voters turned them down when it came to state elective offices. The reformers also placed a host of cumbersome restrictions on party organizations, detailing their structure and various procedures and restricting their ability to raise funds and to influence nominations and elections.

In the same spirit, thanks in part to a state court ruling, California in 1913 went so far as to adopt a cross-filing law that allowed candidates to enter any party primary they wished—for example, to campaign to be both the Republican and Democratic nominee for the office of governor.[62]

This cross-filing system furthered the goal of nonpartisanship. Progressives also liked the plan because it enabled them to run as Republicans as well as members of the Progressive Party and thus maximize their chances of winning. In addition, being able to run as Republicans provided a way for Progressives to stay on the ballot should the Progressive Party suddenly break apart, something it might do any day.[63] Coming at a later date were laws limiting patronage through the establishment of a civil service system where employment was based on merit and those in the system were given job protections.

Though Johnson's time in office resulted in several positive innovations, there was also a black mark: Under pressure he signed on to the Alien Land Law of 1913, which prohibited aliens ineligible for citizenship from owning land in the state. The measure was aimed primarily at Japanese farmers. It was highly popular in California, especially in farming communities, and had been overwhelmingly approved in the legislature by members of both parties. Johnson, with the backing of nearly the entire legislature, signed the anti-alien legislation in 1913. Japan protested the action to President Wilson, who, in turn, asked Johnson and the legislature to reconsider the measure. The president sent Secretary of State William Jennings Bryan to confer with Johnson, but Johnson claimed the law was not discriminatory and ignored the request.[64]

GOVERNOR STEPHENS

Republican William Stephens, who was Johnson's successor as governor and served from 1917 to 1923, operated in a less dynamic fashion than Johnson but consolidated Johnson's work and added a few Progressive measures of his own, especially in the realm of tax legislation. Johnson, though, felt his successor lacked governing skills and vacillated too much—an assessment some regard as totally unfounded and, more than anything, reflective of Johnson's mean-spiritedness.[65]

Stephens was elected for a four-year term on a joint Republican Party and Progressive Party ticket in 1918. He had served as mayor of Los Angeles and, after joining the Progressive Party of Theodore Roosevelt, became a member of the US House of Representatives. Southern California supporters recommended Stephens to Johnson as lieutenant governor following the death of the holder of that office in February 1913. In return for appointing Stephens, Johnson was said to have received a guarantee that a certain newspaper chain would support him in the upcoming election.[66]

Stephens became governor when Johnson left office in March 1917 to take a seat in the US Senate. He was soon confronted with controversy concerning the conviction of two radical union leaders, Thomas Mooney and Warren Billings, for a bombing during a Preparedness Day parade on July 22, 1916, in San Francisco. They were sentenced to be hanged. Critics contended that the trial had been unfair. Stephens disagreed but yielded to pressure from President Wilson and others and commuted their sentences to life imprisonment. Stephens continued to receive demands that he pardon Mooney and Billings and, with these, threats to his personal safety if he did not take such action. He refused to do so. Labor radicals were blamed for a dynamite explosion on December 17, 1919, that damaged the Governor's Mansion. Such events and the fear of more of them contributed to the passage of the state's Criminal Syndicalism Act, supported by Stephens, which was aimed at radical labor unionists, especially the Industrial Workers of the World.

Overall, Stephens was a pragmatist who made policy decisions on the basis of research and fact-finding evidence rather than ideological preconceptions. He liked the mantle of nonpartisanship.[67] He vetoed measures to deregulate public utilities and reorganized governmental agencies to facilitate the implementation of Progressive policies. Like Johnson, he sought to restrict Japanese immigration.

NOTES

1. "Western Radicalism," *The Outlook*, March 30, 1912, 716.
2. On the weakness of parties in the West see Kleppner, "Voters and Parties in the Western States." See also overviews and discussions of various states in Jonas, *Politics in the American West*; and Galderisi et al., *Politics of Realignment*.
3. Griffiths, *Populism in the Western United States*, 293.
4. Goebel, *A Government by the People*, 69–70.
5. While conceding that the railroads had considerable power, scholars have contended that reformers and others greatly exaggerated the extent of the Southern Pacific's control over the state. See, for example, Deverell, "The Varieties of Progressive Experience," 6–7.
6. Griffiths, *Populism in the Western United States*, 3.
7. Olin, *California's Prodigal Sons*, 3.
8. "Assembly Indorses Taft and Gillett," *San Francisco Call*, September 9, 1910, 8. See also "Gillett Fires First Shot for Herrin Machine," *San Francisco Call*, February 28, 1908, 1 (on his closeness to the Southern Pacific); "Gov. Gillett Wins Fight," *Los Angeles Times*, June, 19, 1910, VII-1 (on his campaign against boxing); and "Gov. Gillett Rings True," *Los Angeles Times*, March 26, 1907, II-4 (on his veto of legislation, especially labor bills).
9. Lower, *A Bloc of One*, 18.
10. "The New State Primary Law," *Los Angeles Times*, April 3, 1909, II-4.
11. Weatherson and Bochin, *Hiram Johnson: A Bio-Bibliography*, 3.
12. Weatherson and Bochin, *Hiram Johnson, Political Revivalist*, 3.

13. Lower, *A Bloc of One*, 17.
14. Gunther, *Inside U.S.A.*, 15.
15. "The Impossible Johnson," *Los Angeles Times*, August 16, 1910: II-4.
16. Ibid. The idea that thousands of Democrats had registered as Republicans in order to vote in the primary was also expressed in "Hot Fights in California" *New York Times*, August 15, 1910, 16.
17. Weatherson and Bochin, *Hiram Johnson: A Bio-Bibliography*, 10, 68.
18. "California Party Is All Insurgent," *New York Times*, August 18, 1910, 3.
19. "Lost by the Split: Too Many Republican Candidates," *Los Angeles Times*, August 18, 1910, I-1.
20. Rogin and Shover, *Political Change in California*, 38–44.
21. "California Party Is All Insurgent."
22. "Johnson Nominated for Governor at State Primary," *Los Angeles Times*, August 17, 1910, I-1.
23. Rogin and Shover, *Political Change in California*, 43–44; Shefter, "Regional Receptivity to Reform."
24. Timberlake, *Prohibition and the Progressive Movement*, 166.
25. Interview with James B. Morrow, "The Man Who Tries to Kick a $738,000,000 Corporation out of Politics," *Washington Herald*, January 1, 1911, 1.
26. Quoted in "Dancing and Good Legislation," *Atlanta Constitution*, February 26, 1911, B5.
27. Johnson, "First Inaugural Address."
28. Ibid.
29. Olin, *California's Prodigal Sons*, 30–31; Weatherson and Bochin, *Hiram Johnson: A Bio-Bibliography*, 12.
30. "Scales of Public Opinion Will Weigh Legislators," *San Francisco Call*, January 15, 1911, 1.
31. Lipson, *American Governor*, 51; De Witt, *Progressive Movement*, 63–67.
32. Lower, *A Bloc of One*, 30.
33. Lipson, *American Governor*, 51. See also Beek, *California Legislature*, 193.
34. "Breaks the Record," *Evening Star*, June 6, 1911, 5. This source mentions twenty-one amendments, which is not consistent with other counts of twenty-three.
35. "Three Progressive States," *The Outlook*, May 13, 1911, 43–45.
36. "Breaks the Record."
37. "The Following Constitutional Amendments Are to Be Voted on in October," *Los Angeles Times*, September 10, 1911, II-14.
38. Kent, "Johnson of California," *The Outlook*, February 10, 1912, 313–18. Kent was a California Congressman.
39. Martin, *Ballots and Bandwagons*, 33.
40. Weatherson and Bochin, *Hiram Johnson: A Bio-Bibliography*, 20.
41. Ibid., 21.
42. La Follette, *La Follette's Autobiography*, 244.
43. Weatherson and Bochin, *Hiram Johnson, Political Revivalist*, 57.
44. Ibid., 59.
45. Ibid., 24.
46. Ibid., 14.
47. Ibid., 71–72.
48. Moley, "Knight of Nonpartisanship," 221.
49. Lower, *A Bloc of One*, vii.
50. Ibid., viii.
51. Ibid., 22.
52. Olin, *California's Prodigal Sons*, 170–71.
53. Lower, *A Bloc of One*, 31.
54. Quoted in "Johnson Makes a Hot Argument Advocating Recall of Judges," *Daily Capitol Journal*, February 29, 1912, 1

55. See, for example, Blackford, "Businessmen and the Regulation of Railroads."
56. Olin, *California's Prodigal Sons*, 171.
57. Lower, *A Bloc of One*, 33.
58. Rogin and Shover, *Political Change in California*, 46–47.
59. Mason, "Neither Friends nor Foes," 58; Weatherson and Bochin, *Hiram Johnson: A Bio-Bibliography*, 14.
60. Lower, *A Bloc of One*, 29.
61. Weatherson and Bochin, *Hiram Johnson: A Bio-Bibliography*, 176; Olin, *California's Prodigal Sons*, 176.
62. Putnam, "The Progressive Legacy in California."
63. Olin, *California's Prodigal Sons*, 44.
64. Weatherson and Bochin, *Hiram Johnson: A Bio-Bibliography*, 13.
65. Olin, *California's Prodigal Sons*, 170; Putnam, "The Progressive Legacy in California," 250.
66. Weatherson and Bochin, *Hiram Johnson, Political Revivalist*, 75.
67. Putnam, "The Progressive Legacy in California," 251.

13

AGITATION AND ACTIVITY IN THE NORTHWEST

Chamberlain, West, Rogers, and Carey

Moving along to the Northwest, we start out with Oregon, a pioneer state when it comes to political reform, where we find some very colorful, flamboyant, scene-stealing governors (one specialized in insulting presidents) and reform-minded Democratic governors in a Republican state, wisely downplaying their party affiliation. In Washington State Populists had an early influence on the development of sentiment for reform, including the input of a thoughtful Populist governor, whose views, actions, and problems are given considerable attention here, but it was an all-Republican show when it came to the adoption of policies. With strong support for reform in the legislature governors played a less active or decisive leadership role than in Oregon.

In Montana we find another Populist governor and an extraordinary display of corporate power by the Anaconda Copper Mining Company. In spite of corporate influence, however, there was an impressive amount of reform, the banner year coming in 1907. The story in Idaho includes a labor strike that eventually led to the murder of a governor who had once been elected with the backing of the Populists but also a current of mild progressive reform. In Wyoming we focus on Governor Joseph Carey, who, switching parties, tried to secure political measures that would bring down a conservative business machine and help usher in a new set of leaders who would bring greater development and prosperity to the state.

OREGON: PENNOYER, CHAMBERLAIN, AND WEST

When it comes to political reform in Oregon, mention must be first made of William S. U'Ren, lawyer and Populist-Progressive political activist who promoted a wide variety of measures democratizing the political system and weakening the power of special interests. He began a campaign on behalf of the initiative and referendum in the 1890s, and that finally paid off in the form of a constitutional amendment approved by the voters in 1902. He and other reformers proceeded to use the initiative process to bring a host of changes, including a direct primary, the popular election of US senators, a presidential primary (the first in the nation), a corrupt-practices measure, and the recall of officials. The political reforms that U'Ren campaigned for, commonly known as the "Oregon System," were widely adopted around the country.

On the gubernatorial level reform in Oregon is associated most strongly with three individuals: Democrat-Populist Sylvester Pennoyer (1887–95) and Democrats George Chamberlain (1903–9) and Oswald West (1911–15). All of these governors served at a time when Republicans were generally dominant in the state.

Pennoyer was born in New York, the son of a wealthy farmer who had served in the state legislature. He received a law degree from Harvard and moved to Portland in 1855, where he married, became a school teacher, and a businessman. Demonstrating a talent for making shrewd real estate investments, he wound up a wealthy man. He spent several years as a political writer and working for the Democratic Party.[1] In 1885 he lost a race to become mayor of Portland, but the following year, running on a platform emphasizing the need to exclude Chinese workers from the state, he won the gubernatorial position. As he saw it, "the great producing and laboring classes of our state are being ground down between the upper and nether millstones of corporate power and cheap servile labor." Before long, he warned, "the Willamette Valley will be the home only of rich capitalists and Chinese serfs."[2]

Governor Pennoyer called for controls on railroad and telegraph company rates, the elimination of railroad free passes, an inheritance tax, limits on the use of Pinkerton detectives as private armies, compulsory arbitration for labor disputes, and numerous other reforms in the interest of labor. Under him and with his support the state adopted the Australian ballot and some labor measures, but Republican control of the legislature during both of his terms limited his ability to make legislative achievements. On his own Pennoyer liberally exercised the pardoning power and showed concern for those locked up in the state penitentiary by, for example, abolishing the practice of whipping prisoners. Seeking to protect the power of his office, he opposed the legislature's habit of delegating what he saw as executive authority to commissions beyond the governor's control. He also argued that the courts, state and federal, lacked the constitutional authority to exercise the power of judicial review.

The turning point for Pennoyer in terms of party-switching came in May 1892 when his fellow Democrats, meeting in convention, not only refused his request that they back him as a favorite-son candidate for president at the upcoming national convention but also refused to allow him to lead the state delegation to that meeting. At the same state convention Oregon Democrats passed a resolution endorsing Cleveland, someone Pennoyer despised, in part, because of the president's stand in favor of a single gold standard. Following the gathering he announced that he had left the Democratic Party and was now a Populist. He condemned the Democratic Party for its failure to support the silver cause.

As a Populist, Pennoyer became an even more determined and outspoken opponent of the Cleveland Democrats and even more hostile to Cleveland personally. One illustrative incident came early in 1893 when, in a fit of pique, he turned down a request from the state Democratic Party to use the National Guard cannon to fire a salute in celebration of Cleveland's inauguration as president. Democrats, though, got hold of the cannon and fired it off twenty-two times (Cleveland was the twenty-second president), making sure that the sound was within the governor's hearing range.

In May 1893 Pennoyer received a message from Cleveland's secretary of state asking him to protect the Chinese Americans in Oregon from possible violence because the Chinese Exclusion Act was about to go into effect. He replied: "I will attend to my own business, let the President attend to his" and ignored the request.[3] He also ignored a request from Cleveland to help round up a group of unemployed workers who had hijacked a train to join others in a march on Washington organized by Jacob S. Coxey. Like Populist governors Lewelling of Kansas and Waite of Colorado, he was sympathetic to the "Coxey Army" phenomenon. Later, just out of spite, he refused to accept the date set by Cleveland for a national Thanksgiving holiday, declaring that in Oregon it would be held a week earlier than the president had requested.

Cleveland was a special target, but Pennoyer offended at least one other president. He gained national attention in 1891 by snubbing President Benjamin Harrison, who was visiting the state. He refused to meet the president in a welcoming ceremony at the state line. He reasoned that since the states were sovereign, in Oregon he was a "bigger man" than the president of the United States, and the president would have to come to his office if he wanted to meet.[4]

Contemporary observers characterized Pennoyer as a man of strong opinions who gained attention and churned up public support by doing outrageous things.[5]

Historians Dorothy Johansen and Charles Gates noted that Pennoyer "quickly read the trend of the times and enlisted on the side of some limited reforms."[6] These two historians were far more positive in their evaluations of Chamberlain and West, crediting both of these Democratic governors with accomplishing a considerable amount, even though they had to work with somewhat reluctant Republican legislatures, and giving the office they held a new prestige.[7]

Chamberlain, born in Natchez, Mississippi, the son of a doctor, came to Oregon in 1876 where, after a few years, he began a law practice, won election to the statehouse, became district attorney of Multnomah County, and, in 1891, was appointed by Governor Pennoyer to the recently created position of Oregon attorney general. In the fall of 1891 he won election to that office and served as attorney general until January 1895. In 1902 he ran as a reform candidate for governor, expressing his support for the initiative and referendum proposition that was on the ballot in the same election. The voters chose both Chamberlain and direct democracy, though he managed to win by only a scant 246 votes.

He won again in 1906, this time more comfortably by a margin of 2,494 votes, around 48 percent of the total compared to 45 percent for his Republican opponent. He later resigned as governor to take a seat in the US Senate. He was chosen for that position by the Republican legislature because, under the terms of an initiative measure approved by the voters in the fall of 1908, a majority of the legislators had pledged to vote for the winning candidate in the primary election for the Senate seat that year, and this happened to be Chamberlain.

Being a Democratic governor surrounded by Republicans, he wisely strove for nonpartisanship or bipartisanship. He appointed Republicans to judicial positions and did not openly campaign for a Democratic candidate in a special election to Congress.[8] He also mixed reform with fiscal conservatism. He frequently used his veto power in dealing with a Republican legislature, but on the positive side he was able to secure a railroad commission and various labor and penal reforms in his first term. He was less fortunate in his efforts to increase corporate taxes and regulation or antitrust laws. The voters helped out the Progressive cause in 1904 with the adoption of a direct primary law and several more Progressive measures he supported in 1906.

Throughout his time in office, Chamberlain showed himself to be a strong defender of the Oregon System and a proponent of woman suffrage, reclamation and hydropower projects, conservation, a Progressive income tax, labor regulations, and penal reform. He also backed a campaign led by one of his appointees, future governor Oswald West, against fraudulent land deals.[9] Chamberlain has been judged as a cautious reformer, someone with shrewd political judgment: "Never the early agitator for what later became a popular cause, Chamberlain nevertheless quickly championed reform when the voice of the electorate became clear."[10] Chamberlain has also been viewed as a governor who made what was generally regarded as an unimportant office in Oregon an important one.[11]

Oswald West followed Chamberlain in office. He got there at age thirty-eight and continued the same program of reform. He served but a single four-year term. He was, however, among the most active Progressive crusaders of his time.

Lincoln Steffens described him as a "spectacularly progressive" governor.[12] Like Chamberlain, he stood behind the Oregon System of political reform and was committed to the goal of controlling corporations. To West, "The people must rule the corporations or the corporations will rule the state."[13] He was also active in the causes of prohibition and penal reform.

West was born in Ontario, Canada, and came to Oregon as a baby. His family was poor, and he had little formal education. He started off in a series of low-paying, menial jobs. Early on he was a butcher's boy and sheep herder. Later he rose from an errand boy to a bank teller, took off for six months to search for gold in Alaska, and came back to bank work.[14] A politically active Democrat, West helped out in Chamberlain's successful gubernatorial campaign in 1902. Chamberlain rewarded him in 1903 with a position as state land agent. In that capacity West recovered hundreds of thousands of acres of school lands illegally obtained through a land fraud scheme.[15] He continued to build his reputation as a determined investigator while a member of the Oregon railroad commission.

West's well-publicized investigations helped propel him toward the governorship. In 1910 he won the primary election and became the Democratic candidate for governor. With the backing of Chamberlain and leading Republican Progressives, including US senator Jonathan Bourne, he ran a nonpartisan campaign, barely mentioning his association with the Democratic Party and focusing on the need to defend the initiative, referendum, and direct primary and other political reform measures from their enemies in the legislature.[16] From the start he made no effort to hide his anticorporate views; when announcing his candidacy he declared: "If God had intended corporations to rule over people he would have created the corporations first."[17]

He won with 47 percent of the vote, compared to 41 percent for his Republican opponent. The rest went to two third-party candidates. Commenting on his campaign finances, West noted: "I was elected governor with $3,000. All the money came from my own bank account and that of one friend."[18]

West came into office pushing for Progressive legislation, drawing upon public support and emphasizing nonpartisanship to avert or at least tone down opposition in the Republican-dominated legislature. He nevertheless frequently felt that he had to use the veto power. He vetoed sixty-three bills in 1911 alone.[19] He also threatened to use the initiative as well as the veto to pressure Republicans into supporting Progressive causes and sometimes actually used that device when the legislature refused to act as he wished. This led to laws regarding worker's compensation, banking, and a public utility commission.[20]

As governor he was able to successfully promote business regulation, labor protection, conservation, prohibition, and penal reform. His administration brought greater public utility regulation as well as new controls on bankers, stockbrokers, and loan sharks. For labor came worker's compensation, pensions, and

Figure 13.1. Oswald West. Courtesy of the Library of Congress, Prints & Photographs Division, photograph by Harris & Ewing, LC-DIG-hec-17741.

greater controls on wages, hours, and working conditions. Conservation reforms included beach, forestry, and fish and game protections. He pushed through legislation in 1913 that, in effect, protected the beaches bordering the Pacific Ocean for public use.[21]

Though West sometimes expressed his concern about states' rights, he saw the virtue of federal programs protecting the natural resources of the states. He told his colleagues in 1914 that if the federal government had not taken action and left the job to the states, "the great natural resources of the West would have completely fallen into the hands of large corporations. . . . I am mighty glad the government did put all of these obstacles in the way, in order that we might draw a long breath and realize what fools we have been in the past, and to take steps to pass laws that would throw some protection around the birthright of the people."[22]

Continuing on, he condemned the exploitation of natural resources by large corporations who "think God Almighty gave them the right to own the earth and run it as they see fit" and made the case for public control. This, he told his colleagues, "may be socialism," but he believed that God intended the coal in the earth as well as the air around us to be "for the use of all" and that "when the time comes that the rights of Mr. Rockefeller, or any other of that class, run counter to the rights of the many in controlling these resources, necessary for the comfort of the masses, right then they should be put to one side and the people take control."[23]

West also saw the need for penal reform. He declared that the treatment of inmates in the state prison system was inhumane. Feeling people could do right if given a fair chance, he was liberal in granting pardons, something his opponents used against him.[24] In 1912 he gave four prisoners scheduled for death a reprieve in the hope that voters would abandon the death penalty in the November election, but the voters refused to do so. An unhappy West expressed his disappointment but continued to maintain: "There is no necessity for capital punishment. It is a useless and hideous relic of barbarous and mediaeval ignorance."[25] In 1914, however, the voters abolished capital punishment, much to West's relief, by 157 votes in a referendum.

West also stood out as a strong supporter of prohibition, once going so far as to declare that he wanted to "shoot a bartender."[26] He attracted considerable national attention on New Year's Day of 1914 when, in response to local complaints about lawless behavior and the failure of county officials to do anything about the situation, he declared martial law in a wide-open boomtown in the eastern part of the state named Copperfield. He followed up by sending his personal secretary, Miss Fern Hobbs, and a few National Guard members to the town with the mission of shutting down saloons and gambling houses and securing the resignation of city officials, including the mayor and several council members who were connected with these illegal enterprises.

The governor hoped that the presence of Hobbs, who stood five feet four and weighed under 100 pounds, would lessen the chances of violence. She did not encounter violence, but city officials refused her request that they resign. National Guardsmen proceeded to arrest the officials and to implement martial law, shutting down the saloons and confiscating weapons and gambling equipment. Hobbs left the same day she arrived in Copperfield, but an increased number of Guardsmen stayed on there for several months. Hobbs later said she would not have done this for anyone other than Governor West and would not do it again for anybody.[27]

An Oregon mayor looked at the developments in Copperfield as another example of the "grand-stand administration" of Oswald West, who, in this case, the mayor claimed, had used Hobbs to attract attention to himself. The mayor added: "I believe Mr. West is entirely honest in his aims, but his means are always theatrical. There is everlasting turmoil."[28] West also demonstrated a flair for the theatrical by heading a posse that recaptured a convict he had gone to bat for who had broken parole. He felt morally bound to act because he had misjudged the convict in approving his release.[29]

West was described by contemporaries as a strongly determined, fearless, and peppery individual, a "practical criminologist," and a "militant and advanced progressive."[30] He also had a temper. On one occasion his temper led him to exchange blows with a newspaperman in the capitol rotunda—both wound up on the floor wrestling around and striking each other until someone pulled them apart.[31]

Though largely successful as governor, West chose not to go for another term in 1914. He made an unsuccessful bid for the US Senate in 1918. After this he spent the rest of his career not as a candidate or officeholder but as a practicing lawyer and writer getting involved in all types of political controversies.

WASHINGTON: ROGERS, MEAD, HAY, AND LISTER

John R. Rogers, a Populist-elected Washington governor in 1896, helped establish a reform tradition in his state. Born in Maine, Rogers spent several years moving around the country working as a pharmacist in some locations and a farmer in others. In Kansas he was a well-known Farmers' Alliance leader and became involved in the creation of the Kansas Populist Party. He and his family moved to Washington in 1890.

In 1894 he won a seat in the state legislature as a Populist and proceeded the following year to pursue a variety of reforms, including woman suffrage, mine safety, increased corporate tax assessment, and liberal voting and election laws. He became best known for his sponsorship of the "Barefoot Schoolboy Law," which equalized educational spending among districts in the state, taking money from the wealthier urban districts for use in the poorer rural ones. Turning to writing, Rogers produced a book in 1894 titled *Politics: An Argument in Behalf of the Inalienable Rights of Man*, in which he focused on the abuses of capitalism, associating it with slavery because it also meant the "robbery of labor," condemned inequality, and called for the public ownership of monopolies.[32]

Voters elected Rogers governor in 1896 on a fusion ticket formed by Populists, Silver Republicans, and Bryan Democrats and supported by farmer organizations and organized labor. His victory was viewed with some apprehension. An early historian noted: "Many people shuddered as he entered upon the duties of his office. He refused to ride to his inauguration in a carriage with his predecessor. His austere bearing gave promise of attempts to enforce the doctrines that seemed flamingly fantastic during his campaign speeches, but alarming and revolutionary when he had become the governor."[33]

Rogers, though, soon made it clear that he was going to be moderate and cautious. As he explained in his inaugural address: "In my book I was a propagandist. I said in my preface that I purposely used very plain and emphatic language. I did it to arouse the people. I believe I succeeded. But as Governor of the State I have other duties to perform, and I know that the danger to be apprehended from those who have labored earnestly in a cause is not their lack of honesty, but their lack of judgment. We shall be sincere, but we shall, I hope, be prudent." He said he was also mindful of the importance of not getting ahead of public opinion: "The advance must not be greater than that approved by that public opinion which comes from the general average judgment of all the people of Washington."[34]

Within this boundary he said he would work for measures to improve the quality of life of ordinary citizens, including more equitable taxes, a better educational system, and corporate regulation.

When he came into office, the fusionists had control of both statehouses. Rogers, however, had considerable trouble with the more extreme "middle-of-the-road" Populists in and out of the legislature who disliked his moderation and his failure to repay them for their help in the election with patronage. Rogers wanted to give jobs to Democrats and Silver Republicans as well as Populists in order to build a fusion party. Hard-nosed Populists, on the other hand, wanted him, as a Populist, to use patronage to build the Populist Party. They accused him of actually using it to build his own personal following and his power in the legislature at the expense of the Populists Party. Middle-roaders also objected to Rogers's refusal to back their candidate for the US Senate.[35]

One of Rogers's central goals was to set maximum freight and passenger rates and create a commission to enforce these restrictions. He spoke favorably of public ownership of the rails sometime in the future but for now was willing to settle for regulation.[36] Middle-road Populists, in revolt over patronage and the senatorial question, took it out on the governor by scuttling his proposal for a railroad commission. After the 1897 session Rogers decided to completely isolate the middle-road Populists when it came to patronage, denying appointments he had promised some of them because of their role in the defeat of his commission bill.[37]

In the spring of 1900 Rogers separated himself from the Populist Party, which was now under the control of the middle-roaders, and announced he was now a Democrat. He acted on the belief that by conducting an honest and efficient government he could win reelection without the support of the Populists. Surprisingly to many, he did go on to win reelection in 1900, despite Bryan's defeat in the state and the ability of the Republicans to elect the rest of their state ticket. Apparently aiding his efforts was a reliable and highly effective political organization or "machine" that he had been able to build through patronage appointments.[38] Rogers died shortly after taking office in 1901.

In his time as governor Rogers was able to secure labor protection measures and legislation to support public education and prison system reform. He did not support prohibition, considering it a futile and oppressive effort to legislate morality.[39] Though no revolutionary, Rogers expressed in his writings his concern over the ability of the wealthy few to exploit hard-working people and the poor for their own selfish ends. He felt that "human misery is not inevitable, is not created by defects of character or weak motivation," but springs from the "desire of the wealthy and the strong to seize, under the name of rent, profit or interest, some portion of the product of labor." Engraved on Rogers's tombstone are these words: "I would make it impossible for the covetous and avaricious to utterly impoverish the poor; the rich can take care of themselves."[40]

Rogers's tradition of reform, which was carried on, not by Democratic governors who fought it out with Republican-dominated legislatures, as in Oregon, but by an all-Republican cast until the election of a Democrat in 1912. During much of this period George Cotterill led the Progressive effort in the legislature, bringing about several changes, including a direct primary, woman suffrage, and worker's compensation. Voters elected Cotterill to the state senate in 1906. He was one of three Democrats in the forty-two-member body, but he crossed over to become leader of the Progressive Republicans.

On the gubernatorial level Republican Albert Mead, who had the support of the Great Northern Railway in his campaign for governor in 1904, surprised everyone after the election by supporting legislation to increase railroad property valuations for purposes of taxation and the establishment of a railroad commission. A direct primary also came under his reign. While he sponsored this reform and may have felt it would improve his chances of securing renomination, he failed to win the primary nomination in 1908 and retired from politics.

Reform also came through the administrations of Republican governor Marion Hay, 1909-13. Hay, who had been a successful merchant, stepped up from the position of lieutenant governor to become governor following the death of Samuel G. Cosgrove, who had been elected governor in 1908. The state legislature, dominated by Republicans, adopted many of the reforms it was to adopt during the entire Progressive era in a single legislative session in 1911 while Hay was in office. Coming out of that session were measures regarding the initiative and referendum, worker's compensation, an eight-hour workday for women, and pure food and drugs. The legislature also ratified the Sixteenth Amendment, providing for the federal income tax. Hay, while willing to accept reform, did not take the lead in bringing it about. He had gone on record in favor of some changes, such as the recall, but when it came to others, he was at best lukewarm. Of one leading reform measure, for example, he said: "Should the legislature pass a direct legislation bill, I shall certainly approve it, though I am unable to see where it will do the good its many advocates claim."[41] Overall, he was more concerned with ensuring economy in government and rooting out dishonest state officials than the broader reform program.[42]

Democrat Ernest Lister defeated Hay in 1912 and continued the push for reform. He won again in 1916. Lister was born in England, started out in Washington as an iron molder, became active in his union, and won a seat on the Tacoma city council as a Populist. He went on to manage Populist John Rogers's 1896 campaign for governor and was rewarded with an important position in Rogers's administration. In 1900 he joined Rogers in switching to the Democratic Party. Independent-minded, he rejected offers of free passes from the railroads at a time when such favors were commonly offered and accepted.[43]

His victory at the age of forty-two came in a close election in 1912. He replaced the Democratic nominee, who was forced to drop out because of ineligibility, and

Lister had only a few weeks to make his case. He campaigned like a hurricane around the state and wound up defeating Hay by 622 votes. Like many Democrats that year, his victory was facilitated by divided Republican opposition and the presence of a Progressive Party candidate on the ballot.

In his inaugural speech Lister noted that that public opinion in the state was highly Progressive and that he was a beneficiary of this sentiment.[44] While some editors viewed him as an advanced Progressive, others insisted that "nobody's afraid of Ernest Lister" and had no reason to be because he was "fad proof" and reasonable, and blessed with a full supply of "old fashion horse sense."[45] After Lister died in office in 1919 at age forty-eight, a writer for a paper affiliated with the Nonpartisan League noted that Lister came into office more conservative than Progressive but learned a great deal during his six years in office and "the things that he saw and the fight that he met forced him to become progressive."[46]

Lister had a tough time with the legislature. Many reform bills died, and on eight occasions the legislature overrode his veto of measures they had passed.[47] Not surprisingly, he had no success in his efforts to improve the role of the governor when it came to budgeting and to improve the operation of the legislature by dramatically reducing its size.[48] Finding considerable opposition from conservative Republicans, he worked when he could with the Progressive side of the Republican majority and Democrats. A friend of labor, he pushed for an eight-hour workday, supported the passage of a minimum-wage law for women, and showed considerable courage in vetoing a measure that he felt infringed upon the civil rights of members of the Industrial Workers of the World.

MONTANA: SMITH, TOOLE, AND ANACONDA

Montana, like Washington, had the experience of a Populist governor, Robert B. Smith, who served from 1897 to 1901. Smith, a lawyer from Helena, had failed in 1894 in a bid for Congress as a Populist candidate, coming in ahead of the Democratic candidate but behind the Republican. He had recently left the Democratic Party on the silver issue. He had gained some labor support by defending several hundred idle workers, many of who were on strike against the Great Northern Railroad, and had tried to connect up with Coxey's Army.

Following his successful 1896 campaign as a gubernatorial candidate on a Populist-Democratic ticket, Smith, like Populist victors elsewhere, such as Lewelling in Kansas and Rogers in Washington, attempted to reduce general fears about what their victory meant. Smith stated in an interview before taking office: "No one need feel alarmed that anything very radical or anything sensational will transpire in my administration, if I can help it. Those persons who have been pretending to fear for the business interests of the state if I should be elected governor, were alarmists without cause."[49] Smith, true to his word, proposed only a mild set of reforms. Most of these went nowhere. One failure was a request that the legislature adopt the initiative and referendum, a reform the voters adopted some ten years later.[50]

Along with championing direct democracy Smith called attention to the fact that the corporations, most notably the Anaconda Copper Mining Company, then wrapped up in a trust known as the Amalgamated Copper Company, were evading taxes on fully one-half of the property they possessed. He was unable, however, to do anything about the problem.[51] By 1898 many of his Populist supporters saw Smith as a "band wagon" Populist whose primary interest was in free silver. As in Washington under Rogers and in Kansas under Lewelling, Populists became upset because of Smith's lack of commitment to the broader cause and his tendency to distribute patronage in favor of the Democrats. Smith, having mended his fences, returned to the Democratic Party in 1898.[52]

Corporate control, meanwhile, remained the central characteristic of state politics. This was dramatically apparent in the early 1900s during the administration of Democrat Joseph K. Toole. Missouri-born Toole had been Montana's first governor, elected to that office in 1889. He came back to power in 1900, following Smith, and was reelected in 1904. Prior to becoming governor he had served in the territorial legislature, as territorial delegate to Congress, and as a member of the state's constitutional convention.

Toward the end of his second term as governor Toole experienced a painful reminder about who was in charge. Fritz Heinze, one the state's smaller Copper Kings, was giving the giant Amalgamated Copper Company a great deal of trouble with nagging lawsuits. Heinze was thought to have bribed several judges to throw their decisions his way. Striking back on October 22, 1903, Amalgamated closed down all mining and other operations in Montana, throwing more than 20,000 men out of work and causing an economic panic. The company demanded that Governor Toole call a special session of the legislature to pass a law that would allow the company to take a lawsuit to another jurisdiction if it felt the judge was biased or corrupt.

Toole was anti-Amalgamated but felt he no choice. He called the session, the legislature gave Amalgamated what it wanted, and Amalgamated resumed operations.

Toole had long warned against the growth of monopolies and trusts, saying that they were "moved solely by a love of gain" and willing to do anything to accomplish their objectives.[53] Picking up where Populist governor Smith had left off, in 1903 he called attention to the millions in corporate income that escaped taxation in the state every year.[54] He also led the charge, this time successful, for the initiative and referendum. Noting Oregon's experience with direct legislation, he argued: "It is the sure weapon with which to put to flight the briber and the lobbyist, and drive them, like Hagar, to the wilderness."[55] The voters adopted direct legislation in 1906. In 1907 the legislature, being encouraged by William Jennings

Bryan, who spoke to an assembly of the lawmakers, followed up with the passage of a long list of reforms, including a railroad commission, limits on hours of work for railroad employees, a stronger child labor law, pure food regulations, and an antigambling law.[56]

On the Republican side Joseph Dixon led the Progressive cause in Montana, often in combating the Anaconda Copper Mining Company. His long career as a public official began with his election to the US House of Representatives in 1902 and 1904 and included service in the US Senate from 1907 to 1913. Dixon played an important role as campaign manager for Roosevelt's bid for the White House in 1912 with the Progressive Party.[57]

He won the governorship in 1920 by riding a strong national wave for the Republican Party to defeat Democrat Burton K. Wheeler, a man with solid reform credentials who had the support of the Nonpartisan League. Wheeler, a strong champion of the rights of labor, had also long opposed the Anaconda Copper Mining Company. Montana Republicans depicted the gubernatorial election of 1920 as a life-or-death struggle against the Nonpartisan League, which, they claimed, had taken over the Democratic Party. Eager to "fight sovietism in Montana," they assailed the league and the candidates it supported as "enemies of American institutions and ideals."[58]

In the speech kicking off his campaign, Dixon declared that only the Republican Party stood in the way of a socialist takeover of government in Montana.[59] Dixon, as governor, recommended many reforms but accomplished little because of the opposition generated by Anaconda and the lack of revenues due to the state's poor economy.

While the struggle for reform was difficult, the record in Montana from 1900 down to 1920 was far from barren.[60] Governors, legislators, and, in some cases, voters approved electoral measures dealing with such subjects as direct primaries, the initiative and referendum, woman suffrage, the direct election of senators, the regulation of business enterprises, and socioeconomic issues regarding labor protection, pure food and drug laws, saloons, gambling, and prostitution.

IDAHO: STEUNENBERG, HAWLEY, AND ALEXANDER

In Idaho the Democratic, Populist, and Silver Republican Parties got together in 1896 and were able to secure the election of Frank Steunenberg as governor. Steunenberg, a newspaper editor who had served in the statehouse, came to office as a champion of labor and the "little man," though he was thought to be closer to the conservative side of the coalition than the more Progressive side.[61] He had a peaceful first term, which was mildly successful in regard to labor and health protection reforms. Shortly after his reelection in 1898, however, Populists joined labor leaders in condemning him for declaring martial law and asking President

McKinley to send in federal troops to put down a miners' strike in Coeur d'Alene led by the Western Federation of Miners (WFM). Federal soldiers came to the area, arrested 1,600 strikers and their supporters, including local Populist leaders, and threw hundreds of them into bullpens where they were confined under harsh conditions. Steunenberg left office in 1901, refusing to serve another term, and four years later, while opening the front gate on his home, he detonated a bomb that killed him. A former union member who had since become a paid informer for a mine owners' association confessed to the murder and attempted to implicate three WFM members in the assignation. After a sensational trial the labor leaders were acquitted of the charges against them.

While Progressivism had begun to gain steam about the time Steunenberg left office, the movement was largely obscured by an anti-Mormon campaign that dominated state politics until late in the first decade of the twentieth century.[62] Progressivism had a breakthrough in the 1910 election of Democrat James Hawley as governor. Hawley, a historian as well as a lawyer and politician, was born in Iowa, prospected for gold in California, and started his Idaho political career in the 1870s in the Idaho territorial legislature. He also served as mayor of Boise, winning election in a heavily Republican city. Hawley established himself as a lawyer in criminal cases, both as a defense attorney and a prosecutor. Prominent Idaho politician William Borah once said of him: "Jim Hawley has defended more men and got them acquitted, and prosecuted more men and got them convicted, than any lawyer in America."[63] He was the lead attorney for the state in the Steunenberg assignation trial.

Hawley offered a Progressive platform in his unexpected win in the gubernatorial race in 1910.[64] During his tenure he was able to improve the tax system in a Progressive way through the rigid enforcement of the law requiring assessments at full cash value, a step that increased the tax burden of large property owners. He supported various political reforms, including the initiative, referendum, and recall, which were added to the state constitution.[65] In a close election Hawley went down to defeat in a bid for reelection in 1912, the result of which was seen to have been heavily influenced by the loss of support in Mormon counties prompted by the endorsement by Mormon Church leaders of Taft's reelection as president.[66] Hawley lost two later bids for the US Senate. He was a longtime supporter of woman suffrage.[67]

More reform came under Moses Alexander, elected governor in 1914 and 1916. Alexander, born in Germany, was a prominent clothing merchant who, like Hawley, had served as mayor of Boise. He was also Jewish, which provoked some negative comment but did not do him much damage.[68] He combined fiscal conservatism with support for various causes, including prohibition, suffrage, farm relief measures, and worker's compensation, all of which came to pass during his time in office. He also signed off on a new criminal syndicalism measure aimed at the

Industrial Workers of the World (aka Wobblies). His action on behalf of farmers did not deter the growth of the Nonpartisan League in the state, which in 1918 raided the Democratic primary and nominated its own candidate for governor as the Democratic nominee. The league candidate, though, lost the general election. In 1919 the legislature took several steps, including the repeal of the direct primary law, to make it nearly impossible for the league to take control of a major party again.[69]

CAREY OF WYOMING

Wyoming had a nationally known Progressive governor in Joseph M. Carey. Born in Delaware, this son of a prosperous farmer earned a law degree and turned to politics as a Republican. His help in President Grant's successful campaign for the presidency led to his appointment as US attorney for Wyoming Territory. Later he became associate justice on the territorial supreme court, mayor of Cheyenne, and territorial delegate to the US House of Representatives, where he led the charge to get statehood for Wyoming. Largely in reward for this work on statehood, the state legislature chose him as the state's first US senator, but he fell out of favor with the legislature for a second term because he supported the gold standard over the free-silver standard. For much of his career he feuded with fellow Republican Francis E. Warren, longtime senator from Wyoming who headed the state's Republican Party. Carey was one of those who bolted the Republican national convention in 1912 and helped organize the Bull Moose Party behind Theodore Roosevelt. He decided not to run for reelection in 1914, stayed loyal to the new party, and participated as a delegate to the Progressive national convention in 1916.

In 1910 Carey considered himself an insurgent Republican but ran as a Democrat for governor after he had failed to secure the Republican nomination and after he had worked out a satisfactory platform with the Democrats that called for a direct primary, the initiative and referendum, and an eight-hour workday for women and children. During his campaign he declared that "it is high time, for her own protection, that Wyoming should take her stand with the progressive movement that is everywhere seen and felt in the American Union." He called for political reforms to bring down the political machine run by the Republican old guard, headed by Warren: "These few men have prostituted office and the property of the state for their personal, political and financial gain."[70] Carey repeatedly asserted that the state had been "dwarfed" by the Warren machine and that the adoption of political reform, especially the direct primary, would not only break the machine but put the people in charge and bring to power "energetic men and women" ready to lead in the economic development of the state.[71]

Carey, aware of what was happening in Wisconsin under La Follette, North Dakota under John Burke, and South Dakota under Coe Crawford, wanted

Wyoming to catch up.⁷² He was especially interested in political reforms as found in the Oregon System, which, he hoped, would bring down the Warren machine. He also worked in favor of penal reform, worker's compensation, and blue sky laws but, perhaps fearful of the impact of attracting investment in the state, made no request for legislation regulating corporations. Overall, he offered little in regard to economic or humanitarian reform or conservation and land policy.⁷³

Working with a Republican legislature and a few friendly fellow insurgents, Carey was able to secure a secret ballot, direct primary, and a corrupt-practices act imposing limits on campaign expenditures. A majority of voters supported his proposal for the initiative and referendum, but the vote total was not high enough to meet the requirements of the law. Carey asked for more reforms in 1913 but got little from the legislature, now under control of the faction loyal to Warren. Coming to the end of his term, he said he was proud of his accomplishments, including his use of the veto power to save money, but was sorry he had failed to get some things, especially in the last legislature, including a headless ballot (so that party identification would not be disclosed) and nonpartisan elections for judges.⁷⁴ All in all, though, given the circumstances, Carey's accomplishments were noteworthy.⁷⁵

Carey was a longtime supporter of woman suffrage, which had been written into the state constitution when Wyoming became a state in 1890. His wife Louisa was also active in the cause. In 1895 they entertained suffrage leader Susan B. Anthony at a dinner party in their home in Cheyenne. Among the distinguished guests attending were Senator Warren and his wife—Warren was not altogether persona non grata at the time. Anthony was reportedly much impressed by the reception, and Carey and his wife were remembered by suffrage leaders as "staunch suffragists and old friends of Miss Anthony." Carey was given considerable praise for telling the rest of the country how well woman suffrage had turned out in his state.⁷⁶ Like several other western governors, Carey also believed in states' rights. As he once stated: "I think the government of the United States is going too much into the states and is not permitting the states to depend upon themselves. While I am a Progressive in politics, I think it is right the states should work out their own destinies."⁷⁷

Carey was not a strong leader when it came to building a political organization.⁷⁸ Reform, however, was carried on by others after he left office. Several measures, including labor protection and business regulation, came under the administrations of Democrat John B. Kendrick and Carey's son, Republican Robert D. Carey. Kendrick enjoyed the support of the state's Progressive Party and the elder Carey, whom he followed in office by winning election in 1914. Kendrick was a native of Texas whose rags-to-riches story was one of a penniless orphan who became a millionaire cattleman. He got along very well with the legislature and was successful in securing a public utilities commission, a worker's compensation law, a mothers' pension act, and an amendment to the constitution permitting a loan program to farmers.[79] He resigned his position of governor to go the US Senate.

Carey worked to get his son elected governor in 1918 as part of an effort to reunite the Progressive and Republican Parties in the state. Under Robert Carey Wyoming established a state highway system, but the governor was not able to convince the legislature to go along with an eight-hour workday for women or an income tax. Robert Carey backed Kendrick in his bid for legislative votes to secure a seat in the US Senate in 1914, but the legislature went for Francis Warren instead.

NOTES

1. Griffiths, *Populism in the Western United States*, 118–19.

2. Johnson, *Radical Middle Class*, 95. Pages 119–23 and 128–29 have been drawn upon here for general information on Governor Pennoyer.

3. Quoted in "Short and Tart," *Atlanta Constitution*, May 4, 1893, 1. See also "Pennoyer Is Brash," *Atlanta Constitution*, May 5, 1893, 10.

4. Geer, *Fifty Years in Oregon*, 362. See also "Will Not Go to Meet Harrison: Oregon's Governor Intended to Stand on His Dignity," *New York Times*, April 24, 1891, 4; and "What Pennoyer Is," *New York Times*, May 11, 1891, 2.

5. Geer, *Fifty Years in Oregon*, 333, 377; Bone, *Oregon Cattleman/Governor*, 26.

6. Johansen and Gates, *Empire of the Columbia*, 357.

7. Ibid., 493.

8. Burton, *Democrats of Oregon*, 27.

9. See generally Robbins, "George Chamberlain." See also Piott, *Giving Voters a Voice*, 40, 41, 43. On his support for suffrage see I Harper, *History of Woman Suffrage*, 5:122, 471.

10. Burton, *Democrats of Oregon*, 25.

11. Johansen and Gates, *Empire of the Columbia*, 460.

12. Quoted by Graves, *American State Government*, 322.

13. Johansen and Gates, *Empire of the Columbia*, 461.

14. See generally ibid. As was the case with many events involving West, accounts of the land fraud investigation were carried in eastern papers. See, for example, "Great Land Fraud Plot," *New York Times*, December 3, 1905, 1; and "Bogus Land Titles," *Washington Post*, December 4, 1905, 3.

15. "Notable Oregonians: Oswald West—Governor."

16. Burton, *Democrats of Oregon*, 31–32.

17. "Railroad Commissioner West Announces His Candidacy for Democratic Governor," *Daily Capitol Journal*, July 22, 1910, 1, 8.

18. Graves, *American State Government*, 322, quoting West in "It Costs Too Much to Run for Office," *New York Times Magazine*, April 11, 1948, 20, 58ff.

19. "Oregon History: The Oregon System."

20. Ibid.

21. Ibid.; Johansen and Gates, *Empire of the Columbia*, 462.

22. *Proceedings of the Conference of Western Governors, Held at Denver*, 93.

23. Ibid., 94–95.

24. Jensen, *Pardoning Power*, 61.

25. Oswald West, "Four Die by Popular Vote," *New York Times*, December 14, 1912, 6.

26. "Oswald West (1873–1960)."

27. "The Copperfield Raid," *Literary Digest* January 17, 1914, 93.

28. George Palmer Putnam, mayor of Bend, Oregon, quoted in "Oregon Mayor Here Attacks Gov. West," *New York Times*, January 6, 1914, 10.
29. "Governor Heads a Posse," *Washington Post*, June 24, 1911, 5.
30. "The Democratic Nominee," *Medford Mail Tribune*, October 3, 1910, 4; "West Tells East of Oregon Laws," *Medford Mail Tribune*, December 16, 1911, 12.
31. "Governor Engages in a Fistic Bout with Newspaperman," *East Oregonian*, February 15, 1913, 1.
32. Griffiths, *Populism in the Western United States*, 209.
33. Meany, *Governors of Washington*.
34. "The New Governors," 37–38; Riddle, *Old Radicalism*, 236; Griffiths, *Populism in the Western United States*, 244.
35. Riddle, *Old Radicalism*, 232–35.
36. Griffiths, *Populism in the Western United States*, 245.
37. Riddle, *Old Radicalism*, 237–39.
38. Ibid., 245–51.
39. Ibid., 45.
40. Griffiths, "Populism in the Far West," 236.
41. "Hay Plans Reforms," *East Oregonian*, June 11, 1910, 2.
42. "Progressive (?) Record of Governor Hay," *Labor Journal*, October 25, 1912, 1; Meany, *Governors of Washington*.
43. Ibid.
44. "Tacoma's Son Is Governor Today," *Tacoma Times*, January 15, 1913, 1.
45. "Nobody's Afraid of Lister," *Washington Standard*, January 3, 1913, 4
46. "Governor Ernest Lister," *Nonpartisan Leader*, July 7, 1919, 6.
47. "Review of Work of State Legislature," *Lynden Tribune*, March 18, 1915, 1.
48. W. A. Robinson, "The Governors in 1917," *New Republic*, March 3, 1917, 127–29.
49. Item, *Great Falls News*, November 14, 1896, 1.
50. Griffiths, *Populism in the Western United States*, 300.
51. Toole, *Twentieth-Century Montana*, 206–7.
52. Griffiths, *Populism in the Western United States*, 30.
53. "Gov. Toole, The Trusts, and Direct Legislation," *Rosebud County News*, May 28, 1903, 4; A. H. Barret, "Toole and Victory," *Rosebud County News*, May 12, 1904, 9.
54. Toole, *Twentieth-Century Montana*, 207.
55. Roeder, "Montana Progressivism," 396. See also Piott, *Giving Voters a Voice*, 59.
56. Piott, *Giving Voters a Voice*, 59.
57. See generally Gable, *Bull Moose Years*.
58. "United Republican Party Declares War on League," *Montana Record-Herald*, September 11, 1920, 1.
59. "In Forceful Language Republican Candidate Sounds Campaign Keynote," *Montana Record-Herald*, September 11, 1920, 1, 2.
60. See Roeder, "Montana Progressivism"; and Wheeler and Healy, *Yankee from the West*.
61. "The New Governors," 39.
62. Peterson, *Idaho*, 163; Arrington, *History of Idaho*, 459.
63. Lewis, *Big Trouble*, 289.
64. Martin, "Idaho," 193.
65. "Some New Laws," *Idaho County Free Press*, March 16, 1911, 1; "Is a Great Reform," *Idaho County Free Press*, September 7, 1911, 1; "Idaho Governor Suggests Laws," *Salt Lake Tribune*, January 5, 1911, 9.
66. "Appointment of Senator Will Be Made This Week," *Evening Capital News*, November 7, 1912, 10; "Mormon Fight Again On in Earnest," *Evening Capital News*, November 8, 1912, 1.

67. Arrington, *History of Idaho*, 437; "Idaho's Most Popular Democrat for U.S. Senator," *Evening Capital News*, August 23, 1914, 8.

68. Negative comment on Alexander because of his religion is found in "Alexander an Orthodox Jew," *Clearwater Republican*, October 27, 1916, 1.

69. Lovin, "The Farmer Revolt in Idaho."

70. Joseph M. Carey, "What's the Matter with Wyoming?" Supplement to *Grand Encampment Herald*, October 14, 1910, 1. On the campaign see also "Longs to Be Governor," *Salt Lake Herald-Republican*, September 11, 1910, 1; and "Wyoming Democrats Name Carey," *Norfolk Weekly News-Journal*, September 23, 1901, 5.

71. Peters, "Joseph M. Carey," 260.

72. Ibid., 29–30.

73. Larson, *History of Wyoming*, 334.

74. Remarks of Governor Carey, October 15, 1914, found in *The Progressive Party: Its Triumph Assured and Deserved Its Position in Wyoming* (N.p., n.d.), Joseph M. Carey Papers, Wyoming State Archives.

75. Larson, *History of Wyoming*, 334.

76. Accounts of the involvement of Carey and his wife are found in Anthony and Harper, *History of Woman Suffrage*, 117, 180–81, 184, 207, 224, 318, 449, 851, 998, 1005 (the story of the dinner for Anthony), 1006, and 1007. This unabridged reprint of the 1902 Rochester edition covers various meetings and reports of the National American Woman Suffrage Association over several years. See also Harper, *History of Woman Suffrage*, 5:11, 118 ("staunch suffragists" quote).

77. Carey to Edmund Perkins, December 26, 1913, quoted by Peters, "Joseph M. Carey," 261.

78. Peters, "Joseph M. Carey," 263.

79. Larson *History of Wyoming*, 388; "Progressive Democratic Senatorial Candidates: Kendrick of Wyoming," *The Commoner*, October 1, 1916: 8.

14

THE SOUTHWEST

Shafroth, Bamberger, and Hunt

In the Southwest, our last group of states, we find governors of varying temperaments and talents caught up in issues involving railroads and the mining industry, labor unrest, political reform, woman suffrage, prizefighting, and liquor and gambling control.

In the Colorado discussion we see controversial Populist crusader governor Davis Waite and a line of more moderate Progressive reformers from both major parties culminating in the highly productive administration of Democrat John Shafroth. In Nevada we look at a trio of governors similarly caught up in the Progressive spirit. In Utah Governor William Spry provides an example of a governor close to the dominant political organization who was willing and able to push for various Progressive measures, though he was no friend of labor. Wealthy businessman Simon Bamberger, who represented a departure from Utah politics in terms of religion and party ties, emerges as the state's most outstanding Progressive. In 1911 Progressives came to power in the new states of New Mexico and Arizona. While New Mexico Democrat William C. McDonald served but one largely unproductive term, Arizona Democrat George Hunt was to be elected governor for seven two-year terms and in the earliest of these led in the passage of a considerable amount of Progressive reform.

COLORADO: FROM WAITE TO SHAFROTH

Colorado had the experience, welcomed by some, hated by others, of having Populist Davis Waite as its governor in the 1890s. Wait showed himself a defender of the rights of labor and a foe of drinking and gambling but had great difficulty pushing the Populist agenda through the legislature.

Born in Jamestown, New York, Waite moved around the country practicing law, working for newspapers, and engaging in various business activities. He served in the Wisconsin and Kansas legislatures. In 1878 he came to Colorado; after a two-year stay in Leadville, he moved to Aspen, where he became the owner of a left-wing newspaper devoted to the cause of labor, the *Aspen Union Era*. He developed a reputation as a crusading anticorporate, pro-labor newspaper publisher and editor.[1] He started out as a Democrat before the Civil War, turned Republican after it, and wound up a Populist who helped prepare the Omaha Platform of the national Populist Party. Though the Omaha Platform was of high importance to him, he was not a true believer in one of its most prominent planks, that of free silver. He saw this as of value chiefly in helping Populists win elections.

Waite campaigned for governor in 1892, using as his central themes free silver along with calls for controls on railroads as well as labor reforms such as the eight-hour workday and pledges to eliminate political graft. His election, at age sixty-seven, was a major triumph for the Populist Party. Fusing with the Democrats, the Populists swept the state offices. Waite received 47 percent of the vote in a three-way contest, a strong performance in what had been a reliable Republican state. Two years earlier the Populist candidate for governor had received but 6 percent of the vote.

When it came to legislation, Waite's proposals to the legislature were less revolutionary than might have been expected from his campaign speeches. Even then, he had considerable difficulty in getting anything adopted. Hostile Republicans controlled the house, and there was only a very fragile coalition of Populists and Democrats in the senate. The Populists themselves had rival labor and farming factions. The latter saw little value in the package of labor reforms that Waite was promoting, such as the eight-hour day and employer's liability.

The governor got nowhere with his call for a strong railroad commission (indeed, the legislature even abolished the rather weak one already in existence) and with a somewhat bizarre "Fandango Dollar" scheme that would have made silver dollars coined in Mexico legal tender in the state. Waite successfully pushed for woman suffrage but later regretted it in the belief that women had voted against him in 1894, contributing to his failure to secure reelection. Suffrage leaders acknowledged that there was some truth to this charge.[2] Waite's wife Celia had been an active Populist working to bring women to the party and a leader in the suffrage cause. After the 1894 election she joined her husband in having second thoughts about the value of woman suffrage.[3]

Waite was a religious man, deeply opposed to drinking and gambling. In what is known as the "City Hall War," he attempted to remove two members of the Denver Police and Fire Board that he suspected of taking money to protect illegal gambling operations in the city. He had the authority to hire and fire board members and attempted to remove the two for neglect of duty. They, however, refused to leave. They barricaded themselves in their offices and brought in 300 armed men into the City Hall building to prevent being ousted. Waite responded by ordering National Guardsmen to surround the building. Violence almost erupted but was avoided when Waite agreed to call in federal troops to maintain order until the matter was settled in court.[4] Waite eventually won out in court and appointed new board members who were more effective in driving the gamblers from the city and, in addition, confining prostitution to a segregated district.[5]

Governor Waite established his credentials as a strong supporter of labor by coming to the defense of miners belonging to the Western Federation of Miners during the Cripple Creek Strike of 1894. Unlike Colorado governors before and after him, he refused to intervene on the side of the mine owners and used the National Guard in a neutral fashion to maintain order while he represented the striking miners and negotiated a settlement acceptable to them. His pro-labor position made him a hero to workers and drew praise around the nation from those on the left side of political spectrum. In 1894 Waite also backed workers engaged in a strike against Colorado railroads, called in sympathy with the Pullman strikers.

Like many of the more fully committed Populists and Progressives, Waite felt that capital punishment was not a deterrent to crime and intrinsically wrong. Working with his attorney general, Waite challenged the validity of the penalty. He also used his clemency powers to pardon and alter sentences to avoid putting prisoners to death.[6] He was able to secure renomination from the Populist Party in 1894 but was solidly defeated in the general election.

Waite was a national figure well connected with other reformers of the time. He communicated frequently with other left-leaning governors, including John Altgeld of Illinois, Lorenzo Lewelling of Kansas, and Ben Tillman of South Carolina. Waite and Altgeld were political friends, and Waite backed Altgeld in his stand against Cleveland's actions in the Pullman Strike. He agreed with Lewelling in opposing those Populists who would narrow Populism to the silver issue. Waite, believing in the need for a southerner to head the Populist ticket, proposed giving the People's Party nomination in 1896 to Tillman.[7]

Though he had aroused strong opposition from the conservative faction within the Colorado Populist Party, Waite was able to secure renomination in 1894 without making any concessions to the right. During the general election he continued to have strong support among workers and in mining areas but went down to defeat under a Republican attack that branded him a dangerous radical. One opposing newspaper editor put it bluntly in November 1894: "Waite is a blot upon Colorado's fame and a cancer eating out its vitality."[8] Historian James Wright summed up the election as follows: "There seems little reason to dispute the judgment that the issue in 1894 was clear. Waite challenged the political and economic norms with his unabashed class appeal and with his concept of an active state aiding the oppressed and deprived. He lost."[9]

People in his state saw Waite differently—on one hand, as a demagogue and an anarchist and, on the other, as a new Jefferson or Lincoln.[10] Historians also have had varying thoughts about him. John D. Hicks dismissed Waite as "a man rather advanced in years, headstrong and obstinate. His whole personal appearance as well as the occasional frenzy of his rhetoric suggested the narrow-mined fanatic."[11] Historian David Griffiths was a bit more positive, applauding Waite for his "authentic empathy for workers and the underprivileged" and his "political courage and integrity." Still, he noted, Waite "was short on common sense (perhaps this related to his Biblical absolutism) and lacked the capacity or inclination to think critically about his own premises and actions."[12]

To some extent his speech-making style worked against him. As historian Karel Bicha wrote: "On a podium he thrived on the response of audiences and his utterances were more extreme than his intentions. Enemies regarded him as a madman, and he often played into their hands"[13] A notable example came in an address to a gathering of the Silver League in Denver in 1893 in which Waite declared: "Our weapons are argument and the ballot—'a free ballot and a fair count.' And if the money power shall attempt to sustain its usurpation by 'the strong hand,' we will meet that issue when it is forced upon us, for it is better, infinitely better, that blood should flow to the horses' bridles, rather than our national liberties be destroyed."[14] From this he picked up the nickname of "Bloody Bridles Waite," which was used by his enemies to depict him as a bloodthirsty radical about to stage a violent revolution in Colorado.

Often missing in the evaluations of Waite was his use of humor (though, no doubt, his attempt at humor was not always appreciated). Some of this comes through in a speech he began by complaining about how the press had abused him: "Why it has been published all over the United States and the Dominion of Canada that my wife is Boss. How infernal mean that is, when for the last ten years I have taken every possible means to conceal that fact. But there is one palatable drop in this bitter cup. I know that I have the profound sympathy of nine-tenths of the married men in this vast audience."[15]

Following Waite some reform came under a succession of Democratic governors in the late 1890s and early 1900s, including Alva Adams and Charles S. Thomas, and under Republican Henry Buchtel, who served from 1907 to 1909. Much to the distress of Colorado's insurgent Republicans, a much more active role as innovator fell to the Democrats under John Shafroth, whom Colorado voters chose as their governor in 1908 and again in 1910. Born in Missouri and educated at the University of Michigan, Shafroth came to Denver in 1879, where he set up a law practice and became city attorney. During this period he became familiar with the evils of the political machine in the city.[16] In 1884 he went on to Congress as a Republican. At that time he was no fan of Davis Waite. While running for office, he condemned Waite for waging "a war of extermination against capital" and declared that the governor was "a disgrace to the state."[17]

Shafroth, though, even then was something of a reformer himself. A strong proponent of free silver, he joined several others from Colorado, including US senator Henry M. Teller, in splitting from the regular Republican Party and joining the Silver Republican Party. He was elected to two more terms in the House on the Silver Party ticket. Influenced by William Jennings Bryan, he became a Democrat and returned to Congress for another term on that ticket. This term, however, ended on February 15, 1904, when he resigned on the grounds that, because of voter fraud in his election, he could not honestly claim to have won the contest and asked that the person he defeated be given the office. This action brought him the nickname "Honest John" Shafroth. He came back into the public spotlight in 1907 when he stood out among the attendees to the Denver Public Lands Convention, who repudiated Theodore Roosevelt's conservation policies and condemned federal control of public lands as a violation of states' rights. The 1907 conference gave him a huge boost in seeking the governorship in 1908.[18]

In 1908 he led the "platform Democrats," who firmly stood behind the promised reforms contained in the party platform adopted that year, including the initiative and referendum and the direct primary, and demanded that they be implemented should the party come to power. During his run for governor that year Shafroth picked up the support of a broad coalition of Protestant religious organizations, labor unions, and women's clubs. Shafroth won the governorship in 1908 by four percentage points over his Republican opponent.

During the campaign he maintained a delicate relationship with his sometimes enemy and sometimes friend, Robert W. Speer, mayor of Denver and boss of the Democratic Party machine in that city. Speer was close to the corporations and saw little of value in many of the reforms being pushed by the platform Democrats. Nevertheless, he was pragmatic enough to see the value of getting along with a winning candidate such as Shafroth.[19] During the campaign Shafroth rejected railroad pass offers, noting that the party platform and he personally had pledged to abolish this practice. Despite this, the railroads offered him a free pass following his election. He once again declined.[20]

In his inaugural address Shafroth reminded lawmakers that "while we were in the campaign we represented the party, now we represent the people" and now had a responsibility to implement the policy choices the people had approved, specifically those in the Democratic Party platform.[21] However, he had little success with the legislature in 1909 in regard to the passage of reforms in the party platform. Even William Jennings Bryan, who appeared before the legislature urging reform, could not move the legislators, some of whom saw the proposals, especially the initiative and referendum, as threats to the power of the legislature.[22]

Recounting later events in a letter to Bryan, Shafroth wrote that he had waited "until two weeks before the adjournment of the legislature and then sent a message to them, urging the passage of these measures, and stating to them that if they had honestly changed their minds about the measures that they should resign immediately. They spent the balance of the session abusing me. I had a conference with the recalcitrant members soon after the adjournment of the legislature and found it was impossible to get any votes for the enactment of the laws which we had pledged." In spite of all the opposition, he told Bryan he was going to call a special session prior to the meeting of the state party convention in 1910 and had "great hopes that we will get something real good out of the extra session."[23]

He did indeed have considerable success by calling for a special legislative session in August 1910, which was restricted to focusing on a set of reforms he proposed to the legislature. By calling a special session, Shafroth put the legislators under greater public scrutiny, and this paid off with the passage of several reforms, including the adoption of the initiative and referendum as a constitutional amendment that was later adopted by the vote of the people.[24] In November 1910 Shafroth won reelection with 54 percent of the vote, an eight point lead over his Republican opponent.

Over two terms, Shafroth produce a long, unprecedented list of social, economic, and political reforms, including railroad and utility regulations, direct democracy, the direct primary, direct election of US senators, home rule for municipalities, labor protections for women and children, an eight-hour day for workers in dangerous occupations, factory and coal mine inspections, campaign expenditure disclosure, guarantees of bank deposits, a tax commission, a state conservation commission, and civil service reforms. He also vetoed a bill allowing racetrack betting, opposing it on constitutional and moral grounds. He had made a one-two punch, not uncommon in the period: the first round of reforms focused largely on changes in the political structure, enabling greater citizen input and control, while the second round turned to socioeconomic reforms.[25]

Shafroth, like several governors during this period, was not overly happy with the powers of his office, or lack thereof, and with the legislative policymaking process. Like several other governors, he complained about his inability to enforce the laws—for example, to remove sheriffs and other country officials who were not doing their job enforcing the laws against drinking and gambling or, worse, were running such illegal operations themselves.[26] Though he did not mention the Colorado legislature by name, in 1912 he advanced this thought in a national publication: "There can be no doubt that at the present time there is something seriously wrong as to the manner in which our legislative bodies are constituted." He felt they were dominated by corporate interests and offered direct legislation as a remedy.[27]

Leaders of the National American Woman Suffrage Association praised Shafroth as a "consistent supporter of woman suffrage from the very beginning of the movement" in Colorado.[28] His wife Virginia was also active in the cause. Many women may well have reciprocated by supporting Progressive measures that he and others had proposed. In a report made by Governor Shafroth at the association's convention in 1910, he gave a long list of Progressive laws in Colorado that he said had been adopted through the support of women.[29]

Shafroth is described by his biographers as a chess player, looking ahead to the next move, being especially conscious of how what he might do would affect his or his party's chances in the next election. He also knew how to get along with people with whom he disagreed: "He did not roast opponents; he outthought, outmaneuvered, and outlasted them."[30]

NEVADA: DICKERSON, ODDIE, AND BOYLE

In Nevada Progressivism received a bit of a boost under Governor Denver S. Dickerson. Born in California, the son of a mining engineer, he pursued mining in several states but, upon settling in Nevada, also became engaged in newspaper publishing and using his papers to promote the interests of the Silver Democrats. Dickerson got elected in 1908 on the Silver Democrat ticket as lieutenant governor and became acting governor of Nevada following the death of Governor John Sparks. He accomplished much in a short period, including a raise in the rate of assessment of the property of the Central Pacific Railroad. Also on his agenda was improvement in railroad rate regulation, banking laws, mine inspection, hospital facilities for the mentally ill, and prison reform.

Under Dickerson came a ban on nearly all games of chance in Nevada. Yet Dickerson did not oppose boxing matches in the state, even though many Progressives felt they were immoral. In June 1910 he refused to interfere with a controversial fight in Reno between heavyweight champion Jack Johnson, a black, and former champion James Jeffries, the "Great White Hope," in which Johnson defeated Jeffries. Commenting on the governor's refusal to interfere with the fight, a South Carolina paper passed along the thought that Nevada would allow anything if it would get "a lot of people to stay overnight."[31]

Brooklyn-born Tasker Oddie headed west to seek his fortune in the silver boom in Tonopah, Nevada. In a letter to his mother in 1900 Oddie identified himself as a Bryan man who had moved away from the Republicans nationally on the silver issue: "I always was led to look at a silver man as a fanatic, but, since I have been among them for so long, I have learned to respect their arguments.... Besides, my own interests would be greatly benefitted by free coinage, as I own silver mines, also a quicksilver one, and quicksilver would advance in value with silver."[32] In another letter he added: "I'm not opposed to millionaires, and would like to be one myself, but I am opposed to them using their wealth in crowding corrupt legislation through Congress that will oppress the poorer classes and make them, the millionaires, richer through dishonest means, as is done today. McKinley is a tool in the hands of such men."[33]

Oddie made a fortune as a director of the Tonopah Midway Mining Company and got himself elected to the state senate. In spite of whatever Progressive tendencies he had shown in his correspondence to his mother, during his single term in the state legislature from 1905 to1910 he spent much of his time defending the interests of mine owners.[34] He changed his tune in 1910 when he decided to run for governor and take on Governor Dickerson. He now said he was an insurgent Republican who, in the footsteps of Teddy Roosevelt and Hiram Johnson, stood in opposition to the local "malefactors" of great wealth. He took particular aim at the Central Pacific Railroad. Yet somewhere along the campaign trail he apparently became afraid of appearing too radical and underwent a considerable metamorphosis: "His political colors changed like a chameleon: he stopped being Mr. Nevada Progressive and became Mr. Nevada Chamber of Commerce," eager to boast that he had the confidence of out-of-state investors who could help Nevada's mining industry.[35]

Oddie, in the eyes of his biographer, was a master practitioner "of the rather dubious political art of rhetorical progressivism."[36] Yet after his victory in 1910 he worked with Democrats who controlled the legislature and made some actual if moderate gains in legislation in such areas as worker safety and property reassessment.[37] In 1911 he supported La Follette's National Progressive Republican League and the general Progressive effort to take over the GOP.[38]

Though he considered himself a supporter of Theodore Roosevelt in 1912, he did not endorse the Bull Moose effort in his state, being fearful of its effects on the Republican ticket in Nevada.[39] Oddie lost his bid for reelection in 1914, but did go on to become a US senator from Nevada.

Democrat Emmet Boyle had built a successful career as a mining engineer prior to defeating Oddie in the 1914 gubernatorial contest. He was reelected to another four-year term in 1918. He declined to run for a third term and retired from political life. As governor he continued the moderate reform drive. He helped bring about prohibition, a restructured tax system, and an improvement in the state's worker's compensation law. He worked with trade unionists to create the Office of Labor Commissioners. His term in office also brought improved teacher benefits and a highway department. He used his office to call attention to the problem of lynching and urged national action on the problem.[40]

Boyle, unlike Dickerson, opposed prizefighting and in 1918 would not allow a match between heavyweights Jess Willard and Fred Fulton in his state. Also unlike

Dickerson, he did not object to gambling. In 1915 he signed two bills legalizing racing in the state.[41] Boyle acquired a reputation for being lenient for humanitarian reasons when it came to pardons. He saw long terms of imprisonment likely to cause prisoners to lose self-respect, creating more dangerous criminals on the streets after they were released.[42]

Boyle was especially active in supporting various ideas being floated around the country to improve the performance of state government. For example, he supported the adoption of a legislative council system, as in Wisconsin, to produce better laws and a one-house legislature of relatively few members to improve legislative efficiency.[43] He was a strong advocate of the short-ballot idea. In 1915 he called for making several Nevada offices appointive rather than elective. Boyle argued that the structure needed repair because it fragmented executive authority, with each elected official going his or her own way, and because the people who held these positions were rarely "well fitted for the duties that they have to perform." As a consequence of their lack of qualifications, the governor noted, the state had to hire expensive secretaries to do the actual work. Boyle concluded that no private business would operate this way.[44]

UTAH: MORMONS, LIQUOR, AND BAMBERGER

From the beginning of statehood in 1896 until to 1916, the Republican Party dominated Utah state politics.[45] Up to 1916 all the governors were Mormons as well as Republicans. The leading political figure was Senator Reed Smoot, who held a high position in the Mormon Church and led a machine-like group of current and former federal officeholders he had appointed who were known as the "Federal Bunch."

William Spry won the gubernatorial office in 1908 and again in 1912. He had served in the state senate and, while there, in 1903 helped get Smoot chosen to the US Senate. Though close to Smoot, Governor Spry backed Progressive measures in regard to education, road building, conservation, rail regulation, tax reform, and other matters. He made it clear early on, though, that he favored dealing firmly with labor agitators.[46] He gained national attention, both good and bad, for his refusal to commute the death sentence handed out to Joe Hill (Hillstrom), a labor activist associated with the Industrial Workers of the World who was convicted of murdering a grocer and his son in January 1914. Many contended that Hill did not have a fair trial; Spry disagreed. In 1915 he issued a short reprieve at President Wilson's request on behalf of the Swedish minister, but he refused to commute the sentence to life imprisonment and Hill was executed.[47]

Spry got into trouble in Utah, not for his stand on Joe Hill, but for favoring the local option on prohibition as opposed to a statewide ban. His veto of a prohibition bill did little for him other than receiving a "rousing hurrah for Governor Spry" telegram from Adolphus Busch of the Anheuser-Busch Brewing Company of St. Louis.[48] His stand on prohibition had a great deal to do with his inability to secure his party's nomination for another term. He lost the nomination in a struggle inside the Republican organization to prohibitionist Nephi Morris, a former Teddy Roosevelt Progressive. Spry felt Smoot and other old allies had deserted him.[49] Morris, however, went down to defeat in 1916 to Simon Bamberger, Utah's most prominent Progressive governor, who served from 1917 to 1921. Up to that time he was also the oldest incoming governor in Utah, being seventy-one when he took office as chief executive. He was also the first Democrat, non-Mormon, and person of Jewish heritage to hold the office.[50]

Born in Germany, Simon Bamberger became a wealthy businessman who made his money in railroading, silver mining, the hotel business, and various other enterprises. He served several years on Salt Lake City's board of education. As a member of the state senate he demonstrated Progressive tendencies. Contending that drunkenness was a "social disease and therefore a social responsibility," he proposed a measure requiring county governments to pick up the cost of treatment programs for alcoholics. This one went nowhere and branded him among some people as a radical. Still, he took defeat well, and his sponsorship of the "Drunk Bill" did him no lasting damage.[51]

In 1916 Democratic Party leaders viewed Bamberger as someone who would appeal to Republicans and independent voters as well as Democrats. In nominating Bamberger for governor, Brigham H. Roberts, a prominent member of the Mormon Church hierarchy and a noted orator, made much of his business standing, noting that he had long been one of the "largest paymasters of the state" with excellent relations with those who were in his employ and who now had the support of prominent labor organizations. Continuing on, he said he saw Bamberger bringing proven management skills vital to the office and further praised him for his stand on prohibition as well as his personality and private life, which "will appeal strongly to the home-loving people of Utah."[52]

As for objections that Bamberger was a Jew and German, Roberts dismissed these as ridiculous—he praised the Jews and noted that Bamberger had lived in the United States for fifty years, a nation he had take an oath to defend, and that everything he had was here—his businesses, his family, his home, and his future hopes; it was silly to think of him siding with Germany in case of war. In supporting a Jew, Roberts called up the party members to abandon an unwritten law that the candidate for governor be a Mormon and that other offices be divided between Mormons and non-Mormons.[53]

Bamberger won election in 1916 as part of a Democratic sweep of the state. Wilson carried Utah, and Democrats won all the congressional races, all five state elective offices, and an overwhelming majority in the state legislature.[54] Bamberger appears to have also benefited not only from his position favoring statewide prohibition, an issue that the Republicans had failed to deliver on for several years, but from his appeal to workers, including those in railroad brotherhoods, and the support of some of those who had backed the Progressive Party.[55] To Bamberger the most important fact was that Mormon Church leaders had decided not to get involved in the gubernatorial campaign that year.[56] Following his election he paid a tribute to the Mormon people and pledged he would do everything possible to defend their rights.[57]

During his campaign Bamberger said he was going to push for stronger public utility regulation, improved worker's compensation laws, and prohibition.[58] Aided by a Democratic majority in the legislature, he got all of these plus a flood of other reforms, including a law recognizing the right of workers to join unions, an improved law dealing with child labor, a pioneering securities regulation law (which served as a model for congressional action in the 1930s), increased mine taxation, a corrupt-practices act, and a public health department.

NEW MEXICO: A PROTEST AGAINST MEN AND METHODS

In 1911 forces were at work in the new states of New Mexico and Arizona to bring Progressive administrations into power. In New Mexico Progressive Republicans joined Democrats in electing a successful businessman, William C. McDonald, as the state's first governor.

McDonald was born in New York and spent some time practicing law in Kansas before coming to New Mexico in the late 1880s. He settled in Lincoln County, where he worked as a miner and became a cattle rancher. An active Democrat, he ran for and was elected Lincoln County assessor. He lasted one term, from 1885 to 1887. In his autobiography George Curry, a Republican who had served as territorial governor, described McDonald as "both capable and conscientious" and noted that when McDonald was county assessor, he "made an effective campaign against tax dodgers of whom there were many. Influential cattle men whose assessments McDonald had raised, led a movement to defeat him for re-election, and succeeded."[59]

In 1910 McDonald chaired the Democratic Territorial Central Committee and the following year decided to make the run for governor. It was a rare thing for Democrats to win elections. A conservative political group known as the "Santa Fe Ring" had controlled the Republican Party and territorial politics throughout the territorial period. In 1911, however, conditions were favorable for change. Progressive Republicans did not put a ticket in the field, and several former Republican leaders who had turned Progressive lent their support to McDonald, who ran as a "clean government" candidate opposed to "the rule of graft and greed."[60] During the campaign McDonald also had the support of the state's largest newspaper, the *Albuquerque Morning Journal*. Following the election, the editor of this Progressive Republican paper rejoiced that, with the McDonald victory,

New Mexico is taken bodily from the ranks of the ultra conservative, reactionary states and placed in the van of the progressive commonwealths. We believe there has never been in any state a more striking demonstration of the fact that government is moving back to the people ... that the people of New Mexico have been emancipated from slavery to "party regularity" and are thinking and voting for themselves ... The election was purely a victory for the people. It was a protest, not against party policies or principles broadly speaking, but a protest against men and against methods ... They elected McDonald as the candidate of the people against the bosses.... In the county, as in the state, it was a protest against boss rule, against un-representative political organization, against the irregular and untenable political methods, against czarism and one-man rule.[61]

McDonald won the office with a plurality of 3,000 votes, 51 percent of the total cast. In his first message to the legislature he asked the lawmakers to consider a variety of reforms, including the adoption of a new system of taxation that would value all property in the state, including that of the largest corporations, at its full cash value. He told them: "This is a progressive age. He who lags may be lost."[62] As governor, however, McDonald was not able to accomplish much of anything, other than providing a sound business administration, because of a hostile legislature controlled by Republicans.

Acting on his own, McDonald sprang into action when he learned that boxing promoters were planning to hold a fight in Las Vegas, New Mexico, between heavyweight champion Jack Johnson, a black man, and "Fireman" Jim Flynn, another in the string of "great white hopes" to challenge him. McDonald was quoted as saying: "I have no objection to properly conducted bouts, but if I can stop it I will not permit a contest in New Mexico between a white man and a negro."[63] McDonald, at odds with local officials who wanted the event, attempted to avoid the match by getting the legislature to place a ban on boxing. He failed, but the fight was stopped in round nine in favor of Johnson when the state police captain entered the ring on behalf of McDonald and called it off, declaring it had become a brutal exhibition because Flynn had lost the ability to defend himself.[64]

Whatever his views on race, McDonald stood for law and order when it came to white violence directed at blacks. In June 1912 he held off an attempt of a mob of armed white men to evict blacks from the city of Clovis by sending in mounted police to back up the sheriff. He said he was willing to use all the force necessary to restore order and prevent the recurrence of similar disturbances.[65]

GEORGE HUNT OF ARIZONA

In 1911 Arizona voters elected Democrat George W. P. Hunt to the office of governor. He went on to have a far more successful gubernatorial career than McDonald of New Mexico. After 1911 he won the office six more times, including the elections of 1914 and 1916. In many respects Hunt personified Progressive governors around the country in seeking to democratize the political system and curb the power of large corporations, subjecting them to more public controls. Along with this, and of equal if not greater importance to him, he sought to make the prison system more humanitarian and to abolish the death penalty. More than many other governors he sought to defend the rights of working people.

Hunt had much in common in terms of background and political philosophy with Folk of Missouri, who campaigned for Hunt in 1911, and with Oswald West of Oregon in terms of his views and actions, though he was far less committed than West to prohibition. He served during most of the years when Hiram Johnson was governor of California and expressed his admiration for Johnson's Progressive accomplishments in his state. Arizona, a pioneer state and less bound by tradition than many others, was an ideal place to experiment with the latest ideas in government, and in the period 1910–16 it did a considerable amount of experimentation under Hunt.[66]

Hunt was born in Huntsville, Missouri, a rural settlement named after his grandfather. Raised in virtual poverty, he had very little formal education. He knew what it was to be poor and he never forgot his humble origins. He knew what it was like to be the only child in a classroom not to have a textbook. When he became governor, he made the provision of free textbooks one of his priorities. He settled in Globe, Arizona, in 1881 where he undertook a variety of menial jobs and eventually worked his way up to become a relatively wealthy man as the head of a mercantile and banking firm. Turning to political office in the 1890s, Hunt, like the Populists around him, first focused on curbing the power of the giant railroads, the Santa Fe and the Southern Pacific. Later his attention turned to the large mining corporations, especially Phelps Dodge.

Hunt served as a territorial legislator and, in 1910, president of the convention that shaped the state's first and only constitution, considered by many at the time as a highly Progressive document, with its inclusion of the initiative, referendum, and recall, several labor protections, and a powerful commission to regulate railroads and other public utilities. At the convention he was deeply engaged in state building, putting together what he saw as model state government based on Progressive principles. He wanted Progressivism, in the sense of "modern" or "enlightened" ideas, to undergird every state process and institution.

Coming to the governor's office with the backing of a coalition of workers, farmers, and small businesspeople, Hunt ushered through a host of reforms, many of which the corporate elite opposed. He had campaigned for measures to make corporations pay a greater share of the tax load, thus relieving the burden on small businesspersons, farmers and ranchers, and middle- and lower-income citizens, and to treat their workers more fairly. As governor, Hunt raised the taxes on the mines and railroads, secured the adoption of labor legislation, and came to the defense of striking workers, including, in 1915, thousands of Hispanic mine workers who went on strike in the Clifton-Morenci area along the New Mexico border.

In his inaugural address in 1912 Hunt said he was going to be businesslike and efficiency-minded, but quickly added that he was not going to have a "dollar administration" that neglected the needs and demands of the common people. In his view "government is the people's business" and was to be "administered in the interest of all the people, not only for their material and financial benefit, betterment, and protection, but for their increased pleasure and happiness."[67]

The clergyman who spoke at his inauguration in 1912 called upon the Deity to spare Hunt "the unjust, unreasonable criticism of disgruntled, mugwump Democrats, shrewd and designing Republican politicians and sensational headlines of newspapers."[68] Hunt was not spared. He picked up more than his share of political enemies. He was more than willing to go to war with them and was a sore loser when he lost. Declared the loser in his bid for reelection as governor in 1916, he barricaded himself in the governor's suite and refused to vacate the premises until forced out by a court order. He finally won out in the state supreme court, which declared him the winner after a recount.

Like many Progressives of the period, Hunt had a deep distrust of if not contempt for state legislatures. He feared that they were bound to fall under the influence of special interests without the checks imposed by the initiative, referendum, and recall, campaign finance regulations limiting the size of contributions and requiring disclosure of donors, and strong regulations on lobbying. Hoping to improve the legislative process and bring it more out into the open, he also called for a reduction in the number of legislative seats and the establishment of a one-house legislature. In making the case for the unicameral system he argued in part: "The double legislative branch, with its large membership and many conflicting personal interests, its party prejudices, the low average intelligence in many members, is the most extravagant arrangement possible."[69] The Arizona senate did at one point actually vote to abolish itself, but this suicide measure was shot down in the house, partially out of fear that the senators who would lose their jobs would compete for house seats.[70] After the legislature failed to go along, Hunt took his case to the people via the initiative process, but the voters also rejected the idea.

Unlike many in the West, Hunt had no problem with federal conservation policies protecting the state's natural resources. Hunt declared in a paper written in 1913 for a governors' conference that some time ago state governments in the East "had handed their riches over to a handful of capitalists, while ignoring wage slavery upon a small army of workmen during the process, and at the same time robbing the millions of their rightful heritage. Unpleasant as it may be to admit the truth, the West was for many years going through exactly the same process with reference to its own mineral resources, under the operation of what is called state rights."[71] To Hunt, federal controls had been justified. As governor he went out of his way to protect the public lands given Arizona at statehood.

Penal reform and the abolition of the death penalty engaged much of Hunt's attention. Early in his administration he followed the lead of Tennessee governor Hopper and stayed overnight in prison, locked in a cell with a prisoner. He spent the next day talking to prisoners (though he was sanctioned for doing this at breakfast because no talking was allowed) and prison officials on the need for reforms.[72] Not long after his visit, he closed down underground torture cells used for solitary confinement and eliminated the use of the ball and chain and the silence system. Hunt also liberalized restrictions on mail and the choice of clothing that prisoners could wear, increased food allowances, and gave prisoners the opportunity to reduce the length of their sentences by doing assigned work. His policies on prisoners, however, cost him politically. Some objected that the new policies had made the prison a pleasure resort.

Hunt also took a controversial stand in advocating the elimination of the death penalty. He saw this as "a relic of barbarism," a brutal failure as a deterrent to crime and a practice that smacked of class discrimination: "The more I took into it, the more I am convinced that hanging is the penalty of the poor . . . no man can be hung in Arizona who has plenty of money."[73] In 1916 voters narrowly went along with a proposition to abolish capital punishment but, changing course again, voted to restore it two years later. Hunt used his clemency powers to avoid the application of the death penalty, to undo what he thought was excessive punishment, or simply to reduce the amount of time convicts served on the assumption that long sentences contributed to the bad behavior of those ultimately released. The legislature, however, did not share these sentiments and in 1913 passed a penal code shifting the governor's power in regard to paroles, pardons, commutations, and reprieves to an independent board of pardons and paroles.

Much of what Hunt did or tried to do on prison reform, pardons, and paroles as well as the death penalty was motivated by his quest to come to the aid of the poor, as most of the people caught up in the criminal justice system came from this part of the population. When it came to pardons and paroles, Hunt was fully aware that the lengthy incarceration of the male breadwinners from already struggling families only contributed to the impoverishment of the wives and children left on their own.

On other issues he opposed prizefighting as barbaric but waffled a bit on both woman suffrage and prohibition. He began his career as an advocate of woman suffrage but backed away a bit out of concern for what this might mean at election time. Having a solid base of support among white males, he had little to gain and much to lose by women becoming part of the general electorate. He was not opposed to prohibition—he had suffered at the hands of a father who drank too much—but the cause was not popular with his working-class supporters whose votes he depended upon. When it came to prohibition, where he stood literally depended on where he stood (his position changed from one location to another).

Like the Populists and Socialists with whom he was often in competition for the working-class vote, Hunt used the language of class politics and expressed his concern about the plight of working people and the distribution of wealth. A prime example is a speech he delivered before a highly enthusiastic crowd composed mostly of miners in Bisbee, Arizona, on July 4, 1913, in which he spoke out against the privileged classes' attempts to rule and exploit the masses and against the evils of an economic and political system of "greed backed by power." He condemned the "grinding oppression of the masses" in the modern industrial system and demanded that "labor, which possesses all wealth and makes possible every comfort of life . . . have a greater share of what it creates, and that privilege shall no longer be permitted to seize as much of the profits as its greed dictates." He said he wanted to even things up, "to bring comforts for the homes of the working multitude as it does now in an unequal degree for the homes of the privileged." He called for the triumph of "militant Progressive Democracy," which to him meant, in part, that "this country, its institutions, its resources and its rewards for industry belong to the people whose labor makes them possible." It also involved "the faithful application" of the principal of "equal rights to all and special privileges to none."[74] While he did not seek the cooperative commonwealth of the Socialists as the ultimate goal, his basic outlook was anticorporate and, as his words and actions indicated, strongly working-class in orientation.

Hunt was not a gifted speaker but was able to communicate effectively with people on an individual basis. His personal touch went far in the small-town and frontier society of Arizona at the time. He made a political career by developing friendships. While an idealist and a committed Progressive, he was also a practical politician, willing to use patronage to build up a personal following. He had his limitations. He supported segregated schools for blacks, a literacy test for voting aimed at Hispanics, and restrictions on alien workers and landowners. He held racist views typical of this time and of the people who shared a similar background. On the other hand, he suspended whatever biases he had when it came to defending the rights of workers or those accused or convicted of a crime, regardless of their race, color, or nationality. All in all, he was a middle-class Progressive with strong ties to labor, taking on the appearance of a crude western type, occasionally radical-sounding, who scared more than a few corporate heads and alarmed staid onlookers in the East. Some viewed him as an unpolished, rugged individualist commonly found on the frontier, "a man not to be trifled with, making up in common sense and shrewdness what he lacked in schooling and 'book-learning.'"[75]

NOTES

1. Griffiths, *Populism in the Western United States*, 376–77.

2. During the 1894 campaign, Republicans asked women to help redeem the state from Waite. According to a report presented at a suffrage convention in 1902, many women did rally to the Republican Party and against Waite. See Anthony and Harper, *History of Woman Suffrage*, 520.

3. "Naughty Women, Says Mrs. Waite," *New York World*, November 14, 1894, clipping, Davis Waite Collection, Box 27092, Correspondence Incoming: 1893–95, File 16 (on suffrage), Colorado State Archives.

4. Fritz, *Colorado*, 353–54.

5. Griffiths, *Populism in the Western United States*, 390–91.

6. Ibid., 384.

7. See generally letters in Davis Waite Collection, Box 27092, Correspondence Incoming: 1893–95, Colorado State Archives. See also Griffiths, *Populism in the Western United States*, 394, 408, 413.

8. *Evening Journal*, November 5, 1894, 2, reprint of editorial in the *Denver News*.

9. Wright, *Politics of Populism*, 194–95.

10. Griffiths, *Populism in the Western United States*, 387.

11. Hicks, *Populist Revolt*, 291.

12. Griffiths, *Populism in the Western United States*, 379.

13. Karel D. Bicha, *Western Populism*, 71.

14. "Blood to the Bridles" speech given in 1893, Davis Waite Collection, Box 27023, Folder 16, Colorado State Archives. See also "Blood to the Horses' Bridles," *New York Times*, July 12, 1893, 1.

15. Davis Waite Collection, Box 27023, Colorado State Archives.

16. Leonard, Noel, and Walker, *Honest John Shafroth*, 14.

17. Wright, *Politics of Populism*, 188.

18. McCarthy, "Colorado's Populist Party," 65.

19. Laugen, *Gospel of Progressivism*, 49; and Leonard, *Honest John Shafroth*, 42–43.

20. In a bound volume of letters found in the John Franklin Shafroth Papers, Collection Note 564, History of Colorado Archives, remarks on the 1908 victory are found on pages 740, 743; request for jobs on pages 729, 747, 748, 749, 750, 751; and letters from various railroads on pages 772, 780, 783, 785, and 786.

21. "Party Reform Pledges Must Be Kept, Says Shafroth, Speaks for a Greater State," *Denver Times*, January 12, 1909, 1, Shafroth Family Papers, Box 7, Folder 5, Denver Public Library. See also "Inaugural Address of John F. Shafroth," June 10, 1911, Shafroth Family Papers, Box 7, Folder 45.

22. Leonard, *Honest John Shafroth*, 53.

23. Shafroth to William Jennings Bryan, July 12, 1910, John Shafroth Collection, Box 26731, Folder 4, Colorado State Archives.

24. Leonard, *Honest John Shafroth*, 59.

25. Ibid., 70. See also "Governor Shafroth's Veto of the Race Track Gambling Bill," April 17, 1911, Shafroth Family Papers, Box 7, Folder 45, Denver Public Library.

26. Shafroth raised complaints of this nature at the governors' conference in 1910; see "Governors' Proceedings 1910," page 217, Shafroth Family Papers, Box 7, Folder 45, Denver Public Library.

27. Hon. John F. Shafroth, "Imperative Need of Direct Legislation," *Twentieth Century Magazine*, September 1912, 516–19, Shafroth Family Papers, Box 7, Folder 45, Denver Public Library.

28. Harper, *History of Woman Suffrage*, 5:297.

29. Ibid., 298.

30. Leonard, *Honest John Shafroth*, 74.

31. Item, *Times and Democrat*, June 28, 1910, 2. On Dickerson's administration see Elliot, *History of Nevada*, 248–49.

32. Douglass and Nylen, *Letters from the Nevada Frontier*, 227.

33. Ibid., 238.

34. Chan, *Sagebrush Statesman*, 32–33.

35. Ibid., 44–45.

36. Ibid., 42.

37. Ibid., 32; Elliot, *History of Nevada*, 250.

38. Elliot, *History of Nevada*, 249–50.

39. Eric N. Moody, "Nevada's Bull Moose Progressives," 159, 164, 172.

40. "Nevada Governor Endorses Federal Anti-Lynch Law," *New Journal and Guide*, September 3, 1921, 3.

41. "Would Legalize Nevada Racing," *Washington Post*, February 21, 1915, S4; "Racing for Nevada: Governor Will Sign Bill Creating Commission and Legalizing Betting," *New York Times*, February 20, 1915, 7.

42. Jensen, *Pardoning Power*, 73.

43. Emmet D. Boyle to T. T. Powers, Arizona House of Representatives, February 3, 1915, Emmet D. Boyle Papers, Emmet D. Boyle, Executive Records, Nevada State Division of Archives and Records, Reno, NV.

44. Emmet D. Boyle to W. B. Alexander, Secretary, Nevada Mine Operators Association, December 22, 1914, Emmet D. Boyle Papers, Special Collections Department, University of Nevada, Reno.

45. See, for example, Hainsworth, "Utah State Elections."

46. Roper and Arrington, *William Spry*, 79.

47. For a biography covering the basic events of his career and offering an account sympathetic to Spry, see ibid.

48. Shipps, "Utah Comes of Age Politically," 105.

49. Roper and Arrington, *William Spry*, 203.

50. Alexander of Idaho was the first observant Jew to be elected a state governor; Bamberger was the second. A New York journalist from the *Evening Mail* wrote to Bamberger early in November that the people he worked with were "unanimous in saying that if anyone had offered to bet a week ago that a Jewish Democrat could be elected Governor of the Mormon state of Utah that went for Taft last election, he could have got a 1,000 to 1 proposition." Isaac Russell to Bamberger, November 8, 1916, Governor Simon Bamberger Scrapbook, Utah Historical Society.

51. Peterson and Cannon, *Awkward State of Utah*, 34–35.

52. "Speech of Hon. B. H. Roberts, Nominating Hon. Simon Bamberger for Governor of Utah."

53. Ibid.

54. Jonas, "Utah," 330.

55. Hainsworth, "Utah State Elections," 17, 21–22, 32.

56. "Mormons Quit Politics, Says New Governor," *Los Angeles Times*, November 16, 1916, II-1.

57. "Jews Dine Gov. Bamberger," *New York Times*, December 19, 1916, 3.

58. "Mormons Quit Politics"; Davenport, "The Junction of Jew and Mormon," *The Outlook*, December 20, 1916, 863–64.

59. Henning, *George Curry*, 58–59.

60. "Clean Government," *Eagle*, November 11, 1911, Special Collections, University of New Mexico Library, Albuquerque; Lowitt, *Bronson M. Cutting*, 33, 34, 53.

61. Editorial, "The Lesson of the Victory," *Albuquerque Morning Journal* (ND) (NP), Special Collections, University of New Mexico Library, Albuquerque.

62. "Asks New Tax System", *Kenna Record*, January 24, 1913, 8.

63. "New Mexico Will Not Allow Johnson and Flynn Battle," *Washington Post*, February 9, 1912, 8.

64. Cozzone, "Boxing in New Mexico"; "Prize Fight at Las Vegas a Big Joke," *Arizona Republican*, July 5, 1912, 1.

65. "Second Race Riot in a Fortnight Raises Clovis to Fever Heat," *Albuquerque Morning Journal*, June 10, 1912, 1.

66. Some of what is written here about Hunt is drawn from the author's work in *George Hunt* (Tucson: University of Arizona Press), 2015.

67. "Inaugural Address of Geo. W. P. Hunt, Governor of Arizona," George W.P. Hunt Papers, Arizona Collection, Arizona State University Libraries.

68. *New York Herald-Tribune* article, reprinted in "What Others Say," *Jefferson City Post-Tribune*, December 27, 1934, 4.

69. George W.P. Hunt, "The Single Legislative Branch," 11.

70. "House Tables the Bill to Abolish Senate," *Arizona Gazette*, June 18, 1912, 1.

71. Hunt, "National Control of Mineral Resources," 17–18.

72. Some local editors saw Hunt's overnight stay as political stunt. See, for example, "Governor Hunt's Vaudeville Acts Give Him Plenty of Newspaper Advertising," *Arizona Republic*, March 26, 1912, 5.

73. Message of Geo. W. P. Hunt, March 18, 1912, in McCluskey, comp., *Compiled Messages of Geo. W. P. Hunt and Thos. E. Campbell*, 28.

74. "The Oration of Governor Hunt," *Miner's Magazine*, July 17, 1913, 8.

75. "What Others Say."

15

GOVERNORS AND REFORM

The Record and the Legacy

Governors during the reform period 1890–1920 shared the spotlight with legislators, reporters, muckrakers, academics, labor leaders, social workers, suffragists, prohibitionists, national and local politicians, individual crusaders who never held a major office or any office at all, and leaders of countless reform organizations. Still, governors stood out. They had to deal one way or another with a broader range of reform measures than anyone else. They were vital players in the legislative process and relatively free to promote reform causes in the performance of their administrative duties. This chapter offers some concluding observations about variations in the backgrounds, viewpoints, role in bringing reform, and personalities and styles of the governors involved and general commentary on their path to power, the nature of their job, challenges facing them while in office, what governors thought was needed to improve their ability to do their work, their performance in various policy areas, and the legacy of the reform movement of which they were an essential part.

THE CAST OF CHARACTERS

The governors were a diverse cast of characters. In terms of occupational backgrounds, one finds a great many lawyers, a large number of businessmen, many of whom were very successful, several newspaper owners and editors and former mayors, a few scholars and medical doctors, a preacher, and a riverboat captain.

Many had served in the state legislature, sometimes making a considerable reputation as a reform leader, and several of the most successful governors had served as public prosecutors, sometimes using sensational cases as a springboard to the gubernatorial office.

Some governors were self-made men who were raised in poverty and had only limited formal education. Others came from wealthy and prestigious families and had the best of everything, education included. Several were rich and, to the delight if not the relief of party bosses, used their own resources to finance their campaigns and, while governor, campaigns for particular causes. Some governors were avid and virulent racists. Some were genuine humanitarians who were deeply disturbed by the injustices of capitalism, what was happening to those caught up in the harshness of industrial labor, and who had great sympathy for the poor and powerless. They seemed endowed with what has been termed a "non-ideological moralistic impulse" to help people and make the world a better place.[1] We can see "humanitarian progressivism" with Altgeld of Illinois, Pingree of Michigan, Manning of South Carolina, and many others who combined idealism with practicality and toughness.

When it comes to ideology, we find a wide spectrum of reform governors, from the conservative Mugwumps on the far right to the quasi-socialists on the far left.[2] Most of them, however, seem best described as being in the center of this wide range. They were open-minded, willing to experiment and move away from individualism and laissez-faire but, generally being very practical people, were willing to compromise and were unwilling to move farther than they felt public opinion would permit. Many mixed varying amounts of Progressivism with fiscal conservatism. By leading from the middle or slightly left of center, governors were moderating forces, adding a bit of practicality to the dreams of those on their left. For some governors, especially of the "New South" variety, "Progressivism" may have had less to do with reaching ideological goals than with a simple desire for modernization and catching up with the North.

The governors differed in the scope, intensity, and duration of their commitment to Progressivism. While some looked for a broad range of reforms, others took a more narrow focus, be it on securing reforms democratizing the political system, turning the searchlight on graft, corruption, and the waste of money in state operations, fighting the abuses of corporations, promoting the interests of working people, or dealing with moral problems such as drinking and gambling. Some were largely "rhetorical Progressives" who, although publicizing or building the agenda for reform, did little to actually bring about the reforms they advocated. Governors such as Frazier of North Dakota and Hay of Washington saw considerable reform activity on their watch but had very little to do with it, other than signing off on legislation. Montague of Virginia, though friendly to reform, generally stood back, being unwilling by temperament to get into the rough-and-tumble of fighting for legislation and taking only a limited view of the role of governor in the legislative process.

Others demonstrated their Progressivism by striving for legislation or in making executive decisions regarding such matters as issuing pardons and commutations and employing the National Guard. While some were innovators or initiators of policy ideas, being the first to mount a successful drive for reform, others protected or consolidated the changes that had been made. Some made small contributions, adding a program or two as part of a long crusade to bring about reform. Others added a lot of reforms all at once. For some, Progressivism represented just one phase in their career while others became lifelong true believers.

The timing of governors in becoming Progressives also varied. We find, for example, La Follette, who started out as Progressive seeking office; Wilson, who started out a conservative and became a Progressive when he ran for office; and Pingree, who became a Progressive only after reaching office and finding conditions he felt had to be altered. Those who made an abrupt change around election time often had a tough time convincing others of their sincerity. One can think of Wilson, Folk, and Hughes as "surprise governors" as far as the bosses were concerned, but in these cases the candidates had made their intentions clear—the bosses simply did not believe they really meant what they said or thought that when push came to shove, the candidates could be controlled should they be elected. We find several more genuine "surprise governors" whose switch to Progressivism was unexpected by nearly everybody. One example is Governor Mead of Washington, a candidate backed by the railroads who proceeded to push for increased railroad taxation and regulation.

Populist governors, given the fragile nature of their coalitions, their lack of experience, and their frequent lack of control over the legislative process, were generally agenda builders pushing for reform rather than executives who brought about extensive or significant change. At the core of the movement when it comes to actual reform we find "new" reform-minded Progressive governors who followed the Populists, often borrowing their ideas. In addition to Robert La Follette, Hiram Johnson, and Woodrow Wilson, we find others who deserve recognition, including midwesterners like John Altgeld, Hazen Pingree, Albert Cummins, Joseph Folk, James Cox, Edward Hoch, W. R. Stubbs, George Sheldon, John Burke, and Peter Norbeck; southerners like Hoke Smith, Napoleon Broward, Braxton Comer, Richard Manning, James Hogg, Charles Haskell, Claude Swanson, A. O. Stanley, and Austin Crothers; easterners like Theodore Roosevelt, Charles Evans Hughes, Al Smith, Robert Bass, and Eugene Foss; and westerners such as Oswald West, Joseph Carey, John Shafroth, Simon Bamberger, and George Hunt.

In terms of political personality and style, the material examined suggests several of the more successful new governors, like La Follette, Hiram Johnson, Hughes, Wilson, and Folk come close to fitting the profile of what political scientist James David Barber defined as active-negative leaders.[3] These were very active, highly principled, moralistic, and determined leaders who were also often cold, rigid, vain, and stubborn. They had things to accomplish. They were not out for fun. They were crusaders who saw issues as choices between right and wrong, good and bad, and who saw those who opposed them as dangerous people who had to be beaten. Rather than seeking compromise with their opponents, they worked to wrest power from them, often showing considerable skill as tacticians, and once this was done, implementing a broad agenda. They tended to be far more flexible in running for office than when in office.

Looking at other new governors, one also finds more flexible, pragmatic and happier types, the active-positives such as Governor Theodore Roosevelt who were energetically involved in policy matters and enjoyed politics and exercising the art of political compromise. One might also put John Johnson of Minnesota into the active-positive category—someone who plodded along tinkering with various Progressive ideas, without a general plan of action or broad vision of reform, in a friendly fashion and offending nobody. Some like Dunne of Illinois were dedicated Progressives on most issues but could be criticized for being too nice, not being much of a threat, and trying too hard to get along with the party professionals. The legislative gains of these active-positive types were often less dramatic and extensive than those of the active-negative types because they were less willing to gamble with innovative programs, to present a big package, and to be far more willing to compromise.

Some of the governors are difficult to classify by Barber's typology. In Oswald West of Oregon, for example, we see a highly determined crusader being successful in several areas but also a showman of the Theodore Roosevelt variety who enjoyed the publicity and taking the dullness out of politics. Colorado's John Shafroth comes through as a highly productive chess player, always looking ahead to the next move, who knew how to get along with people who disagreed with him and did so by outmaneuvering them to secure a large package of reforms. Governors Deneen of Illinois, Chamberlain of Oregon, and Rogers of Washington emerge as moderate and cautious reformers, unwilling to press for action until the voice of the people was clear. Some governors saw their essential role to be a simple one of pressing for benefits for their constituents, something they realized was also being done by those whom they opposed. For Governor Stubbs of Kansas, for example, there was nothing personal or essentially wrong in his dispute with the corporations—he as governor represented the interests of his constituents while the corporation leaders represented the interests of the people who employed them.

GETTING THERE

Governors started out in a variety of ways—as self-recruited insurgents building their own campaign organizations against the establishment in their own party, by joining up with an ongoing anti-establishment political organization, or by being recruited and backed by party leaders.

Progressive reformers generally directed much of their wrath against boss control over party nominations in party caucuses or conventions. As illustrated above in the stories of Governors La Follette and Bass, however, boss control for various offices, especially the less popular ones, depended less on their "power" than on the fact that nobody was paying much attention to what they were doing. With a bit of organizing a challenger could rather easily circumvent the local bosses and begin a career as a county attorney or in the state legislature. Though it was more difficult for the office of governor, reform candidates for governor like La Follette, Pingree, and Wilson of New Jersey demonstrated that they could win nominations through convention systems traditionally controlled by the bosses. Several governors, including La Follette, Davis in Arkansas, Montague in Virginia, Catts in Florida, Bass in New Hampshire, and Sheldon in Nebraska, in effect democratized preconvention political campaigning in their states by directly appealing for popular support rather than by simply courting state and local party leaders and through this route were able to circumvent the control of those who led the party organizations.

Still, the direct primary made it considerably easier for the reform-minded to challenge the establishment. It opened the door to mavericks and insurgents hostile to the machines and their corporate client. Hiram Johnson of California, Robert Bass of New Hampshire, and Vardaman of Mississippi were among those immediately benefiting from the adoption of a direct primary system. The Nonpartisan League in North Dakota used the direct primary to nominate slates of candidates in the dominant Republican Party. They found this a much more effective route than forming a third party and put the system to good use in eventually getting Lynn Frazier elected governor. The direct primary proved especially valuable to those gubernatorial candidates opposing the establishment in one-party states where the nominee of the dominant party invariably won.

In many states winning the nomination was all that was actually needed to win the office, but securing the nomination, whether through the convention system or primary system, frequently involved considerable infighting. While state problems frequently became major issues in gubernatorial general election campaigns, outcomes were also often influenced by national political campaigns and issues, especially in presidential years. Race-baiting was useful as a way to get elected in the South but, it might be argued, was not absolutely necessary to secure election and to pursue a Progressive program. For example, Governor Manning of South Carolina did many of things that Governor Bilbo did in Mississippi in regard to taxes, labor protection, and welfare legislation, but without the race-baiting engaged in by Bilbo.[4]

On an individual level, a great many factors went into a successful election. Being identified as not only a Progressive but the most Progressive was essential at the height of the movement—this was the "in" thing. Successful candidates capitalized on the popular rejection of political bosses, state legislatures, and a corrupt political system favoring the special interests. They responded to popular demands for more democracy, openness, and corporate control. In some places being a Scandinavian or a Baptist helped, as did a Folk-like image of a "lone warrior for righteousness." Being seen as a hard-working, upright champion of justice, out to do in evil-doers, was a decided advantage at a time when corruption was a central concern. Also often useful was cultivating an idealized judge-like image of being thoughtful, impartial, and above party and the image of a successful businessperson who had a mastery of managerial, no-nonsense business skills and was so successful and well respected that they could not be considered dangerous, no matter what they said in a campaign.

DOING THE JOB

The early focus of Progressive reformers was on giving the governor greater control over the making of legislation, and, despite the continued grumbling on the part of governors, they had, in fact, by 1915 come a long way toward becoming chief legislators.[5] With this, gubernatorial success and overall competence became evaluated by the voters largely in terms of what governors did or failed to do in regard to securing legislation.

In approaching their legislative tasks the new governors were reformers in a hurry. They generally did not plan on staying long in their position. Some, thanks to term limits, had no choice. Others, term limits or no term limits, could hardly wait to move on to another office, usually the US Senate. With reform sentiment in full swing, being governor became much more of a stepping-stone than a dead-end job for governors with a Progressive bent. But those interested in making a bid for the Senate or the presidency were encouraged to act quickly and to do so by securing dramatic legislative victories. Experience as a prosecutor, as in the case of Hiram Johnson and Folk, and as an investigator, in the case of Hughes, may have carried with it a certain uncompromising toughness later evidenced in dealing with the legislature. As illustrated in Wilson's case, university administration may also have had its own merit as a way of preparing someone to deal with difficult people. Drawing upon his experience with Princeton University, Wilson once told an interviewer that "as compared with the college politician, the real article seems like an amateur."[6]

Having a background in the legislature may have been an asset to governors in giving them important contacts with those still serving, knowledge of the process, and insights on how to best deal with the legislators. On the other hand, their experience in the legislature had not always been pleasant. Those with a Progressive bent had reason to carry over negative attitudes about the legislative process, having been being frustrated in their attempts to win passage of various measures and seeing corruption at first hand, and may well have gone on to the gubernatorial office with strong doubts about whether legislatures could amount to much of anything or do anything worthwhile without extensive reform and the guidance of executive leadership.

Those who came to office without previous political experience had to feel their way around in a new environment—an adjustment especially difficult if they also happened to have been successful businessmen who enjoyed high social and economic status that brought them deference and who were accustomed to running their organizations as they saw fit and if they had been, like Governor Pennypacker, highly respected scholarly judges who saw themselves above the political fray. They found themselves in a much less comfortable, less respectful, and less deferential environment, which included pig-headed legislators, inquisitive reporters, and the sting of press criticism and ridicule. Governors who had been public prosecutors were far more politically experienced and seemingly better prepared to function in a highly political environment.

Reform governors often encountered considerable legislative resistance to their proposals. Some conflict was inevitable. Governors and legislators had different constituencies, and institutional tensions often came between them. The job was more difficult when, as often the case, one or both legislative houses were controlled by members of the opposition party or a hostile faction of the governor's own party. While opposing political bosses may have lost control over the governorship, they often retained considerable clout in the legislature. Beyond this, some legislators could be depended on to instinctively resist assertions of executive leadership. Old-time legislative leaders voiced their resentment of pushy gubernatorial upstarts who challenged the authority and prerogatives of legislators. They resented assertions of gubernatorial power and efforts to influence legislation.

Being a successful chief legislator required a great deal of work, skill, and luck. It also required bargaining, and the governors were generally more than willing to touch bases with or elicit the support of various groups, including businesspeople, whenever their objectives coincided and the situation deemed it necessary. Some of the more successful governors like La Follette and Wilson thought it wise to seek only a few selected reforms at a time. Those who had to work with a legislature dominated by the opposite party wisely chose a nonpartisan or bipartisan approach.

Many gubernatorial candidates and governors tried to get their views in their party's platform so that they could claim popular backing for programs they favored in the event of a party victory and could put additional pressure on party members who were elected on that platform to live up to its promises. The technique sometimes proved successful—for example, when Governor Shafroth called a special session in Colorado in 1910. Often, though, governors discovered that legislators were often far more tied to local concerns in their districts or to the views of machine bosses than the promises made by the state party.[7] Governors too found that many in the legislature believed in the old adage that the platform was something candidates used to get in on, not to stand on.

In establishing their leadership, governors used everything they could give away—jobs, contracts, pardons, free passes from the railroads—and their ability to distribute roads, prisons, and educational facilities around the state to build their parties or personal followings and to influence legislators and other political participants. They had a variety of powers, not unlike those available to contemporary holders of that office, plus some that contemporary governors do not enjoy, such as the use of patronage.

Patronage was useful in securing legislation—the wise practice was to hold off decisions as to what appointments would be made until after the session. Pardons were also useful. In Texas, for example, legislators routinely asked governors for a pardon or a reprieve for clients or constituents in exchange for their vote on legislation.[8] Looking for help, some turned to the universities. The use of the specialists in universities was notable in Wisconsin and elsewhere, though in several states, especially in the South, some governors and other elected officials were "suspicious of the academic mind" and chose not to use these facilities.[9]

The more assertive governors attempted to influence the organization of the legislature and assumed a leading role in initiating legislative ideas, consulting with experts, putting together specific proposals, pushing for their adoption, sometimes appealing for public as well as legislative support, and campaigning for legislative candidates who were on their side and against legislators who opposed them. They used the message power, the veto power, and the powers to call special sessions and make appointments as political tools. Some governors showed unusual skill in getting around the opposition, often being able to work across party lines. They could and did claim to voice the views of the people of the whole state rather than of those in a relatively small legislative district.

They too used the governor's office as a bully pulpit to build up public support for reforms. Indeed, their chief asset in dealing with the legislature may have rested on this support or, more precisely, legislative perception of such support.[10] Hughes of New York was among the governors who saw appealing to the public as his principle tool in dealing with the legislature. As he put it: "The only proper way to hold up a Legislature is to hold it up to public sentiment."[11] Wilson too gave full credit to the force of public opinion in bringing the adoption of his agenda. As noted, in the case of Stubbs in Kansas, the popularity of reform may have effectively offset the governor's lack of understanding of the legislative process, giving him what he wanted all by itself.

Many governors would probably have been more than happy to do without a legislature, but, finding that not to be a viable legal or political alternative, they proceeded to suggest ways that legislatures could be improved so that they could better do their share of the work and be better governing partners, or simply get out of the way of reform. Doing what they could to reduce the influence of special interests on legislative bodies, they called for lobbying reforms. Many also saw the value of establishing legislative reference service bureaus to overcome the limitations on the ability of legislators to make informed decisions and to help produce better, more informed, fact-based legislation—and not coincidentally more Progressive legislation.

Some governors may have shied away from pushing for a reduction in the number of legislators or the creation of a single small legislative body out of fear that this would offend legislators and make it more difficult to secure legislative approval of their proposals. Still, between 1912 and 1919, governors in at least a half-dozen states got behind the idea of adopting a unicameral legislative system as a way of streamlining the legislative process and providing more transparency in the proceedings.[12] Nothing happened, however, until 1934, when Nebraska voters approved a constitutional amendment providing for a one-house legislature.

Taking the task of selecting US senators out of the hands of legislators was still another reform frequently advocated by governors, aimed in part at improving the legislative process. The issue of who was going to be selected to the US Senate often diminished the consideration of more important policy issues in legislative campaigns, led to the buying of legislative votes, and frequently consumed much time and energy during a session, sometimes to the point where there was little or no time left to consider matters of reform or anything else. Serious deadlocks and delays were evidenced, for example, in North Dakota, Oregon, Kentucky, Delaware, and Colorado. In some places legislators as well as governors, hoping to improve the ability of legislators to tend to important business, joined in the call for direct election.[13]

Throughout the period under review governors demonstrated their concern with administrative problems. They spent a great deal of time pointing out deficiencies in state operations, especially the prison system, and the overall need for greater efficiency and economy. They also spent much time complaining about their inability to appoint, supervise, and remove state administrators. They were frequently subject to criticism for the actions of officials they could not control. They also found it difficult to get rid of county and municipal officials whom they felt were incompetent, corrupt, or simply unwilling to enforce state law, especially those relating to liquor and gambling.

Reforms commonly advanced to enhance the governor's status as chief administrator—the short ballot, state government reorganization, and executive budgeting—had a difficult time getting off the ground during the Progressive period, though some progress was beginning to be made by 1920.[14] From many a legislator's point of view, any attempt to further the power of the governor had to be resisted. Governors may have shied away from actively pursuing what appeared to be a hopeless or difficult cause when it came to improving their administrative control through these reforms, deciding that their time and efforts were better directed to other reforms.

CURBING THE BOSSES, PARTISANSHIP, AND DEMOCRATIZING THE PROCESS

Within the broader Progressive movement there was a call for a new kind of politics in which principles and substantive issues would become more important as motivating factors than the desire to win elections and enjoy the benefits of holding power. Many hoped that citizens and elected leaders would come around to ignoring partisanship and view issues as collective problems requiring cooperative action based on solid objective research. Progressive reformers coming from the outside—muckrakers, scholars, leaders of various reform groups concerned with governmental processes—tended to be antiboss and antiparty. They favored elections in which party labels did not appear on ballots as well as civil service reform, and having great confidence in the ability of individual voters to govern directly, they saw great value in direct democracy.

Governors during the Progressive period shared some but not all of these sentiments. They were not invariably antiboss or antimachine. Nor were they antiparty or against partisanship in general, though such sentiments were popular in some places, most noticeably California. One also can question the extent to which they actually strove for civil service reform. One can credit many governors for promoting democratic reforms in elections and the voting rights of women, though the motives are not always clear and the record is somewhat mixed in regard to certain reforms.

Conflict with political bosses was sometimes central to the story of Progressive governors. In several states, however, much was accomplished by governors who got along very well with the bosses. They were not antiboss. They liked, respected, and largely agreed with the views of the leaders to whom they owed their jobs. The bosses, for their part, were not always dead set against reform. If not philosophically on board, they were highly practical, seeing the need to bend with the times and, indeed, sometimes seeing change to be in the short- or long-term interest of their party. Working with the bosses, Al Smith of New York, Claude Swanson in Virginia, and, to a lesser extent, a series of governors in Pennsylvania and West Virginia adopted a wide range of reforms. In some states machine-backed governors did better than antimachine governors in promoting Progressive changes. Having a machine on the side of reform made getting measures through the legislature much easier because the party organizations usually enjoyed considerable strength in these bodies.[15]

Progressive governors around the country—La Follette of Wisconsin, Folk of Missouri, John Johnson of Minnesota, John Burke of North Dakota, Hughes of New York, Bass of New Hampshire, and West of Oregon among them—benefited from the support of voters, legislators, or political leaders who belonged to the other political party. They welcomed and encouraged such support. On the other hand, few governors can be considered crusaders against partisanship in general or eager to forge a party realignment along liberal-conservative lines. Most reform-minded governors worked through a major political party with which they had long associated. They hoped to strengthen the appeal and fortunes of their party by steering it in a more Progressive direction or by keeping it going in that direction. Partisanship and partisan gains were important to them. They had little interest in bringing nonpartisan elections to the state level except when it came to judges.

Nor does it seem that many were actively committed to ending patronage through the adoption of civil service systems. This may help explain why civil service reform hardly got off the ground at the state level during the Progressive period. Civil service seems like something governors who wanted to be considered Progressive felt they had to publicly champion but were not all that eager to actually see adopted. They had little to gain by this type of change. Patronage was useful to them not only as a tool in dealing with legislators but as a means of building and funding, through assessments on the salaries of the people they appointed, their own personal political machines to use in elections; it was also a way of bringing into office people who were not only competent and well equipped to serve but who were loyal to them and the Progressive causes they wished to pursue. From the governor's point of view, there was considerable merit in taking the control of appointments away from political bosses and using patronage to build support for their own campaigns, deal with the legislature, and to hire a supportive staff. There was no sense at all in taking control of appointments away from the bosses, only to turn around and give it to an independent commission.

Progressives in the academic world and some Progressive politicians, as exemplified by governor Hughes of New York, stressed moving through civil service and related reforms into a system in which reliance was placed not so much on politicians but on impartial, independent administrative agencies staffed by politically neutral experts. This "escape from politics" idea, however, appears to have had little appeal for most governors. It further interfered with their ability to control and created the prospect of a larger problem: trying to keep the experts on tap rather than on top.[16]

Governors during the Progressive period often led the way in drives to democratize the political system, though their motives likely were a mixture of idealistic, political, and personal objectives, and the extent of their effort, the nature of the struggle, and extent of success varied around the country. Several governors, as noted earlier, in effect, democratized the convention nomination system in their states by successfully appealing directly to the voters. These and many more governors went on to support the direct primary.[17] Bitter memories about being rejected in past conventions, the desire to come through on a central campaign promise, and longing to make it easier for other Progressives to challenge the establishment were among the influences on their support of the direct primary. In some cases governors faced the determined opposition of party bosses who, with good reason, saw the reform aimed squarely at them. This was true, for example, in New Jersey under Wilson and in New York under Hughes. In other places the direct primary had the support of party leaders who agreed with the governors that it would be beneficial in bringing order and legitimacy to the candidate selection process and in restoring public trust in parties.

The frequent stand of governors for the direct election of US senators was also consistent with democratic theory. It was also consistent with a desire to not only improve the performance of the legislature but to harm the bosses by reducing their ability to control the selection of senators and, through this, influence the distribution of federal jobs in the state.[18] In addition, turning to the voters had value to governors who were anxious to move on to the US Senate and who faced a legislature controlled by the members of the opposing party or by legislators and party bosses in their own party whom they had antagonized.

Many governors appeared willing to back the initiative and referendum.[19] They viewed these as not only vital to democracy but as a way of furthering their agenda by circumventing the legislature or challenging something the legislature had done. Governors West of Oregon and Hunt of Arizona took their case against the death penalty to the voters; though this route was not successful, the initiative at least provided an opportunity to promote the cause. Not all governors, however, favored direct legislation or generally bringing voters directly into the policymaking process. Some, such as O'Neal in Alabama, opposed direct legislation, feeling that it conflicted with executive authority as well as legislative authority.

On the regional level western governors were far more active and enthusiastic in supporting the initiative and referendum and more successful in securing their adoption than governors in other regions. Within the Republican Party one sees this regional difference on direct legislation in the views of Bass of New Hampshire and Hiram Johnson from California. Governors in the South as well as the East generally did not make a strong attempt to secure these reforms, either not believing in them or seeing the battle to secure them as a lost cause. Those who did make an attempt usually found they could not secure legislative or voter support for them. Some, including La Follette and Wilson, were latecomers to the cause of direct legislation, showing more flexibility on the question in an effort to broaden their support in a bid for the presidency.

Governors had different viewpoints on the subject of woman suffrage.[20] Governor Waite of Colorado successfully pushed for woman suffrage but later regretted it in the belief women had voted against him in 1894, contributing to his failure to secure reelection. Some, following him, were fearful about how women might vote. Some saw women voters a danger to their party or personal candidacy. Some feared women voters would bring prohibition. Governors generally either favored both suffrage and prohibition or opposed both of them. Governors, be they Progressives or conservatives in the states first to adopt woman suffrage, many of which were in the West, became nationally known celebrities in advocating that other states follow their lead when it came to suffrage extension and in calling for suffrage on the national level.[21]

A major blemish of the Progressive period was the disfranchisement of black voters in several states, largely in the South—a move supported if not spearheaded by governors in those states, including some who otherwise qualified as Progressive reformers. As historian David Southern once noted, "Seemingly, it never occurred to the egalitarian progressives that disfranchisement of a race might be considered undemocratic."[22]

ATTACKING THE CORPORATIONS, DIFFERENT MESSAGES FOR LABOR

When it came to economic policies, governors often led the push for corporate (especially railroad) regulation and taxation, antitrust legislation, laws cracking down on securities frauds, measures guaranteeing bank deposits, and controls on insurance companies and various public utilities.

Many governors during the 1890–1920 period built their careers by bashing the railroads. This, though, did not amount to an attack on business in general—the railroads and other monopolistic corporations were something special, something that had to be brought under control. In calling for regulation governors were siding not only with farmers and railroad workers but with other elements of the business community—small businesses, merchants, and shippers—that had grievances against the railroads. When it came to the railroads, most new governors disagreed with the Populists before them and shunned public ownership. Some opposed even standing in the way of consolidation, seeing the only problem with the latter being the danger of increased rates, which was something that could be controlled through regulatory action at the state level.[23] Many governors actively worked to limit passenger and freight rates. This was resisted, but the most strongly resisted and impressive thing governors did to the railroads and other large corporations was to increase their tax load, either through legislation or the creation of a tax commission.

Many governors no doubt agreed with Woodrow Wilson, who said in November 1910 that the states, working in a cooperative fashion, could do a better job than the federal government in controlling big business.[24] Many were anxious to protect their turf, or what turf they had in this policy area. For example, governors meeting at the annual Conference of Governors in 1915 strongly protested federal court action that threatened the ability of states to regulate intrastate railroad rates.[25] A few years earlier President Theodore Roosevelt, who favored national regulation of large corporations, received considerable opposition from governors on this subject. In spite of pressure from the president, several Republican governors took a states' rights stand when it came to regulating railroads.[26] Roosevelt was also less than happy with the push of many governors, both Republican and Democratic, most noticeably in the West, for state rather than federal control over conservation policies.[27]

Reformers, including many governors, conducted a long campaign for legislation or state constitutional measures to prohibit railroads from handing out free passes to public officials. Several governors or gubernatorial candidates refused to take passes as a means of showing their opposition to the practice. While the free pass was eventually outlawed virtually everywhere, reformers had a tough time reaching this goal because just about every public official in one way or another was taking advantage of the practice. Even some of the otherwise most reform-minded found the practice useful to them. As illustrated in the case of North Dakota's Governor Shortridge, a Populist, it not only provided governors with free transportation; because they could get passes for other people, it also functioned like having state jobs to hand out and gave them an opportunity to do favors for legislators and other people they were trying to influence or reward.

During the period under review, governors signed off on a great deal of labor legislation, much of which came to them through the efforts of social groups concerned with the rights of women and children or establishing humane working conditions for laborers in general. Labor leaders often saw governors doing the right thing on legislation, but during much of the period under review they generally viewed the actions of governors in regard to labor disputes with considerable alarm. In response to employer calls for help, governors commonly sent in National Guard troops or called for federal troops to put down labor strikes. Powerful corporations demanded protection, and, with a few exceptions, such as Waite in Colorado and Hunt in Arizona, governors complied, showing little tolerance for labor militancy.[28] Workers got legislation but were also put down by military action. Over time, though, governors learned to check things out—rather than sending in the militia at the first call of local officials or employers, they would send trusted militia officers to the strike scene to make their own assessment of the situation. They worried about wasting money and resources and negative feedback from unions and people in the strike area for coming to the aid of the companies. They hoped to appear impartial, and many made the effort.[29]

Some governors worried about the negative effect that state intervention was having on getting men to join the National Guard, a problem that grew as it became increasingly likely that the United States was going to become involved in the war in Europe. Speaking to a gathering of western governors, Governor Samuel Stewart, Democrat of Montana, noted in 1915 that "many men stay out of the local military organizations of different states because they do not want to go out and take part in industrial disputes and, as you might say, take up arms against their own brothers, because that is what it amounts to very often."[30] At the same conference several governors took the position that it was far better that the National Guard not be used to settle industrial pursuits.

SPENDING, MORAL UPLIFT, AND LAW ENFORCEMENT

While reform-minded governors often declared themselves guardians of the budget, they often also took the lead in a drive for greater state spending, especially for education and transportation improvements, but also a variety of other social and public health programs. They hoped to accommodate two contradictory public demands—keeping taxes low and providing more services—by shifting the burden for increased services as much as possible to corporations and wealthy individuals.

During the Progressive period several governors put much effort into battling what they considered to be moral or social evils. In deference to scientific opinion, a common theme of the Progressive period, many governors joined in the effort to fight criminality and bring moral and social improvement by controlling reproduction, and their support was important in the adoption of eugenics legislation. Governors, with some exceptions, such as Pennypacker in Pennsylvania, Marshall in Indiana, and Chamberlain in Oregon, were more than willing to listen to the experts, though in this case the call for action was to be largely discredited.

Governors were divided over the prohibition issue, but, on balance, more appear to have been attracted to the cause than opposed to it. The liquor issue had a strong influence on gubernatorial elections, and governors were forced to stand up and be counted. Still, it was difficult to take a stand one way or another without making enemies, and some firmly and unequivocally took both sides, their current position depending on where they were speaking. Some ardent prohibition supporters like Governor Catts of Florida drank privately. As was the case regarding suffrage, most governors in states where prohibition first took effect warmly endorsed the reform and urged other states to follow suit. In 1919 governors in twenty-six of the twenty-eight states with prohibition laws lauded the benefits of the law and urged other states to adopt similar measures.[31]

Some governors, including Theodore Roosevelt, defended "the manly art" of prizefighting. Roosevelt declared: "I have never been able to sympathize with the outcry against prize-fighters. The only objection I have to the prize ring is the crookedness that has attended its commercial development. Outside of this

I regard boxing, whether professional or amateur, as a first-class sport, and I do not regard it as brutalizing."[32] Many governors, though, did what they could to keep prizefighting out of their states, even though boxing was rapidly gaining in popularity. Governors stood their ground on the basis of their moral objections, focusing on the brutality of the sport and its connection with gambling and criminal elements.

Governors played a crucial role as leaders in the enforcement of state laws regarding liquor, gambling, prostitution, Sunday business closings, and events such as prizefighting. Without strong gubernatorial support, often including the use of troops, state laws of this nature would not have amounted to much of anything in some places. In enforcing these laws governors regularly encountered the opposition of local officials. Local resistance also became a problem in dealing with vigilante activity or in attempting to centralize authority at the state level in regard to tax collection, education, and other programs. Progressive governors were often at war with local officials. While fighting the encroachment of the federal government on state powers, they were often accused of doing the same thing when it came to local powers.

Many governors demonstrated a strong commitment to keeping the peace. They were inclined to act swiftly and with considerable force to restore law and order when dealing with not only industrial disputes but lynching and riots. Some governors, such as Jeff Davis in Arkansas and Coleman Blease of South Carolina, were willing to defend the lynching of African Americans, but most governors heartedly condemned such action and made serious efforts with the use of National Guard troops to protect black prisoners from lynch mobs.[33] Governor Shafroth of Colorado, in repudiation of Blease, articulated the commonly accepted view: "One mob can do more injury to society than twenty murders, because a lynching permeates the entire community and produces anarchy. The influence of mob rule is most reprehensible . . . [it is] our duty as Governors to declare for law and order."[34]

Many governors had legalistic minds that put a high priority on obedience and respect for the law. Many, however, also became well known for their opposition to the death penalty, their liberal use of the pardoning power in the interest of what they considered justice, and for their efforts to make prison systems more humane. Their stands on the death penalty, pardons, and prison reform were often condemned for being soft on crime and thus encouraging violations of the law.

Governors played an especially strong role in the drive to do away with the death penalty in five of the ten states that abolished capital punishment from 1907 to 1910. These were Kansas in 1907 under Edward Hoch, Washington in 1913 under Ernest Lister; South Dakota in 1915 under Frank Byrne, Oregon in 1914 under Oswald West, and Arizona in 1916 under George Hunt.[35] Many used their clemency power to right a wrong, reduce the severity of a conviction, fight off or at least delay the application of the death penalty, and protest against penal conditions such as the use of convict labor. In several cases, such as those involving Joe Hill and Leo Frank, governors did what they could to convince other governors to use their clemency powers. Many appeared to agree with Governor Pennoyer of Oregon that the power to pardon or reduce sentences was "the highest and most necessary prerogative in a civilized government," the exercise of which was of "absolute necessity" as long as courts and juries were not infallible.[36]

Considerable discontent over how governors had used this power, however, prompted a movement toward vesting the authority over pardons and paroles to independent boards. Critics claimed that governors had been too soft-hearted in using their powers or had used them to free or reduce the sentences of undeserving individuals in response to pressure from prominent persons or in exchange for political support or money. Governors may have welcomed sharing or giving up their responsibilities in this area because of the political pressures on them, the gravity of the decisions to be made, and the large number of requests, which meant that they did not have enough time to give each application the attention it deserved.[37]

The penal reform movement in which several governors also played a prominent part aimed to modernize the correctional system by making it both more humane and more scientific. It brought a long list of reforms in prison conditions and the release of prisoners.[38]

BOTTOM LINE AND LEGACY

The new governors, numerous and found throughout the country, were a diverse set of people in terms of backgrounds, ideology, temperament, and skills who played various roles in the development and implementation of reform in the states. Their views, whether shaped by deeply held beliefs, opportunism, or rational self-interest, led them to develop their own approaches to reform and their own particular reform packages. Overall, their performance varied with their personal backgrounds and characteristics and the environment in which they functioned. They generally came out of the Progressive period much stronger as chief legislators, somewhat stronger as chief administrators, a bit wiser in using the militia, and a bit weaker as chief magistrates, especially when it came to their power to pardon.

Governors often voiced their concerns about the encroachment of the federal government on the rights of the states. They acted on the assumption that the states were important units of government and that they, as their chief executives, had a duty to defend their governments. Those with a Progressive record, being proud of their accomplishments and confident in their ability to do more, may well have resented the assertion by proponents of federal action that governors were unable to do what had to be done. With the election of Progressive governors like Woodrow Wilson, some observers saw a victory not only for Progressivism but for states' rights. The hope was that states were improving to the point that there would soon be no need to further shift authority to the federal government. Progressive reform at the state level, however, did little to slow down further centralization. The states were unable to satisfactorily handle giant corporations and national commercial transactions on a state-by-state basis and grew more reliant on federal finances, programs, and leadership.

During the Populist and Progressive era, however, the states had authority—they could act in a variety of areas, and their willingness to do so was of extreme importance to a flood of reformers, organizations, and interest groups that turned to the states seeking change. By and large the states came through. From 1890 to 1920 state governments functioned as exploratory laboratories, often innovating and adopting measures in advance of congressional legislation. They took the lead in reforms regarding corporate regulation, labor rights, direct democracy, campaign regulations, woman suffrage, prohibition, securities regulation, prison reform, and a host of other matters. Progressive governors, throughout the nation, often played a major role in the process of providing models for federal action. Progressive governors going on to the US Senate and, in the case of two of them, the presidency carried the reforms to the national level.

Reform-minded governors throughout the country in the first two decades of the twentieth century also brought needed independence and prestige to the office of governor and aroused interest, confidence, and a sense of excitement in state government. They developed the leadership potential of the office of governor and made state government more relevant to its citizens. They helped shift into an era where more state chief executives began following Al Smith's maxim: "It is the duty of the governor to let the people tell him their troubles."[39]

Governors helped build the image of state governments as innovative, do-something governments. While leaving much to do in the area of civil rights and the rights of workers, they led efforts to bring about a more democratic political system, a more proactive government sensitive to the needs of ordinary people, and a government better prepared to take what action was needed of a regulatory nature or in the provision of public services.

NOTES

1. The phrase "non-ideological moralistic impulse" comes from Phelan, *Grand Master Workman*, 66–67.
2. Yellowwitz, *Labor and the Progressive Movement*, 1.
3. Barber, *Presidential Character*.
4. Kirby, *Darkness at the Dawning*, 41.
5. Lipson, *American Governor*, 50.

6. Needham, "Woodrow Wilson's Views." *The Outlook*, August 26, 1911, 940.

7. Burckel, "Progressive Governors in the Border States," 532. On gubernatorial involvement generally see Leslie Lipson, *American Governor*, 47–63; and Ransone, *Office of Governor in the United States*, 38–72, 157–215.

8. The governor, accordingly, lost a great deal when the power to make such decisions was shifted to an independent Board of Pardons and Appeals. See Gantt, *Chief Executive in Texas*, 152, 242–43.

9. Ransone, *Office of Governor in the South*, 70.

10. See, for example, Mathews "The New Stateism."

11. Harold J. Rowland, "Hughes—Governor," *The Outlook*, February 8, 1908, 308–9.

12. Governors given special recognition for their efforts in regard to the unicameral effort of 1909–19 were Hodges of Kansas, Eberhart of Minnesota, Hunt of Arizona, Lister of Washington, and Norbeck of South Dakota. See Childs, *Civic Victories*, 119–22.

13. Such was the case in, for example, Oregon. See Eaton, *Oregon System*, 92.

14. By 1917 there was considerable activity around the country dedicated to correcting the structural defects of state government through reorganization. Governors commonly called for the need to improve their status as chief administrators. See, for example, Robinson, "The Governors in 1917." A significant breakthrough came that year in terms of a simplified administrative system under Governor Frank Lowden in Illinois.

15. Kirby, *Darkness at the Dawning*, 43.

16. For pioneering work on balancing values of executive leadership, representativeness, and neutral competence see Kaufman, "Emerging Conflicts in Doctrines of Public Administration"; Kaufman, *Politics and Policies in State and Local Government*; and Wright, "Executive Leadership in State Administration."

17. Such was the case, for example, of those governors who assembled at a conference in December of 1910, though they did differ over whether primaries should be closed to party members or open so that party affiliation would not have to be declared. See "All the Governors with One Exception Strongly Favor the Direct Primary," *Atlanta Constitution*, December 7, 1910, 4.

18. Richards, "Half of Our Century," 74.

19. "Governors for Direct Legislation," *The Commoner*, May 13, 1910, 2.

20. Among the governors applauded by the National American Woman Suffrage Association for their support of the woman suffrage cause over the years were Carey of Wyoming; Adams, Shafroth, and Thomas of Colorado; Stubbs of Kansas; Vessey, Byrne, and Norbeck of South Dakota; Brough of Arkansas; Capper, Hoch, and Hodges of Kansas; Cox of Ohio; Dunne of Illinois; and Fort of New Jersey. The wives of Carey, Shafroth, Stubbs, and Byrne were also active in the suffrage movement, as was Mrs. Robert La Follette (Belle Case La Follette). Among those noted for their lack of support were governors Haskell of Oklahoma, Wilson of New Jersey, and James Ferguson of Texas. See material in Anthony and Harper, *History of Woman Suffrage*, vol. 4; and Harper, *History of Woman Suffrage*, vols. 5 and 6.

21. In 1915, for example, governors in suffrage states endorsing the cause on a national basis included Spry of Utah, Capper of Kansas, Dunne of Illinois, Alexander of Idaho, Hunt of Arizona, Lister of Washington, Stewart of Montana, and ex-governors Adams and Ammons of Colorado and Carey of Wyoming. See "Laud Equal Suffrage, Governors Report Success in States Where Women Vote," *New York Times*, August 28, 1915, 7.

22. Southern, *Malignant Heritage*, 45.

23. See, for example: "Railways Help Oregon, Says Governor Geer," *New York Times*, November 29, 1901, 3.

24. "Dr. Wilson Speaks to Many Governors," *New York Times*, November 30, 1910, 3.

25. See "The Governors and the Judge, a Poll of the Press," *The Outlook*, September 30, 1911, 266–68; "The Gathering of the Governors," *The Outlook*, September 23, 1911, 162–66.

26. "Roosevelt Scolded State Executives," *New York Times*, October 22, 1907, 5; "Severe Curtain Lecture," *Idaho Recorder*, October 31, 1907, 2.

27. "State or National Conservation?" *Literary Digest*, September 17, 1910, 425–28.

28. Cooper, *Rise of the National Guard*, 45, 55.

29. Ibid., 55, 148.

30. *Proceedings of the Conference of Western Governors, Held at Seattle*, 29.

31. See "Governors for Dry Laws," *New York Times*, June 2, 1919, 32.

32. Roosevelt, *Theodore Roosevelt*, 41.

33. See generally Cooper, *Rise of the National Guard*.

34. "Blease Says 'To Hell with Constitution.'"

35. See Galliher, Ray, and Cook, "Abolition and Reinstatement of Capital Punishment"; and Filler, "Movements to Abolish the Death Penalty."

36. Johnson, *Radical Middle Class*, 119.

37. Jensen, *Pardoning Power*, 24. For a short but insightful account of the use of the pardoning power of governors in Texas see Gantt, *Chief Executive in Texas*, 150–51.

38. For a report from several governors who reported on progress in their states see "Some Governors on Prison Reform." The article, published by the National Prisoners' Aid Association in New York City, can be found in the Shafroth Family Papers, Box 7, Folder 45, Denver Public Library.

39. Quoted by Glashan, *American Governors*, 151.

BIBLIOGRAPHY

ARCHIVES

Arizona Collection, Arizona State University Libraries, Tempe
    George W. P. Hunt Papers

Colorado State Archives, Denver
    Davis Waite Collection
    John Shafroth Papers

Denver Public Library
    Shafroth Family Papers

Duke University, William R. Perkins Library, Durham, North Carolina
    Socialist Party of America Papers, 1897–1963 (on microfilm)

Historical Research Collection, Wyoming State Museum, Cheyenne

History of Colorado Archives, Steven Hart Library and Research Center, Denver
    John Franklin Shafroth Papers

Idaho State Historical Society, Division of Manuscripts and Idaho State Archives, Boise
    James Hawley Papers
    Moses Alexander Papers

Nevada State Library, Division of Archives and Records, Carson City
    Emmet D. Boyle, Executive Records, Scrapbooks

New Mexico State Records Center and Archives, Santa Fe
   Governor Washington E. Lindsey Collection
   Governor William C. McDonald Collection

State Historical Society of North Dakota, Bismarck
   Biographies of the Governors of North Dakota
   Governor Eli Shortridge Papers
   John Burke Papers
   National Nonpartisan League Papers

Special Collections Department, University of Nevada, Reno
   Emmet D. Boyle Papers

Special Collections Research Center, Syracuse University Libraries, Syracuse, New York

State of South Dakota Archives, Pierre
   Biographical file on Peter Norbeck

Utah Historical Society, Salt Lake City
   Governor Simon Bamberger Scrapbook
   Clipping File

Wyoming State Archives, Cheyenne
   Joseph M. Carey Papers

NEWSPAPERS AND MAGAZINES

Advocate (Topeka, KS)
Afro-American (Baltimore, MD)
Albuquerque Morning Journal (Albuquerque, NM)
Appeal to Reason (Girard, KS)
Arizona Gazette (Phoenix, AZ)
Arizona Republic (Phoenix, AZ)
Arizona Republican (Phoenix, AZ)
Atlanta Constitution (Atlanta, GA)
Barre Daily Times (Barre, VT)
Bennington Evening Banner (Bennington, VT)
Bennington Evening Blade (Bennington, VT)
Bisbee Daily Review (Bisbee, AZ)
Black Hills Union (Rapid City, SD)
Black Hills Union and Western Stock Review (Rapid City, SD)
Brattleboro Daily Reformer (Brattleboro, VT)
Breckenridge News (Cloveport, KY)
Bridgeport Evening Times (Bridgeport, CT)
Broad Ax (Salt Lake City, UT)
Burlington Weekly Free Press (Burlington, VT)
Caucasian (Raleigh, NC)
Central Record (Lancaster, KY)
Chanute Times (Chanute, KS)
Chicago Defender (Chicago, IL)
Clearwater Republican (Orofino, ID)
Coeur d'Alene Press (Coeur d'Alene, ID)
The Commoner (Lincoln, NE)
Cut Bank Pioneer Press (Cut Bank, MT)
Daily Ardmoreite (Ardmore, OK)
Daily Capitol Journal (Salem, OR)
Daily Missoulian (Missoula MO)
Daily Times (Wilson, NC)
Day Book (Chicago, IL)
Democratic Advocate (Westminster, MD)
Denver Star (Denver, CO)
Denver Times (Denver, CO)
Dresden Enterprise and Sharon Tribune (Dresden, TN)
Eagle (Santa Fe, NM)

East Oregonian (Pendleton, OR)
El Paso Herald (El Paso, TX)
Evening Capital News (Boise, ID)
Evening Journal (Alamosa Colorado)
Evening Missourian (Columbia, MO)
Evening Star (Washington, DC)
Evening Times (Grand Forks, ND)
Evening Times-Republican (Marshalltown, IA)
Evening-Times Herald (Marshalltown, IA)
Fairfield News and Herald (Winnsboro, SC)
Forum (New York, NY)
Fulton County News (McConnellsburg, PA)
Grand Encampment Herald (Encampment, Wyoming, WY)
Great Falls News (Great Falls, MT)
Guthrie Daily Leader (Guthrie, OK)
Hartford Courant (Hartford, CT)
Hattiesburg News (Hattiesburg, MS)
Herald and News (Newberry, SC)
Hopkinsville Kentuckian (Hopkinsville, KY)
Hummer (Houston, MS)
Idaho County Free Press (Grangeville, ID)
Idaho Recorder (Salmon City, ID)
Illinois Staats-Zeitung (Chicago, IL)
Iron County Register (Ironton, MO)
Jefferson City Post-Tribune (Jefferson City, MO)
Kansas Agitator (Garnett, KS)
Kansas City Star (Kansas City, MO)
Kenna Record (Kenna, NM)
La Follette's Weekly Magazine (Madison, WI)
Labor Journal (Everett, WA)
Labor World (Duluth, MN)
Lake County Times (Hammond, IN)
Literary Digest Magazine
Little Falls Weekly Transcript (Little Falls, MN)
Los Angeles Herald (Los Angeles, CA)
Los Angeles Times (Los Angeles, CA)
Lynden Tribune (Lynden, WA)
Manning Times (Manning, SC)
Marion Daily Mirror (Marion, OH)
McCook Tribune (McCook, NE)
Medford Mail Tribune (Medford, OR)

Miner's Magazine (Denver, CO)
Minneapolis Journal (Minneapolis, MN)
Montana Record-Herald (Helena, MT)
Mumsey's Magazine
Nation
National Municipal Review
Neshoba Democrat (Philadelphia, MS)
New Journal and Guide (Norfolk, VA)
New Republic
New York Daily Tribune (New York, NY)
New York Times (New York, NY)
New York World (New York, NY)
Newark Post (Newark, DE)
Nonpartisan Leader (Fargo, ND)
Norfolk Weekly News-Journal (Norfolk, NE)
North American Review
North Platte Semi-Weekly Tribune (North Platte, NE)
Norwich Bulletin (Norwich, CT)
Ocala Evening Star (Ocala, FL)
Omaha Daily Bee (Omaha, NE)
Ottumwa Tri-Weekly Courier (Ottumwa, IA)
The Outlook
Palestine Daily Herald (Palestine, TX)
Pensacola Journal (Pensacola, FL)
Public Ledger (Maysville, KY)
Republican News Item (Laport, PA)
Richmond Times-Dispatch (Richmond, VA)
River Press (Fort Benton, MT)
Roanoke Times (Roanoke, VA)
Rock Island Argus (Rock Island, IL)
Rosebud County News (Forsyth, MT)
Salt Lake Herald-Republican (Salt Lake City, UT)
Salt Lake Tribune (Salt Lake, UT)
San Francisco Call (San Francisco, CA)
San Francisco Star (San Francisco, CA)
Socialist and Labor Star (Huntington, WV)
St. Landry Clarion (Opelousas, LA)
Tacoma Times (Tacoma, WA)
Times and Democrat (Orangeburg, SC)
Times Republican (Marshalltown, IA)

Topeka State Journal (Topeka, KS)
United Opinion (Bradford, VT)
Valentine Democrat (Valentine, NE)
Vinita Daily Chieftain (Vinita, Indian Territory)
Washington Herald (Washington, DC)
Washington Post (Washington, DC)
Washington Standard (Olympia, WA)
Weekly Times (Grand Forks, ND)
Willmar Tribune (Willmar, MN)
Worthington Advance (Worthington, MN)

BOOKS, ARTICLES, AND OTHER SOURCES

Abrams, Richard M. *Conservatism in a Progressive Era: Massachusetts Politics, 1900–1912*. Cambridge, MA: Harvard University Press, 1964.

Allen, Lee N. "Charles Henderson (1915–19)." *Encyclopedia of Alabama*. http://www.encyclopediaofalabama.org/article/h-1461.

Ambar, Saladin M. *How Governors Built the Modern American Presidency*. Philadelphia: University of Pennsylvania Press, 2012.

Anthony, Susan B., and Ida Husted Harper, eds. *The History of Woman Suffrage*. Vol. 4. New York: Source Book Press, 1970. Unabridged reprint of the 1902 Rochester edition.

Appleton, Thomas H., Jr. "Augustus Owsley Stanley." In *Kentucky's Governors*, ed. Lowell H. Harrison, 145–48. Lexington: University of Kentucky Press, 2004.

Argersinger, Peter H. *Populism and Politics: William Alfred Peffer and the People's Party*. Lexington: University Press of Kentucky, 1974.

Argersinger, Peter H. *The Limits of Agrarian Radicalism: Western Populism and American Politics*. Lawrence: University Press of Kansas, 1995.

Arrington, Leonard J. *History of Idaho*. Vol. 1. Moscow: University of Idaho Press, 1994.

Arsenault, Raymond O. "Jeff Davis." In *Governors of Arkansas*, ed. Timothy P. Donovan, Willard B. Gatewood Jr., and Jeannie M. Whayne, 115–30. Fayetteville: University of Arkansas Press, 1995.

Baker, Paula. *Curbing Campaign Cash*. Lawrence: University of Kansas Press, 2012.

Baker, Ray Stannard. *Woodrow Wilson: Life and Letters*. Vol. 3, *Governor, 1910–1913*. Garden City, NY: Doubleday, Doran, 1931.

Barber, James David. *The Presidential Character: Predicting Performance in the White House*, 4th ed. Englewood Cliffs, NJ: Prentice-Hall, 1992.

Barnard, Harry. *Eagle Forgotten: The Life of John Peter Altgeld*. New York: Duell, Sloan and Pearce, 1938.

Bartlett, John. *Familiar Quotations*, 14th ed. Boston: Little, Brown and Company, 1968.

Beatty, Jack. *Age of Betrayal*. New York: Alfred A. Knopf, 2007.

Beckel, Deborah. *Radical Reform: Interracial Politics in Post-Emancipation North Carolina*. Charlottesville: University of Virginia Press, 2010.

Beek, Joseph Allan. *The California Legislature*. Sacramento: California State Printing Office, 1960.

Benton, William W. *The Life of Thomas E. Watson*. New York: Val-Ballou Press, 1926.

Berge, George W. *The Free Pass Bribery System*. New York: Arno Press, 1974. Originally published in 1905.

Bicha, Karel D. *Western Populism*. Lawrence, KS: Coronado, 1976.

Black, Edwin. *War against the Weak: Eugenics and America's Campaign to Create a Master Race*. New York: Four Walls Eight Windows, 2003.

Blackford, Mansel Griffiths. "Businessmen and the Regulation of Railroads and Public Utilities in California during the Progressive Era." In *Growth of the Regulatory State, 1900–1917*, ed. Robert F. Himmelberg, 1–13. New York: Garland Publishing, 1994.

Blair, Diane D. *Arkansas Politics and Government*. Lincoln: University of Nebraska Press, 1988.

Bone, Arthur H., ed. *Oregon Cattleman/Governor, Congressman, Memoirs and Times of Walter M. Pierce*. Portland: Oregon Historical Society, 1981.

Bowers, Claude G. *Beveridge and the Progressive Era*. Cambridge, MA: Riverside Press, 1932.

Boyce, Everett Robert, ed. *The Unwanted Boy: The Autobiography of Governor Ben W. Hooper*. Knoxville: University of Tennessee Press, 1963.

Boyer, William W. *Governing Delaware: Policy Problems in the First State*. Newark: University of Delaware Press, 2000.

Brooks, Clayton McClure, ed. *A Legacy of Leadership: Governors and American History*. Philadelphia: University of Pennsylvania Press, 2008.

Brooks, Glenn E. *When Governors Convene: The Governors' Conference and National Politics*. Baltimore: John Hopkins University Press, 1961.

Browne, Waldo R. *Altgeld of Illinois*. New York: B. W. Huebsch, 1924.

Bruce, Andrew A. *Nonpartisan League*. New York: Macmillan, 1921.

Bryant, Keith L., Jr. *Alfalfa Bill Murray*. Norman: University of Oklahoma Press, 1968.

Bryce, James. *The American Commonwealth*. Philadelphia: J. D. Morris and Co., 1906.

Buck, A. E. *The Reorganization of State Governments in the United States*. New York: Morningside Heights, 1938.

Buenker, John D. *Urban Liberalism and Progressive Reform*. New York: Charles Scribner's Sons, 1973.

Burckel, Nicholas C. "From Beckham to McCreary: The Progressive Record of Kentucky Governors." *Register of the Kentucky Historical Society* 76 (October 1978): 285–306.

Burckel, Nicholas C. "Progressive Governors in the Border States: Reform Governors of Missouri, Kentucky, West Virginia, and Maryland." PhD diss., University of Wisconsin, 1971.

Burdick, Usher L. *History of Farmers' Political Action in North Dakota*. Baltimore, MD: Wirth Brothers, 1944.

Burns, Michael. "The Legislative Reference Movement in Ohio: From Progressive Ideal to Session Satisfying." *University of Toledo Law Review* 32 (Summer 2001): 485–507.

Burton, Robert E. *Democrats of Oregon: The Pattern of Minority Politics, 1900–1956*. Eugene: University of Oregon, 1970.

Burts, Robert Milton. *Richard Irvine Manning and the Progressive Movement in South Carolina*. Columbia: University of South Carolina Press, 1974.

Casdorph, Paul D. *Republicans, Negroes, and Progressivism in the South, 1912–1916*. University: University of Alabama Press, 1981.

Cash, W. J. *The Mind of the South*. New York: Vintage Books, 1941.

Cesare, Austin T. "Connecticut and the Progressive Era, 1895–1920." MA thesis, Southern Connecticut State University, 2004.

Chan, Loren Briggs. *Sagebrush Statesman: Tasker L. Oddie of Nevada*. Reno: University of Nevada Press, 1973.

Cherny, Robert W. *Populism, Progressivism, and the Transformation of Nebraska Politics, 1885–1915*. Lincoln: University of Nebraska Press, 1981.

Chessman, G. Wallace. *Governor Theodore Roosevelt: The Albany Apprenticeship, 1898–1900.* Cambridge, MA: Harvard University Press, 1965.

Childs, Richard S. *Civic Victories.* New York: Harper and Brothers, 1952.

Childs, William R. *The Texas Railroad Commission.* College Station: Texas A&M University Press, 2005.

Chrislock, Carl H. *The Progressive Era in Minnesota, 1899–1918.* St Paul: Minnesota Historical Society, 1971.

Christman, Henry M., ed. *The Mind and Spirit of John Peter Altgeld: Selected Writings and Addresses.* Urbana: University of Illinois Press, 1960.

Clanton, O. Gene. *Kansas Populism.* Lawrence: University Press of Kansas, 1969.

Colburn, David R., and Richard K. Scher. *Florida's Gubernatorial Politics in the Twentieth Century.* Tallahassee: University Presses of Florida, 1980.

Coletta, Paolo E. *William Jennings Bryan.* Vol. 1. Lincoln: University of Nebraska Press, 1964.

Cook, James F. *The Governors of Georgia*, 3rd ed. Macon, GA: Mercer University Press, 2005.

Cooper, Jerry. *The Rise of the National Guard.* Lincoln: University of Nebraska Press, 1997.

Cooper, John Milton, Jr. "Why Wisconsin?" *Wisconsin Magazine of History* 87 (Spring 2004): 14–15.

Cotton, Alice R. "Robert Brodnax Glenn." *NCPedia.* https://www.ncpedia.org/biography/glenn-robert-brodnax.

Coursey, O. W. *Who's Who in South Dakota.* Vol. 2. Mitchell, SD: Educator Supply, 1916.

Cox, James M. *Journey through My Years.* New York: Simon and Schuster, 1946.

Cozzone, Chris. "Boxing in New Mexico." *NewMexicoHistory.org.* http://newmexicohistory.org/people/boxing-in-new-mexico.

CQ Guide to U.S. Elections, 5th ed. Washington, DC: Congressional Quarterly Press, 2005.

Crandlemere, Cynthia. "Edward Hull Crump: A Political History." *Bridgewater Review* 5 (1987): 11–14. http://vc.bridgew.edu/br_rev/vol5/iss2/7.

Crew, Robert E., Jr. "Gubernatorial Leadership: Testing a Preliminary Model." *Social Science Journal* 35, no. 1 (1998): 15–27.

Crooks, James B. *Politics and Progress: The Rise of Urban Progressivism in Baltimore, 1895 to 1911.* Baton Rouge: Louisiana State University Press, 1968.

Crow, Jeffrey J., and Robert F. Durden. *Maverick Republican in the Old North State: A Political Biography of Daniel L. Russell.* Baton Rouge: Louisiana State University Press, 1977.

Danelski, David J., and Joseph S. Tulchin, eds. *The Autobiographical Notes of Charles Evans Hughes.* Cambridge, MA: Harvard University Press, 1973.

Dennis, Michael. *Lessons in Progress, State Universities and Progressivism in the New South, 1880–1920.* Urbana: University of Illinois Press, 2001.

Deverell, William. "The Varieties of Progressive Experience." In *California Progressivism Revisited*, ed. William Deverell and Tom Sitton, 1–11. Berkeley: University of California Press, 1994.

De Vou, Mary R. "Delaware." In *The History of Woman Suffrage.* Vol. 6, ed. Ida Husted Harper, 86–103. New York: J. J. Little and Ives, 1922.

De Witt, Benjamin Parke. *The Progressive Movement: A Non-Partisan, Comprehensive Discussion of Current Tendencies in American Politics.* Seattle: University of Washington Press, 1968. Originally published in 1915.

Dittmer, John. *Black Georgia in the Progressive Era, 1900–1920.* Urbana: University of Illinois Press, 1977.

Douglass, William A., and Robert A. Nylen, eds. *Letters from the Nevada Frontier: Correspondence of Tasker L. Oddie, 1898–1902.* Norman: University of Oklahoma Press, 1992.

Dowdy, G. Wayne. *Mayor Crump Don't Like It: Machine Politics in Memphis.* Jackson: University Press of Mississippi, 2006.

Duffy, John J., Samuel B. Hand, and Ralph H. Orth, eds. *The Vermont Encyclopedia.* Lebanon, NH: University Press of New England, 2003.

Dulles, Foster Rhea, and Melvin Dubofsky. *Labor in America: A History,* 4th ed. Arlington Heights, IL: Harlan Davidson, 1984.

Eaton, Allen H. *The Oregon System.* Chicago: A. C. McClurg, 1912.

Elliot, Russell R. *History of Nevada,* 2nd rev. ed. Lincoln: University of Nebraska Press, 1987.

Erickson, Nels. *The Gentleman from North Dakota: Lynn J. Frazier.* Bismarck: State Historical Society of North Dakota, 1986.

Faulkner, Harold Underwood. *The Quest for Social Justice, 1898–1914.* New York: Macmillan, 1931.

Feldman, H. "The Direct Primary in New York State." *American Political Science Review* 11 (August 1, 1917): 494–518.

Fenton, John H. *Midwest Politics.* New York: Holt, Rinehart, and Winston, 1966.

Ferrell, Henry C., Jr. *Claude A. Swanson: A Political Biography.* Lexington: University Press of Kentucky, 1985.

Filler, Louis. "Movements to Abolish the Death Penalty in the United States." *Annals of the American Academy of Politics and Social Science* (November 1952): 124–36.

Finan, Christopher M. *Alfred E. Smith: The Happy Warrior.* New York: Hill and Wang, 2002.

Fishback, Price V., Rebecca Holmes, and Samuel Allen. "Lifting the Curse of Dimensionality: Measures of the State's Labor Legislation Climate in the United States during the Progressive Era." *Labor History* 50, no. 3 (August 2009): 313–46.

Fite, Gilbert Courtland. *Peter Norbeck: Prairie Statesman.* Pierre: South Dakota State Historical Society Press, 2005. Originally published in 1948.

Flint, Winston Allen. *The Progressive Movement in Vermont.* Washington, DC: American Council on Public Affairs, 1941.

Flynt, Wayne. *Cracker Messiah: Governor Sidney J. Catts of Florida.* Baton Rouge: Louisiana State University Press, 1977.

Folsom, Burton W., Jr. *No More Free Markets or Free Beer: The Progressive Era in Nebraska, 1900–1924.* Lanham, MD: Lexington Books, 1999.

Fortenberry, Charles N., and F. Glenn Abney. "Mississippi, Unreconstructed and Unredeemed." In *The Changing Politics of the South,* ed. William C. Havard, 472–524. Baton Rouge: Louisiana State University Press, 1972.

Fox, Jean M. *"I Went to the People . . .": Fred M. Warner, Progressive Governor.* Farmington Hills, MI: Farmington Hills Historical Commission, 1988.

Fritz, Percy Stanley. *Colorado: The Centennial State.* New York: Prentice-Hall, 1941.

Gable, John Allen. *The Bull Moose Years: Theodore Roosevelt and the Progressive Party.* Port Washington, NY: Kennikat Press, 1978.

Galderisi, Peter F., Michael S. Lyons, Randy T. Simmons, and John G. Francis, eds. *The Politics of Realignment: Party Change in the Mountain West.* Boulder, CO: Westview Press, 1987.

Galliher, John F., Gregory Ray, and Brent Cook. "Abolition and Reinstatement of Capital Punishment during the Progressive Era and Early Twentieth Century." *Northwestern School of Law Journal of Criminal Law and Criminology* 83 (Fall 1992): 538–76.

Gantt, Fred, Jr. *The Chief Executive in Texas: A Study in Gubernatorial Leadership*. Austin: University of Texas Press, 1964.

Geer, T. T. *Fifty Years in Oregon*. New York: Neal Publishing, 1912.

Geiger, Louis G. *Joseph W. Folk of Missouri*. Columbia: Curators of the University of Missouri, 1953.

George, Alexander L., and Juliette L. George. *Woodrow Wilson and Colonel House: A Personality Study*. New York: Dover Publications, 1964.

Ginger, Ray. *Altgeld's America*. Chicago, IL: Quadrangle Books, 1958.

Glaab, Charles N. "John Burke and the North Dakota Progressive Movement, 1906–1912." MA thesis, University of North Dakota, 1952.

Glaab, Charles N. "John Burke and the Progressive Revolt." In *The North Dakota Political Tradition*, ed. Thomas W. Howard, 40–65. Ames: Iowa State University Press, 1981.

Glashan, Roy R., comp. *American Governors and Gubernatorial Elections, 1775–1978*. Westport, CT: Meckler Books, 1979.

Goble, Danney. *Progressive Oklahoma: The Making of a New Kind of State*. Norman: University of Oklahoma Press, 1980.

Godshalk, David Fort. *The 1906 Atlanta Race Riot and the Reshaping of American Race Relations*. Chapel Hill: University of North Carolina Press, 2005.

Goebel, Thomas. *A Government by the People: Direct Democracy in America, 1890–1940*. Chapel Hill: University of North Carolina Press, 2002.

Goldfarb, Stephen J. "The Slaton Memorandum: A Governor Looks Back at His Decision to Commute the Death Sentence of Leo Frank." *American Jewish History* 88 (2000): 325–39.

Goodwin, Lawrence. *The Populist Moment*. New York: Oxford University Press, 1978.

Gosnell, Harold F. *Boss Platt and His New York Machine*. Chicago: University of Chicago Press, 1924.

Gould, Lewis L. "Progressive Era." *Handbook of Texas Online*. https://tshaonline.org/handbook/online/articles/npp01.

Gould, Lewis L. *Progressives and Prohibitionists: Texas Democrats in the Wilson Era*. Austin: University of Texas Press, 1973.

Grantham, Dewey W., Jr. *Hoke Smith and the Politics of the New South*. Baton Rouge: Louisiana State University Press, 1958.

Grantham, Dewey, W., Jr. *Southern Progressivism: The Reconciliation of Progress and Tradition*. Knoxville: University of Tennessee Press, 1983.

Graves, W. Brooke. *American State Government*, 4th ed. Boston: D. C. Heath, 1953.

Green, James. *The Devil Is Here in These Hills: West Virginia's Coal Miners and Their Battle for Freedom*. New York: Atlantic Monthly Press, 2015.

Griffiths, David B. "Populism in the Far West, 1890–1900." PhD diss., University of Washington, 1967.

Griffiths, David B. *Populism in the Western United States, 1890–1900*. Vol. 1. Lewiston, NY: Edwin Mellen Press, 1992.

Gross, Donald A. "Governors and Policymaking: Theoretical Concerns and Analytic Approaches." *Policy Studies Journal* 17 (Summer 1989): 764–87.

Gubernatorial Elections, 1787–1997. Washington, DC: Congressional Quarterly, 1998.

Gunn, John W. "Awakening of Farmers Is Shown in Growth of Nonpartisan League." *Appeal to Reason*, September 6, 1919, n.p.

Gunther, John. *Inside U.S.A.* New York: Harper and Brothers, 1947.

Hahn, Harlan. *Urban-Rural Conflict: The Politics of Change*. Beverly Hills, CA: Sage Publications, 1971.

Hainsworth, Brad E. "Utah State Elections, 1916–1924." PhD diss., University of Utah, 1968.

Haller, Mark H. *Eugenics*. New Brunswick, NJ: Rutgers University Press, 1963.

Hamilton, John J. *The Dethronement of the City Boss*. Freeport, NY: Books for Libraries Press, 1971. Originally published in 1910.

Hand, Samuel B. *The Star That Set: The Vermont Republican Party, 1854–1974*. Lanham, MD: Lexington Books, 2002.

Hand, Samuel B., Jeffrey D. Marshall, and D. Gregory Sanford. "'Little Republics': The Structure of State Politics in Vermont, 1854–1920." *Vermont History* 53 (1985): 141–66.

Harlow, Victor E., and Arrell M. Gibson. *Harlow's Oklahoma History*, 5th ed. Norman, OK: Harlow Publishing, 1967.

Harper, Ida Husted, ed. *The History of Woman Suffrage*. Vols. 5 and 6. New York: J. J. Little and Ives, 1922.

Harris, David Alan. "Braxton Bragg Comer, 1907–1911." In *Alabama Governors*, ed. Samuel L. Webb and Margaret E. Armbrester, 175–81. Tuscaloosa: University of Alabama Press, 2001.

Haas, Edward F. "Bourbonism, Populism, and a Little Progressivism, 1892–1924." In *Louisiana: A History*, 6th ed., ed. Bennett H. Wall and John C. Rodrigue, 256–79. Chichester, UK: Wiley-Blackwell, 2013.

Heffernan, Nancy Coffey, and Ann Page Stecker. *New Hampshire: Crosscurrents in Its Development*, 3rd ed. Hanover, NH: University Press of New England, 2004.

Heinemann, Ronald L. "Andrew Jackson Montague (1862–1937)." *Encyclopedia Virginia*. http://www.EncyclopediaVirginia.org/Montague_Andrew_Jackson_1862–1937.

Helms, Winifred G. *John A. Johnson, The People's Governor: A Political Biography*. Minneapolis: University of Minnesota Press, 1949.

Henning, H. B., ed. *George Curry, 1861–1947: An Autobiography*. Albuquerque: University of New Mexico Press, 1958.

Hicks, John D. *The Populist Revolt*. Lincoln: University of Nebraska Press, 1961. Originally published in 1931.

Hill, Michael. "Thomas Walter Bickett, Governor: 1917–1921." *NCPedia*. http://ncpedia.org/biography/governors/bickett.

Hill, Michael. "William Walton Kitchen." *NCPedia*. https://www.ncpedia.org/biography/governors/kitchin.

Hirst, David W. *Woodrow Wilson, Reform Governor*. New York: D. Van Nostrand, 1965.

"History of Direct Democracy in Delaware." *Ballotpedia*. https://ballotpedia.org/History_of_direct_democracy_in_Delaware.

Hohenstein, Kurt. *Curbing Corruption: The Making of the American Campaign Finance System*. DeKalb: Northern Illinois University Press, 2007.

Holcombe, Arthur N. "Organizing Democracy." *New Republic*, July 7, 1917, 268–71.

Holli, Melvin G. *Reform in Detroit: Hazen S. Pingree and Urban Politics.* New York: Oxford University Press, 1969.

Hollingsworth, J. Rogers. *The Whirligig of Politics: The Democracy of Cleveland and Bryan.* Chicago: University of Chicago Press, 1963.

Holmes, William F. *The White Chief: James Kimble Vardaman.* Baton Rouge: Louisiana State University Press, 1970.

Hormell, Orren. *Maine Public Utilities.* Municipal Research Series 7. Brunswick, ME: Bowdoin College, Bureau for Research in Municipal Government, 1927.

Howe, Edward T., and Donald J. Reeb. "The Historical Evolution of State and Local Tax Systems." *Social Science Quarterly* 78, no. 1 (March 1997): 109–21.

Hoy, Suellen Monica. "Samuel M. Ralston: Progressive Governor, 1913–1917." PhD diss., Indiana University, 1975.

Hunt, George W.P. "National Control of Mineral Resources." In *Proceedings of the Conference of Western Governors Held at Salt Lake City, Utah, June 6. 7, 1913*, 17–18. Denver, CO: Smith-Brooks Printing, 1913.

Hunt George W.P. "The Single Legislative Branch." *Welfare: A Journal of Social Progress* (October 1913): 11.

Hunter, Carey J. "Governor Kitchin: The Man and the Principles That Guide Him." *Carolina Democrat*, December, 22, 1911. http://digital.ncdcr.gov/cdm/ref/collection/p249901coll37/id/3617.

Isaac, Paul E. "The Problems of a Republican Governor in a Southern State: Ben Hooper of Tennessee, 1910–1914." *Tennessee Historical Quarterly* 27, no. 3 (Fall 1968): 229–48.

Jackson, Frederick H. *Simon Eben Baldwin.* New York: King's Court Press, Columbia University, 1955.

Jensen, Christen. *The Pardoning Power in the American States.* Chicago: University of Chicago Press, 1922.

Jensen, Richard. *The Winning of the Midwest.* Chicago: University of Chicago Press, 1971.

Johansen, Dorothy O., and Charles M. Gates. *Empire of the Columbia: A History of the Pacific Northwest*, 2nd ed. New York: Harper and Row, 1967.

Johnson, Christopher R. *The Governors of North Dakota.* Minot, ND: J&B Entertainment, 1994.

Johnson, Hiram. "First Inaugural Address." January 3, 1911. *Governors' Gallery.* http://governors.library.ca.gov/addresses/23-hjohnson01.html.

Johnson, Robert D. *The Radical Middle Class.* Princeton, NJ: Princeton University Press, 2003.

Johnson, Tom L. *My Story.* Edited by Elizabeth J. Hauser. New York: B. W. Huebsch, 1911.

Jonas, Frank H., ed. *Politics in the American West.* Salt Lake City: University of Utah Press, 1969.

Jonas, Frank H. "Utah: The Different State." In *Politics in the American West*, ed. Frank H. Jonas, 326–79. Salt Lake City: University of Utah Press, 1969.

Jones, Alton DuMar. "The Administration of Governor Joseph M. Terrell Viewed in the Light of the Progressive Movement." *Georgia Historical Quarterly* 48, no. 3 (September 1964): 271–90.

Kantrowitz, Stephen. *Ben Tillman and the Reconstruction of White Supremacy.* Chapel Hill: The University of North Carolina Press, 2000.

Karr, Carolyn M. "Henry D. Hatfield." *The West Virginia Encyclopedia.* http://www.wvencyclopedia.org/articles/280.

Kaufman, Herbert. "Emerging Conflicts in Doctrines of Public Administration." *American Political Science Review* 50, no. 4 (December 1956): 1057–73.

Kaufman, Herbert. *Politics and Policies in State and Local Government*. Englewood Cliffs, NJ: Prentice Hall, 1963.

Kaylor, Earl C., Jr. *Martin Grove Brumbaugh*. Madison, PA: Fairleigh Dickenson University Press, 1996.

Key, V. O., Jr. *Southern Politics in State and Nation*. New York: Alfred A. Knopf, 1950.

Keyssar, Alexander. *The Right to Vote: The Contested History of Democracy in the United States*. New York: Basic Books, 2000.

Kirby, Jack Temple. *Darkness at the Dawning: Race and Reform in the Progressive South*. Philadelphia: J. B. Lippincott, 1972.

Kleppner, Paul. "Voters and Parties in the Western States, 1876–1900." *Western Historical Quarterly* 14 (January 1982): 49–68.

Klotter, James C. "William Goebel." In *Kentucky's Governors*, ed. Lowell H. Harrison, 134–36. Lexington: University of Kentucky Press, 2004.

Koenig, Louis W. *Bryan: A Political Biography of William Jennings Bryan*. New York: G. P. Putnam's, 1971.

Kolko, Gabriel. *Railroads and Regulation, 1877–1916*. Princeton, NJ: Princeton University Press, 1965.

La Follette, Robert M. *La Follette's Autobiography*. Madison: University of Wisconsin Press, 1960.

La Forte, Robert Sherman. *Leaders of Reform: Progressive Republicans in Kansas, 1900–1916*. Lawrence: University Press of Kansas, 1974.

Lambert, Louis E. "The Executive Article." In *Major Problems in State Constitutional Revision*, ed. W. Brooke Graves, 185–99. Chicago: Public Administration Service, 1960.

Larsen, William. "Andrew Jackson Montague: Virginia's First Progressive." In *The Governors of Virginia, 1860–1978*, ed. Edward Younger and James Moore, 159–69. Charlottesville: University Press of Virginia, 1982.

Larsen, William. *Montague of Virginia: The Making of a Southern Progressive*. Baton Rouge: Louisiana State University Press, 1965.

Larson, T. A. *History of Wyoming*. Lincoln: University of Nebraska Press, 1978.

Laugen, R. Todd. *The Gospel of Progressivism: Moral Reform and Labor Wars in Colorado, 1900–1930*. Boulder: University Press of Colorado, 2010.

Ledbetter, Calvin R., Jr. *Carpenter from Conway: George Washington Donaghey as Governor of Arkansas, 1909–1913*. Fayetteville: University of Arkansas, Press, 1993.

Leff, Mark H. "Consensus for Reform: The Mothers' Pension Movement in the Progressive Era." *Social Science Review* 47 (September 1973): 397–417.

Leonard, Stephen J., Thomas J. Noel, and Donald L. Walker Jr. *Honest John Shafroth*. Denver: Colorado Historical Society, 2003.

Lewis, J. Anthony. *Big Trouble*. New York: Simon and Schuster, 1997.

Link, Arthur S. "Portrait of the President." In *The Philosophy and Policies of Woodrow Wilson*, ed. Earl Latham, 3–27. Chicago: University of Chicago Press, 1958.

Link, Arthur S., ed. *The Papers of Woodrow Wilson*. Vols. 16, 22, 23, and 24. Princeton, NJ: Princeton University Press, 1974–1977.

Link, Arthur S., and Richard L. McCormick. *Progressivism*. Arlington Heights, IL: Harland Davidson, 1983.

Lipson, Leslie. *The American Governor from Figurehead to Leader*. Chicago: University of Chicago Press, 1939.

Lisenby, Foy. *Charles Hillman Brough: A Biography*. Fayetteville: University of Arkansas Press, 1996.

Lisenby, Foy. "Charles Hillman Brough." In *The Governors of Arkansas: Essays in Political Biography*, ed. Timothy P. Donovan, Willard B. Gatewood Jr., and Jeannie M. Whayne, 150–56. Fayetteville: University of Arkansas Press, 1995.

Lockard, Duane. *The New Jersey Governor: A Study in Political Power*. Princeton, NJ: D. Van Nostrand, 1964.

Lombardo, Paul A., ed. *Century of Eugenics in America*. Bloomington: Indiana University Press, 2011.

Lough, Alexandra W. "Hazen S. Pingree and the Detroit Model of Urban Reform." *American Journal of Economics and Sociology* 75, no. 1 (January 2016): 58–85.

Lovejoy, Allen Fraser. *La Follette and the Establishment of the Direct Primary in Wisconsin, 1890–1904*. New Haven, CT: Yale University Press, 1941.

Lovin, Hugh T. "The Farmer Revolt in Idaho, 1914–1922." *Idaho Yesterdays* (Fall 1976): 4–15.

Lower, Richard Coke. *A Bloc of One: The Political Career of Hiram W. Johnson*. Stanford, CA: Stanford University Press, 1993.

Lowitt, Richard. *Bronson M. Cutting: Progressive Politician*. Albuquerque: University of New Mexico Press, 1992.

Luconi, Stefano. *The Italian-American Vote in Providence, Rhode Island, 1916–1948*. Vancouver, British Columbia: Fairleigh Dickinson University Press, 2004.

Macdonald, Austin F. "American Governors." *National Municipal Review* 16, no. 11 (November 1927): 715–19.

Macdonald, Austin F. *State and Local Government in the United States*. New York: Thomas Y. Crowell, 1955.

Macmahon, Arthur W. "Woodrow Wilson: Political Leader and Administrator." In *The Philosophy and Policies of Woodrow Wilson*, ed. Earl Latham, 100–122. Chicago: University of Chicago Press, 1958.

Magruder, Nathaniel F. "Thomas Walter Bickett, 1869–1921." *Documenting the American South*. http://docsouth.unc.edu/wwi/bickettashe/bio.html.

Malone, Michael P. *The Battle for Butte*. Seattle: University of Washington Press, 1981.

Marcosson, Isaac F. "Bass of New Hampshire." *Munsey's Magazine*, February 1911, 624–30.

Margulies, Herbert F. *The Decline of the Progressive Movement in Wisconsin, 1890–1920*. Madison: State Historical Society of Wisconsin, 1968.

Marshall, Thomas R. *Recollections of Thomas R. Marshall*. Indianapolis, IN: Bobbs-Merrill, 1925.

Martin, Boyd A. "Idaho: The Sectional State." In *Politics in the American West*, ed. Frank H. Jonas, 181–200. Salt Lake City: University of Utah Press, 1969.

Martin, Ralph G. *Ballots and Bandwagons*. New York: New American Library, 1964.

Mason, Mary Ann. "Neither Friends nor Foes, Organized Labor and the California Progressives." In *California Progressivism Revisited*, ed. William Deverell and Tom Sitton, 57–71. Berkeley: University of California Press, 1994.

Mathews, John M. "The New Role of the Governor." *American Political Science Review* 6 (1912): 216–38.

Mathews, John M. "The New Stateism." *North American Review* 193 (June 1911): 808–15.

Maxwell, Robert S. *La Follette and the Rise of the Progressives in Wisconsin*. New York: Russell and Russell, 1973. Originally printed in 1956.

McCarthy, Michael G. "Colorado's Populist Party and the Progressive Movement." *Journal of the West* 15 (January 1976): 54–75.

McCluskey, H. S., comp. *Compiled Messages of Geo. W. P. Hunt and Thos. E. Campbell, Governors of Arizona from 1912 to 1923 Inclusive*. Phoenix, AZ: N.p., 1924.

McCormick, Richard L. *From Realignment to Reform: Political Change in New York State, 1893–1910*. Ithaca, NY: Cornell University Press, 1981.

McCulley, Richard T. *Banks and Politics during the Progressive Era*. New York: Garland Publishing, 1992.

McGee, W. J. *Proceedings of a Conference of Governors in the White House, Washington, D.C., May 13–15, 1908*. New York: Arno Press, 1972.

McGerr, Michael. *A Fierce Discontent: The Rise and Fall of the Progressive Movement in America, 1870–1920*. New York: Free Press, 2003.

McLean, Joseph E. "Early Modern Governor." *National Municipal Review* 46 (January 1957): 20–22.

Meany, Edmond S. *Governors of Washington, Territorial and State*. Seattle: University of Washington, 1915. https://www.sos.wa.gov/library/publications_detail.aspx?p=30.

Mehrotra, Ajay K., and David Shreve. "'To Lay and Collect': Governors, Fiscal Federalism, and the Political Economy of Twentieth-Century Tax Policy." In *A Legacy of Innovation: Governors and Public Policy*, ed. Ethan G. Sribnick, 48–75. Philadelphia: University of Pennsylvania Press, 2013.

Merrill, Horace Samuel. *Bourbon Democracy of the Middle West, 1865–1896*. Baton Rouge: Louisiana State University Press, 1953.

Miller, William D. *Mr. Crump of Memphis*. Baton Rouge: Louisiana State University Press, 1964.

Millspaugh, Arthur, C. "Direct Primary Legislation in Michigan." *Michigan Law Review* 15, no. 1 (November 1916): 21–37.

Moley, Raymond. "Knight of Nonpartisanship: Earl Warren." In *The Politics of California: A Book of Readings*, ed. David Farrelly and Ivan Hinderaker, 220–28. New York: Ronald Press, 1951.

Moody, Eric N. "Nevada's Bull Moose Progressives: The Formation and Function of a State Political Party in 1912." *Nevada Historical Society Quarterly* 16, no. 3 (Fall 1973): 157–79.

Moore, Waddy W. "George Washington Donaghey." In *The Governors of Arkansas: Essays in Political Biography*, ed. Timothy P. Donovan, Willard B. Gatewood Jr., and Jeannie M. Whayne, 134–38. Fayetteville: University of Arkansas Press, 1995.

Morlan, Robert L. *Political Prairie Fire*. Minneapolis: University of Minnesota Press, 1955.

Morton, Richard Allen. *Justice and Humanity: Edward F. Dunne, Illinois Progressive*. Carbondale: Southern Illinois University Press, 1997.

Munroe, John A. *History of Delaware*, 4th ed. Newark: University of Delaware Press, 2001.

Musslewhite, Lynn, and Suzanne Jones Crawford. *One Woman's Political Journey: Kate Barnard and Social Reform, 1875–1930*. Norman: University of Oklahoma Press, 2003.

Nevins, Allen, ed. *Letters of Grover Cleveland, 1850–1908*. Boston: Houghton Mifflin, 1933.

"The New Governors: A General Survey of Their Personal and Political Characteristics." *The Outlook*, January 2, 1897, 35–45.

Newton, Earl E. *The Vermont Story*. Burlington, VT: Lane Press, 1949.

Noble, David W. *The Progressive Mind, 1890–1917*. Minneapolis, MN: Burgess Publishing, 1981.

Noble, Ransom E., Jr. *New Jersey before Wilson*. Princeton, NJ: Princeton University Press, 1946.

Nolette, Paul. "Litigating the 'Public Interest' in the Gilded Age: Common Law Business Regulation by Nineteenth-Century State Attorneys General." *Polity* 44 (2012): 373–99.

Norbeck, Peter. "For the Whole Family, South Dakota's Sane Legislation Helps Ambitious Farmers to Succeed." *Country Gentleman*, February 14, 1920, n.p.

"Notable Oregonians: Oswald West—Governor." *Oregon Blue Book*. http://bluebook.state.or.us/notable/notwest.htm.

Nye, Russel B. *Midwestern Progressive Politics*. East Lansing: Michigan State University Press, 1959.

Olin, Spencer C., Jr. *California's Prodigal Sons: Hiram Johnson and the Progressives*. Berkeley: University of California Press, 1968.

Olson, James C., Ronald C. Naugle, and John J. Montag, eds. *History of Nebraska*, 4th ed. Lincoln: University of Nebraska Press, 2015.

"Oregon History: The Oregon System." *Oregon Blue Book*. https://sos.oregon.gov/blue-book/Pages/facts/history/state-oregon.aspx.

Orr, Oliver H., Jr. *Charles Brantley Aycock*. Chapel Hill: University of North Carolina Press, 1961.

Osborn, Chase S. *Iron Hunter*. Detroit, MI: Wayne State University Press, 2002.

"Oswald West (1873–1960)." *Oregon History Project*. https://oregonhistoryproject.org/articles/historical-records/oswald-west-1873-1960/#.XENSHLj_DMA.

Pegram, Thomas R. *Partisans and Progressives, Private Interests and Public Policy in Illinois, 1870–1922*. Urbana: University of Illinois Press, 1992.

Peirce, Neal R. *The New England States*. New York: W. W. Norton, 1976.

Pennypacker, Samuel W. *The Autobiography of a Pennsylvanian*. Philadelphia: J. C. Winston, 1918.

Percy, William Alexander. *Lanterns on the Levee: Recollections of a Planter's Son*. New York: Alfred A. Kopf, 1941.

Perman, Michael. "Joseph F. Johnston, 1896–1900." In *Alabama Governors*, ed. Samuel L. Webb and Margaret E. Armbrester, 149–56. Tuscaloosa: University of Alabama Press, 2001.

Peters, Betsy Ross. "Joseph M. Carey and the Progressive Movement in Wyoming." PhD diss., University of Wyoming, 1971.

Peterson, Charles S., and Brian Q. Cannon. *The Awkward State of Utah: Coming of Age in the Nation 1896–1945*. Salt Lake City: University of Utah Press, 2015.

Peterson, F. Ross. *Idaho: A Bicentennial History*. New York: W. W. Norton, 1976.

Phelan, Craig. *Grand Master Workman: Terence Powderly and the Knights of Labor*. Westport, CT: Greenwood Press, 2000.

Pickens, Donald K. *Eugenics and the Progressives*. Nashville, TN: Vanderbilt University Press, 1968.

Pillsbury, Samuel H. "Understanding Penal Reform: The Dynamic of Change." *Northwestern School of Law Journal of Criminal Law and Criminology* 803 (Fall 1989): 726–80.

Piott, Steven L. *Giving Voters a Voice: The Origins of the Initiative and Referendum in America*. Columbia: University of Missouri Press, 2003.

Piott, Steven L. *Holy Joe: Joseph W. Folk and the Missouri Idea.* Columbia: University of Missouri Press, 1997.

Postel, Charles. *The Populist Vision.* New York: Oxford University Press, 2007.

Proceedings of the Conference of Western Governors, Held at Denver, Colorado, April 7, 8, 9, 10, and 11, 1914. Denver: Smith-Brooks Printing, 1914.

Proceedings of the Conference of Western Governors, Held at Salt Lake City, Utah, June 6, 7, 1913. Denver: Smith-Brooks Printing, 1913.

Proceedings of the Conference of Western Governors, Held at Seattle, Washington, May 18, 19, and 20, 1915, and at Portland, Oregon, September 22, 1915. Olympia, WA: Frank M. Lamborn, 1916.

Proctor, Samuel. *Napoleon Bonaparte Broward: Florida's Fighting Democrat.* Gainesville: University of Florida Press, 1950.

Pulley, Raymond H. *Old Virginia Restored: An Interpretation of the Progressive Impulse, 1870–1930.* Charlottesville: University Press of Virginia, 1968.

Pusey, Merlo J. *Charles Evans Hughes.* Vol. 1. New York: Macmillan, 1951.

Putnam, Jackson K. "The Progressive Legacy in California." In *California Progressivism Revisited*, ed. William Deverell and Tom Sitton, 247–68. Berkeley: University of California Press, 1994.

Ranney, Austin. *Cursing the Mischiefs of Faction: Party Reform in America.* Berkeley: University of California Press, 1975.

Ransone, Coleman B., Jr. *The Office of Governor in the South.* University: Bureau of Public Administration, University of Alabama, 1951.

Ransone, Coleman B., Jr. *The Office of Governor in the United States.* University: University of Alabama Press, 1956.

Reiter, Howard L. "The Bases of Progressivism within the Major Parties." *Social Science History* 22 (Spring 1998): 83–116.

Remele, Larry. "Power to the People: The Nonpartisan League." In *The North Dakota Political Tradition*, ed. Thomas W. Howard, 66–92. Ames: Iowa State University Press, 1981.

Reynolds, John F. *Testing Democracy: Electoral Behavior and Progressive Reform in New Jersey, 1880–1920.* Chapel Hill: University of North Carolina Press, 1988.

Rice, Bradley Robert. *Progressive Cities: The Commission Government Movement in America, 1901–1920.* Austin: University of Texas Press, 1977.

Richards, Alan R. "Half of Our Century." In *The Fifty States and Their Governments*, ed. James W. Fesler. New York: Alfred A. Knopf, 1967.

Richardson, James D. *A Compilation of the Messages and Papers of the Presidents, 1780–1897.* Vols. 8 and 9. Washington, DC: Government Printing Office, 1898.

Riddle, Thomas W. *The Old Radicalism: John R. Rogers and the Populist Movement in Washington.* New York: Garland Publishing, 1991.

Ridge, Martin. *Ignatius Donnelly: The Portrait of a Politician.* St. Paul: Minnesota Historical Society Press, 1991.

Robb, Thomas Bruce. *The Guaranty of Bank Deposits.* Boston: Houghton Mifflin, 1921.

Robbins, William G. "George Chamberlain (1854–1928)." *Oregon Encyclopedia.* https://oregon encyclopedia.org/articles/chamberlain_george_1854_1928_/#.V-2A6sLrvIU.

Robinson, Elwyn B. *History of North Dakota.* Lincoln: University of Nebraska Press, 1966.

Robinson, W. A. "The Governors in 1917." *New Republic*, March 3, 1917, 127–29.

Rodgers, Daniel T. "In Search of Progressivism." *Reviews in American History* 10 (December 1982): 113–32.

Roeder, Richard B. "Montana Progressivism, Sound and Fury—and One Small Tax Reform." In *Montana's Past: Selected Essays*, ed. Michael P. Malone and Richard B. Roeder, 391–404. Missoula: University of Montana, 1973.

Rogin, Michael Paul, and John L. Shover. *Political Change in California: Critical Elections and Social Movements, 1896–1966*. Westport, CT: Greenwood Publishing, 1970.

Roosevelt, Theodore. "The Manly Virtues and Practical Politics." *Forum* (July 1894): 551–57.

Roosevelt, Theodore. *Theodore Roosevelt: An Autobiography*. New York: Charles Scribner's Sons, 1925.

Roosevelt, Theodore. "True American Ideals." *Forum* (February 1895): 743–50.

Roper, Donald M. "The Governorship in History." In *Governing New York State: The Rockefeller Years*, ed. Robert H. Connery and Gerald Benjamin, 16–30. New York: Academy of Political Science, 1974.

Roper, William L., and Leonard J. Arrington. *William Spry: Man of Firmness, Governor of Utah*. Salt Lake City: Utah State Historical Society and University of Utah Press, 1971.

Rosenburg, R. B. "Emmet O'Neal (1911–15)." In *Alabama Governors*, ed. Samuel L. Webb and Margaret E. Armbrester, 182–87. Tuscaloosa: University of Alabama Press, 2001.

Rothman, David J. *Conscience and Convenience: The Asylum and its Alternatives in Progressive America*. New York: Aldine, de Gruyter, 2002.

Sage, Leland L. *A History of Iowa*. Ames: Iowa State University Press, 1974.

Sarasohn, David. *The Party of Reform: Democrats in the Progressive Era*. Jackson: University of Mississippi Press, 1989.

Sarasohn, Stephen B., and Vera H. Sarasohn. *Political Party Patterns in Michigan*. Detroit, MI: Wayne State University Press, 1957.

Scales, James R., and Danney Goble. *Oklahoma Politics: A History*. Norman: University of Oklahoma Press, 1982.

Schlesinger, Joseph A. *How They Became Governor*. East Lansing: Governmental Research Bureau, Michigan State University, 1957.

Schmelzer, Janet. *Our Fighting Governor: The Life of Thomas M. Campbell and the Politics of Progressive Reform in Texas*. College Station: Texas A&M University Press, 2014.

Schott, Matthew J. "John Parker." *Encyclopedia of Louisiana*. https://www.knowlouisiana.org/entry/john-parker.

Schott, Matthew J. "Luther Hall." *Encyclopedia of Louisiana*. https://www.knowlouisiana.org/entry/luther-hall.

Schwantes, Carlos. A. *Coxey's Army: An American Odyssey*. Lincoln: University of Nebraska Press, 1985.

Shafroth, John F. "Imperative Need of Direct Legislation." *Twentieth Century Magazine* (September 1912): 516–19.

Shaw, Albert. "Theodore Roosevelt as Political Leader." In *The Works of Theodore Roosevelt, Memorial Edition*, ed. Hermann Hagedorn, 16:xi–xxxviii. New York: Charles Scribner's Sons, 1925.

Shefter, Mark. "Regional Receptivity to Reform: The Legacy of the Progressive Era." *Political Science Quarterly* 98 (Fall 1983): 471–76.

Shipps, Jan. "Utah Comes of Age Politically." *Utah Historical Quarterly* 35, no. 2 (Spring 1967): 91–111.

Simkins, Francis Butler. *Pitchfork Ben Tillman: South Carolinian.* Baton Rouge: Louisiana State University Press, 1944.

Skocpol, Theda, Marjorie Abend-Wein, Christopher Howard, and Susan Goodrich Lehmann. "Women's Associations and the Enactment of Mothers' Pensions in the United States." *American Political Science Review* 87 (September 1993): 686–701.

Smith, Alfred E. *Up to Now: An Autobiography.* New York: Viking Press, 1929.

Socolofsky, Homer E. *Arthur Capper: Publisher, Politician, and Philanthropist.* Lawrence: University of Kansas Press, 1962.

"Some Governors on Prison Reform." *The Review* 2 (March 1912): 2–18.

Southern, David W. *The Malignant Heritage: Yankee Progressives and the Negro Question 1901–1914.* Chicago: Loyola University Press, 1968.

Spargo, John. "Report of the Nonpartisan League of North Dakota and Various Other States," n.d. Socialist Party of America Papers, Reel 140, 6, Perkins Library.

"Speech of Hon. B. H. Roberts, Nominating Hon. Simon Bamberger for Governor of Utah." *Proceedings of the Democratic State Convention Held at Ogden, Utah, August 18, 1916,* 15–22. Salt Lake City: Century Printing, 1916.

Sribnick, Ethan G., ed. *A Legacy of Innovation: Governors and Public Policy.* Philadelphia: University of Pennsylvania Press, 2013.

Startt, James D. *Woodrow Wilson and the Press: Prelude to Presidency.* New York: Palgrave, Macmillan, 2004.

Steffens Lincoln. *The Shame of the Cities.* New York: Hill and Wang, 1957. Originally published in 1904.

Steffens, Lincoln. *The Struggle for Self-Government.* New York: Johnson Reprint, 1968. Originally published in 1906.

Steinberg, Alfred. *The Bosses.* New York: New American Library, 1972.

Stephenson, George M. *John Lind of Minnesota.* Port Washington, NY: Kennikat Press, 1971. Originally published in 1935.

Stonecash, Jeffrey M., Mark D. Brewer, R. Eric Peterson, and McGee Young. "Politics, Alfred Smith, and Increasing the Power of the New York Governor's Office." *New York History* 85, no. 2 (Spring 2004): 149–79.

Stromquuist, Shelton. *Reinventing "The People": The Progressive Movement, the Class Problem, and the Origins of Modern Liberalism.* Urbana: University of Illinois Press, 2006.

Swanberg, W. A. *Citizen Hearst.* New York: Bantam Books, 1971.

Thelen, David P. *The New Citizenship: Origins of Progressivism in Wisconsin, 1885–1900.* Columbia: University of Missouri Press, 1972.

Timberlake, James H. *Prohibition and the Progressive Movement, 1900–1920.* Cambridge, MA: Harvard University Press, 1963.

Tindall, George Brown. *The Emergence of the New South, 1913–1945.* Baton Rouge: Louisiana State University Press, 1967.

Toole, K. Ross. *Twentieth-Century Montana: A State of Extremes.* Norman: University of Oklahoma Press, 1972.

Trottman, Nelson. *History of the Union Pacific.* New York: Ronald Press, 1923.

Tucker, David M. *Mugwumps: Public Moralists of the Gilded Age.* Columbia: University of Missouri Press, 1998.

Tucker, Gary J. *Governor William E. Glasscock and Progressive Politics in West Virginia.* Morgantown: West Virginia University Press, 2008.

Tumulty, Joseph P. *Woodrow Wilson As I Know Him.* Garden City, NY: Garden City Publishing, 1925.

Unger, Nancy C. *Fighting Bob La Follette: The Righteous Reformer.* Chapel Hill: University of North Carolina Press, 2000.

Urban, Wayne J. "Progressive Education in the Urban South." In *The Age of Urban Reform: New Perspectives on the Progressive Era*, ed. Michael H. Ebner and Eugene M. Tobin, 131–41. Port Washington, NY: Kennikat Press, 1977.

Wagner, Robert L. "Charles A. Culberson." *Texas Politics Project.* https://texaspolitics.utexas.edu/archive/html/exec/governors/07.html.

Walker, Jack L., Jr. "The Diffusion of Innovations among the American States." *American Political Science Review* 63 (September 1969): 880–99.

Ware, Alan. *The American Direct Primary: Party Institutionalization and Transformation in the North.* Cambridge, UK: Cambridge University Press.

Warner, Hoyt Landon. *Progressivism in Ohio, 1897–1917.* Columbus: State University Press for the Ohio Historical Society, 1964.

Weatherson, Michael A., and Hal W. Bochin. *Hiram Johnson: A Bio-Bibliography.* New York: Greenwood Press, 1988.

Weatherson, Michael A., and Hal W. Bochin. *Hiram Johnson, Political Revivalist.* Lanham, MD: University Press of America, 1995.

Wetmore, Claude. *The Battle against Bribery.* St. Louis, MO: Pan-American Press, 1904.

Wheeler, Burton K., and Paul F. Healy. *Yankee from the West.* Garden City, NY: Doubleday, 1962.

White, Frank F., Jr. "Edward Warfield (1848–1920)." *Archives of Maryland, Biographical Series.* http://msa.maryland.gov/megafile/msa/speccol/sc3500/sc3520/001400/001476/html/1476bio2.html.

White, Frank F., Jr. *The Governors of Maryland, 1777–1970.* Annapolis, MD: The Hall of Records Commission, 1992.

White, Richard D., Jr. *Roosevelt the Reformer: Theodore Roosevelt as Civil Service Commissioner, 1889–1895.* Tuscaloosa: University of Alabama Press, 2003.

White, William Allen. "Free Kansas, Where the People Rule the People." *The Outlook*, February 24, 1912, 407–14.

White, William Allen. "Political Signs of Promise." *The Outlook*, July 15, 1905, 667–70.

Wilkins, Robert P. "Alexander McKenzie and the Politics of Bossism." In *The North Dakota Political Tradition*, ed. Thomas W. Howard, 3–39. Ames: Iowa State University Press, 1981.

Willoughby, William F. *The Movement for Budgetary Reform in the States.* New York: D. Appleton for the Institute of Government Research, 1918.

Wilson, Carol O'Keefe. *In the Governor's Shadow: The True Story of Ma and Pa Ferguson.* Denton: University of North Texas Press, 2014.

Wilson, Woodrow. "The Law and the Facts." *American Political Science Review* 5, no. 1 (February 1911): 1–11.

Wish, Harvey. "Altgeld and the Progressive Tradition." *American Historical Review* 46 (July 1941): 813–31.

Woodward, C. Vann. *Origins of the New South, 1877–1913.* Baton Rouge: Louisiana State University Press, 1971.

Wright, Deil S. "Executive Leadership in State Administration." *Midwest Journal of Political Science* 11, no. 1 (February 1967): 1–26.

Wright, James Edward. *The Politics of Populism: Dissent in Colorado*. New Haven, CT: Yale University Press, 1974.

Wright, James. *The Progressive Yankees: Republican Reformers in New Hampshire, 1906–1916*. Hanover, NH: University Press of New England, 1987.

Yellowwitz, Irwin. *Labor and the Progressive Movement in New York State, 1897–1916*. Ithaca, NY: Cornell University Press, 1965.

Zainaldin, Jamil S., and John C. Inscoe. "Progressive Era." *New Georgia Encyclopedia*. http://www.georgiaencyclopedia.org/articles/history-archaeology/progressive-era.

INDEX

Abbeville (SC), 100
Abrams, Richard, 196
Adams, Alva, 237, 271n20, 271n21
Addams, Jane, 39
Addicks, J. Edward, 186
African Americans (blacks, negroes), 28, 31, 33, 77, 94, 96, 97, 98, 99, 100, 101, 102, 105, 106, 107, 110, 117, 118, 120, 121, 122, 123, 125, 128, 129, 134, 135, 136, 137, 143, 145, 149, 178, 186, 245, 249, 268; education of, 98, 118; Progressivism and, 33; prohibition and, 31. *See also* Jim Crow laws; lynching; racial conflict; racism; riots; segregation; voter discrimination
Alabama, 22, 95, 96, 108–110, 118, 119, 147, 176, 264
Albany (NY), 158
Albuquerque Morning Journal, 244
Aldrich, Chester, 24, 26, 83, 208
Aldrich, Nelson W., 188
Alexander, Moses, 228, 251n50, 271n21
Alien Land Law, 211
alien workers, 249
Allison, William Boyd, 57, 59
Altgeld, John Peter, 8, 22, 37, 38–43
Amalgamated Copper Company, 226
America First, 118
American Tobacco Company, 138, 139
Ammons, Elias, 271n21
Anaconda Copper Mining Company, 215, 226, 227

Anthony, Susan B., 230
anti-alien legislation, 211
Anti-Saloon League, 83, 147, 205
antitrust policy, 23, 24, 30, 39, 44, 59, 60, 66, 67, 69, 71, 80, 82, 114, 120, 124, 125, 126, 129, 136, 138, 139, 194, 218, 265
Appleton's Booklovers Magazine, 86
Arizona, ix, 23, 28, 29, 32, 108, 114, 201, 234, 244, 245–249, 264, 266, 268, 271n12, 271n21
Arkansas, 104, 114, 119–123, 157, 268, 271n20
Aspen (CO), 235
Aspen Union Era, 235
Atlanta (GA), 104, 105
Atlanta Constitution, 65, 105, 117
Atlanta Journal, 104
Augusta (ME), 194
Austin, Horace, 9
Australian ballot, 47, 216. *See also* secret ballot
Aycock, Charles Brantley, 135, 136

Bailey, Joseph, 126
Baker, Ray Stannard, 168, 175
Baldwin, Simeon, 23, 194–195
Ball, Thomas, 127
Baltimore (MD), 95, 142, 144
Bamberger, Simon, 234, 243–244, 255
banking, 9, 30, 79, 89, 148, 164, 187, 240, 246
Baptist(s), 118, 119, 120, 121, 258
barbed wire case, 57

294 INDEX

Barefoot Schoolboy Law, 222
Barnard, Kate, 129, 130
Bass, Robert P., 24, 25, 34n17, 192–193, 255, 257, 263, 264
Baton Rouge (LA), 104
Beach, Rex, 86
Beaver, James, 182
Behrman, Martin, 103
Bell, Theodore Arlington, 205
Berge, George W., 82
Bicha, Karel, 237
Bickett, Thomas, 136–137
big business, 6, 58, 126, 129, 135, 202, 209, 265
Bilbo, Theodore Gilmore, 95, 101–102, 257
bill drafting, 6, 69
Billings, Warren, 212
biracial alliances, 22
Birmingham Cotton Mills, 108–109
Bismarck (ND), 85, 86
Black Horse Cavalry, 158
Black, Frank S., 155
Blaine, James G., 19, 154, 194
Blair, Diane, 119, 120
Blease, Coleman Livingston, 95, 98–99, 100, 104, 118, 122, 176, 268
blue law, 154. *See also* Sunday closing laws
blue sky law(s), 30, 79, 80, 84, 230
Boise (ID), 228
Boise, Horace, 57
bombings/explosions, 37, 40, 142, 212
Borah, William E., 228
Boston (MA), 195, 196, 201
Boston and Maine Railroad, 192
Bourbons, 7, 94, 100, 102, 134, 137
Bourne, Jonathan, 219
boxing, 190, 240, 245, 268. *See also* prizefighting
boycott(s), 203, 207
Boyle, Emmet D., 241–242
Bradley, William O'Connell, 137–138
Brayton, Charles R., 181, 188–189
bribes, 4, 8, 50, 64, 145, 175, 186, 188, 261
Brotherhood of Railway Trainmen, 196
Brough, Charles H., 114, 122–123, 271n20
Broward, Napoleon Bonaparte, 22, 114, 115, 116–117, 255
Brown, Joseph E., 106
Brown, Joseph M., 106, 107
Brumbaugh, Martin, 185
Bryan, William Jennings, 20, 21–22, 24, 37, 41, 42, 51, 52, 60, 62, 65, 66, 68, 75, 80, 81, 83, 104, 107, 115, 120, 121, 127, 129, 130, 138, 154, 155, 163, 169, 176, 208, 211, 223, 227, 228, 239, 240. *See also* Bryan Democrats
Bryan Democrats, 7, 18, 21, 67, 85, 222
Bryant, Keith L., 129
Bryce, James Lord, 8, 16n9
Buchtel, Henry, 237

Bull Moose Party, 17, 25, 26, 140, 195, 208, 229, 241. *See also* Progressive Party
bullpen(s), 141, 228
Burckel, Nicholas, 9, 140
Burke, Andrew, 84
Burke, John, 22, 76, 85–86, 229, 255, 263
Burlington and Grant Northern Railroad, 58
Burlington Railroad, 82
Burnquist, Joseph, 63
Busch, Adolphus, 242
Butler, Ed, 63, 64
Byrne, Frank, 89, 90, 268, 271n20

California, x, xi, 9, 24, 25, 28, 202–212
Cameron, Simon, 182
campaign finance regulations, 6, 28, 48, 78, 86, 89, 96, 110, 158, 174, 196, 219, 230, 239, 247
Campbell, Thomas M., 126
Canada, 219, 237
capital punishment, 32, 43, 71, 221, 236, 248, 268. *See also* death penalty
capitalism, 124, 222, 254
Capper, Arthur, 79, 80, 271n20, 271n21
Carey, Joseph M., 12, 24, 25, 98, 215, 229–231, 255, 271n20, 271n21
Carey, Robert D., 230–231
Carmack, Edward, 147
Catholic(s), 31, 114, 118, 119, 189, 195, 197
Catts, Sidney J., 114, 115, 118–119, 257, 267
Central Pacific Railroad, 240, 241
Chamberlain, George, 216, 217, 218–219
Cheyenne (WY), 229, 230
Chicago (IL), 24, 37, 40, 41, 89
Chicago and Northwestern Railroad, 89
child labor, 31, 39, 53, 71, 72, 77, 82, 96, 98, 101, 103, 104, 108, 109, 117, 129, 148, 183, 185, 193, 197, 210, 227, 229, 239, 244, 266
Childs, Richard S., 29
Chinese, 110, 216, 217
Chinese Exclusion Act, 217
Chrislock, Carl H., 60
Churchill, Winston (novelist), 192
Cincinnati (OH), 141
City Hall War, 236
civil rights, 225, 270
civil service, 6, 19, 28, 29, 42, 51, 69, 80, 154, 168, 175, 183, 195, 206, 207, 210, 211, 239, 262, 263
Civil War, 12, 43, 44, 96, 134, 182, 185, 235
Clark, Champ, 66
Clark, William A., 5
class conflict/divisions, 31, 39, 44, 58, 94, 95, 98, 100, 104, 120, 129, 134, 144, 204, 230, 237, 248, 249
Clayton Act, 23
Cleveland Democrats, 7, 18, 21, 22, 41, 67, 81, 86, 107, 167, 169, 217
Cleveland (OH), 67

Index

Cleveland, Grover, 7, 22, 62, 67, 96, 97, 98, 104, 110, 120, 125, 135, 145, 154, 167, 217
Clifton-Morenci (AZ), 247
Clovis (NM), 245
coal mining industry/conditions, 23, 59, 79, 84, 90, 110, 140, 141, 142, 185, 220, 239
Cobb, William, 193–194
Coeur d'Alene, 228
Colby, Everett, 168
Colorado, 22, 26, 28, 32, 41, 60, 201, 202, 217, 235–240, 256, 259, 261, 264, 266, 268, 271n20, 271n21
Colquitt, Oscar, 126
Comer, Braxton Bragg, 22, 96, 108–110, 255
Commoner, The, 68, 80, 107
Commons, John R., 51
Confederate Army, 134
Conference of Governors, 12, 176, 266
Connecticut, 23, 194–195, 197n1
conservation, 12, 53, 103, 109, 117, 118, 163, 183, 192, 203, 206, 210, 218, 219, 220, 230, 238, 239, 242, 247, 266
Consolidated Gas Company, 158
convent inspection law, 119
convict labor leasing system, 32, 110, 269
Cook County (IL), 38
Cooper, Duncan, 147
Copper County Strike, 47
Copper Kings, 226
Copperfield (OR), 221
Cornwell, John J., 142
corporate control of government, 51, 84, 136, 138, 197, 202, 226
corporate regulation, ix, 20, 100, 101, 115, 170, 223, 258, 270
corporate taxation, ix, xi, 4, 27, 39, 44, 45, 46, 48, 58, 68, 82, 89, 107, 138, 140, 146, 192, 193, 218, 222, 224, 226, 244, 245, 255, 265
corruption in government, 4, 5, 6, 11, 13, 21, 30, 56, 63, 65, 70, 71, 103, 105, 121, 143, 145, 148, 154, 158, 163, 188, 189, 195, 209, 254, 258, 259
corrupt-practices legislation, 6, 28, 43, 48, 58, 63, 68, 72, 89, 104, 106, 122, 139, 142, 143, 144, 158, 174, 175, 193, 195, 209, 216, 230, 244
Cosgrove, Samuel G., 224
Cotterill, George, 224
Cox, James M., 23, 56, 67, 68–69, 255, 271n20
Coxey, Jacob S., 19, 217
Coxey's Army, 19, 77, 125, 217, 225
Craig, Locke, 136
Crawford County (KS), 79
Crawford, Coe, 89, 229
criminal justice system, x, xi, 32, 46, 77, 248
criminal syndicalism measures, 212, 228
Cripple Creek Strike, 236
Crocker, Richard, 153
cross filing system, 211

Crothers, Austin, L., 142, 143–144, 256
Cruce, Lee, 129, 130
Crump, Edward H., 147–148, 151n59
Cuba, 116, 117
Culberson, Charles, 126
Cummins, Albert B., 23, 56, 57–59, 66, 208, 256
Curry, George, 244
Curtis, Chester, 194
Czechs, 88

Dane County (WI), 48
Darrow, Clarence, 38, 40, 41, 42
Davidson, James O., 52–53
Davis, Bob, 170
Davis, Jeff, 104, 114, 119–121, 122, 257, 268
Davis, Jefferson, 120
Davis, Robert W., 117
Davis, Westmoreland, 146–147
Dawson, William O., 139–140
Dayton Daily News, 68
death penalty, xi, 4, 32, 71, 77, 197, 221, 246, 248, 264, 268, 269. *See also* capital punishment
Decatur (IL), 40
Delaware, 181, 185–187, 229, 261
Democratic Party, 5, 19, 20, 21, 22, 25, 38, 39, 42, 61, 62, 65, 66, 68, 69, 76, 80, 85, 89, 99, 100, 102, 104, 108, 110, 115, 116, 118, 122, 123, 125, 127, 130, 135, 136, 137, 138, 142, 144, 146, 147, 163, 169, 171, 178, 191, 196, 203, 217, 219, 225, 226, 239, 243. *See also* Bourbons; Bryan Democrats; Cleveland Democrats
Deneen, Charles, 42, 43, 256
Denver (CO), 62, 237, 238
Denver Fire and Police Board, 236
Denver Public Lands Convention, 238
Des Moines (IA), 57, 58
Detroit (MI), 43, 44, 45
Dickerson, Denver S., 240–242
Dickson, Edward A., 203
direct democracy, 80, 121, 128, 152, 174, 176, 178, 193, 197, 202, 206, 207, 210, 218, 226, 239, 262. *See also* initiative; referendum; recall
direct election of U.S. Senators, 68, 142, 145, 195, 203, 227, 239, 264
direct legislation, 28, 52, 60, 68, 71, 88, 121, 224, 226, 240, 264. *See also* initiative; referendum
direct primary, 12, 26, 27, 42, 45, 46, 48, 49, 50, 51, 58, 63, 66, 69, 77, 78, 82, 86, 89, 95, 100, 104, 116, 136, 138, 144, 161, 163, 173, 174, 184, 185, 191, 192, 194, 195, 203, 216, 218, 219, 224, 229, 230, 238, 239, 257, 264. *See also* nominating conventions
Dix, John A., 163, 173
Dixon, Joseph M., 227
Donaghey, George W., 114, 121–122
Donnelly, Ignatius, 59
du Pont, Francis, 186

INDEX

du Pont, Henry A., 186
du Pont, T. Coleman, 187
Dunne, Edward, 23, 37, 42–43, 66, 108, 256, 271n20, 271n21
Durbin, Winfield Taylor, 69, 71
Duval County (FL), 116

Eagle, James R., 199
Eberhart, Adolph, 62, 271n12
Eccles (WV), 142
economy in government, 29, 72, 80, 102, 157, 170, 203, 224, 261
education spending, xi, 3, 26, 40, 80, 100, 101, 104, 106, 107, 108, 109, 110, 119, 123, 127, 134, 135, 136, 146, 222, 267
Elkins, Stephen, 139, 140
employer's liability laws, 206, 235
employment bureaus, 210
Emporia Gazette, 65
Essex County (NJ), 169, 176
eugenics/sterilization, 4, 31, 70, 203, 267
Everglades (FL), 116, 117
executive leadership, 9, 11, 146, 167, 173, 174, 177, 259
extradition, 12

factory regulation and inspection, 4, 31, 39, 53, 59, 129, 136, 164, 187, 188, 239
Fagan, Mark M., 168
Fandango Dollar, 235
Farmers' Alliance(s), 20, 81, 84, 88, 104, 125, 222
Fayetteville (AR), 122
Federal Bunch, 242
federal funds, 117, 119, 270
federal lands, 4
Federal Reserve System, 23
Federal Trade Commission, 23
federal troops, 23, 41, 123, 228, 236, 266
Felker, Samuel, 23, 193
Ferguson, James Edward ("Pa"), 114, 127–128, 270n20
Ferguson, Miriam ("Ma"), 128
Ferrell, Henry, 146
Ferris, Woodbridge, 23, 147
Flagler, Henry M., 115, 116, 117
Fletcher, Allen, 191
Florida, 22, 96, 114, 115–119, 257, 267
Flynn, Jim, 245
Flynt, Wayne, 115
Folk, Joseph W., 12, 13, 22, 56, 63–67, 246, 255, 258, 263
Fort, John Franklin, 168, 271n20
Foss, Eugene, 196–197, 255
Foster, Murphy J., 102
Frank, Leo, 43, 108
Frazier, Lynn, 76, 86, 87, 88, 254, 257
Free Coinage League, 81

free coinage of silver, 20, 41, 104, 108, 138, 226, 235, 238, 240
free textbooks, 115, 246
Fulton, Fred, 241
fusion tickets, 22, 81, 83, 84, 85, 88, 105, 134, 189, 222, 223

Galveston (TX), 127
gambling, xi, 4, 31, 66, 67, 70, 89, 147, 148, 161, 190, 192, 221, 227, 234, 235, 236, 239, 242, 254, 261, 268
Garvin, Lucius, 22, 188–189
Gates, Charles (writer), 217
Gates, Charles (governor), 191
Geiger, Lovis, 66
George, Henry, 154
Georgia, 22, 32, 43, 96, 104–108, 120
German Socialists, 51
Germany (Germans), 37, 38, 39, 88, 139, 228, 243
Gilchrist, Albert W., 118
Gillette, James, 203
Glasscock, William E., 24, 26, 139–141, 208
Glenn, Robert B., 136
Globe (AZ), 246
Glynn, Martin H., 163
Goddard, Robert, 189
Goebel, William, 137–138
good government reformers (goo-goos), 7
Gorman, Arthur Pue, 142
Gould, Jay, 154
governors: administration and, x, 7, 29–30, 69, 189, 261–262, 269; backgrounds and political careers of, 53, 253, 254, 256–258; budgeting and, 30, 69, 80, 84, 109, 110, 121, 126, 147, 162, 187, 189, 225, 261, 268; clemency powers of, 3, 236, 248, 268, 269; development of the office, 7–13; emergence of the reform-minded, 18–26; executive leadership and, 9, 11, 146, 167, 173, 174, 177, 259; getting elected, 115, 256–258; impeachment of, 121, 127, 128, 163, 164, 185; legislation and, 258–262, 269; motives and behavior, 14–15, 36; nature of the job, 12, 258–262; new, xi, 10, 11, 255, 256, 258, 265, 269; pardoning power use of, x, 32, 37, 40–42, 46, 71, 98–99, 121, 122, 126, 127, 133, 135, 138, 141, 147, 149, 196, 212, 221, 242, 248, 255, 260, 268, 269; parole and, 39, 203, 221, 248, 269; patronage use of, 51, 69, 86, 88, 103, 118, 175, 178, 223, 226, 260, 263; political personalities and styles, 255–256; Populist types, 37, 75, 88, 202, 215, 216, 217, 222, 225, 227, 255; Progressive types, 13–15, 67, 70, 71, 95, 241, 255, 253–256; recall of, 88; regional differences in conditions and performance, 13, 36–37, 56–57, 75–76, 94–96, 114, 133–134, 152–153, 18–182, 201–202, 215, 234, 264; short ballot movement and, 29–30; terms of, 16n9, 197n1; veto power use of, 7, 19, 40, 58, 70, 81, 84, 101, 110, 121, 126, 127, 129, 139, 147, 154, 161, 174, 177, 184, 185,

189, 193, 194, 197, 212, 218, 219, 225, 230, 239, 242, 260. *See also individual governors and specific policy areas*
Granger(s), 9, 11, 30, 36, 37, 47, 48, 57
Grantham, Dewey, 103
Graves, W. Brooke, 9
Great Northern Railroad, 58, 126, 225
Greenback Party, 134
Griffiths, David, 237

Hadley, Herbert S., 24, 26, 63, 67, 208
Haines, William, 194
Hall, Luther, 103
Hamburg (SC), 96
Hamburg Massacre, 96
Hanley, Edward, 68
Hanly, James Franklin, 69–70
Hanna, L. B., 11
Hanna, Mark, 45
Harding, Warren G., 68, 69
Harmon, Judson, 22, 23, 56, 67–68
Harper and Brothers, 169
Harper's Weekly, 169
Harrisburg (PA), 183
Harrison, Benjamin, 154, 217
Harvey, George, 169
Haskell, Charles, 114, 128, 130, 255, 271n20
Hatfield, Harry D., 139, 140–142
Hawley, James, 228
Hay, Marion, 224–225, 254
Haymarket bombing, 37, 40, 41
Hearst, William Randolph, 158, 159, 160, 163
Heinze, Fritz, 226
Henderson, Charles, 130
Heney, Francis, 204
Hepburn Act, 24
Hewitt, Abram, 154
Hicks, John D., 237
Higgins, Francis, 157, 158
Higgins, James Henry, 189
highway(s), 26, 102, 110, 119, 186, 231, 241. *See also* road building
Hill, Joe (Hillstrom), 242
Hispanics, 33, 247, 249
Hobbs, Fern, 221
Hoch, Edward W., 76, 77–78, 255, 268, 271n20
Hodges, George, 78, 79–80, 271n12, 271n20
Hogg, James Stephen, 22, 41, 123–126, 176, 255
Holcomb, Silas A., 81
home rule, 206, 239
honesty and efficiency types, 7
Hooper, Ben, 147–149
Hoople (ND), 87
House of Governors, 12
House of Mirth, 158
House of Southern Governors, 13
Howell, Clark, 105

Hudson County (NJ), 170
Hughes, Charles Evans, 9, 13, 23, 106, 153, 157–162, 165, 168, 172, 181, 210, 255, 258, 260, 263, 264
Hull House, 39
Humanitarian Progressivism, 100
Hunn, John, 186
Hunt, George W.P., 23, 108, 114, 234, 245–249, 271n2, 271n21
Huntsville (MO), 246

Idaho, 11, 22, 26, 31, 201, 215, 227–229
Illinois, 8, 22, 23, 27, 28, 36, 37–43, 62, 108, 115, 125, 138, 154, 236, 254, 256
immigrants, 31, 79
income tax: federal, 23, 42, 161, 194, 224, 264; state, 27, 44, 53, 101, 103, 129, 218, 231
independents, 7, 148, 189
indeterminate sentencing, 32, 39, 148
Indiana, 22, 31, 57, 62, 69–72, 184, 267
individualism, 3, 7, 21, 210, 254
industrial commission, 88, 164
Industrial Workers of the World, 212, 225, 229, 242
inheritance tax, 39, 50, 72, 216
initiative, 3, 20, 21, 26, 28, 34n28, 43, 47, 52, 66, 69, 83, 88, 96, 110, 121, 174, 176, 186, 194, 196, 197, 201, 202, 206, 207, 209, 216, 218, 219, 224, 226, 227, 228, 229, 230, 238, 239, 246, 247, 264, 303. *See also* direct democracy; direct legislation
insurance regulation, 4, 30, 58, 77, 79, 88, 89, 96, 110, 117, 120, 123, 148, 158, 164, 265
insurgents, xii, 6, 18, 23, 24, 48, 56, 57, 58, 59, 75, 77, 78, 82, 83, 86, 87, 89, 101, 191, 192, 205, 229, 230, 237, 241, 256, 257
Interstate Commerce Commission, 66, 79, 85
Iowa, 23, 36, 51, 56, 57–59, 82, 208, 228
Irish, 88, 162, 195, 197

Jackson, Andrew, 7
Jacksonian Democracy, 7
Jacksonville (FL), 116
Japanese, 211, 212
Jefferson, Thomas, 237
Jeffries, James, 240
Jennings, William Sherman, 114, 115–117
Jews (Jewish), 108, 228, 243, 251n50
Jim Crow laws, 33, 77, 117, 119, 129, 137, 143
Johansen, Dorothy, 217
Johnson, Grove, 203, 204
Johnson, Hiram, x, 8, 9, 23, 24, 25, 29, 68, 202, 203–211, 212, 241, 246, 255, 257, 258, 264
Johnson, Jack, 240, 245
Johnson, John A., 22, 56, 60–62, 85, 176, 256, 263
Johnson, Tom, 20, 67–68
Johnston, Joseph F., 108
Jones, Mary Harris ("Mother"), 141
Jones, Samuel, 67, 68, 155
Jug Bill, 148

Kansas, 22, 24, 28, 29, 31, 32, 36, 41, 75, 76–80, 129, 130, 155, 201, 208, 217, 222, 225, 226, 235, 236, 244, 256, 260, 268
Kansas City (MO), 5, 67
Kelley, Florence, 39
Kendrick, John, 230–231
Kentucky, 12, 133, 137–139, 176, 261
Keys, E. W., 48
Key, V.O., 98
Kitchin, William, 136
Kittredge, Alfred Beard, 89
Knights of Labor, 20, 38
Ku Klux Klan, 96, 139

La Follette, Belle Case, 52, 271n20
La Follette, Robert M., 8, 24, 37, 47–53, 56, 58, 65, 69, 192, 229, 255, 257
labor legislation, 31, 60, 79, 161, 190, 191, 210, 247, 266. See also child labor; factory regulation and inspection; mine inspection; minimum wage; worker's compensation
Labor Party, 119
labor theory of value, 129
Larrabee, William, 57, 58
Lawler, Daniel, 59
Lawrence, Mass., 196
Lea, Preston, 186
Leadville (CO), 235
Lease, Mary Elizabeth, 75
Lee, Andrew, 88–89
Leedy, John W., 77
legislative reference bureau (service), 30, 43, 51, 69, 261
Lemke, William, 87, 88
Lenroot, Irvine L., 52
Lewelling, Lorenzo, 1, 76–77, 217, 225, 226, 236
Lewis, Vivian, 171, 172
lieutenant governor, 52, 62, 84, 90, 102, 110, 158, 163, 197, 205, 207, 211, 224, 240
Lincoln (NE), 176
Lincoln County, NM, 244
Lincoln Party, 189
Lincoln Republicans, 191, 192
Lincoln, Abraham, 182, 237
Lincoln-Roosevelt League, 203, 204, 206
Lind, John, 60–61, 176
Lindsey, W. E., 11
Link, Arthur, 178
Lipson, Leslie, 9
liquor control, 31, 70, 79, 83, 89–90, 97, 106, 107, 117, 119, 120–121, 122, 130, 139, 146, 147, 148, 188, 190, 192, 234, 261, 267, 268. *See also* local option; prohibition
liquor dispensaries, 97, 117
Lister, Ernest, 224–225, 268, 271n12, 271n21
literacy test, 106, 146, 249
Lloyd, Henry Demarest, 38, 39

lobbying regulation, 6, 20, 47, 50, 51, 66, 69, 72, 78, 79, 82, 86, 89, 104, 107, 115, 121, 125, 126, 139, 140, 158, 173, 188, 190, 192, 195, 204, 226, 247, 261
local option on liquor, 31, 105, 139, 171, 185, 242
Lodge, Henry Cabot, 156, 196
Long, Huey, 103
Los Angeles (CA), 211
Los Angeles Times, 62, 204
Louisiana, 95, 102–104, 121
Louisville and Nashville Railroad, 109, 138
Lowden, Frank, 271n14
Lower, Richard, 209
Lowndes, Lloyd, 142, 144
lumber interests, 47, 48
Lutherans, 39
lynching, x, 32, 40, 41, 66, 95, 97, 98, 99, 100, 104, 108, 118, 121, 125, 133, 135, 136, 137, 139, 146, 241, 268

Madison (WI), 48
Mann, William, 146
Manning, Richard Irving, I, 99
Manning, Richard Irving, III, 95, 99–100, 254, 255, 257
Marion, Kansas, 77
martial law, 137, 140, 221, 227
Martine, James, 172, 173
Martin, Thomas Staples, 145, 146
Maryland, 133, 143–144, 145
Massachusetts, 7, 195–197, 197n1
Massillon, Ohio, 19, 80
mayor(s), 37, 43, 44, 45, 63, 67, 68, 88, 103, 110, 147, 149, 154, 155, 158, 159, 168, 184, 189, 190, 194, 199, 212, 216, 221, 228, 229, 238, 253
McAlester (OK), 130
McCormick, Richard L., 157
McCreary, James B., 138, 176
Macdonald, Austin, 13
McDonald, Mike, 38
McDonald, William C., 23, 234, 244–245
McGovern, Francis E., 24, 37, 53
McKenzie, Alexander, 84, 86
McKenzie Pass, 86
McMillan, James, 43, 44, 45
Mead, Albert, 224, 255
Memphis (TN), 95, 147, 148, 149
Methodist, 57, 70
Mexico, 65, 235
Mickey, John H., 82
Militant Progressive Democracy, 249
Miller, Charles, 187
Milliken, Carl, 194
Milwaukee (WI), 49, 51
mine inspection, 139, 142, 222, 239, 240
mine owner's association, 228
minimum wage, 196, 225

Index

Mississippi, 32, 95, 100–102, 103, 104, 122, 143, 218, 257
Moley, Raymond, 208
Montague, Andrew Jackson, 144–146, 176, 254, 257
mothers' pension laws, 27, 231
Mooney, Thomas, 212
Morehead, John, 84
Morehead (MN), 85
Moreland Act, 162
Morgan, J. P., 139
Mormons, 228, 242, 243, 244
Morris, Nephi, 243
Morrow, Edwin, 139
Morton, J. Sterling, 21
Muckrakers, 26, 253, 262
Multnomah County (MS), 218
Murphy, Charles, 163, 164, 165
Murray, Bill, 129
Murray (KY), 139
murder(s), 40, 96, 105, 106, 108, 125, 133, 136, 138, 142, 147, 160, 163, 203, 215, 228, 238, 242, 268. *See also* lynching; riots
Muskogee (OK), 128
Mugwumps, 19, 39, 254
middle of the roaders (mid-roaders, middle-roaders), 20, 33
Missouri, 5, 12, 13, 22, 24, 32, 37, 56, 63–67, 155, 208, 226, 238, 246, 263
Minnesota, 9, 22, 26, 29, 32, 36, 37, 56, 59–63, 84, 85, 176, 256, 263
Marshall, Thomas R., 22, 57, 70–71, 267
Michigan, 23, 24, 26, 37, 43–47, 238, 254
Montana, 22, 23, 26, 28, 201, 202, 215, 225–227, 267
monopoly/monopolies, 13, 20, 21, 23, 30, 40, 45, 47, 52, 59, 60, 79, 104, 128, 138, 158, 177, 191, 203, 222, 226, 265. *See also* antitrust policy; big business
Maine, 23, 31, 43, 193–194, 197n1, 222
McKinley, William, 20, 23, 42, 45, 50, 60, 155, 156, 160, 228, 241

Natchez (MS), 218
Nation, Cary, 177
National American Woman Suffrage Association, 240
National Civil Service Reform League, 29, 175
National Guard, 183, 217, 221, 236, 255, 266, 267, 269. *See also* state militia
National Progressive Republican League, 24, 241
Native American, 33
Nebraska, 20, 21, 22, 24, 36, 75, 80–84, 155, 176, 208, 258, 261
Nelson, Knute, 59
Nevada, 31, 201, 234, 240–242
New England Telephone Company, 190
New England, 13, 181, 189, 190, 192
New Hampshire Direct Legislation League, 193
New Hampshire, 23, 24, 25, 31, 191–193, 197n1, 257, 263, 264
New Haven Railroad, 195
new idea men, 168, 178
New Jersey Federation of Labor, 170
New Jersey, x, xi, 9, 14, 23, 24, 167–178, 181, 183, 257, 264
New Mexico, 23, 201, 234, 244–245, 246, 247
New Orleans (LA), 95, 102, 103
New Orleans Good Government League, 103
new south, 95, 133, 137, 146, 254
New York Times, 42, 45, 61, 76, 164, 204
New York, 7, 13, 18, 19, 23, 29, 41, 42, 62, 78, 106, 125, 153–165, 172, 173, 181, 185, 190, 201, 203, 210, 216, 235, 260, 263, 264
Newark (NJ), 169
Newark Star, 176
Newport (RI), 190
Newton (NC), 104
nominating conventions, 6, 27, 47, 50, 51, 82, 95, 100, 116, 145, 149, 257, 263, 264. *See also* direct primary
nonpartisan elections, 28, 68, 206, 210, 230, 263
Nonpartisan League, 18, 26, 63, 86, 225, 227, 229, 257
nonpartisanship, 28, 81, 211, 212, 218, 219
Norbeck, Peter, 76, 90–91, 255, 271n12, 271n20
North Carolina, 22, 104, 133, 134–139
North Dakota, 11, 22, 23, 31, 32, 36–37, 75, 76, 84–88, 91, 201, 254, 257, 261, 263, 266
Northern Securities Trust, 23, 60
Northern, William, 104
Norwegians, 52, 59, 88
Norwood, C.P., 119
Nugent, James, 170, 173, 175, 176
Nye, Russell, 36, 59, 61

O'Neal, Emmet, 96, 110, 264
O'Neal, Edward, 110
Oakland (CA), 202
Oddie, Tasker, 240–241
Odell, Benjamin, 152, 156, 157, 158
Ohio, 19, 20, 22, 23, 56, 67–69, 83, 128, 271n20
Oklahoma, 29, 114, 121, 128–130, 201, 271n20
Olin, Spencer, 209
Olney, Richard, 19
Omaha Platform, 235
Omaha, Nebraska, 20
one-house legislature, 6, 28, 29, 80, 242, 247, 261. *See also* unicameralism
Oregon System, 216, 218, 219, 230
Oregon, 22, 28, 32, 41, 60, 173, 174, 201, 202, 215, 216–222, 224, 225, 226, 246, 256, 261, 263, 264, 267, 268, 269
Osborn, Chase S., 24, 26, 37, 45–47
Our Penal Machinery and Its Victims, 38
Ouster Law, 149
Owen, Rubert Latham, 130

INDEX

Paint and Cabin Creek (WV), 140, 141
Pardee, George, 202–203
Paris (TX), 125
Parker, Alton B., 22, 24
Parker, John, 103
parole, 32, 39, 80, 203, 221, 248, 269
party machines, 4, 5, 6, 10, 11, 14, 19, 37, 38, 42, 44, 48, 49, 57, 60, 63, 64, 67, 78, 86, 89, 95, 96, 102, 103, 133, 135–136, 139–140, 143, 145, 146, 152, 153, 155, 161, 167–169, 170, 172, 174, 175, 176, 182, 184, 185, 187, 188, 192, 196, 197, 202, 204, 206, 210, 215, 223, 229–230, 238, 242, 257, 260, 262, 263. *See also* political party bosses
patronage, 5, 6, 10, 19, 29, 39, 51, 69, 70, 82, 86, 88, 103, 118, 153, 164, 175, 178, 211, 223, 226, 249, 260, 263; federal, 44, 98, 156. *See also* civil service
Patterson, Malcolm R., 133, 147
Pattison, Robert, 182
Pawtucket (RI), 189
Peffer, William A., 76
penal reform, 27, 43, 69, 119, 121, 137, 218, 219, 221, 230, 248, 269. *See also* prison reform
Pendergast, Thomas, 5, 67
penitentiary, 65, 101, 120, 127, 130, 216
Pennewill, Simeon Selby, 187
Pennoyer, Sylvester, 41, 216–218, 269
Pennsylvania Manufactures Association, 182
Pennsylvania Railway Company, 140, 183
Pennsylvania State Police, 183
Pennsylvania, 23, 31, 57, 70, 101, 140, 181, 182–185, 194, 259, 262, 267
Pennypacker, Samuel, 70, 101, 182–184, 194, 259, 267
Penrose, Boies, 182, 184, 185
People's Party. *See* Populist Party
Percy, Alexander, 101, 102
Percy, Le Roy, 101
Perkins, Frances, 164
Pharr, John Newton, 102
Phelps Dodge Corporation, 246
Philadelphia (PA), 182, 183, 184, 185, 186, 201
Philipp, Emanuel L., 53
Phillips County (AR), 123
Pingree, Hazen S., 23, 37, 43–46, 52, 56, 66, 155, 254, 255, 257
Pinkerton detectives, 216
Pittsburgh (PA), 182
Plaisted, Frederick, 23, 194
Platt, Thomas Collier, 153, 155, 156, 157, 158, 160
Pleasant, Ruffin, 103
Poe Amendment, 142
political party bosses, xii, 5–6, 8, 14, 27, 38, 47, 48, 49, 52, 58, 63, 66, 142, 143, 152, 153, 155, 158, 159, 160, 161, 162, 163, 164, 167, 168, 169, 170, 171, 172, 174, 175, 176, 177, 181, 182, 183, 196, 204, 245, 254, 255, 257, 258, 259, 260, 262, 263, 264. *See also* party machines
poll taxes, 146

Populism, 105, 119
Populist Party, 20, 22, 36, 37, 41, 59, 202, 222, 223
Populists, ix, xii, 3, 4, 7, 10, 11, 18, 19, 20, 21, 22, 30, 38, 41, 51, 56, 58, 59, 60, 75, 76, 77, 81, 82, 84, 85, 86, 87, 88, 89, 94, 95, 96, 97, 102, 104, 105, 106, 201, 202, 215, 216, 222, 223, 224, 225, 226, 227, 228, 234, 235, 236, 246, 249, 255, 265, 266, 270
Portland (ME), 194
Portland (OR), 17, 216
positive liberalism, 153, 165
Pothier, Aram Jules, 189–190
Powers, Caleb, 138
Poynter, William A., 81–82
presidential primary/primaries, 14, 24–25, 42, 46, 86, 216
prison reform, xi, 4, 11, 32, 38, 39, 43, 46, 58, 69, 101, 110, 127, 130, 147, 148, 149, 196, 210, 216, 221, 223, 240, 246, 248, 261, 268, 269, 270
private armies, 216
prizefighting, xi, 31, 126, 190, 203, 234, 241, 248, 268
Proctor, Fletcher, 190
Proctor, Redfield, 190
Progressive era, 12, 31, 56, 181, 201, 224, 270
Progressive movement, x, xi, 3, 33, 36, 50, 67, 94, 168, 190, 195, 208, 229, 262
Progressive Party, 25, 50, 71, 83, 103, 157, 163, 189, 191, 193, 208, 211, 225, 227, 230, 244. *See also* Bull Moose Party
Progressivism, 14, 30, 33, 46, 47, 56, 66, 68, 98, 100, 103, 123, 126, 145, 146, 168, 176, 193, 202, 228, 240, 241, 246, 254, 255, 270
Prohibition Party, 70, 118
prohibition, 10, 31, 57, 70, 71, 77, 83, 85, 86, 96, 97, 100, 102, 104, 106, 108, 109, 110, 117, 118, 119, 122, 123, 127, 128, 129, 130, 133, 136, 139, 146, 147, 148, 149, 154, 171, 178, 185, 187, 188, 194, 202, 204, 219, 221, 223, 228, 241, 242, 243, 244, 246, 248, 249, 253, 265, 267, 270
property tax(es), 61, 62, 82, 88, 240
prostitution, 31, 227, 236, 268
Prouty George, 190
public health, x, 13, 47, 58, 122, 136, 139, 244, 267. *See also* pure food and drug laws
public land, 116, 164, 238, 248
public utility regulation, 4, 30, 43, 53, 68, 71, 72, 78, 79, 123, 129, 141, 142, 144, 148, 160, 168, 174, 192, 194, 195, 197, 207, 209, 212, 219, 230, 244, 246, 265
Pulitzer, Joseph, 65
Pullman strike, 19, 41, 44, 125, 236
pure food and drug laws, 24, 42, 104, 117, 140, 148, 224, 227
pure food laws, 58, 77, 106, 126, 183, 227
Pusey, Merlo, 160, 161, 162

Quay, Matthew, 182, 183, 184

Index

racetrack gambling, 66, 161, 239
racial conflict, xii, 13, 15, 32, 35, 118, 121, 123
racism, x, xii, 33, 94, 95, 96, 101, 115, 121, 176, 249, 254
railroad commission(s), 30, 50, 51, 57, 58, 71, 85, 88, 103, 106, 109, 110, 124, 125, 168, 190, 192, 207, 209, 218, 219, 223, 224, 227, 235
railroad passes, 4, 58, 66, 81, 82, 85, 86, 89, 106, 126, 148, 183, 192, 207, 216, 224, 238, 260, 266
Ralston, Samuel M., 71–72
Ranney, Austin, 27
Rasin, Isaac Freeman, 142, 143
recall, 3, 6, 88, 201, 202, 206, 207, 209, 228, 246, 247; of judges, 28, 128, 176, 207, 209, 216, 224. *See also* direct democracy
Reconstruction, 96, 115, 134, 147
Record, George L., 24, 168, 170, 174
red shirts, 135
rednecks, 120
referendum, 3, 20, 21, 28, 34n28, 43, 47, 52, 66, 69, 83, 88, 96, 110, 121, 174, 176, 186, 194, 196, 197, 201, 202, 206, 207, 209, 216, 218, 219, 224, 226, 227, 228, 229, 230, 238, 239, 246, 247, 264. *See also* direct democracy; direct legislation
Regular Democratic Organization, 102, 103
regular Republicans, 48, 58, 148, 160, 186, 193
Reiter, Howard, 14
reorganization of state agencies, 12, 28, 29, 30, 80, 162, 165, 190, 212, 261, 271n14
Republican Party, 6, 18, 22, 24, 26, 37, 42, 43, 44, 47, 48, 57, 58, 60, 61, 70, 76, 84, 86, 87, 89, 97, 134, 140, 149, 153, 154, 157, 158, 159, 167, 168, 175, 182, 183, 184, 185, 186, 188, 189, 190, 191, 192, 196, 204, 208, 211, 227, 229, 238, 242, 244, 257, 264. *See also* insurgents; Mugwumps; new idea men; regular Republicans; Silver Republicans;, stalwarts; standpatters
rhetorical Progressive, 14, 95, 241, 255
Rhode Island, 22, 181, 188–190, 197n1
riots, x, 4, 32, 95, 105, 123, 128, 135, 268
Ripley, Edward, 79
road building, 19, 32, 118, 144, 146, 242
Roberts, Brigham H., 243
Robinson, Joseph T., 122
Rockefeller, J. D., 40, 125, 126, 220
Rogers, John R., 222–224, 225, 226, 256
Rome (NY), 164
Roosevelt, Theodore, 2, 12, 13, 14, 18, 21, 22, 23, 41, 42, 47, 52, 53, 65, 67, 82, 83, 84, 89, 90, 103, 109, 117, 128, 140, 141, 149, 153–157, 158, 159, 160, 162, 163, 165, 172, 182, 183, 192, 193, 195, 208, 211, 227, 229, 241, 243, 255, 256, 266, 267
Root, Elihu, 153, 159
Rough Riders, 155
Rowell, Chester H., 203
Ruef, Abe, 204

Russell, Daniel Lindsay, 133, 134–135
Rye, Thomas Clark, 149

Sage, Leland, 57
Saint Peter (MN), 60
Salt Lake City (UT), 243
San Francisco (CA), 203, 204, 210, 212
Santa Fe Railroad, 79, 246
Santa Fe Ring, 244
Sarasohn, David, 196
Sawyer, Philetus, 49
Scandinavians, 51, 56, 59, 63, 90, 258
Schurz, Carl, 154
Scofield, Edward, 48, 49
secret ballot, 38, 47, 100, 216, 230. *See also* Australian ballot
segregation, 33, 66, 94, 117, 118, 119, 128, 143, 146, 178, 236, 249. *See also* Jim Crow; separate coach laws
separate but equal, 33
separate coach laws, 125, 137
Seven Sisters legislation, 177
Seventeenth Amendment (U.S. Constitution), 28
Shafroth, John F., 22, 234, 237–240, 255, 256, 259, 268, 271n20
Shafroth, Virginia, 240
Sharp, Harry, 70
Shaw, Albert, 157
Sheldon, George, 82–83, 255, 257
Sherman Antitrust Act, 59
Sherman Silver Purchase Act, 19, 21
Shilling, George A., 39, 40
short ballot, 28, 29, 69, 103, 206, 261
Shortridge, Eli, 84, 85, 86
silver issue, 19, 20, 21, 22, 41, 96, 97, 104, 108, 120, 137, 138, 217, 225, 226, 229, 235, 236, 238, 240, 241. *See also* free coinage of silver
Silver League, 237
Silver Republican Party, 22
Silver Republicans, 22, 60, 88, 222, 223, 227, 238
Simmons, Furnifold, 135, 136
Sixteenth Amendment, U.S. Constitution, 224
Slaton, Jack, 43, 107, 108
Smith, Alfred E., 153, 163–165, 255, 262, 270
Smith, Henry, 125
Smith, Hoke, 22, 96, 104–108, 120, 255
Smith, James, 169, 170, 172–173, 174, 176, 183
Smith, John Walter, 142
Smith, Milton, 109
Smith, Robert B., 225–226
Smoot, Reed, 242, 243
Socialist Party of America, 26
Socialists, 38, 51, 90, 188, 227, 249, 254
South Carolina, 22, 95, 96–100, 104, 117, 122, 125, 135, 236, 240, 254, 257, 268
South Dakota, 22, 23, 25, 26, 28, 29, 32n17, 37, 75, 76, 88–91, 229, 268, 271n12, 271n20

Southern Pacific Railroad, 124, 125, 202, 203, 204, 205, 206, 209, 246
Southern Railroad, 105
Southern, David, 265
Sparks, John, 240
Speer, Robert W., 238
Springfield (IL), 42
Springfield (MO), 66
Spry, William, 234, 242–43, 271n21
Square Deal, 156, 192
St. Louis, 20, 63, 65, 66, 243
St. Louis Post-Dispatch, 65
St. Paul (MN), 85
St. Peter Herald, 61
stalwart(s), 6, 48, 50, 53
Standard Oil Company, 40, 67, 103, 115, 125, 129, 130
standpatters, 6
Stanley, Augustus O., 133, 138–139
state constitutional convention(s), 26, 27, 67, 87, 97, 108, 110, 128, 129, 164, 165, 226, 246
state constitutions, 7, 26, 66, 68, 69, 71, 87, 88, 97, 98, 102, 106, 114, 121, 128, 129, 135, 136, 142, 143, 144, 145–146, 161, 185, 191, 206, 207, 228, 230, 231, 239, 246, 261, 266
state land, 115, 229
state militia, x, 41, 66, 79, 130, 135, 136, 137, 140, 187, 189, 196, 266, 270. *See also* National Guard
state tax commission(s), 27, 62, 77, 89, 100, 102, 109, 138, 140, 239, 265
states' rights, 145, 161, 230, 238, 248, 266, 269, 270
Staunton, Virginia, 169
Steffens, Lincoln, 8, 10, 48, 50, 64, 188, 219
Stephens, William, 211–212
Steunenberg, Frank, 227–228
Stewart, Samuel, 23, 267, 271n21
street railways (cars), 30, 106, 137
strikes, 19, 23, 41, 44, 47, 64, 96, 109, 110, 125, 140, 141, 142, 164, 189, 196, 197, 215, 225, 228, 236, 247, 266
structural reformers, 3, 7
Stuart, Edward, 184
Stubbs, Stella, 79
Stubbs, Walter R., 24, 76, 78–80, 208, 255, 256, 260, 271n20
Sullivan, Roger, 62
Sulzer, William, 23, 153, 163–164, 185
Sunday closing laws, 66, 123, 154, 268
Swanson, Claude, A., 144, 145–146, 255, 262
Sweden, 62
Swedish 60, 61

Tacoma, Washington, 224
Taft, William Howard, 18, 22, 23, 24, 25, 59, 67, 84, 89, 128, 140, 141, 149, 162, 185, 187, 193, 208, 228
Taggart, Thomas, 62, 70, 71
Tammany Hall, 19, 62, 102, 153, 160, 163, 164, 165
tariff issue, 23, 58, 62, 182, 195

tax equalization, 39, 45, 46, 62, 102, 110, 118, 119, 126, 170
Teller, Henry M., 238
tenant farmers (sharecroppers), 98, 99, 123, 127, 137
Tener, John, 184, 185
Tennessee, 31, 32, 63, 65, 133, 147–149, 188, 248
Terrell, Joseph M., 104
Texas Traffic Association, 124
Texas, 22, 32, 41, 51, 114, 121, 123–128, 176, 260
third parties, 18, 25, 26, 87, 94, 201, 219, 257
Thomas, Charles S., 237, 271n20
Three Friends, 116
Tillman, Benjamin Ryan, 22, 95, 96–98, 99, 100, 104, 117, 118, 123, 125, 135, 236
tobacco industry, 136, 138, 139, 187
Tonopah (NV), 240
Tonopah Midway Mining Company, 241
Toole, Joseph K., 226–227
Townley, Arthur C., 26, 87
Townsend, John Gillis, Jr., 187
Trammell, Park, 118
Trenton (NJ), 173, 174
Triangle Shirtwaist Company fire, 163
Tumulty, Joseph, 169, 170

U'Ren, William, 173, 174, 216
unicameralism, 29, 80, 247, 261, 271n12. *See also* one-house legislature
Union Pacific, 82, 84
Union Republicans, 186
United Mine Workers, 110, 141
United States Civil Service Commission, 154
United States Congress, 13, 19, 21, 23, 24, 28, 48, 59, 60, 69, 89, 117, 138, 142, 144, 146, 147, 160, 163, 175, 196, 218, 225, 226, 238, 241, 243, 244, 270
United States Constitution, 24, 28, 41, 161, 194
United States Steel Corporation, 62
Utah, 28, 201, 234, 242–244, 271n20
Utica (NY), 159
Utter, George H., 189

Van Sant, Samuel, 60
Van Wyck, Augustus, 155
Vardaman, James K., 95, 100–102
Vermont Marble Company, 190
Vermont, 31, 190–191, 197n1
Vessey, Robert, 25, 34n17, 89–90, 271n20
vigilante(s), 4, 32, 33, 69, 98, 101, 147, 268
Virginia, 24, 133, 144–147, 169, 176, 254, 257, 262
voter discrimination, 33, 94, 97, 102, 105, 106, 121, 122, 127, 129, 134, 135, 136, 137, 142, 143, 144, 145, 146, 185, 186, 265
voter fraud, 102, 143, 186, 188, 189

Wagner, Robert F., 163
Waite, Celia, 235
Waite, Davis H., 41, 217, 234, 235–238, 264, 266

Wall Street, 46
Wallace, A. J., 205
Walsh, David I., 196, 197
Warfield, Edwin, 142–143, 144, 145
Warner, Fred, 46
Warren, Francis, 229, 230
Washington, DC, 19, 24, 37, 52, 96, 136, 156, 182, 217
Washington (state), 11, 22, 23, 28, 29, 32, 201, 202, 215, 222–225, 226, 254, 255, 256, 268, 271n12, 271n21
Washington Post, 188
Washington, Booker T., 122
Watson, Thomas E., 104, 105, 106, 107
Weaver, James, 84, 104
welfare, 27, 31, 257
West Virginia, 24, 133, 139–142, 208
West, Oswald, 216, 218–222, 246, 255, 256, 268
Western Federation of Miners, 47, 228, 236
Wheeler, Burton, K., 227
White Cap, 69
White Cappers, 101
white supremacy, 94, 97, 100, 110, 118, 135, 136, 145
White, Albert B., 139
White, William Allen, 10, 65
Wichita, Kansas, 76
Willamette Valley, 216
Willard, Jess, 241
Willson, Augustus E., 12
Wilmington (DE), 186, 187
Wilmington (NC), 134, 135
Wilson, Woodrow, x, 8, 9, 11, 21, 23, 25, 41, 57, 66, 75, 122, 163, 167–178, 185, 193, 196, 255, 265, 270, 271n20
Wisconsin Idea, 51
Wisconsin, x, xi, 8, 9, 23, 24, 26, 27, 30, 36, 37, 39, 47–53, 59, 68, 69, 78, 82, 84, 201, 229, 235, 242, 260, 263
woman suffrage, 10, 28, 46, 52, 69, 79, 80, 85, 89, 96, 103, 110, 119, 123, 127, 128, 139, 142, 178, 187, 195, 197, 207, 210, 218, 222, 224, 227, 228, 230, 234, 235, 240, 248, 264, 265, 270
Woodward, C. Vann, 138
worker's compensation, 4, 31, 43, 46, 53, 68, 69, 71, 72, 79, 84, 86, 103, 139, 140, 141, 142, 174, 191, 192, 193, 195, 197, 207, 210, 219, 224, 228, 230, 241, 244
Wright, James, 193, 237
Wyoming, 12, 24, 25, 28, 98, 201, 215, 229–231

Yerkes, Charles T., 40

Ziegenhein, Henry, 63